Unaccustomed to Fear

A BIOGRAPHY OF THE LATE

GENERAL ROY S. GEIGER, U.S.M.C.

BY
R O G E R   W I L L O C K
Colonel, USMCR

Privately Published

ROGER WILLOCK   PRINCETON, N. J.

The Marine Corps Association is
grateful to the Marine Corp Historical
Foundation for recommending this
book for reprinting for todays
Marines.

Reprinted by
The Marine Corps Association
Quantico, Virginia
May 1983

LIBRARY OF CONGRESS CATALOG NUMBER 68-22840

MANUFACTURED IN THE UNITED STATES OF AMERICA

ISBN 0-940328-05-4

Acknowledgements

For a line officer even to attempt to relate the life and times of a naval aviator—and one of the Marine Corps most illustrious pilots at that—requires a certain amount of courage and at least a word of explanation.

Back in the mid-1930's there used to be an expression frequently overheard at small arms ranges on Marine Corps posts at home and abroad to the effect that a sailor with a rifle or an automatic pistol ashore was a particularly dangerous individual—to friend or foe alike. This was predicated on the theory that bluejackets away from their normal surroundings armed with lethal weapons were downright unpredictable, prone to make mistakes and to disregard basic safety regulations, and in essence were considered a distinct menace to any other law-abiding persons in the immediate vicinity.

For many months past the writer has felt a close kinship with those apocryphal seamen of three decades past. His over-all knowledge of aviation affairs being somewhat restricted it was necessary from the very start to seek technical advice and professional guidance to offset his ignorance of many of the fundamentals and to spare him from the pitfalls which otherwise would have exacted their toll in due course in the writing of the tale. Aside from reading everything pertinent to the general as well as the specific subject upon which the writer could lay his hands, numerous individuals, Navy, Marine Corps, and civilian employees of the naval establishment, ranging from four-star Generals and former Wing, Group, and Squadron Commanders of the Pacific War through longtime Crew Chiefs and Radiomen, veterans of Haiti, China, and Nicaragua, and on down the line to lowly "wing washers" and "nut busters,' were contacted either in person or by interchange of lengthy, detailed correspondence. In this respect notable assistance was rendered by two senior Master Sergeants, specialists in the fields of aviation maintenance and ordnance, assigned to the staff of the Marine Corps Museums at Quantico, who devoted the better part of at least one summer in their spare time with some degree of success to pound into the writer's skull some of their vast store of accumulated knowledge of the technicalities of the flying machines of the "stick and string" era—the old *DeHavilland* scout-bombers, the *Curtiss Hawks* and *Falcons,* the versatile *Vought Corsairs,* and the early *Boeing* fighters.

Similarly, every conceivable aid, comment, and constructive criticism was cheerfully tendered by scores of persons who literally made the time available to search their personal files for letters and photographs to clarify this point and to correct an error that had worked its way into the typescript. My debts and obligations to those many splendid persons are legion. At the risk of unintentionally omitting the name of any individual, I should like to make specific mention of the following without whose assistance and encouragement General Geiger's biography could not have been written: Generals A.A. Vandegrift, O.P. Smith, and V.E. Megee; Lieutenant Generals L.E. Woods, M.H. Silverthorn, L.B. Puller, E.W. Snedeker, and A.L. Bowser, Jr.; Major Generals W.P.T. Hill, F.O. Rogers, B.F. Johnson, W.L. McKittrick, W.S. Brown, and J.C. Munn; Brigadier General J.R. Cram; Captains, U.S. Navy, H.B. Grow and R.G. Pennoyer; Colonels W.A. Lee, R.J. Johnson, R.D. Heinl, Jr., J.P. Wagner, Jr., J.H. Magruder III, and D E. Schwulst; Captain R.B. Asprey; Master Sergeants R.R. Emmons, George McGarry, and W.F. Gemeinhart; First Sergeant Edward Abrams; Mr. H.I. Shaw and Mr. D.M. O'Quinlivan, both of Washington, D.C., Mr. J.H. Moss of East Point, Georgia, and Mr. W.T. Larkins of Concord, California.

As for the laborious task of editing and amending the initial draft of this biography I am deeply indebted to five persons, all eminently well qualified for that exacting mission: Lieutenant Generals F.L. Wieseman and R.C. Mangrum; Brigadier General F.P. Henderson; The Reverend P.C. Holnback of Princeton, New Jersey, formerly a naval aviator who served aboard escort carriers in the Pacific, and Mr. C.D. Tuska, also of Princeton, whose flying days commenced in that early era when the Army's aviation components were part of its Signal Corps.

I am especially grateful to a former Marine

non-commissioned officer, then Technical Sergeant (Aviation) John Donato, sometime maintenance mechanic and radio operator of then Colonel Geiger's command aircraft at Quantico in the mid-1930's. Indirectly Donato was the cause of my undertaking the assignment many years after our first meeting. While assigned to a Latin-American Republic in the capacity of an Assistant Naval Attache', about four months prior to the Japanese raid on Pearl Harbor, I had occasion to join the Naval Attache' and his Crew Chief on a flight from Bogotá, Colombia, to the Panama Canal Zone. Midway between the jungles of the Atrato River valley and the Naval Air Station at Coco Solo, our *Beechcraft* light transport encountered as violent a series of thunder-and-lightning storms as I was ever to experience before or since anywhere in the tropics: so heavy the downpour and so terrific the force of the winds I marveled at the ability of the plane to remain aloft.

Sitting next to Donato and strapped into our seats I could not refrain from remarking that I sincerely hoped that our pilot knew where he was and that he could bring us safely to our destination. Not one whit disturbed by the rocking of the plane Donato looked at me with disgust and retorted; "Lieutenant, don't you worry about the storm or Colonel Johnson up front. Hell, he flew with Geiger. Storms didn't bother old *Jiggs* none. All his Squadron pilots learned their navigation from him. We'll get there when we get there, and that's that." And as if to add insult to injury Donato reached into a paper bag and proceeded to bite into a very large combination salami and cheese sandwich laced with garlic, and with an aroma whose intensity was only matched by the sheets of rain beating on the outside of the fuselage.

For the remainder of our tortured passage Donato gave me a running account of Colonel Geiger's prowess as a naval aviator and as a leader, and for the duration of our tour of duty in Colombia enlivened our successive flights by his colorful recitals of Colonel Geiger's feats of renown in the air as well as on the ground. I was inclined to take many of them with a grain of salt. Months later I learned that the information Donato had imparted had not been elaborated upon appreciably, and at length I came to the conclusion that General Geiger's biography deserved to be written not just for the benefit of those of his generation but also for the edification and entertainment of those who succeeded him.

Apart from the recollections of General Geiger's immediate

associates was the invaluable assistance extended by his family. To his wife, Eunice Thompson Geiger, his daughter, Joyce Geiger Johnson, and his son, Colonel Roy Stanley Geiger, Jr., U.S. Army, are due my profound appreciation. It was thanks to them that not only were the General's private correspondence and photographs placed at my disposal, including his flight log books and the originals of all of his official orders and citations, but in addition they were willing to share with me—without reservation—their memories of many of the intimate details of their daily "Life with Father." Moreover, my grateful thanks are due for the hours they devoted reading the typescript and for assisting me to interpret correctly the many-sided structure of General Geiger's personality.

Lastly, I owe a supreme debt to my wife, to whom this book is dedicated—for her patience, forbearance, and understanding throughout the protracted period of time it required to write this biography.

Roger Willock

Princeton, New Jersey
1968

vi

Preface

To that generation of Americans whose youth and formative years took place in the mid-1920's there is no denying that among its more fascinating aspects was the comparatively rapid development of commercial aviation, then in its infancy, including a growing public awareness of its potentialities. Not that other thrills galore were lacking, for the motor car had opened up new vistas; the overt flaunting of the National Prohibition Amendment by gangsters and rum-runners was daily making front-page headlines; the *Charleston* and the *Black Bottom* had seemingly limitless variations; and wet-battery radio sets had begun to pose a serious threat to the continued sale of Victrola records. The motion picture moguls in their Hollywood fastness were quick to sense the changing tenor of the times. Although the public appetite for war films and plays momentarily had been rendered somewhat jaded from a chronic overdose of muddy boots and barbed wire, bad language and bloody bayonets, a solution for falling receipts at the box office was devised by the simple expedient of introducing a third dimension, the air above us. Thus, by climbing out of the trenches into the cockpits, accompanied by realistic orchestrations far beyond the capabilities of the player-piano or the skilled fingers of a pipe organist, the audience could thrill to the sight and sound of simulated aerial combat. Hereafter, Saturday nights at the *Bijou* or Sunday matinees at the *Strand* meant clutching tightly to the undersides of gum-encrusted, red plush seats, meanwhile on the flickering screen thin-lipped pilots in refurbished fighter aircraft of World War I vintage sprayed their adversaries with Brownings and Spandaus; *Fokkers* and *Albatrosses* were machine-gunned to shreds with utter abandon, to crash-land in columns of greasy smoke and pillars of livid flame with almost monotonous regularity; and the badly battered but somehow still manageable *Sopwiths* and *De Havillands* limped back to the friendly airdrome to allow our hero to rejoin his Squadron comrades and to partake of liquid refreshment at a conveniently located Mess. Exhausted but sated after this hour-long stirring spectacle the viewers staggered forth from the theaters to the streets, bound and determined at all cost not to miss next week's aerial dogfight.

For the more adventuresome there was usually a makeshift landing strip at the nearest fair grounds or picnic grove, where, for a price you could sample the real thing. This was the haunt of that rugged individualist, the barnstormer, that daredevil with his leather jacket and flying helmet, his laced boots and oil-stained breeches, his goggles and silk scarf. When not engaged in taking apart his flying machine and putting it together again, or, dangling by his ankles, head down, at 1,000 feet elevation from beneath the landing gear of a Curtiss *Jenny,* which had invariably seen better days, that aerial acrobat could be prevailed upon to take his head out of a crankcase long enough to fly you "Low over Trenton, ten bucks for ten minutes," or to treat you to a bird's-eye view of "Downtown Des Moines for a double sawbuck." You paid cash on the line in advance, no refund in case of breakdown or a change of heart, and absolutely no guarantee of a smooth landing, right side up. Back on the ground when it was all over, you really had something to talk about and could impress your friends with your rather risqué feat, for in the 1920's those who had flown were almost as few in number as those who piloted what then passed for airplanes in that era of the open cockpit and the fabric fuselage, the wooden struts and the wire wheels.

There were others, of course, actively engaged in the aviation game with far more at stake then the war birds of movieland zooming over Burbank or the stunt fliers staging spectacular displays above Miami's shimmering strands. With little more than road maps and magnetic compasses to guide them lonely Air Mail pilots by day strove to clear the Alleghenies and the Rockies. By night they strained to catch a faint glimpse of the chain of beacons across the Great Plains, alone under the stars with only the wind whistling through the guy wires and the drone of their throbbing motors to keep them company. Aeronautical designers and engineers pored long over blueprints and drafting boards in their quest to build aircraft of greater endurance and reliability, while down in Haiti and Santo Domingo young Marine Lieutenants, seeking to keep the peace in those troubled lands, daily flew reconnaissance flights and experimented with glide bombing techniques against fleeting groups of armed bandits. And finally in May 1927, after a non-stop flight of more than thirty hours aloft over water, Captain Charles A. Lindbergh electrified a watching world by his successful crossing of the Atlantic from west to east in his tiny monoplane. Not since the Wright brothers' historic achievement of the early 1900's had the public's interest and enthusiasm in man's mastery of the air been so aroused. Overnight the *Lone Eagle* and his *Spirit of St. Louis* became and were to remain for more than a decade not only symbols of American prowess in the aviation field and heady stimulants to the progressive development of that industry, but also served as a tremendous inspiration to an entire generation of imaginative and impressionable American youth seeking an outlet for its creative abilities. So far-reaching were the effects and so pronounced the scope of Lindbergh's accomplishment, a case may be made that his exploit was not to be overshadowed until the advent of the American astronauts and their successful encirclement in orbit of the Earth, some thirty-five years or roughly a generation after his history making, transatlantic flight.

Regardless of their status or their just claims to fame, these aviators, be they stunt fliers or test pilots, yesterday's war eagles or today's jet jockeys and outer space men, seem impelled by a common motive and possessed of a profound belief. Flying to them is basically a challenge: not only would they dare to fly, but in so doing they would venture to the limit, discovering in the sheer enormity of their daring additional strength and overpowering incentive. In the early days they played it by ear, living from day to day by their wits, flying by the seat-of-their-pants. As long as there was money for gasoline and oil the true barnstormer was content; as long as his airship held together any test pilot worth his salt would continue the power dive at full throttle. Dirty weather was no cause to ground the Air Mail; guerrilla rifles did not deter low-level strafing runs in the tropics of the Caribbean. Admittedly, their chosen profession was and continues to remain a hazardous one with comparable financial benefits far less forthcoming than its inherent perils, yet at least to the pioneers of aerial flight, they regarded their lot neither as a task nor a chore but simply thought of it as lots of fun with plenty of excitement and fresh air thrown in for good measure.

The real old-timers, the "old, bold pilots" had, as the airmen of the present retain, a common, all-embracing faith and a certain zest for living which appears to satisfy their needs, sustaining them in moments of adversity, driving them on to seek loftier goals. Fundamentally a matter of trust, their creed stresses self-confidence on the part of the individual flier, coupled with reciprocal respect for and between those various persons, agencies, and mechanical contrivances which seek to keep him airborne in defiance of Mr. Newton's celebrated Law of Gravity. Naturally, a pilot must have faith in himself and in his acquired skills. Similarly, he must have faith in those who design and build his airplane and its engine as well as in those who service and maintain it. And he must also have faith in his companions to act in harmony as members of a team, to assist him to accomplish his mission, and to give him a helping hand in time of need. For assuredly in the case of combat aviation, a compound must be blended from two contradictory elements: on the one hand, pilots are essentially individualists and must be treated accordingly if they are to perform at their best; on the other hand, they must be simultaneously trained to live, to think, and to act as a troupe of acrobats and as group participants working for the mutual good of a tactical organization in which all share, equally, success or failure. Hence, in learning to fly, men learn not to fear by conquering their doubts, and in their surmounting natural, physical forces which would impede their flight, they gain the necessary confidence to enable them to defeat their national enemies, in time of war, in aerial combat.

As a consequence, airmen have earned to a degree the right to live a little bit apart from their contemporaries who pound the gravel and the sod, and their activities are not infrequently associated with a certain aura of glamor. The skeptics and the spoil-sports occasionally view their behavior, particularly tendencies toward aloofness and casual indifference, disregard of caution and outright exhibitionism, with rather a jaundiced eye, forgetful of the fact that young men engaged in any dangerous occupation, who have cause to suspect they may be cut down summarily and without warning, are inclined to get the most out of life while they live, and are not overly concerned with public opinion. Nor should it be overlooked that if the gladiators of Rome and the toreadors of Madrid were scheduled to face death in the afternoon, pilots have a running blind date with the *Grim Reaper*, subject to call at any hour of the clock, day or night. Therefore, if they elect to avail themselves of the creature comforts of normal living when such amenities can be procured in their off- duty hours, there is patently no valid reason to deny them this harmless privilege.

Divested of its external trappings, the popular misconceptions of the aviator's life of opulence reveal to the contrary, a singularly demanding existence. Technical proficiency is taken for granted, and if self-discipline and self-reliance are required attributes, so, too, are energy and drive, ingenuity and imagination. Moral courage and physical stamina are vital qualities; determination and perseverance are paramount. Perhaps no other individual is more acquainted with loneliness than a fighter pilot, a solitary aviator in a high-performance combat airplane, lined up at the edge of the strip awaiting take-off. From the moment he adjusts his throttle and releases his brakes until such time as he switches off his ignition on his return to a landing field or a carrier's deck he will be riding side by side with sudden death as a constant companion. And those who have literally been hurled into space by a steam catapult will tell you that braced in the cradled flying machine, waiting for the man to pull the trigger, is a sensation closely akin to being shot at by a firing squad.

The "Riders of the Sky," especially the airmen of the era of trial and error, experiment and improvisation, are of a separate race. Neither they nor their successors felt disposed to consult the artificial guidance and counsel of the psychiatrist or the psychoanalyst; their way of life was diametrically opposed to the notion of those who are "Riders of the Golden Couch." As boys they grew up to become men, willing to assume risks, with an aggressive outlook rather than an apathetic approach regardless of the difficulties. Security and the soft life had little appeal; built-up life insurance policies and built-in fringe benefits were but secondary considerations in their choice of profession. Their outlet for their pent-up energies was to soar through the atmosphere; their limit the endless horizon.

To attempt to select the one individual who best typifies the spirit of the pioneers of aviation is well-nigh impossible. So much depends on personal choice and prejudice; so many of the best qualified contenders for the title achieved distinction for such diverse reasons it becomes a matter of relativity. But among the select few no name stands out in greater prominence than that of the late General Roy S. Geiger of the Marine Corps. He was not the first naval aviator to win his wings but rather the forty-ninth. He was not the first Marine officer to be officially designated a pilot but rather the fifth. Throughout his long and distinguished career in his Corps he thought of himself primarily as a line officer, additionally qualified as a naval aviator. From the very beginning he had a keen appreciation of the closely connected roles of the fighting man on the ground and his counterpart in the air, with but one mission and one common aim. So pronounced were his versatile feats and so outstanding his leadership he was a legend while he lived. Above all he served as an inspiration to at least one generation of Marines, on sea, on land, and in the air, to those who fought in two world conflicts and in a score of expeditions from China to Nicaragua. And after his death he continued to remain a glowing inspirational symbol to his onetime lieutenants destined to win further laurels in far distant Korea.

Foreword

Before the Pacific War, General Geiger was known primarily as one of the early Marine Birdmen, who had learned to fly after serving some ten years as a ground trooper. This preparatory service was spent as a junior officer on a variety of assignments, including sea and foreign service. Thus he learned the basic tenets of a Marine officer and the ground rules of minor tactics for ground forces, which gave him a decided advantage over those officers who had entered directly into the aviation branch of the Corps.

Geiger's relative seniority in the aviation branch assured him an almost unbroken chain of command billets, which experience early developed a noteworthy command presence and promoted professional recognition among his contemporaries. During the rare intervals when subordinate assignment threatened, the canny Geiger managed a selection to attend one or another of the war colleges. Thus, when opportunity beckoned to high command during the early Pacific War, Geiger – on the record – was simply the best qualified candidate. Those few who thought otherwise were unable to make a case against him. History records in the annals of Bougainville, Guam, Peleliu and Okinawa, the wisdom attending his selection.

As for the personality factor: For years prior to 1941, Roy Geiger had been a living legend in Naval and Marine aviation circles. After the war, this reputation had spread throughout the Naval service and within those command elements of the Army serving in the Pacific area. Within the amphibious commands, Geiger was known as the hard-driving landing force commander whose highly mobile command post ashore could always be found where the action was hottest.

Geiger exuded command presence and physical vitality; he was reticent in speech and reserved in manner, impulsive in action yet thorough in preparation. He demanded much of his subordinates and had small patience with those who failed to measure up. On the other hand, he never forgot those who had served him well throughout the years. He was a difficult man to know, especially for juniors. . .to be raked by that glacial twenty-yard stare was indeed a terrifying experience for the unwary, far more effective than was the usual "ten days hack."

Yet, for the favored few who did get to know him better and to understand his shifting moods, friendship with Roy Geiger was a rare experience, to be tasted and savored like old wine. Normally without small talk and seemingly devoid of a sense of humor, when among friends he liked and trusted Geiger could relax and be socially delightful. As a young bachelor officer, he was inclined to be prankish, an attribute not always acceptable to his seniors; as a mature officer, this trait became evident in his sometimes impish tendency of speech and action. Whatever his mood of the moment, he retained the affection of his social friends, as did he hold the respect and loyalty of his military juniors.

Notwithstanding Geiger's elevation to high rank among major task force commanders, he never forgot that in Marine aviation circles he would always remain the "OLD MAN," respected and admired by all those who wore wings, a commanding figure who, despite his obstreperous interludes, never lost that essential of leadership — the ability to inspire. Two generations of Marine pilots literally followed him to hell and back; other generations will be likewise inspired by this biography.

Geiger continued to fly well into his fifties because he loved the "wild blue yonder" and the challenge entailed. He was indeed a competent military pilot, especially in bad weather where his superior skill in instrument flying carried him safely through many dangerous situations.

He preached and practiced the theory of close air support for the Marine ground forces, and fretted at the misuse of Marine aviation units on what should have been Army Air Force missions. He was the mentor for those of us engaged in working out a reliable air support control system, which efforts finally materialized on Okinawa.

Throughout Geiger's aviation career he punctiliously insisted on recognition of his status as an officer of the Marine Corps line, qualified to command ground troops as well as aviation units. He effectively resisted any tendency to overlook his lineal seniority. To the last, he wished to be remembered as a Marine officer with a special qualification. So be it. That qualification which carries the golden wings is very special indeed, but Geiger never allowed the aviator's insignia to outshine the globe and anchor.

Roy Geiger's luck held to the last. At war's end he was approaching the age of retirement when he was stricken by a deadly ailment. The vigorous body which had carried him safely through thousands of hours of stormy skies and through countless exposures to enemy gunfire finally succumbed to Death's call. Though a shock to his family and host of friends, his demise was perhaps fortuitous — it would be difficult to imagine Roy Geiger as an invalid on the retired list.

1983   **General Vernon E. Megee, USMC (Ret)**

Appreciations

I first met General Geiger over thirty years ago, when he was a major, and during all of my experience with him, he occupied a command status. It is difficult to visualize him as a junior officer but, of course, he had been. As a matter of fact, he enlisted in the Marine Corps in November 1907, after receiving a law degree from Stetson University in Florida. Born on January 25, 1885, he was nearly 23 years of age when he entered the Marine Corps. After a little over a year in the ranks, he was commissioned a second lieutenant on February 5, 1909.

Service as a company officer included a tour of sea duty aboard battleships; foreign duty in Nicaragua, where he served as an artilleryman; and in China and the Philippines. After seven years duty as a line officer, in March 1916 he went to Pensacola as a student naval aviator, successfully completed the course and was designated a naval aviator in June 1917. He was the fifth Marine officer to be designated a naval aviator.

A year later found him commanding a bombing squadron in France as a part of the First Marine Aviation Force. For distinguished service in leading bombing raids against the enemy, he was awarded the Navy Cross, the first of many decorations for bravery and leadership.

The period between World War I and II found him serving in various aviation command assignments in Haiti, Nicaragua and the United States, as well as a tour in Washington as Officer in Charge, Marine Corps Aviation. General Geiger, cognizant of the unity of ground and air forces, and stimulated by his seven years experience as a ground officer, determined he would establish himself as an expert on the ground as well as in the air. To this end, he laid out for himself a plan of education. In 1925, he graduated from the Command and General Staff School, Fort Leavenworth. In 1927 he served as an instructor at the Marine Corps Schools. In 1929 he graduated from the Army War College. Between 1929 and 1941 he completed the Senior and the Advanced Courses at the Naval War College. Thus, in four professional institutions of learning, represented by the Army, the Navy and the Marine Corps, he acquired the basic knowledge of combined arms and the practice of higher staff and command functions, which he displayed so well during World War II.

The outbreak of World War II found the General in command of the First Marine Aircraft Wing, which he later led on Guadalcanal. During this period, he performed feats of extraordinary heroism which earned for him his second Navy Cross. Arriving on Guadalcanal less than one month after the landing, he established his headquarters in the "Pagoda," a wooden shack only 200 yards from the runway of Henderson Field, the main target for Japanese air and naval units. Commanding all the air on Guadalcanal, consisting of Army and Navy as well as Marine units, he molded together an organization on the field of battle that performed magnificently. At one time when morale was ebbing due to enemy action, weather, and lack of planes and supplies, he took off in an SBD from a field that some thought inoperable, dropped bombs on an area containing Japanese troops, and returned safely. He was 57 years of age at the time and this demonstration on the part of the "old man" had its desired effect on the young pilots.

The spring of 1943 found him back in Washington as Director of Aviation, but not for long. On October 15, 1943, he departed Washington for the South Pacific to assume command of the I Marine Amphibious Corps, which he led in the Bougainville operation, and for which he was awarded his first Distinguished Service Medal. Although there were ground officers competent by rank and training to assume command of the I Amphibious Corps, the selection of General Geiger, an aviator, was generally applauded throughout the Marine Corps.

He led this Corps, later redesignated III Amphibious Corps, with distinction in the invasion and recapture of Guam; in the assault and capture of the southern Palaus; and in the assault and capture of Okinawa. For these operations, he was awarded his second and third Navy Distinguished Service Medals and Distinguished Service Medal by the Army. It was while in command of the Corps on Okinawa that he succeeded while in command of the Tenth U.S. Army upon the death in action of its commander, Lieutenant General Buckner, and thus became the first and only Marine to command a United States Field Army. It was while on Okinawa that he was promoted to the rank of Lieutenant General, the first Marine aviator to advance to that rank.

As soon as the fighting was over on Okinawa, early in July 1945, he assumed duties as Commanding General, Fleet Marine Force, Pacific, where he served until his return to the United States in November of 1946.

During Christmas leave at his home in Pensacola in January 1947 he suddenly became ill. Flown to Naval Medical Center, Bethesda, he lingered but a short time and died on January 23, 1947. He was buried two days later on his 62nd birthday. General Geiger was slated for retirement for age only a week after his death. Due to decorations received in action against an enemy, he would have been promoted on the retired list to the rank of four-star general. The 80th Congress did so promote him to that rank posthumously.

Along with his determination, he was a man of few words and direct action. No beating about the bush with him, no words and phrases capable of two interpretations. When General Geiger announced his position or stated his views, none within hearing could misunderstand. I recall his action in one instance which illustrates his determination. When he departed Washington in 1943 for his second tour in the Pacific, he made a mental vow that he wouldn't return until he had seen Tokyo. Invited to be present on USS *Missouri* for the surrender ceremonies, he was in Tokyo Bay, but until the ceremony and certain formalities were completed, Americans were not permitted to enter Tokyo. Knowing that he was due to depart soon after the ceremonies, he and his aide contrived to visit the American Embassy in Tokyo before permission had been granted to enter the city.

On every battlefield in the Pacific, front line troops were accustomed to seeing their Corps Commander daily. He landed on D-Day on Bougainville, Guam, Peleliu, Anguar and Okinawa. Many a younger aide and battalion commander were tired from following him over the coral, hills and jungles of front line combat.

During the trying days of planning and amphibious assault, he displayed great patience with his staff and subordinates. Realizing they had many duties, he let them work out their problems without interference. By this display of confidence, he inspired his subordinates to maxium efforts. Nevertheless, he had his own ideas when staff work should be completed, and woe betide the staff officer who was delinquent.

Long ago he realized that aviation was not something separate, but a part of the Marine Corps. In the Quantico days of Smedley Butler, Geiger's aviators drilled and worked on projects other than aviation. Frequently it was his battalion that carried off honors on inspections or occupied the position of honor at parades. Whatever he considered worth doing, he considered worth doing well, be it playing volleyball, flying a plane, fighting Japanese, or, yes, making a liberty.

Punctuality was another attribute of his. He was always on time — usually a little early. Old-timers in aviation recall how he required his pilots to be punctual insofar as take-off time was concerned; and further recall that it was not uncommon to see pilots who were late for a take-off summoned from their cockpits and awarded one day's arrest for each minute of tardiness.

Old-timers in aviation also recall the many, many instances of determination and flying skill wherein he displayed his ability and willingness to fly any mission which he assigned to another.

Yes, the name Geiger conjures memories of an indomitable person and a great military leader.

1983   **Lieutenant General M.H. Silverthorn, USMC (Ret)**
                        General Geiger's Chief of Staff

In recent years much has been written and discussed pertaining to the extraordinary discoveries of new knowledge which have occurred throughout this twentieth century. When one looks back to the turn of the century and finds that the first powered aircraft flight would not be made for another four years, the true magnitude of the developments to come is spotlighted. In its first eight decades, the twentieth century has left little untouched or unchanged by a gradually accelerating pace of discovery. By the fifth decade, this acceleration had become almost an explosion and it was said that the amount of new knowledge accumulated in one year was greater than the total accumulation in all the previous years of recorded history. By the middle of the century, to cite only a few major examples, intercontinental air transport was commonplace, the jet age had begun, unclear energy was beyond theory and the first orbital probes of space exploration were within reach.

With its technological upheavals, however, the twentieth century also saw two worldwide wars, one in the second decade and the other in the fifth. Both were of an order of violence, destruction and geographical dimension previously unknown to man. Whether these cataclysmic events stimulated or inhibited the technological revolution is still open to debate. It seems certain, however, that the political, sociological, economic and moral effects of the two world wars will be factors of influence for the foreseeable future.

It was into this epochal century of world history that Roy Stanley Geiger made his entrance in January 1900, the month of his fifteenth birthday. He was an unusually practical, industrious, alert and responsible young man. His character was in no small way shaped by the untimely death of his father when he was but seven years of age. These characteristics, already strongly evident, were whetted and solidified by the need for all seven children to help their mother and each other on a daily basis. This was accomplished through all sorts of household jobs for the younger ones, and by extra after-school jobs as each grew older. There was a goal to the unity of family effort beyond daily routine necessity, however. Mrs. Geiger's leadership and close supervision of her seven children resulted in all of them achieving a college education. This in itself was a major accomplishment under very difficult circumstances, to say the least. For young Roy, these formative years let him open the new century with a strong sense of the objective, an attitude that nothing worthwhile came for free, and a keen understanding of the values of teamwork and cooperative effort under centralized control and direction. He was remarkably fitted therefore to encounter, as they came, each of the unprecedented developments and extraordinary events of the century which lay before him.

In a brief essay it is not easy to set forth the complete significance of the total impact that General Geiger had on the U.S. Marine Corps, and particularly on Marine Aviation. In the preceding paragraphs, the nature of the times in which he lived his almost forty years as a Marine has been highlighted, and the basic characteristics which he brought to this environment have been touched upon. It suffices to say that the unique combination of this highly motivated Marine with the racing developments across all the years of his Marine Corps career was to be one of the most fortuitous match-ups of Marine Corps history.

Colonel Willock has done a masterful research job in bringing the details of General Geiger's life and his Marine Corps career into chronological perspective. In so doing, he has painted an extremely accurate portrait of Geiger the man, his personality and mannerisms, his likes and dislikes, and his dogged determination to achieve whatever objective he set, for self or for Corps. In this regard, the substance of Chapter One could well be the framework for a set of principles to be religiously followed for assurance of an outstanding Marine Corps career. It should be required reading for any young person aspiring toward a successful life as a Marine.

In absorbing this exceptionally well done biography of a very exceptional Marine, the reader should take special care not to slough over some highly important points. For example, one should not miss the fact that Geiger had acquired almost eight years of experience as a ground officer, including action in Nicaragua, before being designated as the forty-ninth Naval Aviator. This becomes of importance in combination with the exploratory nature and newness of aviation at the time of his assignment for training. It gave him the capability to evaluate the uses of aviation in the improvement of ground combat effectiveness from the beginning of his aviation experience; and perhaps even more importantly, it gave him the basis for his view of aviation as an integral arm of the Marine Corps under Marine command and control, a view from which he never wavered throughout his life. Uniquely, within Marine Aviation, he spent his entire career in command positions, from World War I to Guadalcanal.

There were other early and senior Marine aviators, but whenever a pilot of that lengthy period used the term, "the old man," he invariably meant only Geiger. It was more than just seniority that gave him this preponderance of command assignments. It was also the fact that when he was not "with troops," he was constantly alert for the next opportunity to return to command. A fallout of this unique assignment pattern is embodied in the fact that Geiger was more often than anyone else very visible to his pilots and to his troops. This made for maximum inspirational effect on the entire command at any given time for superior performance. It was not the "pat-on-the-back" or "cheer-leader" type of inspiration, but more that of the "living legend" variety. No comment at all after a given evolution signified approval, but a nod of the head with an almost inaudible grunt was practically a commendation.

One last point the reader should not miss is also related to the constancy of command factor. It permitted Geiger to set his objectives for Marine Aviation and to then take the actions which would equip the units of his command to meet his chosen goals. An example is found in his early appreciation of the values of instrument flying in extending and fully realizing the potential of combat aircraft. He began with the "needleball-airspeed" augmentation of the traditional "seat-of-the-pants" method in the biplane Marine Corps. He was so proficient at it in those days of minimum airway aids or none, that the popular saying in the squadrons was to the effect that "the old man has homing-pigeon blood." In any case, he pursued the goal of instrument flying proficiency for the Marine Corps by procuring one of the earliest models of the Link Trainer and installing it in one of the hangars at Turner Field, Quantico. It was required utilization for all squadron pilots and was the start of the general proficiency level that is so commonplace today.

I was particularly fortunate to serve under General Geiger in fighter squadrons at Quantico during the pre-war years, and again in the Pacific as Operations Officer of the Fighter Commands at Guadalcanal and Bougainville. To me and my fellow officers he was so special that "living legend" doesn't really say it all. I know that without question he is the "Father" of Marine Aviation and always will hold that honored position. In a recent discussion with General Gerald C. Thomas of World War I, World War II and Korea fame, he gave me his measure of General Geiger in this way:

"We have always understood that John A. Lejeune was the greatest of all Marines. So the question then comes, 'Who was the second greatest?' Well, I divide my idea about it between Holland Smith and Roy Geiger. . .great Marines, and I won't choose between them, but I loved old Geiger."

I commend Roger Willock most highly for preserving for posterity this outstanding account of General Geiger's life.

1983   **Major General John P. Condon, USMC (Ret)**

Having been his aide and pilot in the combat zone and seeing him under conditions of tension and relaxation, to me General Geiger is the ideal Marine for all times. A man of few words--but if you were involved--you had better remember them!

Our first meeting occurred while I was engineering officer with VMSB-131, temporarily at the Naval Air Station, Coronado, California, on our way to Guadalcanal. LtCol Paul Moret, our commanding officer, returning from headquarters of the wing, came out to the Officers Club swimming pool and asked, "Who has flown twin engine aircraft?" No one spoke up! On looking over the group, he finally said, "Jack, you flew twin engine Beechcraft when you were with the Civil Aeronautics Authority." I replied, "I have very little time--less than 50 hours." He replied, "Report to the Chief of Staff immediately," which I did.

There, General Woods told me that "General Geiger was getting a plane to fly to Guadalcanal, was ready to go and needed a pilot. He is waiting to talk with you."

I entered and was greeted from his desk with his famous 20-foot stare, saying that, "I am looking for a plane to fly to Guadalcanal. What do you think of a DC-3?" This came without warning, but quickly remembering earlier squadron discussions of the Guadalcanal area--mostly water with the scattered, rugged Solomon Islands, I replied, "Considering the large water area under combat conditions where runways can be bombed out, have you considered an amphibian?" Again, the 20-foot stare and, "You mean something like a PBY-5A?" I said, "Yes." He replied, "General Woods will make all the arrangements--you be ready to go, immediately, to the factory in San Diego to pick one up--that is all." He continued working at his desk.

General Geiger always rode in the co-pilot's seat and very early I appreciated his flying ability. We were on instruments and I had been flying for about three hours when suddenly he said, "You take a rest, I'll fly for a while." He took over the controls and he really amazed me with his precision on instruments when I considered how little time he had to do this type of flying. He had a sixth sense.

His Marine philosophy to me is summed up in his statement, "There are two places to be if you want to succeed in the Marine Corps--in time of peace, go to school and prepare for war--in time of war, get to the front and apply what you have learned."

Heroes to General Geiger were "People who prepared themselves and who were at the right place at the right time."

When General Woods gave me the instructions for picking up the PBY-5A, he also said, "Jack, General Geiger has decided to make you his aide. Being a major, you won't be paid any more but he doesn't want the extra person in the combat area." This changed my whole life and set up a most unique friendship.

1983   **Brigadier General Jack R. Cram, USMC (Ret)**
General Geiger's Aide and Pilot

Contents

Chapter I

Meet Me on the Pier

Located some forty miles south of the capital at Washington and fronting the Potomac River is one of the nation's most important naval installations, the United States Marine Corps Base at Quantico, Virginia. Presently the site of the Marine Corps Schools, this extensive land tract has served in many diverse capacities and has undergone numerous faceliftings as well as changes of name since ground was initially broken there in the spring of 1917 for the construction of a training center for an Advanced Base Force. In the autumn of 1921, this post, then officially designated the United States Marine Barracks, Quantico, was commanded by Brigadier General Smedley D. Butler. Its principal function at that time was to provide the home station and training grounds for headquarters and troop elements of the East Coast Expeditionary Force, the Third Marine Brigade. Despite its rather imposing title, this organization under command of Colonel Robert H. Dunlap, was considerably understrength due to budgetary limitations prevailing as an aftermath of the First World War.

Its foremost components were the remnants of two rifle regiments and an attached machine gun battalion which had served overseas as a part of the Second Division, AEF, reinforced by a composite artillery regiment, signal, engineer, and searchlight companies, and a small aviation detachment. The last mentioned unit, the 1st Aviation Group, consisted of two aircraft squadrons, each of twelve airplanes, largely *DeHavilland* and *Vought* light bomber—observation scouts, and an active division of three kite balloons. Composed of approximately 20 commissioned officers and 370 enlisted men, and commanded by Major Roy S. Geiger, this group centered its activities around a landing strip at Reid,

1

immediately south of and adjacent to Quantico, pending completion of a combination flying field and seaplane base within the confines of the main reservation. It represented roughly one half of the total strength of Marine Corps Aviation, the remainder being more or less equally divided between the First and Second Marine Brigades, serving on expeditionary duty, respectively, in Haiti and Santo Domingo, plus a very small aviation contingent stationed on the remote Island of Guam in the Marianas.

Similar to its commanding officer, the majority of the squadron pilots comprising the 1st Aviation Group had previously flown in combat in France and Belgium with the Day Wing of the Northern Bombing Force aside from many additional hours aloft in the Caribbean Republics. During the spring of 1921 these war-wise Captains and Lieutenants had participated in a series of cross-country flights, and in the summer of that year they had taken an active part in the aerial bombardment of obsolete German and American battleships off the Virginia Capes. In September they commenced a rigorous training program involving gunnery practice and night flying runs in preparation for field maneuvers and tactical exercises, scheduled to be held the following month in the Wilderness region of Virginia, in which the 1st Aviation Group had been assigned the all important mission of providing close air support for the ground forces of the Third Marine Brigade.

Intent on making a good showing and demonstrating conclusively to the Brigade Commander and the umpires the value of close liaison between air and land forces, even under conditions of mock warfare, Major Geiger strove to his utmost to train his squadron pilots thoroughly for their contemplated operations. Granted that aircraft and their water-cooled engines of the early 1920's were comparatively more reliable than their wartime counterparts, the improvements which had been effected nevertheless left a great deal to be desired. Instrument flying as contrasted to contact, or aerial navigation dependent on actual observation of the terrain, was still in such rudimentary stages that it was generally regarded more as a novelty than as an accepted technique. And if low-level strafing and glide bombing were attended with a certain degree of risk, any attempt at formation flying or intricate aerial maneuver after dark, in fog, or in other circumstances of reduced visibility was considered a decidedly hazardous undertaking.

A born leader, Major Geiger displayed ample proof of his mettle by personally setting an example. Night after night he led off successive flights from the take-off strip at Reid, performing difficult and frequently dangerous aerial evolutions himself in his *DH-4B* or *VE-7* before permitting his junior officers to engage in such work. The searchlight company at Quantico being anxious to get in a little night practice, the 1st Aviation Group accordingly obliged the lamp operators by acting as targets of opportunity, soaring back and forth across the autumn skies, attempting to evade the searching beams of light. Under the group leader's tutelage an effective procedure was devised wherein pilots caught in the rays simply rolled their planes over on their backs, and then pulled out in the opposite direction. Although such diversionary tactics were quite good enough for most of the fliers, there was one aviator among their midst who favored a more spectacular solution. A recent newcomer to Marine Aviation, this officer, Captain John A. Minnis, had already established an enviable reputation as a distinguished line officer, having been awarded the Navy Cross for gallantry in action on the Western Front. Seeking other fields to conquer and not content with the squadron's accepted system of evasion, he championed the notion of diving straight into the lights on the ground at full power, and then pulling up abruptly at the last possible moment short of a head-on collision. His contemporaries attempted to dissuade him from a stunt they viewed as overly reckless and fraught with peril, but he was stubborn in his beliefs, and resolved that given the opportunity he would put his plans to actual test. In time he got his chance, and on the evening of 23 September 1921, while flying over the Potomac, alone in a *VE-7,* he discovered to his sorrow and to the dismay of his comrades that he had grossly overextended the capabilities of his aircraft not to mention his limits as a pilot.

*   *   *   *   *   *   *   *   *

As far as Major Geiger was concerned that day has not differed greatly from any other. Arriving at Reid field just prior to Morning Colors, he spent the forenoon at his field desk in a makeshift office in the corner of a hangar attending to the usual pile of paperwork. His afternoon was devoted to a careful inspection of the aircraft of that division scheduled to take off after dusk in a night flying exercise, and to a final briefing of those pilots who were to participate in the problem. As the evening shadows fell and as the lights of the post began to twinkle, he climbed into the cockpit of his *VE-7* (No. 5671), revved up its slowly turning motor, signaled for the wheel chocks to be withdrawn, and took off with a roar. Fifteen minutes later he was back on the strip, and after a brief word of warning to the group of assembled pilots to steer clear of the direct beams of the searchlights which had just been switched on, jumped into his automobile, and headed home for a late supper. On his return to his residence, Quarters No. 18 on the Main Post at Quantico, he quickly shifted from uniform to civilian clothes, and then sat down before the table in the dining room, eagerly anticipating the first hot meal of the day.

Although it was long past her bedtime, for it was almost half-past eight, the Major's three-year-old daughter, Joyce, had persuaded her parents to permit her to remain up late so that she could watch the searchlights. Seated on a low stool in her night clothes, clutching a small puppy and swathed up to her chin in a blanket, for the evening was cool, the little girl peered skyward from her special spot just outside the back door; inside the house her baby brother lay peacefully asleep in his crib while her mother busied herself in the kitchen. Having already downed a generous helping of steak and potatoes, the Major was just about to attack a large slice of his favorite desert, lemon cream pie, when he put down his fork, abruptly pushed away from the table, and walked over to look out the front door.

From the worried look on his face, his wife realized that he was quite disturbed; however, Eunice did not question him, knowing full well that if he were so inclined he would discuss the matter in due course. She had not long to wait, for turning about, her husband said, "Honey, there's something wrong up there tonight. I can feel it. The motors sound all right, the weather's clear, and all that, but I just don't like it."

"Well," she replied, "You've done everything you can, taught them all you know. They'll make out. By the way, who's up there this evening?"

"The usual crowd. Hardly a division. Only Minnis, Rogers, and Farrell. Sanderson and Palmer, too. I'm not worried about Tex or Walter, Sandy and Hoke. But I hope the other fellow

4

knows what he's doing. It's hard to say what's wrong, but I know I've got to get back out to the field before something happens."

Back in the bedroom, buckling up his leather puttees, the Major momentarily paused as he heard the unmistakable sounds of an aircraft engine at full throttle, of an airplane in an all-out power dive. As he hastened into the corridor, hat in hand, the little child outside the house squeezed the puppy so hard he whimpered, fascinated at the sight of a rapidly descending plane aimed straight at the searchlights at the river's edge, caught head-on within their blinding rays. Rising from her stool she ran around in front of the quarters, pointing toward the Potomac and calling loudly, "Look, Daddy, look!" Within seconds there was a terrific *whump* as the plane plummeted into the river raising a cloud of spray and flying debris.

The post siren shattered the sudden stillness in the wake of the crash. Buttoning up his blouse, the Major called over his shoulder: "Get somebody to look after the children. I'll get a ride. You take our car and meet me on the pier."

Out in the street he commandeered an automobile leaving the nearby Commissioned Officers' Mess, and to its startled driver he ordered: "Take me to the Post Dock, quick as you can!" At the pier he boarded the first launch with engine running and coxswain at the tiller. "Let's go!" he said, and as the helmsman cast off the lines and yanked the bell cord, Lieutenant Farrell made a pier-head jump into the departing motor boat in time to join his commanding officer.

Clear of the boat basin the launch headed upstream at full speed while the two officers forward in the bow began to search the murky waters with an electric torch. Shortly thereafter they found what they were looking for: a few scattered bits of floating wreckage and a prominent oil slick. Stripping to his shorts and shivering in the cold for a breeze had spring up, the Major hesitated not an instant. Without a second's thought he plunged deep into the Potomac. A few moments later his head broke the surface as he returned to gasp for air. "Can't see a thing, but I'll find it," he called. After a second attempt he rose again, shaking his head to clear it of water, and shouted, "Over this way, Farrell, I think I've got it. Give me a hand, we've got to get a line down there fast!"

Working frantically the two officers repeatedly dove or swam

5

down underwater thirty feet and more, pausing only briefly to replenish their lungs on the surface. By this time other small craft had arrived at the scene of operations. Out of the darkness came the unmistakable voice of the Commanding General, "Geiger, what's the situation?" Swimming over to the General's launch, Geiger hung on to the gunwale long enough to reply, "Located the plane but have to feel our way. Forward section seems buried deep in the mud. Engine has sheared off its mount and has been thrust back into the cockpit. Pilot's pinned underneath. I'll do the best I can to get him out, General." "All right, Geiger, go ahead," Butler barked, "but watch out, we don't want to lose another Marine out here tonight in the middle of this river."

With time at a premium now for the Major was literally turning blue from the cold, he made half a dozen additional descents, each of several minutes duration. Finally, he rose for the last time from the river's bottom, arms deeply scratched, blood pouring from cuts on his face and chest. Thrashing the water and gasping for breath, he called out, "I'm holding his body between my legs, but for God's sake, General, don't ask me to bring up what's left to the surface." Quick as a flash came the answer, "Hang on, Major, we'll take over," whereupon several persons jumped overboard at once to support the exhausted diver and to relieve him of his gruesome burden. "Well done, Geiger, that's quite enough for tonight. Get out of the water. That's an order, understand," Butler commanded. So spent he could barely nod his head by way of acknowledgement, the Major suddenly felt himself being lifted bodily out of the river, and almost before he realized what had happened, found himself stretched out prone on the floor boards in the stern cockpit of the General's launch.

Back at the Post Dock, Colonel Dunlap, who had accompanied General Butler to the scene of the crash and had witnessed the recovery of Minnis' body, decided it was no time for half measures. Well aware of his senior's pronounced views on the subject of hard liquor, for the General was an avid teetotaler, Dunlap took one look at Geiger, and made up his mind to risk the General's ire, come what may. Turning to the Major's wife, who was waiting at the pier, the Colonel asked, "Mrs. Geiger, have you any whisky at your quarters?" "No, at this moment we do not," she replied. "Well, I'll tell you what to do," Dunlap continued, "Drive back to my house. Ask Mrs. Dunlap to give you that decanter which she will find in the inside left corner of the buffet in our dining room. You take it, and return to your quarters as fast as you can. Get a fire blazing in your living room fireplace. Dig up all the blankets you can lay your hands on, and wait for us. We'll take care of your husband, don't you worry."

That night the lights in Quarters No. 18 burned brilliantly until the wee hours of dawn. Not only did the Major stay one jump ahead of an acute case of double pneumonia, so drastic was the nature of the "first aid" administered, he felt inclined to report for duty at Office Hours the following morning. Somehow he was prevailed upon to rest up and to recharge his batteries; nevertheless, so potent were his recuperative powers he drove out to Reid field the second day after Minnis' fatal accident. Realizing that their commanding officer was still living on sheer momentum if not his nerves, and that it would be the height of folly for him to fly, the pilots ganged together and talked the *Old Man* out of his attempt to don flight clothing. Just to play it safe they conveniently arranged to have his plane deadlined for an engine check, although it was quite obvious its motor at that precise moment no more needed attention than General Butler's official automobile required a wash and polish. They could not keep him grounded indefinitely, of course, and if you will check Major Geiger's personal flight log book, you will note recorded that on 25 September 1921 he flew for forty-five minutes in *VE-7* (No.5965), the group leader of a formation flight at the military funeral of the late Captain Minnis.

*   *   *   *   *   *   *   *   *

The spectacular events surrounding the terminal act of Captain Minnis' flying career have been deliberately selected for analysis for the primary reason that the particular incident and its aftermath serve to bring into striking focus many of the outstanding character traits of his immediate superior, Major Geiger. Naturally, there were other occasions which exemplify to their fullest the distinctive mannerisms and singular qualities of the latter officer at various stages of his colorful service life. There was, for example, the episode at Camp Elliott in 1913, when Second Lieutenant Geiger astounded the onlookers by his high-diving and swimming feats in the Panama Canal, a performance carried out under express orders of the Camp Commander, Major Smedley D. Butler. But he was only twenty-eight years of age at that time, and comparatively speaking, it was too early in his career to draw over-all conclusions from a single, melodramatic event. By the same token, there were any number of incidents which transpired in the Pacific Island Campaigns of the Second World War, wherein General Geiger, first as a Wing Commander, then as an Amphibious Corps Commander, and finally as an Army Commander, demonstrated conclusively his marked abilities as a dynamic, aggressive, and fearless combat leader in positions of great responsibility, invariably under duress. But by that time he was in his late fifties, the die had long before been cast, and he was largely a living legend, a man who could be depended upon to surmount the unpredictable and to achieve the impossible in his stride.

On the other hand, in 1921 at Quantico, at age thirty-six, Major Geiger was physically in his prime. Approximately one third of the way through his service career, he had already won an eminently satisfactory reputation as a line officer as well as a naval aviator. He was an individual of whom a great deal was expected, and his conduct immediately prior to, during, and after the Minnis incident gave him abundant opportunity to prove himself worthy of the trust and confidence reposed in him by his superiors and his associates.

Examine carefully the actions of this pilot which culminated in his nighttime plunge into the Potomac to extricate from a wrecked and submerged aircraft the body of a fellow comrade. Here in essence is an aviation group leader who has conscientiously trained the members of his command to carry out their assigned missions in the proper manner. Not content to sit idly by on the sidelines or at rear area headquarters directing this and ordering that, he has personally taken part in all of the evolutions, the leader of the pack in which he sets the pace and takes the followers over the course. Throughout his life Geiger was never known to have asked or commanded another to attempt anything which he was not first willing to test himself. He turns the pack loose to fend for themselves only after he is convinced that the individuals know what they are doing and can handle the situation. Once committed to an operation it does no good to fret about the outcome: never a worrier, Geiger was not one to counsel his fears nor to fall prey to unnecessary mental anguish and anxiety. It was not a devil-may-care attitude, nor lack of concern, nor outright indifference, but rather one of security gained through self-confidence and self-discipline. Well aware that accidents can and do happen and that well calculated plans all too frequently go astray, he was optimistic enough to hope for the best, on the alert for the unforeseen, ready to employ alternate plans to meet changing circumstances.

He was quick to sense trouble. A man with highly developed imaginative powers, he was blessed with extrasensory perception bordering on that of the proverbial "Woman's Intuition." So prescient was he, he could often foretell events or predict their outcome with uncanny accuracy. So sensitive was his private, built-in radar detection system, he could readily spot deceit or fraud, or unmask a charlatan, with the minimum of circumstantial evidence. At one point in his career, for instance, Geiger served as a member of a Board of Investigation convened to uncover the facts surrounding the mysterious and rather suspicious disappearance of a Marine aircraft at an outlying field. Confronted with the pilot of the missing plane, Geiger sized him up at first glance, and after casually listening to the latter's opening remarks, peremptorily cut him short with the interjection, "You're lying!" Forthwith, he was able to prove within a matter of hours what he had suspected: that the plane had not crashed as reported, but rather had been deliberately flown into a swamp, whereupon by prior agreement it had been acquired—for a set price—by a civilian test pilot and stunt flier. In much the same fashion with the aid of his extraordinary insight, Geiger sensed that Captain Minnis had committed an error of judgement, and he knew only too well what would be the end result.

Once the matter has gotten out of control and the plane has struck the river, Major Geiger doesn't waste time trying to figure out what to do. Nor does he collapse with indecision when faced with a sudden, unexpected emergency. Throughout his life he was always regarded as a very positive individual. To him the worst thing an officer could do was to do nothing. He always felt that it was infinitely better to try something—anything—than to sit and stew, and that once having made a decision it should be prosecuted with full force and determination, trusting things would eventually turn out all right. His reaction to the crisis is typical. He does not despair, nor wring his hands, nor run to the telephone to consult with the Officer of the Day as to what should be done and by whom. He makes a quick mental estimate of the situation, decides on a course of action, and runs out to implement it as fast as he can. So confident does he feel as to its successful outcome, he asks his wife to meet him on the pier.

He improvises as he goes, taking full advantage of every opportunity, and somehow makes his way to the scene of the accident. When he arrives at the spot he doesn't vacillate. He knows there's not one chance in a million that the downed pilot could have survived the crash and the immersion, but it has always been traditional in his Corps that every effort will be made to save a man's life or to rescue him from peril, and if this be impossible, at least to recover his remains. So over the side he plunges knowing full well that he is perhaps the best swimmer on the Post, the one man at that moment who might be able to do more than any other. This is not recklessness nor rashness in the extreme. Neither is it cheap showmanship. It is more a matter of calculated audacity, formulated on the conviction that as the leader it is incumbent on him to set the example plus the fact that basically he was responsible for Captain Minnis being in the plane that evening.

He is cognizant of all of the risks of the undertaking. The river is deep, the currents unknown. The water is cold, the slimy mud is treacherous. With no light to guide him underwater he cannot see; his only sensory feeling is restricted to that of touch. He doesn't know exactly where the target lies; he can only imagine what he will find if he is fortunate enough to locate the sunken plane. Time is running out and haste is vital, but that does not bother him: he was always one who performed best under pressure. He perseveres and at length finds what he is searching for. Making use of all available resources, for an efficient leader must be sufficiently clever and creative to make the most with what he has got at hand, Major Geiger puts into play his capable assistant, Lieutenant Farrell, also a powerful swimmer, and then proceeds to carry out his plans.

Geiger's commanding officer arrives at the scene. He is quickly briefed on the situation, and approves the Major's concept of the pending operation. It is now high time to commit his reserves: from now on it's all or nothing. Drawing on his tremendous physical energy and strength Geiger employs his unique skills to the utmost of his ability. His resolution and

10

dogged determination pay dividends; his stamina, intrepidity, and moral courage return the value of his investment in full. He succeeds in his mission, and only breaks off the action when it is quite evident there is no more he can do. He will not leave the water until he is ordered to come out. Then and only then is he drawn from the Potomac utterly exhausted from his exertions, to be laid upon the deck gasping for breath, muscles twitching from overstrain.

General Butler and Colonel Dunlap were excellent judges of character and human behavior. In this case they knew their man particularly well, for they had campaigned together in the field for many years in many far off places. Their diagnosis of the Major's symptoms and their recommended prescription for his recovery may be regarded in hindsight as overly rigorous, but they were highly effective and were tailored to fit the man. The waiting ambulance at the Post Dock was spurned. The Post Hospital with its white sheets and its nurses, its medicines and its sedatives, was not the place for a person of Major Geiger's disposition. He was invariably scornful of any sickness or weakness. An exponent of physical fitness, ever mindful of the state of his health—he was in all probability never gravely ill for more than a day in his life until a few weeks before his death—he had a passionate distrust and dislike of physicians and surgeons. Had the doctors gotten their hands on him at Quantico, they would have put him to bed and kept him in it for days, under observation; it might have been weeks before they would have released him to fly again. So his friends spared him that ordeal: with the aid of a Corpsman they patched up his wounds on the end of the pier; bundled him up and got him into an automobile; and took him back to where he belonged, to his wife at his quarters. In familiar surroundings they double-dosed him with tonic of their own choice (and brand), and although it is conceded that if the shock-treatment may have been primitive, and the prognosis based on hope rather than on scientific medical deduction, the desired results were achieved on schedule with few if any lingering, post- operative after-effects.

There is no lengthy period of convalescence for the patient. The Major was never one to feel sorry for himself. Inclined by nature to be somewhat impulsive and impatient, he disdained idleness, and he became easily bored if he had nothing to do. Inherently cheerful he was always eager to get back to work, willing to tackle the job at hand, and in this instance he was champing at the bit to get back into harness once more. This tendency was one of his well known trade-marks. Perhaps it is best summed up in the following observation of one of his close friends: "Roy had a remarkable animal vitality." Repeatedly throughout his career Geiger demonstrated an amazing ability to bounce back into battery regardless of the amount of punishment he had suffered. Long after most of his contemporaries had fallen by the wayside, he was still up and about. When he could stand it no longer he could lie down like a dog, and after a short nap could awaken, refreshed and revitalized, all set to start all over again. For he was relatively impervious to fatigue, and he was immensely strong. He never reached the limits of his endurance until almost the day of his death, and he was never tired himself for any protracted period.

Thus, in many respects, his recovery of Captain Minnis' body from the depths of the Potomac was just another challenge which he met and mastered in his own fashion. His entire life as an aviator was a challenge: he piloted aircraft and engaged in free ballooning not simply because he yearned to fly or to soar through space, and enjoyed it, but rather because it was fundamentally a test of his skills. He seemed to love danger for its own sake. Undoubtedly, he took the longest and often the most fantastic chances, but he thrived on excitement, and he did many things seemingly to experience the mere thrill of doing them.

He also worked hard, desperately so, at most everything he attempted. He had an uphill struggle as a lad to acquire an education; he had no end of difficulty securing a commission in the Marine Corps. Even at the very beginning of his aviation career, as his flight instructor at Pensacola will attest, it was a very near thing. Contrary to common belief, Lieutenant Geiger was by no means a "natural pilot." He had to fight to earn his wings; subsequently, he flew with a firm and forceful hand rather than a light touch at the controls. Likewise, he struggled with might and main to accumulate the very best technical education in his selected profession. Not only did he successfully complete complicated courses of instruction at both the Army and Naval War Colleges, he was also a Distinguished Graduate of the Army's Command and General Staff School. He threw himself heart and soul into his studies, and he literally slaved over his books and his maps in his efforts to excel. And years later, perhaps no other General Officer in the Pacific worked harder than Roy Geiger intent on learning and applying the tools of his trade, or utilized their staffs more efficiently than he from Guadalcanal through to the end at Okinawa.

In everything he did, he played to win, for he was not content to finish in Second Place nor was he satisfied with any Second Prize. In this respect a trace of vanity undeniably is present; however, any born leader normally strives to surpass his contemporaries quite aside from the fact that Geiger was a commissioned officer of that branch of the naval service long known to demand perfection as a matter of course. A superb pilot and instrument flier, he was likewise an accomplished athlete and a versatile sportsman. In addition to his aquatic prowess he was a skilled horseman: he had a good seat, jumped well, and was an enthusiastic polo player. He was a crack shot on the rifle range, especially as a junior officer. To qualify as *Marksman* or *Sharp-shooter* was not sufficiently distinguished for him: Roy Geiger had to shoot *Expert Rifleman* or turn in his Springfield. He loved athletic sports and contests of any sort for relaxation as well as for physical conditioning. He particularly enjoyed volley ball, and in competition he hated to lose. In this game as well as others which he played, he was very critical of his own performance, and he never tried to cover up his mistakes by blaming his partners.

He could not excel at everything, of course. One activity he could never master was golf, although he most certainly worked at it conscientiously for years. Some people play golf for exercise, and others for fun and pleasant conversation. Geiger played the game for vengeance. Par for the course in his case had little to do with the number of strokes taken, but was measured in units of time: the number of hours it took him to hack his way around eighteen holes. Whether or not he ever broke through into the high eighties at Quantico's links is open to question (he could be deadly around the green), but he could break at least one golf club in the rough or in a sand trap on a single summer's afternoon. As for his golf balls, they had a difficult choice: a very short life and a merry one—being driven hopelessly out of bounds and lost forever, or, a long and punishing career—being hammered into frayed cubes, ultimately to die the Death of One Thousand Cuts. But if the Geiger mantelpiece were barren of trophies for match or medal

13

play, he could take pride in other lines of endeavor, for he played a fair hand at bridge, and he enjoyed the reputation of being a highly skilled and most astute operator at the poker table. Completely noncommittal and composed with his chilly-eyed stare, he could maintain a poker-faced front indefinitely, and he was always considered a formidable opponent in most any card game.

From a strictly professional point of view Roy Geiger never enjoyed playing Second Fiddle in any man's orchestra nor did he perform at his best in a subordinate capacity, in the back row. A measure of conceit enters the picture here; yet, the explanation seems to lie more in his independent nature than in his intolerance of restraint and impatience of detail. Given a position of responsibility or a free hand to run affairs as he saw fit, he would seize the opportunity, take the initiative, pick up the ball and run the length of the field. As second-in-command or relegated to a subsidiary role, Geiger seldom displayed either the enthusiasm or the zeal which he could be counted upon to impart were he the designated leader. He was not cut out to be a staff officer for the reason that he preferred to be actually doing things—flying, marching, shooting, or maneuvering—rather than sitting around a conference table or in a tent talking about what he was going to do or making up lists of things he was going to need. Petty administrative details bored him. Discussions and debates were not to his liking, for he was inherently a quiet and taciturn individual, especially when he had something on his mind; moreover, he was essentially more interested in the practicalities of the moment or the problem at hand than he was listening to another expound on the theoretical aspects of future possiblities or eventualities. Noted for his spirit of friendly cooperation, Geiger nevertheless was too outspoken to have been classed as an organizational-man, and far too direct in his approach to have adopted any party line or championed any platform for the sake of convenience or conformity. And he was far too much of an individualist ever to have been a convincing yes-man.

But out in front, like the leader of a band, Geiger seemed to shine. There is a bit of showmanship in most aviators, and he was enough of an exhibitionist that he liked not only to display his wares but also to show them off with no holds barred whenever opportunity knocked. He drove his automobiles the same way he piloted his planes—hard and fast—with a certain flair tending toward the dramatic. There is no denying a streak of childishness existed in his adult make-up, but it had been so channeled in his case as to become an asset. His colorful trait was imparted into many things: for example, his forceful and buoyant personality was injected into all of his written orders. Nobody made up his mind for him. He consulted with his staff, made his own decision, and told them *what* he wanted to do. From then on it was up to them to figure out *how* to do it in accordance with their commander's basic desires. Although he frequently disagreed with his subordinates he was invariably loyal to them; he gave them considerable latitude, and seldom interfered, but he demanded results. In some instances he bore a grudge against those few individuals whom he though were not bearing their proper share of the load, or whose conduct had been such that he had lost confidence in them. Generally speaking, it may be said that he had his own ideas about completed staff work, but if he drove his staff hard, he drove himself to a greater degree. Consequently, his operation orders were noted for their clarity, conciseness, and accuracy, the entire work indelibly stamped with the individuality of the commanding officer. Geiger set the over-all tone and style; the tactical units of his command became infected by the confidence and enthusiasm radiated by their leader; thereafter, there was little to concern him other than his supervisory functions as an executive making sure that what had been approved and ordered was in fact being carried out.

Geiger was no headquarters commander. Time and again throughout the Pacific Campaigns he astonished his superiors as well as his subordinates by personally showing up at the most unlikely spots at the most unlikely times. Advance outposts, forward observation posts, and other sites open and exposed to enemy fire were his specialty. As an Amphibious Corps Commander at Peleliu, General Geiger landed on the beach on D-Day prior to the arrival of the Commanding General of the First Marine Division. He insisted on visiting the command posts of two of its three rifle regiments heavily committed and under intensive fire, and it was only with great difficulty that the Assistant Division Commander was able to persuade him from making his way forward to the third element, struggling to maintain a toe hold in a gap in the lines, more or less in a no-man's land. Again, at

Okinawa, he could not be restrained from moving his Corps command post nearer to the enemy front lines than those of the field headquarters of his two Divisions. So anxious was he to get closer to the Japanese homeland than any other member of his command, he accompanied an advance combat patrol during the fighting at Okinawa. In substance, Geiger was not the type to order "Go there!", but rather one who said, "Follow me!" as a matter of principle. He was bound and determined to get to Tokyo before the fighting was over, and in this he was eminently successful. On 1 September 1945, the day before the official Japanese surrender ceremony was consummated, General Geiger turned down the offer of a tour of Yokohama, electing instead to drive inland to the Emperor's Palace at the capital. He drove through the city unchallenged, and at the grounds of the American Embassy arranged to have the Swiss custodian sign a document attesting his presence at Tokyo, thereby enabling him to win a personal wager he had made some months before with other high-ranking American officials. There was more than impishness involved in this incident—it was in large part a mixture of resourcefulness and determination.

Roy Geiger's personality was a most complex one, for in the main the man was a bundle of contradictions. He was noticeably unpredictable: no one, not even his wife or his intimate friends, knew with any degree of certainty what was on his mind, what were his intentions, or what might be his reactions to any given situation. Normally high-spirited and vivacious, his hearty air and outgoing manner could easily give way to moodiness were he not physically or mentally occupied. At times he could be cold and calculating, completely detached and analytical in his approach, as unemotional as a lawyer. In this respect he showed strong traces of his legal mind and training, for he had a fantastic memory for details, provided they pertained to a subject in which he was interested. He could sight-scan countless pages of intricate technical data or complicated professional texts, pick out the salient facts, and remember most of them thanks to the retentive powers of his photographic mind. On the other hand he could evidence complete disinterest, or resort to snap judgement; moreover, it was uniformly difficult for him to remember person's names despite the fact that he might have been working closely with those individuals for extended periods of time.

16

Usually blunt and gruff, close-mouthed and inclined to converse in monosyllables, when he was so inclined he would say what he liked or what displeased him in no uncertain terms and at considerable length. He was not afraid to talk back to higher authority if he were convinced that he was in the right, and he did not hesitate to employ straight-from-the-shoulder tactics to make himself understood or to get what he wanted. In this his attitude was strikingly similar to that of his lifelong friend, General Butler, for both officers had a reputation for speaking their minds and taking positive action, ready to take the consequences and to assume all blame and responsibility for their deeds.

Curiously enough, despite the fact that Roy Geiger is most commonly thought of or associated with his feats as a naval aviator, he uniformly regarded himself as a line officer endowed with extra, special qualifications as a pilot. He prided himself on the fact that either as a squadron leader, group, or wing commander he could march or drill, shoot or skirmish in the field, as well as any line officer attached to a comparable sized ground element, and he found it difficult to understand why infantry and artillerymen considered his achievement as rather unusual. To some it seemed strange that a Marine pilot could command an Amphibious Corps not to mention an Army in combat, but General Geiger felt equally at home on a cruiser or battleship as he did taking off from a carrier's deck or landing a free balloon in a farmyard, and he saw nothing odd about his rifleman's ability to crawl forward along a communication trench or to bed down for the night in a foxhole.

He was never a self-seeking officer. He refrained from requesting special duty assignments, taking the good with the bad as a true professional soldier. He did not seek favors nor did he pass out praise and awards indiscriminately. He asked for little. He was never known to be a scrounger, and he was definitely not the acquisitive type to amass possessions merely because they bore no identifying marks or whose ownership otherwise could not be established. He was primarily interested in getting his fair share of what he had justly earned or to which he was normally entitled. He was noted for his punctuality and his personal neatness. Unlike many other pilots he was proud of his turnout, and he avoided wearing his uniform as if it were an ordinary suit or a set of garage man's overalls.

"Life with Father" as applied to the Geiger household was a strenuous ordeal for all parties concerned. When the master of the manor was in residence there was no doubt as to who ruled the roost. "Daddy" could be counted upon to put on quite a performance. The show went on regardless of the hour of the day or the season of the year; living under the same roof with him made the other occupants feel as if they were spectators constantly attending a three-ring circus or a comic opera. Father's appetite was such that he could eat or drink practically anything that could be swallowed. He could consume a quarter of watermelon as kind of an in-between-snack, and he had a weakness for five-layer, grape jelly cakes with thick white frosting. When he was not away on maneuvers or flying cross-country, two different desserts had to be prepared daily: one for lunch, one for evening dinner. At the Commissioned Officers' Mess at Quantico the stewards soon learned that the conventional *pie a la mode* was not substantial enough to suit Colonel Geiger. So they concocted a triple threat, *pie a la Geiger,* two scoops of ice cream on the largest slice of pastry available, and they stood by for orders whenever he entered the dining room. Asked if he desired something to drink, Geiger's unvarying response, "Oh, just hand me the biggest and the coldest," became one of his special identification remarks. He could smoke anything that could be set alight and would burn, and his consumption of cigars would have delighted a tobacco grower's association. For more than fifteen years his friend and admirer, the late Generalissimo Rafael Trujillo Molina, President of the Dominican Republic, saw to it that regardless of where Geiger was stationed or what he was doing, he was always kept amply supplied with boxes of Santo Domingo's choicest (and strongest) rolled leaf.

Laughter and zestful living accompanied the Geiger quarters from Miami to Philadelphia and from Quantico to Port-au-Prince. "Daddy" thrived on entertainment; took a prominent part in all the antics; stayed out late at stag parties; and every now and then got involved in rough-and-tumble horseplay. He knew how to relax, and he thoroughly enjoyed himself in his off-duty hours. If some people live life right up to the hilt, Roy went right on through to the outer end of the handle. As far as he was concerned there was a time for work and a time for play, but he was careful to keep the two apart, and other than a few youthful escapades and brushes with higher authority as a junior Lieutenant, he managed to keep out of trouble. There was method in his madness, so to speak, for a person of his temperament had to have some release from his tensions, and periodically he had to blow off steam. Behind the backdrop of comedy and high jinks, tragedy constantly hovered: whenever an aviator sat down to a meal he could ponder over the distinct possibility it could be his last, for risk was an ever present feature of his profession even in time of nominal peace.

Obviously, "Home on the Range" within the Geiger domain was not all beer and skittles. Having elected to pursue his career on an "I'll fly it, or smash it" basis, added to the "slam-bang-crash" tenor of his daily living, made the senior partner a difficult person with which to live for any lengthy period. Granted that his temper was generally stable and under control, and that he was tolerant of others' limitations and whims, Geiger at times could be very demanding if not downright unreasonable. Quick to forgive mistakes and patient with his professional subordinates, he could demonstrate marked impatience within the family circle, and occasionally he displayed a notable lack of comprehension of domestic affairs.

For example, he found it very hard to understand why it was necessary for him to provide such things for his children as dancing and music lessons, sporting gear or costumes, camping uniforms and related equipment. Summer vacations or trips away from home for the youngsters were outright luxuries to him. Financially restricted as a youth, he had had to forego many of the natural and normal pastimes and games of his companions, and he felt that others were not necessarily entitled to special privileges which he had been denied. Thrifty and frugal, he held on to his money as if each expenditure might bankrupt the family; only on rare occasions was he inclined to splurge. Likewise, his sense of musical and artistic appreciation being somewhat limited, the notion of paying out hard-earned funds for private instruction in such fields was regarded with unconcealed skepticism.

Within the household, his wife became the buffer between the youngsters and their father. Eunice brought them up; looked after their health and their needs; repeatedly pleaded their case for the little extras they yearned for, including a small allowance, and tried to keep them from unduly upsetting their father. Although

19

the children were frequently puzzled by their father's attitude, there existed a strong bond of friendly affection within the family circle, and the son and daughter adored and respected both their parents. As for Eunice, she had her hands full ministering to the demands of her many-sided husband. Throughout their married life she never failed him, and he in turn was equally devoted to her.

In a variety of ways Eunice played a vital role in furthering her husband's professional career. At the service schools which he attended, when he was too tired to read anymore, she would pick up his texts and read to him by the hour, far into the night. She assisted him with his graphic presentations and sketches, in shading and color-contouring the many required maps, and spent hours in libraries and files looking up references and checking research data for his formal papers. She helped him assemble the material as well as write his speeches, and she lent a helping hand when it came to handling his voluminous correspondence. But transcending all these tasks was the most delicate one of all: that of trying to control a restless and impetuous mate. This never ending assignment she was able to perform with all the finesse of a skilled diplomat.

A cold-blooded realist in some respects, Geiger was nevertheless an incurable romanticist in just as many others. Uninhibited to a pronounced degree, he really preferred the simpler things of life. He had a fondness for pets: the Geiger residence at times could assume the aspect of a small menagerie so numerous were the dogs and the cats, the caged birds and the parrots. He liked to listen to the children sing, around the piano while their mother played after dinner. He had no well developed hobbies, but he liked to ride horseback, to swim, and to fish. Every now and then he enjoyed attending a motion picture show. Other than his professional reading he took some interest in historical biographies, but his true love was focused on the pulp magazines: detective stories and mysteries, western travel and adventure tales. An avid Sax Rohmer fan, he was particularly fond of the doings of the celebrated Dr. Fu Manchu. He became so engrossed in that wily Oriental gentleman that it formed the basis of an anecdote known far and wide throughout the stretches of the South Pacific. An aviator attached to his command, a Major Petras, quite innocently found himself the victim of Geiger's dry sense of humor. Repeatedly he had asked permission to take part in air strikes. Just as regularly his requests were turned down without explanation. At his wits' end trying to ascertain the reason for the constant denial, the Major went directly to General Geiger and asked him the cause. Grinning from ear to ear, the latter finally supplied the answer: as Dr. Fu Manchu took delight in saying, "No, Dr. Petri," so, too, did Geiger enjoy responding, "No, Major Petras," for the close similarity between the two names, in his opinion, was too intriguing to let such a rare opportunity go by unused.

Cynical about some things, Geiger was just as sentimental about others. He had his own system of personal identification in his correspondence with his wife and children: "all my love and loyalty" preceding his signature indicated the letter was genuinely his. Two long blasts followed by two short toots on the automobile horn meant that "Daddy" was coming up the drive—in a hurry. And if a plane flying low relatively near the Geiger residence four times gunned its engines—two long followed by two short—it meant that Father was at the controls. On Christmas morning the entire family was treated to champagne before breakfast—partial compensation for the parents having stayed up most of the night to trim the tree—and Geiger always took care to remember to scratch the soot on the back of the fireplace with a poker so that he could show the children where Santa Claus had slipped. Motoring back and forth to Florida in the family car, to amuse the children and to relieve the monotony he would pull over into the left lane if traffic permitted, and continue driving on the wrong side as long as possible, accompanied with much horn-blowing and exaggerated hand signals to imaginary cars. Asked for an explanation for this antic, his stock answer, "Oh, I'm just practicing passing" never varied. And if on his automobile outings his wary eye could detect the presence of a wayside antique store before his wife noticed it, down would go the accelerator right to the floor boards for he hated to stop once he got out on the open road. "Life with Father" was usually confusing and often had its harrowing moments, but nobody could complain that it was ever dull.

He was remarkably naive in certain ways. Informed that he had been promoted from the rank of Colonel to that of Brigadier General, Geiger was very concerned about the required changes to his dress uniforms. After having proudly worn sky blue trousers with wide scarlet stripes on their outside seams for some thirty-two years, he had become very much attached to that arrangement, and the notion of turning them in to be replaced by an all dark blue set which matched the color of his dress blouse was not at all appealing. In the long run, of course, things worked themselves out in one fashion or another if not for the best: Uniform Regulations were not slighted, and General Geiger no longer needed to worry, for within two months of his promotion the events at Pearl Harbor and elsewhere in the Pacific put all of his dress uniforms back in his foot locker with the mothballs "for the duration."

Thus, Roy Geiger represented many different things to many people. He was not easy to know; hence some persons thought of him as strictly a cold fish, an uncommunicative lone wolf with an habitual, penetrating bellicose stare (with which he could cut a man down to size in a single glance), and with a smile grimmer than a warden's handshake. Some individuals unquestionably were literally scared stiff of the man, and were noticeably uneasy in his presence. They were ordinarily those who had had some sort of a difference of opinion with the *Old Man,* or had gotten out of line, and had been put back in their place, and they were the type prone to regard him as brash and opinionated, hard-driving and heavy-handed. But nobody took anything for granted with the man. If he liked you and believed in you, figuratively speaking, he would have taken his shirt off his back, folded it neatly, and given it to you. Conversely, if he thought you were deceitful or otherwise deserving of disdain, he was quite capable—ready, willing, and eager—to rip your shirt off your back, roll it up into a wad, and throw it right back in your face.

Because he was so positive in his views and so direct in his actions, because he was a man of strong likes and dislikes, many of Geiger's mannerisms undeniably were annoying to certain types of individuals. At times he was so cocksure of himself, his attitude tended almost to arrogance. After all, he was one of those rare persons who could have walked into any restaurant, sat down and ordered a plate of scrambled eggs and bacon with a pot of chocolate sauce, or called for a bowl of chili powder to put in his strawberry milkshake, and he would have gotten them without hesitation. A head waiter did not need to be a genius to recognize

Roy Geiger as a man who knew precisely what he wanted, and was going to get it regardless of what others thought about the matter. A man of Geiger's cut could not escape making enemies. He had his share of detractors, but it is interesting to note that despite his treatment of his subordinates, without exception all maintained their deep sense of devotion and loyalty to their superior, for they respected his ability as an officer and his word as a gentleman.

To a very select few Roy Geiger was addressed as *Jiggs.* To a slightly larger group he was referred to—but not addressed—as *Rugged Roy.* But from the lowliest wing-washer or nut-buster to the highest echelon of the commissioned ranks, men thought of him as a fearless leader and organizer, perhaps the sole pilot of the Marine Corps, who, during his lifetime, flew or commanded practically every type of aircraft, balloon, or aviation unit (of his branch of the service) that ever existed. His feats of daring and the performance records which he established during his thirty years as a naval aviator placed him securely in the category of those who were quite *unaccustomed to fear.* His greatest contribution to his Corps was that of inspiration. He did not invent or champion any particular model of airplane or related equipment, and with the exception of his profound interest in instrument flying, neither was he a devotee of any specialty or technique, although as far as doctrine is concerned, he was one of the earliest officers to recognize the inestimable value of close air support, and constantly worked to perfect that system. His contribution in the main pertained to the moral or spiritual side as contrasted to the material. Men thought of him as a living symbol, and by setting personally the example for others to emulate, he supplied the one ingredient —morale— which cannot be invented or developed, mass-produced or stock-piled, in time of war, like a conventional weapon.

Napoleon's oft-quoted Maxims include a notation that "Soldiers will follow anybody who wins battles." Perhaps a Twentieth Century Corollary in the same vein might read: "Airmen will follow any combat pilot who leads the flight and gets results." And as far as Marine Corps Aviation is concerned, while he lived no one set a faster pace or flew higher than Roy Geiger.

23

Chapter II

I Can Run Faster

On a hot summer's day in 1898 a rather bored and freely perspiring telegraph operator in a small Florida town stared dully at the now silent receiver on his desk, and after checking the hour with the wall clock, slipped off his green eye shade, and reached for his battered straw hat. It was high noon, not a breath of air was stirring, and the silence of his dingy office was disturbed only by the constant buzzing of half a dozen large black flies. Looking forward to a tall glass of beer and a sample of the free lunch on the counter down the way at the *Palace,* he was halfway to the door when he heard someone knock.

"Come in," he called, whereupon he found himself confronted with a lanky youth about thirteen years of age, freckle-faced and barefoot. Simply attired in white shirt and trousers, it was quite noticeable that if the boy's clothing were frayed and worn in places it was remarkably clean.

"Well, what do you want, son?" asked the telegraphist.

"It's about a job," the boy answered. "I was told you wanted somebody to deliver messages."

"You look big enough to handle it. Guess your parents don't object. All right, get back here for work in an hour, and park your bicycle under the shed."

"Well, Sir," the youth replied somewhat hesitantly, "I don't own one, but I can manage just as well."

"In that case, until you can get a bicycle let's just forget it. Middleburg isn't Jacksonville or Tampa. Down here the Company expects its messengers to furnish their own transportation."

"Look, Mister, give me a chance. Those fellows on their bicycles take all day. I can run faster than they can ride!"

"Sonny, I'm not going to argue with you. Anybody knows a boy on a bicycle can get places quicker than he can on foot. Now if you don't mind it's my lunch hour."

Blocking the doorway the lad stood his ground. "Try me anyway, it won't cost you anything. I know short cuts and back alleys, places you can't ride a bicycle. I know most of the people here and where they live. I'll prove it to you if you'll only let me show you."

"You're a stubborn one, you are," the operator continued. Lifting a message form from a wire basket, he wrote the exact time of day in one of the spaces provided for that purpose, and turning toward the youth ordered: "All right, we'll find out. Take this sheet to Swanson's saw mill out on the west side of town. Get old man Swanson or his foreman to write in this box the time you hand him this paper, and have him sign it. Then you get back here with it as fast as you can. After that, we'll see."

Less than an hour later, smoking a long Cuban cigar and attempting to fan himself with his hat, the telegraph operator returned to his office. To his surprise he found the youth waiting for him, sitting calmly on the front door sill, message in hand. The telegraphist took one look at the hour of delivery and the signature. He whistled softly, and then said, "How did you do it, boy? Bet you got a ride out there from some teamster."

"No," retorted the lad, "just like I told you, I ran out there, and I ran right back. I didn't stop on the way, and nobody gave me a lift. Now, how about that job?"

"All right, young fellow, you're hired. The regulations don't say how the messages are supposed to be delivered just as long as they get there. Next time the Inspector comes by there will probably be a fuss of sorts, but we'll worry about that when it happens. From now on you're working for *Western Union,* but don't forget, in these parts I'm the boss. Here's a booklet which tells you what to do. And remember two things you won't find in it. If somebody gives you something when you hand 'em a message, you'll split that tip fifty-fifty with me. And the first complaint I hear about you, out you go. Get me?"

"Yes, Sir, I understand," the boy replied enthusiastically. "No sense standing here in the hot sun talking," he continued, "If you've got something for me to do, I'd like to get started, right now."

This little incident which Geiger delighted to relate in later years is rather revealing, for if nothing else, it is indicative of many of the traits which he developed during his formative years. His boyhood was a continual struggle against adversity. It took all the determination and tenacity he could muster to surmount the obstacles; it also taught him to live by his wits and to try to turn every little opportunity, no matter how insignificant, to his advantage. He had little choice in the matter—it was "sink or swim"—and throughout his period of adolescence financial security was conspicuous by its absence, and austerity prevailed instead.

Compared to the large number of facts and legends surrounding Roy Geiger's adult life in general and his service career in particular, there is a notable dearth of detail, verbal as well as written, concerning his years as a youth in northeastern Florida. There appear to be several reasons for this unusual situation. In the first place, there are presently very few surviving, close relatives. Most of them as they grew up were forced at an early age to seek their livelihood elsewhere, and they moved away, more or less permanently. Secondly, the town in which Geiger was born, Middleburg, and the general region in which he lived as a lad, Clay County, have changed materially since the turn of the present century. At one time the area was the heart of a thriving timber cutting and export business, but after the land had been thoroughly worked over and chopped right down to the stump, such local prosperity as had been temporarily accumulated, departed just as rapidly. Thereafter, the community was abandoned to drowse along in its vanished glamor, relatively isolated and off the beaten track of progress, surpassed by more up-and-coming towns with better transportation facilities enabling them to corner the trade needs of the region. There was consequently neither the energy nor the need to maintain detailed records of a setting living on its memories. Lastly, Geiger for one reason or another never felt called upon to make other than scant reference to his youth, although throughout his life he was always an enthusiastic promoter for the State of his birth. His explanation was less a matter of desire to forget, or determination to conceal, the period in question because of the difficulties he experienced, but rather more one of indifference or disinterest on the grounds that he considered the circumstances so prosaic and uneventful, they simply were not worth mentioning.

Despite these restrictions the basic information pertaining to his family background can readily be determined from such sources as are currently available. Roy Geiger's ancestors had been in North America for almost two centuries prior to his birth. Of Austrian descent they had set foot ashore on one of William Penn's proprietory land grants along the Delaware River about 1690; however, it would appear that the cold and blustery weather associated with the Philadelphia region in winter was altogether too similar to the ice and snow of the Alps from which they had recently departed, for by the early 1700's they had begun to migrate southward from Pennsylvania and Delaware along the Atlantic Coast through the Carolinas to Georgia. As the frontier was pushed back gradually from the water's edge, and the land further to the south was opened up to colonization, either by the elimination of Indian tribes or by treaty with Spain, in company with other bands of settlers they had crossed the border into Eastern Florida during the first quarter of the 19th Century. Roy's grandfather, Marion Francis Geiger, was born within that Territory; likewise, his father of identical name was born within the State of Florida, a native of Middleburg.

At the termination of the Civil War that portion of northeastern Florida radiating outward from Jacksonville for a distance of some twenty-five miles became the site of marked agricultural and commercial activity. The introduction of the railroad to the region plus the utilization of canals, and navigable tidal rivers and estuaries, provided the means to transport Florida's magnificent stand of timber from interior groves to deep-water shipping points. The wooded lands of northern New England having been progressively denuded of their larger trees, and the lumber mills of Georgia and South Carolina then in ruins or otherwise inoperative as the result of the recently fought conflict, Florida's virgin forests of pine and live-oak and her extensive tracts of cedar and cypress stood waiting for the woodman's axe. To satisfy the booming Northern market for housing and shipbuilding the logging trade was introduced almost overnight to the banks of the St. John's River, and a lively business in related naval stores, principally, tar and turpentine, was developed simultaneously in that general area.

Roughly twenty miles southwest of Jacksonville and about

one half that distance west and inland from the port of Green Cove Springs on the St. John's, the little town of Middleburg found itself caught in the meshes of this sprawling timber cutting industry. Although its permanent population did not then exceed five hundred persons, schools and churches sprung up alongside modest homes and stores, and a degree of commercial prosperity was achieved in due course. Married to Josephine Prevatt, Marion Francis Geiger decided that the locality was as good as any other in which to rear a family, and in time the couple became the proud parents of four sons and three daughters.

The next to the youngest child, christened Roy Geiger, was born at Middleburg on 25 January 1885. Some fifteen years after his birth the boy asked that he be given a middle name. It appears that Roy was attempting to avoid confusion between himself and a distant cousin of identical name, with whom he had been thrust into daily contact, and of whom he was not especially fond (perhaps it was because his relative was a preacher). His mother accordingly assented, whereupon the youth became Roy Stanley Geiger. As a youngster he led a busy and active life in a bustling community; also at an early age he showed a distinct tendency to wander about on his own. In one instance, the lad then being five years old, he came near to frightening his mother half out of her mind. Reported missing a frantic search was made of the neighborhood, and at length Roy was discovered under the family residence, leaning against a chimney foundation, firmly holding between his two small hands a wriggling black snake seeking its freedom. Several years later, Roy had another chance engagement with a serpent, this time with a diamond-back rattlesnake. Bitten on his bare leg from beneath a board sidewalk, he was not treated by a druggist until after the snake had been killed (at Roy's insistence), and it was a very near thing for by that time the boy had fainted.

A member of what could probably be best described as a moderate income class, for his father served as a local Tax Assessor as well as the Superintendent of Clay County Schools, he engaged in all of those pursuits that a growing boy would normally be expected to enjoy in a small town. He liked to hunt and to fish, to ride horseback and to swim in the creeks and streams, and there was always something interesting to observe at the livery stable or something to be learned at any one of the dozen-odd steam, saw mills in the vicinity. In 1892, when the boy was but seven years of age, his father passed away suddenly, leaving his wife with heavy responsibilities to maintain and educate a large family. This she was able to accomplish, although at considerable self- sacrifice, but somehow—and to her everlasting credit—she managed to secure a college education for all of her children, each of whom eventually entered the teaching profession.

Largely left to his own resources at a comparatively early age, Roy was forced to take himself seriously as a youth. To assist his mother hold the household intact, he, along with his brothers at once realized the necessity of becoming self-supporting, and he sought such employment as was available after school hours or during his vacations. He ran errands about town for merchants; worked at odd jobs (10 cents per hour) for a local lumber company; and in time served as a messenger boy at the town telegraph office. He was obliged to turn in all of his earnings to his mother, and he had little if any free time to spend with his companions. Despite the drudgery, there was some outlet for his pentup energies. Between the age of eight and nine he decided that somehow he was going to learn to fly. Borrowing a pair of feathered turkey wings, which his mother had set aside for use as "dusters," he wired them to his upper arms, and then jumped from atop the woodshed with the expectation of gliding smoothly to an eggshell landing in the sand. To his dismay, he plummeted eathward like a falling stone, managing to break his arm in the process after he had fetched up hard against an upright chopping block. Understandably, further attempts at aerial flight had to be postponed indefinitely, and it was not until two decades later that Roy was finally able to gratify his boyhood ambition.

Among other incidents of his formative years was a rare example of courage and family devotion. One of his sisters, Lily, was stricken with a severe attack of typhoid fever. Roy's mother, at that time, was suffering acutely from a heart disorder, and was in no position to assist her ailing daughter. With the exception of Roy, the girl's other brothers and sisters felt helpless to cope with the situation. Roy immediately took it upon himself to nurse his sister back to good health, and for over three months was in constant attendance. Working alone he never deserted his patient; she subsequently completely recovered, and the family physician gave Roy sole credit for saving his sister's life. Naturally, this loyalty strengthened the bond between Roy and Lily, and they were devoted to one another throughout their lives.

Determined though Roy's mother was to do her best for her children, her over-zealousness in certain affairs was heartily resented by the boys of the family. It appears that the lady was bound that one of her sons should become an accomplished violinist, and from the eldest to the youngest each in turn was forced—much against their will—to take music lessons. The net result was that sooner or later each of her sons openly rebelled at the enforced instruction, even resorting to such extreme measures as running away from home. No exception to the trend set by his elder brethren, when Roy at age eleven found himself the current target of his mother's musical aspirations, he, too, packed up his few personal belongings, and made tracks for the railway line. Not only did he abhor the thought of becoming a fiddler, he was equally concerned with what he considered to be an inequitable distribution of the joint responsibility to provide for the family larder, inasmuch as he felt that he was being asked to contribute far more than his fair share.

For quite some time it had become customary at Middleburg for small boys to board outbound freight and lumber trains, and to "bum" rides back and forth to outlying localities. It was generally regarded as a relatively harmless (if dangerous) pastime, and for the most part railroad personnel blinked an eye at this irregularity. Hence, for Roy it was an easy matter to run down to the nearest lumber loading point or watering stop, and to climb within the rods and braces underneath the car platforms of a halted train. Concealed from the eyes of a vigilant brakeman, he proceeded in such fashion as far away as Jacksonville. There, at the freight yards, he transferred to another train, and continued his way north until he eventually reached Chicago. It took him almost two months to complete the trip, meanwhile his mother hounded railway officials incessantly to locate and to retrieve her errant son. Roy managed to evade his pursuers, and in all probability would have arrived at his destination far sooner had he not been put off a train at Cincinnati, thereby causing him a week's delay before he could figure out a way to board a departing, westbound freight, outside the railroad yard limits and beyond the clutches of alert watchmen and railway detectives.

Once in the "Windy City" Roy went directly to the address

of his older brother Ellis. The latter, forewarned by letter from his mother what had transpired at Middleburg, had reason to suspect that Roy ultimately would terminate his cross-country tour in Chicago, and had long been expecting the youth's arrival. Taking the lad under his protective wing, Ellis saw no reason for Roy to neglect his education just because he had run away from home, and promptly enrolled his younger brother at the nearest public school. At Ellis' insistence Roy took on part time jobs after school hours to help pay for the expenses of his return trip to Florida. When school let out the following spring, Ellis escorted his brother to the depot, paid for his ticket, and put him aboard a passenger coach. Just to make sure that he would arrive safely at Middleburg, Ellis had made prior arrangements to have Roy placed under the custody of railway officials all along the route, and for the duration of his trip, Roy was passed along from one railroad conductor to another until he finally left the train at the siding in his home town.

Reunited with his mother and sisters Roy soon adjusted anew to the familiar routine of life in a small Florida community. After his recent experience, however, there was one welcome change: no longer was he threatened with the prospect of taking violin instruction. Furthermore, his exciting excursion and temporary absence from his immediate surroundings had opened his eyes not only to the vastness of the country of which he was a junior citizen, but also to the countless opportunities beyond the confines of his restricted, provincial setting. To supplement the limited chances of employment offered to a boy of his years at Middleburg, as he grew older and stronger he sought work at Green Cove Springs. There, he was able to find a variety of jobs: helping to operate the logging trains, assisting the yard crews to skid the massive timber balks on to the cutting platforms at the saw mills, or sorting and poling logs in the wet-storage basins and booms along the shores of the St. John's River. Such work was not only extremely hard but was equally hazardous: early in his teens he suffered a severe cut on one of his legs from a heavy logger's peavey which had slipped out of his control while engaged in assembling a timber raft. Temporarily incapacitated by the accident, it scarred him for life, but he never complained nor lost his nerve, and as soon as he could walk again, he reported back for work at the loading slips.

In the autumn of 1902, at age seventeen, Roy felt that he had set aside enough money to take care of his room and board at the Florida State Normal School, then situated at De Funiak Springs. During the following two years he underwent instruction there, and periodically participated in practice teaching in small rural schools. It is of interest to note from photographs taken at that time that he wore a prominent pince-nez, his explanation for this affectation being that at least it made him appear older to some of his more advanced pupils. Later, he served as the Principal of Palatka (Clay County) Junior High School, and after a single term there was awarded a statement quaintly phrased in the tenor of the time, attesting that he "gave general satisfaction." In any event, there was no question as to his ability as an instructor, for his official Teacher's Certificate, signed by a relative and dated 10 June 1905, authorized the holder to practice that profession unreservedly throughout Clay County.

Having successfully climbed up the bottom rungs of the ladder, Roy forthwith decided he might as well try for the top in his search for higher education. Commencing in 1904 he attended a three-year course at John B. Stetson University at Deland, and three years later was granted his certificate as a Bachelor of Laws, as of 28 May 1907. His period of study at Deland was a trying one in many ways: to earn the funds for this specialized education he acted briefly as an accountant, and in the evenings when by all rights he should have been studying, he traveled about the neighborhood, checking entries and balancing the accounts in the cash books of local merchants who paid him a pittance for that task. In the meantime, in April 1906, he was appointed a Notary Public, "in and for the State at large," and exactly a year later, he was admitted to the Bar and licensed to practice in the Circuit Court. In May 1907, he was admitted to the Supreme Court, and to round out the picture completely, during that same year he finally was granted admission to the Federal Court.

At age twenty-one Geiger suddenly found himself in the highly enviable position of being not only a qualified teacher but also a licensed attorney, despite the fact that this accomplishment had been attained at considerable cost in many ways: he had had to deny himself of many pleasures, and as he was soon to learn, he had come dangerously near to imperiling his general health and well-being. Never one known to procrastinate, he did not choose to hang around Deland aimlessly admiring himself or waiting for a wealthy client to fall into his lap, but rather began to look about for a likely locale which might prove profitable as well as interesting. In his opinion Middleburg was too small and too insignificant to attract or to support another lawyer, and remembering his former activities at Green Cove Springs, which by that time had worked up to a population of some three thousand citizens, he decided that the latter spot would be the more desirable place to display his legal shingle. Consequently, in the summer of 1907 he returned to open his practice there, little realizing that his active career as a lawyer in the State of Florida would only last for four months.

During that interlude he handled very few cases and had only two clients of any real importance. Unfortunately, it was crystal clear that both were guilty—a fact that bothered Roy immensely as a matter of principle. He soon lost patience with them, and grew increasingly intolerant and contemptuous of their deceitful ways. Disgusted with their attitude and somewhat disillusioned with the turn of events, for he had no desire to associate with persons who had already fallen afoul of the law and had only turned to him to defend them from what they otherwise justly deserved, he began to regard his future as an attorney with noticeable misgivings. Discouraged and desirous of a change, he made a second trip to Chicago, to consult with his brother Ellis, who was fast making a name for himself in his local political arena.

It is not definitely known what prompted him to take the step which turned out to be one of the most vital decisions of his entire life, but it is very much a matter of official record that on 2 November 1907, Roy enlisted as a Private in the United States Marine Corps, to serve for four years, at St. Paul, Minnesota. Unquestionably, the unremunerative and distasteful aspects of a legal career in a small Florida community were disturbing; moreover, by nature restless and impulsive, sooner or later he would have found such work far too confining. Under the circumstances, being ready for a change of scenery and manner of employment, he was correspondingly ripe for any opportune transformation. He found it in the presence of a Recruiting Sergeant, and the lure of travel and adventure added to the prospect of an active and orderly life out of doors, not to mention the appeal of military uniform, won him over in short order.

When he made his original inquiry at the Recruiting Station it was with the hope of securing a commission. Following a preliminary physical examination by the Naval Medical Officer, it was pointed out to him that his physical defects were so grave as to preclude any chance of his acceptance as an officer-candidate; in fact, he appeared as a more likely applicant for admission to a clinic than for entry to Officers' School. In later years Geiger delighted to list his alleged disqualifications if for no other reason that quoted out of context they made him appear more dead than alive. They were seven in number: he had flat feet, hence he would be unable to drill or to march properly; he was double-jointed at the knees to the degree he could not stand up straight, or come to attention in the prescribed regulation manner, with his knees together; he was not of sufficient height (he then measured 5ft. 6½in.); he was somewhat underweight (he then tipped the scales at about 140 pounds); he had a heart murmur; he was suffering acutely from eyestrain; and several of his back teeth were either missing or had not yet dropped into place (the inference being that he would have difficulty grinding up what then passed for rations). Presented with such an alarming bill of medical findings the average man might well have turned on his heels and walked away—or gone over in the corner, sat down, and asked for a glass of water—but this unexpected disclosure was precisely the sort of thing to whet Geiger's competitive spirit. After all, if he had been able to out-run any boy in town, if he were rugged enough to hold his own in company with tough loggers and perform such heavy work as that employment demanded, and he could swim and dive like an otter, he was by no means a weakling or a hopeless physical specimen. As for his defects, there was little he could do to alter basically the frame and structure which nature had provided him, but he was convinced that he could grow in stature and put on weight if he could exercise, sleep, and eat regularly. As for his eyes, he was certain that if he could get his head out of a law book or a pile of legal briefs for six months, his normal vision would return. All he asked for was that the officials give him a chance to correct his more conspicuous failings.

Also in his favor were his charm and his spirit. He was a clean-cut, good looking young man, full of enthusiasm and desperately anxious to join up; he had a likeable personality, and his aggressiveness made a distinctly favorable impression from the very start. If nothing else here was a promising candidate with most unusual educational and professional qualifications, especially for one of his age, and it seemed to the officials a shame to turn down such a versatile prospect. They talked the matter over among themselves—doubtless they took into consideration their ability to meet their assigned quota of recruit enlistments for that month—and eventually they compromised to the degree they permitted Geiger to enlist with the tacit understanding that at some future, unspecified date, provided he could meet all of the physical requirements and otherwise attain an outstanding performance record, he might apply from the ranks for a commission in the Marine Corps. This arrangement was quite satisfactory to Roy—one gathers that as of that moment he made up his mind that nothing was going to prevent him from some day becoming a commissioned officer on his own merit—whereupon he picked up the pen and signed his enlistment contract with a flourish. Characteristically, within the blank space on the form which indicated the recruit's former occupation, he modestly inserted one word: clerk.

In retrospect, one wonders if Roy had any idea of what he had let himself in for. Other than his two trips to Chicago there is no evidence that he had traveled to any degree outside his home State. In 1907, the average American citizen had only a rather vague idea of the Marine Corps and its functions; in fact, other than at the nation's largest seaports with their accompanying navy yards, Marines were seldom seen ashore within the continental limits of the United States. Concerning Florida there were small detachments of Marines serving at the naval stations at both Pensacola and Key West, and it is altogether possible that Geiger might have observed them at their barracks at one of those locations. Granted that the Corps had gained favorable publicity for its exploits at Guantanamo Bay in Cuba during the Spanish-American War, for its operations in the subsequent Philippine Insurrection, and for its participation in the Boxer Rebellion in North China—all of which had been prominently aired in the nation's press—compared to the Army and the Navy the size of the Marine Corps in the first decade of the present century was so relatively minor, comparatively few civilians were aware of the nature of its routine activities.

Although the authorized strength of the Marine Corps for the

Fiscal Year ending 30 June 1908 was set at 9,520 enlisted men, its average actual strength for that period totaled approximately 8,500 rank-and-file. Some 270 Marine officers were then serving on the active list. In that twelve month interval there were roughly 5,100 first enlistments, some 425 recruits being provided monthly from a score of recruiting stations scattered across the nation. About one third of the entire strength of the Corps—90 officers, 3,000 enlisted—manned Marine Barracks and receiving ships, and furnished guards, at ten navy yards and major naval installations on the east coast, and at two similar naval activities on the west coast. In addition to these security duties, they maintained naval prisons; others served on recruiting duty and at depots, or acted in staff or clerical capacities at Headquarters at Washington. Of the forces attached to the home stations the largest concentration of troops was to be found at Norfolk and Philadelphia Navy Yards, in readiness for expeditionary duty in the general Caribbean area, or, for the purpose of forming a mobile brigade to seize, consolidate, and defend such advance naval bases as might be required by the Atlantic Fleet.

Slightly more than one third of the Marine Corps—120 officers and 3,100 enlisted personnel—was then serving abroad. At Camp Elliott in the Panama Canal Zone, a battalion of 400-odd was employed supervising local elections, maintaining peace and order, and was trained and equipped to serve as an independent expeditionary force in Nicaragua in case of need in that troubled land. The 1st Provisional Regiment, some 40 officers and 900 enlisted, was stationed in Cuba, the majority at or near Habana, the remainder at a dozen outlying posts throughout the Island, serving as part of the Army of Cuban Pacification under terms of the Platt Amendment. In the Philippine Islands 60 officers and 1,600 men composed the First Brigade, with Brigade Headquarters and the Second Regiment at the naval base at Cavite on Manila Bay, while the First Regiment formed the garrison at the naval station to the northwest at Olongapo on Subic Bay. The mission of this insular group was quite comprehensive. In addition to providing security forces for the naval facilities, they frequently engaged in field operations and patrolling activities; they acted as a ready reserve for expeditionary duty in the Far East, including the furnishing of troops for the Legation Guard at Peking, China; and they supplied personnel for Marine detachments aboard vessels of the Asiatic Fleet as well as for the small contingents stationed on the Pacific Islands of Guam and Midway. The final portion of the Corps on foreign service numbered 10 officers and 200 enlisted Marines comprising the barracks detachments at San Juan and Culebra, Puerto Rico, at Guantanamo Bay, Cuba, at Honolulu, Territory of Hawaii, and at Sitka, Alaska.

The balance of the Marine Corps or a little less than one third—60 commissioned officers and 2,400 rank-and-file—served afloat, furnishing Marine detachments for some forty combatant and auxiliary vessels of the Navy. Aboard twenty battleships, Marines manned one of the deck and gunnery divisions of each vessel, acted as a guard and as the nucleus of the ship's landing party. They performed similar duties aboard six large armored cruisers, four fast scouts or protected cruisers, five light cruisers, and five patrol vessels. Herein, it is of passing interest to note that from December 1907 until January 1909, the Marine guards of some sixteen battleships enjoyed the rare chance of a lifetime occasioned by the voyage around the world of four divisions of the United States Fleet on its celebrated good will tour.

At the time of Geiger's enlistment, pay scales were determined by the Act of March 1889, modified by certain provisions contained in the Act of June 1906. Under their stipulations, the monthly pay rates for Privates and Corporals were set at $13.00 and $15.00, respectively. These figures were subject to an increase of 20% for foreign service, and to the standard deduction of 20 cents monthly for the Hospital Fund. For those who could demonstrate proficiency on the target range, additional qualification pay was provided monthly to enlisted personnel: *Expert Rifleman,* $3.00; *Sharpshooter,* $2.00; and *Marksman,* $1.00. Admittedly, such modest augmentations appear almost infinitesimal; however, to single men in barracks the ability to shoot well made all the difference financially between living and barely existing so low were the regulation pay rates. Interestingly enough, at that time the lowest ratings in the Navy, Apprentice Seamen and Mess Attendants, 3rd Class, were paid $16.00 per month, meanwhile a Native Cook of the Insular Force in the Philippines was tendered the same stipend as a Private of Marines, or $13.00. Twice a month the Paymaster made his rounds, and the average Marine during his first enlistment seldom walked away from the pay table with more than $5.00, cash in hand, after other checkages had been defrayed. Fortunately for Geiger, in 1908 the Pay Acts were further amended to the extent Privates and Corporals received $15.00 and $21.00, respectively; moreover, rifle qualification pay was increased proportionately to new totals of $5.00, $3.00, and $2.00. Thereafter, 50 cents per day (12-hour day, at that) and "all found" remained the regulation rate for Marine Privates until the advent of the First World War, when Congress, in an unguarded moment of patriotic generosity, doubled the amount to $1.00 "for the duration."

In 1907 there were no central recruit Depots in the sense that Parris Island and San Diego were later developed for primary indoctrination and instruction. Those who enlisted east of the Mississippi River were generally sent to either Norfolk or Philadelphia Navy Yard, while those who joined west of that arbitrary dividing line were ordered to Mare Island, California. Such basic training as was then given to recruits laid strong emphasis on the purely practical rather than on the theoretical side: regardless of the post or station to which a newly enlisted man reported, his Company Commander, after a cursory inspection invariably turned to the First Sergeant or the Gunnery Sergeant and said, "Take this man out and make a Marine out of him." Limited rudimentary schooling on the drill square and on the parade ground followed, and depending on the individual aptitude and patience, interest and personal eccentricities, of a man's instructor, the recruit somehow learned the tricks and the tools of his new trade. It was a rough-and-tumble existence; there was no coddling; and a man stood or fell depending on the strength of his fists as well as of his moral fiber.

By today's standards, the average enlisted man's lot of the early 1900's was indeed Spartan, but the troops were volunteers who largely set their own code of conduct. They regarded themselves as professional mercenaries in which the appeal to their pride and the challenge offered by their profession far outweighed the amount of their pay, and the military pomp and glamor of their parades and elaborate ceremonies served to offset in part the rigid discipline, inferior quarters, and sub-standard diet which formed the backbone of their normal existence. Promotion came slowly, and not only had to be earned but frequently had also to be fought for: if the majority of the troops were at least superficially hard-boiled, not a few, notably among the non-commissioned ranks, were inherently tough. Illiteracy was far from unknown, and even the language barrier at times was a problem. Aliens and emigrants, fresh off the liners from Europe, could and did enlist at earliest opportunity, and away from the parade ground or the rifle range one could hear spoken any one of half a dozen foreign tongues, Gaelic and Scandinavian, Teutonic and Slavic, predominating in that order. Nevertheless, the age of regimentation and classification had commenced to transgress the roots of rugged individualism, for on 1 July 1907, the Marine Corps along with the rest of the naval establishment formally adopted the Fingerprint System of Identification for all first enlistments.

Geiger entered the picture at a most opportune time. In place of the Krag-Jorgenson, the Marine Corps had begun to issue the newer clip-loading, bolt-action Springfield Rifle, Model 1903, and by 1909 the latter with its accompanying bayonet had become the regulation individual weapon for Marine riflemen. With the gradual addition of light supporting arms, principally, Gatling and Colt-Browning Machine Guns, and 3 in. field artillery pieces, and the availability of some stocks of engineer and signal equipment, specialized instruction became mandatory. To meet the complexities of naval ordnance, a degree of booklearning and technical knowledge were required in lieu of the previous hit-or-miss methods based exclusively on practical experience. The new trend naturally met with some opposition, but in time the printed training manuals and the more formal atmosphere of the classroom were recognized as essential features of the training program. And if the tobacco-chewing Drill Sergeants on the parade ground were concerned with their future, the clerks at Headquarters upstairs in the Mills Building faced even keener competition against the inroads of the machine age: the introduction of typewriters numbered the days of hand-written records and accounts heretofore laboriously penned in Spencerian style, while the prospect of a telephone on each desk was equally disturbing. Meanwhile, down at the post stables the draft animals and the officers' mounts contemplated with mixed emotions the sights and sounds of increasing numbers of motor vehicles, and the farriers and wheelwrights, saddle makers and blacksmiths, went about their daily tasks with worried looks.

Apparently, Geiger adjusted to his new profession as readily as a duck takes to water. He was doubly fortunate in his station assignments. Other than a brief interval at Norfolk and short tours on rifle ranges in Maryland, he spent almost all of his period of enlisted service at the Marine Barracks at Washington's Eighth and "Eye" Streets. The residence of the Commandant as well as of other General Officers of the Corps on duty at Headquarters, then as at present the post was the show piece of the Marine Corps. Noted for its spit-and-polish manners, its strict discipline, its neat and ordered way of life, the troops assigned there were very definitely a cut above average. They had to be: in addition to intricate ceremonies and colorful parades at scheduled times, every man was figuratively "on parade" every moment he stood his tour of guard duty, and the Formal Guard Mounts themselves were quite an impressive show, requiring countless hours of preparation aside from their execution.

Along with his companions in arms Private Geiger actively participated in all of the daily drills and formations as well as in other routine duties and activities at that busy post. Barracks life did not visibly coarsen him as it might well another of weaker character, nor was he debased by the inevitable brawling, constant profanity, and other questionable behavior displayed by the meaner element among his associates., that minority group which seems attracted to the military life and exists in most military organizations despite ruthless attempts to eradicate it. He stayed very much by himself, shunned the misfits and the dissatisfied, and when he was not engaged in sports devoted much of his off-duty time to conscientious study of military texts. As a result, he maintained his dignity and sense of self-respect, and his fellows came to regard him as a quiet, serious, and reserved individual to be left unmolested, for he was a scrappy little fighter, slow to anger but handy with his fists if sufficiently aroused. He never asked for special favors, but went where he was sent, and carried out his fair share of assigned tasks without complaint. Otherwise, he went about his own business in a cheerful and cooperative manner.

Such conduct and attention to duty could not long pass unnoticed. So well was he regarded by his superiors, he was soon recommended for promotion. This of itself at that time was not an easy feat. For a man to make the grade of Corporal (that of Private 1st Class was then nonexistent) usually took all four years of his first enlistment: "one stripe, one hashmark." Even then he had to be a man of exceptional merit and demonstrated ability. He had also to be lucky, for there were few vacancies. The average non-commissioned officer (and there were less than 1,300) remained on active duty in the Corps more or less indefinitely; as a rule openings occurred only as a consequence of a death or a retirement within its ranks. Without question Geiger's unusual educational qualifications were of paramount importance, although by the same token jealous persons might have viewed such talents antagonistically. In any case, he won his advancement in near record time—after seven months of "on-the-job-training." His Certificate of Appointment to Corporal, effective 2 June 1908, was signed by none other than the tenth Commandant of the Marine Corps, George F. Elliott, who, incidentally, but a week before had been promoted from Brigadier to Major General, and was doubtless then feeling so elated with his own recent advancement, it was a pleasure to take time off from other official duties to sign the warrant of a lowly Corporal.

Proudly sporting his Corporal's chevrons, Geiger spent the summer of 1908 preparing himself for the coming ordeal. In September he was officially notified that he had been designated by the Secretary of the Navy to take the series of professional examinations for appointment to commissioned rank, scheduled to take place in late October. These he passed with flying colors; moreover, on this occasion he was certified as sound in body by the Naval Medical Board, who noted with favor the correction of certain of Geiger's previous physical defects, and gave him waivers on the few irregularities he was powerless to change.

The culmination of fifteen months of strenuous application to duty and devotion to an ideal finally arrived on 4 February 1909. On that date Geiger was advised by General Elliott that he had been honorably discharged (as a Corporal) to accept an appointment as a commissioned officer of the Marine Corps. His actual Certificate of Honorable Discharge, signed by Lieutenant Colonel James E. Mahoney, Commanding Officer of the Marine Barracks at Washington, shows that Corporal Geiger was graded "Excellent" in *Character* and "Honest and Faithful" under *Remarks,* the highest grades that could be extended at that time. The document further attests that he was "Paid in Full, $53.00," and indication that Geiger had a favorable balance in his uniform

41

clothing allowance as well as some accrued leave. The following day, 5 February, Geiger accepted his commission as a Second Lieutenant of the Marine Corps, and was accordingly sworn in at Washington, his date of rank being 20 January 1909. His formal Commission, dated 30 January 1909, is rumpled and heavily stained from the spilled contents of champagne glasses, and ring-marked from the bottoms of brandy and whisky decanters, for in those days what was known as "wetting down a commission" was a full-fledged (and quite damp) ritual, which, if it required several evenings to get the job done properly, similarly called for several days for the participants to recover as best they could from its after-effects.

Immensely elated with himself and displaying his brand-new gold bars on his shoulder straps, Roy returned to Florida for three weeks' well earned leave before reporting under orders for instruction at the Marine Officers' School of Application. Prior to 1909, the forerunner of what later was to be termed the Basic School was located at the Marine Barracks at the Naval Academy, at Annapolis, Maryland. Some consideration was given to shifting its locale north to New London, Connecticut, but during the winter of 1908—09 the authorities at Washington decided that the Marine Barracks at the Naval Station at Port Royal, South Carolina, was better fitted to serve as the site of a school of instruction for newly commissioned officers. If nothing else, the chosen spot did have a more equitable year-round climate for outdoor training and target shooting. Situated on low and flat Parris Island the mere remoteness of the selected place was probably another important factor, for its general isolation was such that students could find little to distract them from their work, the nearest temptation of any consequence being Savannah, Georgia, many hot and dusty miles to the south.

A member of the first class convened at Port Royal, Second Lieutenant Geiger in company with 50-odd fledgling officers called themselves "The Mixed Pickles." Like Mr. Heinz' well known "57 Varieties," they too had been drawn from all over the nation with varying backgrounds and widely diverse experiences. Commanded by Lieutenant Colonel Eli K. Cole, the School of Application carried on its roster of staff and students the names of many individuals who in later years were to achieve outstanding records during their long service careers. Among them was the

Adjutant, First Lieutenant Clayton B. Vogel, a future Adjutant and Inspector of the Marine Corps, while Second Lieutenant Alexander A. Vandegrift in time became its eighteenth Commandant, and the first to be promoted to four-star rank. Five of the officers present were future Marine pilots, all destined to win laurels in the field of naval aviation: Lieutenants Alfred Cunningham and Edward Brainard, along with Roy Geiger, eventually were to become renowned Directors of Marine Aviation; Bernard Smith and Francis Evans were among the original pioneers of the naval air arm, and both in time were to attain enviable reputations as highly skilled pilots.

The aim of the School of Application was to educate and train junior officers to become efficient Platoon Leaders as well as to enable them to perform such other duties as were normally assigned to Company Grade Officers aboard ship, in the field, or in garrison. A ten-month course, the scope of instruction was most comprehensive covering a wide range of professional subjects. Included were field engineering and military topography, naval and military law, administration, organization, and signals. Naval ordnance and gunnery, and service afloat, were important topics. Much stress was given to drill and command, and to the operation and firing of small arms—on the target range as well as musketry problems. To round out the picture, many hours were devoted to scouting and patrolling, and to tactical exercises under field conditions.

Then as now, young Lieutenants during their basic period of training quickly established reputations which were to accompany them from station to station throughout their careers. Habits and distinctive mannerisms—good as well as bad—acquired on the drill fields at Parris Island were to reappear in the same fashion and with notable regularity at other times and other places, and similar to his designated serial number and his staff returns, an officer's character, once definitely established and demonstrated for all to view, became a permanent part of him, seldom subject to change and retained wherever he went. In Geiger's case he made his mark early in the game. An avid sports' enthusiast, he excelled at swimming and diving. The only man on Parris Island who could manage to swim against the incoming Atlantic tides in Port Royal Bay, his aquatic ability won him the first of his nicknames: *Rugged Roy*. He could spend hours on end in the water, swimming effortlessly, and whenever possible, he would go down to the beaches at Hilton Head to enjoy the surf-bathing. So marked was his endurance it was immediately noticed and admired by Cunningham and Evans, and as will be subsequently related, so favorable an impression was made they deliberately selected Geiger as their choice of candidates for flight instruction a few years later when the Naval Air Station at Pensacola was activated.

Geiger applied himself wholeheartedly to his studies, and stood high in his class. This was indeed fortunate for while at Port Royal, Geiger had his first brush with the law. Had he not already achieved a reputation as an excellent student and a responsible young officer, he might well have found himself in serious trouble. In March 1909 he received permission to visit nearby Beaufort. This was granted, but once "ashore" Roy changed his mind and went to Savannah. He was unlucky that day for he was observed by some member of the staff of the School, who promptly turned him in. Brought before his Commanding Officer, Roy was admonished for his dereliction, and just so he would not forget, Colonel Cole gave him thirty days' restriction to the confines of the Barracks and the School. Roy was never at his best when he was penned in like a caged animal, and such curtailment of his freedom of action annoyed and irritated him. Boredom led to apathy and moodiness. He commenced to brood about his misfortunes, and during the third week of his period of restriction, so great was the tension, he decided to drown his sorrows. Caught red-handed in the act of drinking with enlisted men, Geiger found himself facing a grave Charge of "Conduct Unbecoming an Officer", with two attached Specifications both equally damaging. To make a bad situation even worse, he had compounded the severity of his offenses by committing them while serving sentence for a prior indiscretion, an unpardonable sin by any standards, and a serious error of judgement on his part.

There was little he could do in his own defense. As a lawyer he realized that the weight of the evidence against him would be impossible to contradict or to surmount; that it would be unwise even to submit a plea of *Not Guilty*. Rather than antagonize his jurors, Roy decided that the only sensible thing to do was to admit his guilt openly, and to take whatever medicine was served out. Such an attitude softened the Courts' hearts, for the members, had they been so minded, would have been entirely within their rights had they recommended that Roy's commission be revoked. Instead, having considered his otherwise fine record at the School, scholastically as well as athletically, and his forthright and frank admission of the error of his ways, they relented to the extent he was awarded punishment consisting of ten days' arrest, confined to quarters.

Geiger was nobody's fool. He knew how far he could go, where, and when to head in. He had narrowly escaped disaster; thereafter, for the remaining eight months of the course he walked a very straight and narrow path. The incident was regrettable in several respects. It had now become a matter of official record in his file jacket. Furthermore, it prevented him from receiving what otherwise assuredly would have been a rating of "Excellent" on the first Fitness Report. For the period under consideration Colonel Cole noted that since Geiger's punishment in April, he had consistently maintained a clear record, and had stood well in the forefront of his class. But it was equally obvious that the episode had not been forgotten: under *General Conduct and Bearing,* Geiger was graded "Tolerable," if nothing else an indication that the Commanding Officer of the School of Application looked upon the attitude and behavior of one of its Second Lieutenants with some misgiving.

In all probability, Roy was not overly concerned—he was not prone to cry over spilled milk—and as a young officer, fresh out of school, in December 1909 all the world seemed waiting for the taking. Under orders to join the Marine Detachment of the *USS Wisconsin,* Geiger was granted a weeks' leave over Christmas, with instructions to report for duty aboard that battleship at Brooklyn Navy Yard not later than 27 December. For the moment he had a chance to look about and to survey his position after a protracted interval of intense concentration and competition. Under the Act of 11 May 1908, his annual base pay as a Second Lieutenant was set at $1,700.00. 10% additional was granted for foreign duty. As for his allowances, he was provided with Public Quarters consisting of two furnished rooms, or a monthly cash payment of $12.00 per room, which could be paid to those of his rank not actually serving with troops, or, living off a post or station. If he were assigned to duty or to an organization requiring that he be mounted, his horse would be furnished by the Government, or he could receive a sum of $150.00 annually if he provided one

45

suitable mount at his own expense, and $200.00 if he maintained two horses.

Aside from his ability to acquire financial security, Geiger was a member of a society marked by dependability and reliability, and there was a basic assurance of certainty and continuity in the mere conformity of his well regulated and orderly way of life. In the decade immediately prior to the First World War, what was then known as "Principle" was a highly esteemed attribute. It was an attitude which championed the notion that there was a "right way to do things." A person was expected to think along safe channeled lines. Anything spectacular was viewed with reserve if not distrust; change did not necessarily mean progress; and mere activity was not to be confused with usefulness or productivity. Applied specifically to the armed services, it was an era of "Considered Opinion." Careful deliberation went into every decision of importance, for there was yet sufficient time to think things out, and if a man were asked to express his views on a matter, his opinion was not given lightly.

As for the Marine Corps of 1909—10, although its strength had shown a modest increase to meet the demands placed upon it by the progressive enlargement of the Navy, it was still so small that as far as the officers were concerned, in a very short time everybody got to know everything there was to know about everyone else. The Staff consisted of the Major General Commandant backed up by 29 officers assigned to the Adjutant and Inspector's, Quartermaster's, and Paymaster's Departments. The Line was made up of 304 commissioned officers, of which 35 were of Field Grade, and the remainder about equally divided numerically in the ranks of Captain, First and Second Lieutenant. Although the terms of Executive Order No. 969 of 12 November 1908 had removed Marine Detachments from all naval vessels, the provisions of the Naval Appropriations Act of 1910, passed by Congress on 3 March 1909, just as emphatically reinstated the Marines to their traditional functions and duties aboard ship. As before, approximately one third the entire strength of the Corps was detailed for service afloat, and it was to the Marine Guard of one of the units of the Atlantic Fleet that Geiger was assigned. Secure in his conviction that he was happy in his new found profession which had so much to offer, and eagerly looking forward to his first tour of sea duty, Lieutenant Geiger passed through the main gate at Brooklyn Navy Yard on a snowy morning two days after Christmas 1909, and finally located his ship, the *USS Wisconsin,* snugly lying alongside Pier 8.

Chapter III

Flash of Empire

Lieutenant Geiger's first tour of sea duty as the junior officer of *Wisconsin's* Marine Detachment, commanded by Captain Theodore E. Backstrom, USMC, was destined to endure no longer than his former, brief career as a practicing attorney. It was not his fault that his service aboard that vessel was cut short in the early spring of 1910, but rather his misfortune to have been assigned to a ship that had rapidly reached the end of her usefulness. Authorized two years before the outbreak of the Spanish-American War, *Wisconsin* was fast approaching obsolescence at the time of her initial commissioning in 1901, and within five years was to be rendered practically obsolete, so vast had been the technological changes introduced in that short space of time in the basic design and construction of large warships and in the related fields of naval ordnance and marine engineering. For *HMS Dreadnought*, Admiral John A. Fisher's brilliant creation and the Royal Navy's pride and joy, had sounded the death knell for every battleship afloat, regardless of nationality, at the time of her launching in 1906, and *Wisconsin* along with her two sister ships, *Alabama* and *Illinois*, found herself considerably out of date, undergunned, and underpowered, relegated to a second string role, momentarily biding her time, and waiting for the ship-breaker's cutting torch.

With her prominent main battery turrets at the extremities of her mountainous armored, central citadel, her low freeboard at the stern, her twin towering stacks placed abreast, and her lofty boat cranes, *Wisconsin* presented an unusual silhouette. From a distance at anchor she resembled more a segment of a metropolitan electric

48

power and light plant, which had somehow slid off its shore foundations into the bay, to reappear at low tide as a semi-waterlogged island, than a 12,000-ton American man-of-war. Back from her lengthy voyage around the world and with Brooklyn Navy Yard her nominal home port, *Wisconsin's* days of active duty were running out. A unit of the 4th Division of the Atlantic Fleet under command of Captain Ben W. Hodges, USN, there was little to keep her occupied, for tactically speaking, she was no longer capable of keeping pace with the newer and far more powerful vessels as they left their builders' yards. Operationally, her function was limited to that of serving as a mobile floating classroom for seamen-gunners and firemen. In the summer months she sloshed up and down the Atlantic Coast, periodically putting in at the larger seaports extending northward from Newport, Rhode Island, to Rockland, Maine, to replenish her coal bunkers and to permit her crew occasional week-end liberty ashore. As a respite from New England's winter gales, January through March was usually spent in fleet exercises at the Southern Drill Grounds offshore from Cuba's Guantanamo Bay.

This annual period of firing practice at sea and on the rifle range ashore was eagerly looked forward to by the 60-odd members of *Wisconsin's* Marine Guard. It provided them the opportunity to compete with the naval crews jointly manning the ship's secondary batteries, and to engage in competition in a variety of athletic contests from racing whaleboats to boxing bouts. Swimming and diving were important features of the sports' program, and her Lieutenant of Marines could be counted upon to win every coveted trophy available in those popular events. Geiger thoroughly enjoyed every moment of his ship's stay in Caribbean waters, and soon won the reputation of being able to swim completely around his vessel at anchor faster than any other contestants. He also achieved no little notoriety for his endurance feats on Saturday afternoons while the fleet units in the harbor leisurely swung about their mooring buoys.

From high atop one of *Wisconsin's* boat skids Geiger delighted to dive over the side, whereupon he would swim about the anchorage, visiting in succession every major vessel present there. Oblivious to the potential dangers of man-eating sharks and voracious barracuda, on arrival alongside a ship's accommodation ladder he could depend on being loaned dry clothing permitting him to make a hasty change of attire before facing the Officer of the Deck. Once past that official, the next stop was the Wardroom to sample the wares of the Wine Mess. He had many friends aboard the battleships and cruisers of the Atlantic Fleet, and they were always happy to stand treat if Roy felt inclined to swim over for a friendly chat.

In this respect, it should be mentioned that in 1910 the Navy was still "wet," at least to the degree that commissioned officers afloat or ashore could purchase and consume alcoholic beverages from such small stocks as were maintained in Officers' Messes in the interest of convenience and economy. This traditional source, which was based on the premise that an officer was a gentleman and as such would not abuse a privilege, was to continue for another four years. At that later date, the Secretary of the Navy, Mr. Josephus Daniels, with a stroke of his pen did away with an age-old custom, for his "Bone Dry Order" (Navy General Order No. 99, effective 1 July 1914) brought compulsory prohibition to warships' afterguards, greatly to the consternation and righteous indignation of those who held that it was grossly unfair and not quite a sporting thing to deny jack-tar his tot after his day's work had been done. Whether Mr. Daniels' decision was motivated by a weak stomach, by the sincerity of his personal moral convictions, or by downright political expediency was shortly to become the subject of much heated discussion; however, in the long run his controversial action made little difference, for with the eventual ratification of the National Prohibition Amendment after the First World War, the Navy along with the nation at large had no other choice but to climb aboard the water wagon.

But at Guantanamo Bay back in 1910, such a state of affairs was only a remote threat on the horizon, far from an accomplished fact. Provided the sun had passed well over and beyond the yardarm, there was no objection to liquid refreshment for officers off watch, but it was well understood that one held one's liquor under any and all circumstances, and overindulgence was very definitely frowned upon. In Geiger's case, if a man had the energy and the strength, not to mention the endurance, to swim about from ship to ship until darkness fell, and with timeout only for a quick glass, he was regarded as an individual to be admired, for comparatively few persons have the requisite physical stamina to stand such strain. Considering that normally eight battleships or armored cruisers of the Atlantic Fleet dropped anchor simultaneously in Cuban waters, not infrequently ten, and occasionally a dozen, by the time Geiger had completed his rounds and had returned to *Wisconsin's* gangway, he was more than ready for a four-course meal and a good night's rest.

Like many things, these and other pleasant aspects of an unhurried era all too quickly came to an end. In late March *Wisconsin* was back once more at Brooklyn, where her complement was paid off and disbanded. A makeshift maintenance crew took her north to the Navy Yard at Portsmouth, New Hampshire, and during the month of April she was laid up there "in reserve," her active career finished for all time. As for Lieutenant Geiger, he reported to the Naval Hospital at Brooklyn for minor surgery, and on his release was assigned to the Marine Barracks at that Navy Yard. The following month he was detached, and ordered to proceed to Mare Island, California. At the last moment his orders to the West Coast were revoked, and he was sent instead to Port Royal, South Carolina, for duty under instruction in an Advanced Base Course. On completion of that brief period of schooling, in June, he was ordered to the Marine Barracks at the nation's capital. Throughout the summer of 1910 he served on temporary additional duty at the rifle range at Winthrop, Maryland, as an instructor and line coach to recruits brought there from Norfolk and Philadelphia. Finally, in September, he was reassigned to sea duty, and returned to Brooklyn once again, this time under orders to join the 80-man Marine Detachment of the *USS Delaware,* then fitting out for an extended tour of service.

Contrasted to his experiences aboard *Wisconsin,* Geiger's service afloat in *Delaware* was altogether as different as night is from day. This latter vessel was a true dreadnought in the literal use of the term, and at the time of her commissioning in the late spring of 1910, she was unquestionably the largest, fastest, and most powerful warship not only of the United States Navy but also of any foreign naval power. With twice *Wisconsin's* size and complement, horsepower and operating range, *Delaware's* main battery of ten 12 in. rifles in five twin turrets could doubtless have blown her earlier contemporary out of the water with a single salvo. By this date the American Navy was second in magnitude only to that of Great Britain, and the appearance on the scene of

Delaware together with her soon-to-be-launched sister vessel, *North Dakota,* in time was to cause officers of the Royal Navy to sit up and take notice of this product of Yankee shipyards on the other side of the Atlantic Ocean.

They did not have to wait long to get a good look at this monster of some 22,000 tons displacement, capable of steaming at a maximum speed of 21½ knots, employing a mixture of fuel oil and pulverized coal to fire her fourteen boilers. In October 1910, *Delaware* departed from Hampton Roads for Weymouth, England, on her first overseas cruise. She remained on display there, along with other units of the 1st Division of the Atlantic Fleet, for three weeks, thereby affording British naval architects a fine opportunity to look her over and to make comparisons, meanwhile part of her crew took the train to visit London. During the month of December, *Delaware* crossed the English Channel to pay a similar duty call at Cherbourg, France. A few fortunate persons managed to spend Christmas liberty at Paris, but the authorities at Cherbourg wisely decided that they would be stretching their luck too far were they to permit large numbers of American sailors ashore in a foreign port on a New Year's Eve. Accordingly, on 31 December, *Delaware* weighed anchor, and ten days later after an uneventful trans-Atlantic passage, poked her sharp stem into the fleet anchorage at Cuba's Guantanamo Bay.

So pleased were the officials at Washington with her stellar performance abroad, they decided to put her on the southern circuit. Their decision was predicated on several important factors. The Chilean Minister to the United States having recently passed away, the Chilean Government discovered to its embarrassment that it momentarily had no means of returning Sênor Cruz' body to the land of his ancestors for appropriate burial there, having neither an adequate navy nor merchant marine of note. Consequently, *Delaware* being currently unassigned and more or less free to go where she wished, it was decided to press her into service as a seagoing hearse for the deceased diplomat. Secondly, there was the practical matter of business closely allied with international power politics. At that time all three of the major South American nations—Argentina, Brazil, and Chile—were openly shopping about in their efforts to acquire oceangoing battleships of the dreadnought class for their fast growing navies. Argentina had already contracted with the Fore River Shipbuilding Company of Massachusetts for the construction of two mighty dreadnoughts, *Rivadavia* and *Moreno,* each of 28,000 tons displacement. This had been deliberately done to counter the previous purchase by Brazil from British firms of her two dreadnought battleships, *Minas Gerais* and *São Paulo.* Fearful lest her national dignity suffer were she to be outclassed by her neighbors and rivals, Chile let it be known that she was in the market for at least two super-battleships, and then retired smugly to the sidelines to watch American and British shipbuilders try to underbid one another. Such an arrangement was perfectly agreeable to naval constructors of those two nations, who were anxious to experiment with certain innovations pertaining to ordnance, armor plate, and marine power plants, providing, of course, they were done at the expense of third power. It was therefore logically reasoned that were an American dreadnought to visit Chilean ports on a good will mission, it might possibly influence the prospective purchaser to conduct business with Bethlehem Steel rather than with Armstrong, Whitworth and Company.

Last and by no means a minor consideration were the complicated logistical aspects of *Delaware's* pending cruise. In 1911 the Panama Canal was yet far from completion, and a roundtrip voyage from Norfolk to Valparaiso, Chile, meant a 17,000-mile jaunt around the southern tip of the Western Hemisphere or two transits of the dangerous Straits of Magellan. For a single vessel of *Delaware's* size and fuel consumption to attempt this, unescorted by colliers or supply ships, capable of effecting normal maintenance at sea not to mention "running repairs" in the event of machinery breakdown or navigational mishap, was far from an easy task. As things transpired, on the outbound passage a stop was made at Brazil's Rio de Janeiro for coal and water, and a second was arranged at Punta Arenas within the Straits for provisioning. As for the return trip, once the ship had coaled and victualed at Valparaiso, *Delaware* thereafter touched briefly at Rio a second time for fuel bunkers, and from thence continued back to Boston non-stop and under full power, much to the elation of her builders and to the satisfaction of the Navy Department in general, all of whom were most favorably impressed by her brilliant achievement, unmarred by mechanical failure or other unforseen incident.

The outward-bound leg of *Delaware's* cruise to Chile was

largely an ordeal for her Marine Guard. At least one half of the Detachment stood constant Vigil over the coffin of the late Minister, laid in state in one of the ship's Flag cabins, and Lieutenant Geiger shared watch and ward with his immediate superior, Captain Thomas H. Brown, USMC, on this solemn duty throughout the month of February. Long before the vessel reached the Straits of Magellan the Marine Guard felt that through close, physical associationship with the deceased, they were practically on speaking terms. By early March, when they had finally arrived at Valparaiso and had ceremoniously unloaded his body on to the pier, they had figuratively worked up to a shaking hands relationship with the former diplomat, so intimately had they become attached to his remains. Naturally, it was not all work and no play, for there were liberty parties and shore entertainment at Rio on the way down and back; moreover, *Delaware* remained in port at Valparaiso for ten days in March to give all hands a good chance to stretch their shore legs and to take in all the local sights.

Little did they realize at that time what was in store for them; that their South American interlude was just a warming-up exercise for far more spectacular events. Granted that *Delaware's* presence in Chile had not been sufficient to sway the sympathies of the latter country's Navy Department in favor of buying American-made dreadnoughts (for the British successfully undercut their Yankee rivals in competitive bidding), she was nevertheless the showpiece of the United States Navy. While in dry dock at Boston Navy Yard in early May, it was disclosed that she had been expecially selected to represent the nation at the Coronation Review in honor of His Britannic Majesty, King George V, scheduled to be held at Spithead on the Solent, off the Isle of Wight, on 24 June 1911. Forthwith, every effort was devoted to refurbishing *Delaware* from the cap of her main truck to her keel in anticipation of this unusual assignment.

As for the Coronation Review, it was stated in the London press that it was the largest and most powerful gathering of British warships ever known, and was a fitting close to the stately ceremonies of Coronation Week. At that performance no less than 167 ships of the Royal Navy were assembled at Spithead, the senior vessel present being *HMS Neptune,* Flagship of the Home Fleet. The British representation consisted of 8 battleships and 4 large battle cruisers, all of the dreadnought category, some 40 cruisers of various types and 80 destroyers and torpedo boats, not to mention a dozen-odd naval auxiliaries and an equal number of submarines. Also present were the two Royal Yachts, *Victoria and Albert,* and *Alexandra,* as well as the Admiralty Yacht *Enchantress.* Eighteen foreign men-of-war, including *Delaware,*flying the flags of the principal European and Asiatic powers and the American Republics, dropped anchor in the Solent. As finally constituted the combined fleet occupied a space of 18 square miles, the ships being moored in successive, parallel lines, each 6 miles long. The main event, of course, was the passage down the anchored columns of the Royal Party aboard *Victoria and Albert,*on which occasion every ship, regardless of size or type, successively fired a Royal Salute of 21 Guns in honor of the newly crowned King-Emperor.

Delaware was by far the largest of the foreign warships in attendance. Her Marine Guard was kept on the run on the quarterdeck incident to parades and formations for visiting dignitaries. In addition to official calls and other ceremonial occasions, the evening social events included formal dinners and dances. Throughout the afternoons there were frequent opportunities for informal gatherings in the Wardrooms of all of the larger vessels. In fact, one gathers that if a large amount of saluting powder was shot up in the form of white smoke, an equal quantity of champagne corks popped out of the necks of their bottles at an almost unprecendented rate. After ten days of festivities, the social calendar took on the aspect of an endurance contest, each nation trying to outdo another, with no one desiring to be the first to break up the party. Lieutenant Geiger stuck it out to the bitter end, but in time even he succumbed to what must have amounted to sheer physical exhaustion.

Returning to *Delaware* from a dinner aboard an English ship the final night of the Coronation Review, Geiger was reported by the officer of the Deck to have been slightly awash, the inference being that if he had not drunk wisely at least he had drunk well. *Delaware's* Commanding Officer, Captain Charles A. Gove, promptly awarded the vessel's Lieutenant of Marines ten days' suspension from duty, and ordered him to submit a statement explaining his conduct. On 1 July 1911, while making the return trans-Atlantic passage from Spithead to Boston, Geiger submitted his written explanation, which, unfortunately for him, was not accepted as satisfactory by his superiors, and was to hang threateningly like a sword over his head for many months to come. In substance, he claimed that the dinner in question had occurred after a week of official entertainment, at which time he was physically in no condition "to stand the drink which was pressed upon me on that occasion, and of which I felt it my duty to partake."

This mixture of candidness and logic apparently was not to the liking of Captain Gove. He could have tolerantly accepted Geiger's account in the spirit in which it was given, and let it go at that. Perhaps he was under strain from the weight of his recent responsiblilities; perhaps, he, too, was suffering from a bad attack of jangled nerves after the exhausting round of gala festivities in British waters. In any event, he made an issue out of the incident by giving Geiger an unfavorable Fitness Report, wherein it was quite evident the Captain of the *Delaware* regarded his Lieutenant of Marines as flippant if not impertinent. In time this report wound up on the desk of the Major General Commandant, who had no other choice but to refer the matter again to Geiger's attention for comment, accompanied with the admonition that the Lieutenant so conduct himself in the future as to preclude "the necessity on the part of your commanding officers of rendering adverse fitness reports on fitness in your case."

Once again, in October 1911, *Delaware* then being at Brooklyn Navy Yard, Geiger was ordered to resubmit his explanation of the incident at Spithead. As before the Lieutenant stubbornly stuck by his guns as he saw no reason to alter his original version. His reply to Captain Gove was brusque and to the point: "I have no further statement to make other than that made on 1 July 1911." Ordinarily the entire affair should have been allowed to die quietly on the vine, for Geiger had long ago been summarily punished for his temporary indiscretion. On the other hand, the episode had gradually snowballed into a mass of correspondence and endorsements, all of which had now become part of Geiger's official record. The whole business was by no means over and done with. Four years later, as will be subsequently related, when Geiger's name was brought before a Marine Examining Board preliminary to his promotion to the rank of First Lieutenant, the Secretary of the Navy, Mr. Daniels, felt called upon to make additional comment on the Spithead dinner party.

In the winter of 1911–12, however, Lieutenant Geiger was not going to worry unduly about either the past or the future. There were too many other pleasant things to do at the moment, *Delaware* having returned to the Southern Drill Grounds to engage in routine tactical exercises. By the time his ship had steamed north to Narragansett Bay in the late spring, his tour of duty afloat had been completed. On 15 May 1912, he was detached from *Delaware,* then at the Naval Training Station at Newport, under orders to report to the Marine Corps Recruiting Office on New York City's East 23rd Street.

Assistant Officer-in-charge to Captain Harold C. Snyder, USMC, Geiger's stay in Manhattan during the summer months of 1912 was suddenly terminated by assignment to Expeditionary Duty in Nicaragua. This was not exactly an unexpected development, for throughout that summer things had been progressively going from bad to worse in that Central American Republic, to the degree that American intervention became practically mandatory to stave off outright anarchy and to restore some semblance of law and order. Herein, the Conservative party under the leadership of President Adolfo Díaz found itself face to face with an armed uprising led by the Liberal opponent, Benjamin Zeledon, aided and abetted by Luis Mena, a former Minister of War and the dominant member of a Conservative splinter group violently opposed to Díaz' financial dealings with the United States. Besieged at the nation's capital Managua, President Díaz was so hard pressed to defend himself against the rebels he was in no position to guarantee effective protection of American citizens and their property, hence his request that the United States come to his support.

Concerned with the safety of his Legation, the American Minister at Managua at once cabled for assistance. In August, a detachment of bluejackets from the *USS Annapolis,* then at anchor in the seaport of Corinto, was put ashore to assume the duties of a Legation Guard at Managua. The capital continuing to remain under intermittent bombardment by the Liberals, a battalion of Marines under command of Major Smedley D. Butler was hastily transferred from Camp Elliott in Panama, to Managua, to reinforce the Legation Guard there, and to keep the railroad open between the capital and Corinto on Nicaragua's western coast. But even the presence of Butler's troops was not sufficient to overcome the rebel threat, and by the end of August the clarion call had to be sounded for additional help.

On orders from Headquarters at Washington, an expeditionary force of some 30 officers and 750 enlisted Marines was hurriedly organized at Philadelphia Navy Yard for duty in Nicaragua. Commanded by Colonel Joseph H. Pendleton, this so-called 1st Provisional Regiment consisted of headquarters and two battalions manned by personnel drawn from the Advance Base School as well as from Barracks Detachments of various East Coast Navy Yards. Second Lieutenant Geiger, nominally on temporary additional duty from his Recruiting Billet at New York, found himself assigned to E Company of the Second Battalion. On 24 August 1912, along with the rest of Pendleton's Regiment, he embarked on the transport, *USS Prairie,* at Philadelphia, and sailed the same day for the Panama Canal Zone. A week later, following its arrival at Cristobal and crossing of the Isthmus to Balboa on the Pacific, the expeditionary force boarded the *USS California* for the final leg of the passage to Corinto.

On 4 September the troops disembarked there in the midst of a very critical situation. Under the over-all command of Rear Admiral William H. Southerland, USN, Pendleton's Regiment was given the mission of opening the railroad its entire length, all the way south to Grenada, denying its use to the Liberal revolutionists, and otherwise by its show of strength to impress the rebels with the futility of their cause. The Second Battalion was immediately dispatched to Léon, about one third of the distance to Managua, with orders to suppress rebel activities locally; meanwhile, Pendleton with the First Battalion continued on to the capital with the intention of pushing onward to Grenada. During the month of September, Geiger remained with his battalion, commanded by Lieutenant Colonel Charles G. Long, in the Léon area. This unit faced a difficult task, for part of Léon was still held by the Liberals. All roads leading to that community had to be carefully guarded lest the revolutionists receive ammunition, food stocks, or reinforcements from the surrounding region. Aside from constant patrolling was the ceaseless problem of preventing the rebel troops from occupying threatening positions which would menace the uninterrupted operation of the railroad.

Meantime, Butler's Separate Battalion and Major William N. McKelvy's First Battalion of the Provisional Regiment were jointly employed by Colonel Pendleton for the relief of Grenada. After numerous delays this was accomplished during the latter part of September: Mena turned the half starved city over to the Marines, and after agreeing to surrender himself and to the disarming of his troops, was given safe passage out of the Republic. With Mena disposed of, Pendleton at last was able to concentrate his forces against Zeledon, who with a force of some 800 rebels had taken a strong defensive position on the rail line near Masaya, approximately midway between Managua and Grenada.

Refusing all offers of a peaceful settlement and scornful of the weak-hearted attempts of Nicaraguan Federal troops to dislodge him, Zeledon proceeded to dig himself even more deeply into a natural geographic barrier provided by a thickly wooded ridge between the two hills, Coyotepe and Barranca. In preparation for a frontal assault against the Liberal stronghold (the trenches were protected by barbed-wire entanglements), Pendleton brought from Léon two batteries of light artillery and their Marine gun crews, and commenced a steady bombardment of the principal rebel strong points atop Coyotepe. At dawn on the morning of 4 October, a composite force of three battalions of Marines, and sailors from *Annapolis* and *California,* took the Coyotepe-Barranca hill mass by storm, and after a brisk 40-minute fire fight drove the rebels completely from their trenches, Zeledon being shot in the melee by one of his own followers when he attempted to desert them. After learning of the Americans' successful seizure of Coyotepe and the rout of the rebels, the Nicaraguan Federalists worked up enough courage to attack Masaya, which they promptly put to fire and sword, thus wiping out the few remaining Liberal sympathizers.

A member of assault force at Coyotepe, Lieutenant Geiger for the first time in his service career experienced armed combat against enemy opposition in the field. Within a week's time he was back again at Léon where he took part in several skirmishes between the American troops and Nicaraguan rebels fighting a last ditch stand. Although the back of Liberal resistance had been irreparably broken, there still existed scattered bands of former revolutionists, who, as armed brigands or outlaws continued to challenge the stability of the Conservative regime. To disarm them as well as to reassure the confidence of the rural population in the prestige of the central government, a number of small expeditions were sent from Managua to outlying regions to the north. During the latter part of October Geiger accompanied a mixed detachment of Marines and sailors sent to Matagalpa to put on a show of force designed to bolster the strength of the Conservative party.

Early in November the American naval forces began their withdrawal from Nicaragua. By the end of that month Colonel Pendleton and the bulk of the Provisional Regiment, in addition to Major Butler's Battalion, were on their way back to Panama. Colonel Long's Battalion continued to remain at Léon, while a company of Marines commanded by Captain Robert O. Underwood was detailed to serve more or less indefinitely as the Legation Guard at Managua. A member of this latter force, some 4 officers and 100 enlisted men, Lieutenant Geiger spent the month of December 1912 at the Republic's capital attempting to enforce the terms of an uneasy peace. Despite the best efforts of local dissident factions to create an incident, the Guard was successful in its mission. In time, Geiger along with his Commanding Officer was to receive an official Letter of Commendation from the American Minister, Mr. George T. Weitzel, for his outstanding performance of duty at Managua during that trying period.

By mid-January 1913 Geiger was stationed at Camp Elliott at Bas Obispo, about fifteen miles from the City of Panama at the end of the Culebra Cut. Under orders to form a 100-man detachment for further transfer from the Canal Zone to Mare Island Navy Yard, he remained on duty at Panama until early spring. As before the Camp Commander was Major Smedley Butler. Aware of Geiger's feats as a swimmer and diver, Butler ordered the young Lieutenant to participate in various aquatic sports and contests in competition with Army units also stationed in the Zone. Geiger was only too happy to oblige accordingly; moreover, he achieved a very distinguished record swimming ashore from barges and tug boats with their mooring warps, when it became necessary for them to come alongside a convenient bank to load firewood for their furnaces. His reputation as an expert diver, however, shortly forced him to request a transfer, for it soon became evident that were he to continue his specialty, he

60

might well imperil his own safety.

In this case, as the coping blocks were set higher and higher in position at the entrances to one of the Canal locks, Butler informed Geiger that he expected him correspondingly to increase the height of his dives. A little basic arithmetic demonstrated that within a month's time Geiger would have to undertake a plunge more normally associated with the talents of a professional, daredevil high-diver at Atlantic City's famed Steel Pier. There being no evidence that Butler intended to restrict the limits to a height more in keeping with Geiger's capabilities, the latter reasoned that the best way out of this ticklish situation was to get himself sent elsewhere. This he was able to arrange (for he was still technically on temporary additional duty from the Recruiting Station at New York), and on 20 March 1913, much to Geiger's relief he embarked aboard the *USS Buffalo,* at Balboa, as the detachment commander of a detail posted to the Marine Barracks at Mare Island.

Following a month's tour of duty in California, in June Geiger was detached from Mare Island, and was ordered to report to the Second Regiment, First Marine Brigade, then stationed in the Philippines. By mid-July he had joined the Brigade Headquarters at Cavite Navy Yard, south of the City of Manila. Commanded by Colonel Charles A. Doyen, Headquarters' personnel included in its roster such prominent officers as Major Henry L. Roosevelt, later an Assistant Secretary of the Navy under President Franklin D. Roosevelt, his cousin, and First Lieutenant Holland M. ("Howlin' Mad") Smith, years later destined to become the senior Marine Amphibious Corps Commander in the Pacific Theater during the Second World War. Later that month, Roy joined the Second Regiment under canvas at the Olongapo naval station on Subic Bay.

Under command of Lieutenant Colonel Lawrence H. Moses, the Second Regiment conducted routine field training, tactical exercises, and garrison duty in its assigned locale, and from time to time made available small detachments to man Marine Guards serving aboard vessels of the Asiatic Fleet as well as at the American Legation at Peking, North China. Herein, the Brigade as a whole served as a mobile force-in-readiness for expeditionary duty anywhere in the Far East in much the same manner that the Marine Battalion at Panama was kept on a stand-by basis for commitment in case of emergency in Central America or in the Caribbean. Until the development of the Navy Yard at Pearl Harbor and the creation of its Marine Barracks in July 1914, the Marine Corps maintained a field force in the Philippines throughout the decade following the Spanish-American War. Thereafter, other than the permanent Marine Guards at the Cavite and Olongapo naval stations, and at Guam, the Marines were largely concentrated at or near Honolulu in the Hawaiian Islands.

In time, it became Geiger's turn to serve his tour in the Orient, and in September 1913 he sailed aboard the SS *Loonsang* for Tientsin, his ultimate destination being Peking. Transferred to A Company of the Second Regiment, Geiger joined the Legation Guard at the northern capital of the Republic of China on the 22nd day of that month. His posting to that organization came at a most interesting period, and he was indeed fortunate to have had the opportunity to observe at first hand a series of rather colorful and spectacular developments in the fabulous history of the Celestial Empire.

In the wake of the overthrow of the Manchu Dynasty in 1911, a no-holds-barred struggle for power broke out between various Chinese political groups, all vying for control of its residue, and a chronic state of unsettled conditions accompanied by violence descended upon that unhappy land. Actual fighting and other disturbances erupted at Hankow and Shanghai; at Peking, so pronounced was the general disorder and unrest, the Commander-in-Chief of the United States Asiatic Fleet deemed it expedient to call upon the First Marine Brigade in the Philippines to furnish reinforcements. The Legation Guard at Peking, normally maintained at one-company strength, was thereupon practically doubled in size to permit it to protect American interests in that remote area. In fact, so grave had become the situation in 1912, it had been necessary to bring north by rail from its compound at Tientsin a detachment of the United States Fifteenth Infantry. By the time Lieutenant Geiger arrived at Peking things had largely quieted down; nevertheless, it was thought that it would be advisable to keep the Legation Guard at two-company strength.

Composed of 9 Marine Officers, 1 officer of the Navy Medical Corps, and some 200 enlisted Marines, the Legation Guard under the command of Major Dion Williams led a very active life.

Geiger's Company was commanded by Captain William P. Upshur, Second Lieutenant David L. Brewster being one of its two Platoon Leaders. Similar to all junior officers—then as at present—Roy quickly fell heir as the most recently joined member to a never ending series of additional duties, all of which were designed to increase his technical knowledge, and otherwise kept him so busy around the clock he could not find time to get into trouble. During his two-and-one-half-year tour of duty, at one time or another he served at Post Treasurer, Post Athletic Officer, and Recorder of a Marine Examining Board. Thanks to his legal background he frequently acted as Recorder of Summary Courts-Martial, and as Assistant Judge Advocate of General Courts-Martial. An *Expert Riflemann* he was a member of the Post Rifle Team, and on several occasions at both Peking and Tientsin, fired with the winning Marine team which defeated not only the best shots the Fifteenth Infantry could put on the line, but also the British marksmen of the *Gloucestershire Regiment* and the *South Wales Borderers.* In one of his rifle matches, Geiger placed sixteenth with a score of 92 out of a possible 105.

Denied the opportunity for swimming and diving, other than during the periods of summer encampment at Peitaho on the Gulf of Chihli, Geiger more than made up for the temporary loss of their enjoyment by his feats as a horseman. In May 1915, he relieved Lieutenant Brewster as Commanding Officer of the Mounted Detachment, a position which he held until January 1916. He enjoyed the "Horse Marines" tremendously, and in time became not only a skillful and aggressive polo player but also an expert steeplechase rider and an ardent cross-country enthusiast. Similarly, he participated in many hunting excursions and field trips to outlying territories, north of Peking. During a portion of each summer it was customary to establish a Hot Weather Camp some ten miles distant from the capital in the Western Hills. The annual hegira to that spot was always a welcome respite from the heat and dust of the city and from the monotony of drills and guard duty, which otherwise in large part provided the daily bill of fare of the Marines stationed to stand watch over Peking's celebrated Legation Quarter in the Tartar City.

Surmounting these pleasures were limitless opportunities to visit the gardens and lakes within the tinted walls of Peking's Imperial City, and to inspect at leisure the statues and palaces of the former Ming and Manchu Emperors contained inside the confines of the central stronghold, the Forbidden City. Further afield were the ancient tombs and exotic temples—now in ruins—while forty miles away by rail to the north stood one of the Wonders of the World, a portion of the Great Wall at Nankou Pass. Closer at hand and ever present were the fascinating bazaars and markets of the Chinese or Native City. The local currency being practically worthless, and the rate of exchange for the American dollar having attained unprecedented heights, enlisted men as well as officers could figuratively live like Oriental potentates on their meager service pay. Consequently, with servants and housing, travel and entertainment, dirt cheap, there was almost no end of things to see and to do if one were so inclined and could obtain liberty or local leave from his superiors.

Another unusual feature of service with the Legation Guard was the chance to become acquainted with men of outstanding caliber. A privileged group, personnel of the Marine Guard were selected with care, for it was a much sought assignment, and especially in the case of its commissioned officers, a successful tour of duty with that command was generally considered a highly favorable entry in one's service record. Many enduring friendships were consequently developed, particularly among the younger officers. Applied to Geiger, it was during his tour at Peking that he became friendly with Lieutenant Brewster to the degree that it was more than mere coincidence that both of them shortly were to embark on their future careers as Marine aviators. As for the enlisted men, they were more than a little proud of their associationship with this select segment of their Corps, and they constantly strove to outdo their contemporaries, the dozen-odd guard detachments of European and Japanese soldiers performing corresponding security duties within Peking's Legation Quarter. Figuratively enjoying the "Life of Reilly" the troops behaved very well, having no desire to be transferred under a cloud to other, more prosaic duties elsewhere, the general tranquility of their existence only being disturbed by an occasional resort to fisticuffs in a barroom or a native bazaar, followed by the inevitable consignment to the Guard House.

For Lieutenant Geiger his entire period of service in North China was a most interesting and enjoyable interlude. As a young bachelor, he along with his fellow officers had ample opportunity to engage fully in the gay social whirl of Peking's diplomatic set with its balls and its dinner parties, its race meets and its lawn fetes. The only dark spot on its otherwise unclouded horizon was occasioned by an incident of the past which managed to catch up with him. On 26 April 1915, he received a rather caustic note from Secretary of the Navy Daniels (complete with that gentleman's cramped signature) which threw up on the table once again all the details of Geiger's imprudent conduct at the now infamous dinner party at Spithead four years before. In this communication Mr. Daniels informed Geiger that he had been found qualified for promotion to the rank of First Lieutenant by Marine Examining Boards at Washington and Peking, and had been so recommended. The Secretary, however, apparently could not abstain from making mention of the unfavorable entry in Geiger's Fitness Report, rendered by Captain Gove of the *Delaware,* for he stated that the Navy Department in accepting the recommendation of the Examining Boards that Geiger be promoted "only took favorable action because your record subsequent to the date of the offense noted above has been excellent." Mr. Daniels continued to the effect that Geiger's single lapse of discretion would not warrant denial of his promotion, but again admonished the young Lieutenant for his impropriety, and finally signed off with the remark: "The Department anticipates that with this warning your future conduct will be such as is commensurate with the high standards of the Naval Service." Needless to say, Geiger had long since learned the error of his ways; thereafter, such official correspondence as he was to receive in the future from the Office of the Secretary of the Navy were uniformly congratulatory citations for outstanding performance of duty in peace as well as in time of war.

At long last—after some six and one-half years in grade—on 16 June 1915 Second Lieutenant Geiger exchanged his gold bars for the silver ones of a First Lieutenant. His actual commission, incidentally, was dated 25 January 1916, and his date of rank shown as of 16 May 1915. This was a most important milestone in Geiger's career. No longer a probationary officer, he had now completed two tours of sea duty, and had successfully engaged in foreign service in the field—in Nicaragua and Panama, in the Philippines and in North China. For these latter periods in time he was to be awarded the Nicaraguan Campaign Medal (1912), the

Expeditionary Medal for Nicaraguan service (1913), and a subsequent award of the Expeditionary Medal for his tour at Peking,China (1914). He had therefore experienced a wide variety of line duty aboard ship as well as in the field, and within bounds he was now free, if he so desired, to undertake staff assignments or to enter into the realm of specialized study beyond that of infantry or artillery.

Little did he know it at that time that his name was currently being considered for what was regarded as a most unusual posting for a young Marine Lieutenant. On 6 November 1915, First Lieutenant Alfred A. Cunningham, the pioneer pilot of Marine Corps Aviation, then serving at the Naval Aeronautic Station at Pensacola, Florida, submitted an official letter to Colonel John A. Lejeune at Headquarters in which he stated: "Having canvassed all of those who appear to be suitable for aviation, in order of desirability, I would place Geiger No. 1 on the list—and Brewster—if he can pass the physical examination, with assurance he would make a good showing." Herein, it is known that Cunningham had previously discussed the possibility of assigning Geiger to aviation training with Lieutenant Francis T. Evans (the fourth Marine officer to win his wings, in early 1916), for, as will be recalled, both of them had remembered Geiger for his swimming ability at Port Royal, and as such had an exceptionally high regard for his courage, tenacity, and physical endurance. As far as they were concerned Geiger had the essential qualifications to become a successful aviator, and there was no doubt in their minds that of all the potential candidates for basic flight instruction, Roy was best suited to meet the demanding challenge.

Whether or not Geiger personally corresponded with Cunningham on the matter has not been positively determined; nevertheless, the odds favor such a presumption. In any event, there is no record that Geiger officially requested a transfer to flight school. On 15 January 1916, he received orders at Peking directing his detachment and instructing him to proceed to the Continental Limits of the United States for further orders. It was not until his arrival at San Francisco, California, exactly two months later, that he learned for the first time that he had been directed to report to the Marine Corps Aviation Section of the Navy Flying School at Pensacola to commence his initial flight instruction.

His return trip across the Pacific was not without incident. Departing from Peking on 19 January, he arrived a week later at Nagasaki, Japan. Government shipping momentarily being unavailable he had to bide his time, "on the beach" as it were, for almost a month, awaiting the arrival at Nagasaki of the United States Army Transport *Sheridan,* bound for San Francisco. During the intervening weeks he had his first opportunity to observe the Japanese residents at least of the extreme western portion of the Island of Kyushu, but he was unable to visit the main Island of Honshu until nearly thirty years later on the occasion of the Japanese Surrender at Tokyo Bay at the close of the Second World War. Notwithstanding this protracted time interval it would appear that Roy got involved in a little private war of his own commencing as early as January 1916, in which he scored over his Japanese opponents by a double, technical knock-out.

An altercation with a ricksha-man over an exhorbitant fee soon progressed from an interchange of words to an exchange of blows. The appearance of two Japanese policemen on the scene having placed Geiger at a distinctly numerical disadvantage, he quickly resolved the problem by banging their two heads together so hard they were rendered *hors de combat* summarily; meanwhile, the owner of the ricksha, loudly bewailing his misfortune, ran off to summon further assistance. Realizing that common sense took precedence over valor, Geiger beat a hasty retreat, and managed to get back aboard ship before the Riot Squad of the local constabulary arrived at the gangway. Even this was a near thing for the Police insisted on searching the vessel, and Geiger had to go into hiding—and to remain *sub rosa*—for several days until the affair blew over. Under the circumstances, when the *Sheridan* finally slipped her mooring lines, if the Japanese authorities were glad to be rid of Geiger's presence at Nagasaki, no less eager was the young First Lieutenant to bring to a close his first, direct and personal acquaintance with Japanese officialdom.

Chapter IV

The Marine and his Flying Machine

On 31 March 1916, Lieutenant Geiger reported for duty at the Naval Aeronautic Station at Pensacola, Florida. Assigned to the Marine Aviation Section of the Navy Flying School, the Commanding Officer, Lieutenant Commander Henry C. Mustin, USN, forthwith officially designated Geiger "a student naval aviator for duty involving actual flying in aircraft, including balloons, dirigibles, and aeroplanes, in accordance with the Act of Congress approved 3 March 1915." The terms of that bit of legislation (the Naval Appropriations Act of 1915) are of more than passing interest, for they provided the basic authorization and the necessary additional funds for the training of not more than thirty naval aviators not exceeding the rank of Lieutenant Commander of the Navy or of Major of the Marine Corps. As student fliers they were allowed 35% extra "flight pay," those who became qualified pilots thereafter were granted an increase of 50% beyond their base pay as long as they remained on active flight duty. Accordingly, the Major General Commandant of the Marine Corps ordered the organization of a Marine Aviation Company of 10 commissioned officers and 40 enlisted men to establish the Marine Aviation Section of the Navy Flying School at Pensacola, and it was to that command that Geiger was initially posted on his return to the United States from the Orient.

Despite its high-sounding title, Pensacola's Naval Aeronautic Station in the spring of 1916 was not exactly an imposing installation for it was still very much in its infancy, and its training facilities were rather rudimentary. The latter consisted in the main of a number of buildings at the Naval Station proper, converted for use as classrooms and machine shops, while directly across Pensacola Bay to the south along the inner, sandy shores of Santa Rosa Island, there had been erected half a dozen large canvas tents which served as hangars for the training seaplanes. The actual "flying machines" were a dozen-odd basic trainers–biplanes with primitive ailerons or flexible warping wings, mounted on crude pontoons, and powered by single-engine "pushers." A "shotgun wedding," so to speak, between an enlarged kite and a motor cycle, these fragile (and quite temperamental) float planes were soon to be destroyed in the fall of 1916 by a tropical hurricane of considerable intensity, whereupon they were replaced by the slightly more stable $N-9$ Curtiss seaplane trainers. The station was not then provided with "land aeroplanes;" however, several free balloons were maintained for basic instruction in that specialized field of air transportation.

At the time of Geiger's arrival at Pensacola, three of the Marine Corps' total of four qualified naval aviators were attached to the Marine Aviation Section of the Navy Flying School. Heading the list was First Lieutenant (shortly to be promoted to the rank of Captain) Alfred A. Cunningham, who had soloed as far back as August 1912 at Marblehead, Massachusetts, thus becoming the first Marine Officer to win his golden wings. The second Marine aviator, First Lieutenant Bernard L. Smith, was then serving at the American Embassy at Paris as an Assistant Naval Attaché. Number 3, First Lieutenant William B. McIlvain, who had accompanied Smith on their aerial flights as part of the First Brigade Maneuvers at Culebra during the winter of 1913–14, was also present at Pensacola, together with Number 4, First Lieutenant Francis T. Evans. Not only was Evans destined to become Geiger's principal flight instructor, but also within a year's time he was to undertake and to complete successfully a unique experiment which assured him enduring fame in the annals of naval aviation. In February 1917, Captain Evans astounded the experts at Pensacola by looping a $N-9$ float plane *Jenny* not just once but twice, and after having deliberately forced his flimsy aeroplane into a spin, managed to pull it out of its spiral descent when only a few hundred feet above the surface of the Bay, a spectacular feat as well as a valid contribution to the science of aviation which in time was to be marked by a belated award of the Distinguished Flying Cross. In addition to Geiger, these three qualified pilots and some twenty enlisted men who served as mechanics and riggers comprised the Marine Aviation Section in the summer of 1916; the following year their number was increased by two with the assignment to flight training of First Lieutenant David L. Brewster and Warrant Officer Walter E. McCaughtry.

Although the Major General Commandant of the Marine Corps had extended formal recognition of the embryonic naval air arm by his creation of the Marine Aviation Company and his authorization of its use with Advanced Base Forces or expeditionary troops, in 1916, thus establishing the fundamental concept that Marine aircraft were tactical weapons developed for use with landing forces, the pilots not infrequently were regarded with noticeable reservation in certain circles. This tendency on the part of some of their contemporaries, afloat and ashore, was understandable, for comparatively few line officers of either the Navy or the Marine Corps at that time were wholeheartedly convinced that flying machines were here to stay. To their minds aviation was looked upon more as a novelty, if not an expensive and quite unreliable toy, of questionable value and practicability, and as for those who would volunteer to fly seaplanes, they were considered mere truants who were not bearing their fair share of the load. Considering that in the early days of naval aviation the latter were very few in number, of necessity they were placed on the defensive, for their selected specialty undeniably was very much of a sporting proposition, a mixture of "controlled insanity" on the one hand, counterbalanced by acquired technical skills on the other. In this respect their lot did not differ materially from the aviation pioneers of a later generation—the rocketeers and the guided missilemen, the astronauts and the explorers of outer space—who similarly elected to assume calculated risks in the game of nerve and scientific experiment against the unknown.

Far from being a handful of hare-brained faddists or air buffs, the overwhelming majority of the birdmen of the decade immediately preceding the First World War were conscientious individuals who had chosen to fly because it represented a challenge: a desire to join a combat arm with a future rather than one with only a past. Once aerial combat came into its own in the skies over the Western Front, a subsidiary motive entered the picture: a partial revival of the spirit of chivalry in warfare wherein a man could actually see and match wits with his adversary as an individual, as contrasted to the elimination of an opponent by long-range shelling or the use of poison gas. Overriding these considerations, of course, was the plain and simple fact that the pilot of an aeroplane or a free balloon was largely a man on his own, free to fly like a bird, limited only by his technical proficiency and the capability of his aircraft, and at least until the perfection of air-to-ground communication, unhampered by rigid control from higher authority. As a consequence and if nothing else it was a fine training ground for the development of self-confidence: if a land vehicle suffered a breakdown, the driver could dismount and walk; if a ship foundered, a man might launch a raft or could attempt to swim to safety; but if an aeroplane got out of control the pilot had two choices—he could ride it down or bail out if he wanted to take a chance with what then passed for a parachute.

In Geiger's case the motive for his entering naval aviation has not been unequivocally established. When questioned on the matter, he apparently saw no need to go into greater detail than his stock rejoinder, "Oh, I just wanted to fly, that's all." Doubtless the element of risk had great appeal to him for he was temperamentally impetuous and always inquisitive of new techniques and developments. Extraordinarily prescient throughout his life, it is quite within the bounds of reason to assume that if he were quick to sense an advantageous opportunity to expand the scope of his professional interests, he was equally alert to foresee the future, limitless potentialities of the then undeveloped air arm, especially as applied to its use in conjunction with conventional ground and sea forces.

In March 1916, however, the degree and manner of his deliberation were of secondary importance, for Geiger was introduced to aerial flight the very day he reported for duty, and he was far too occupied learning the intricacies of his new trade to ponder unduly over the reasons why. In that era basic flight training was a lengthy affair, measured in terms of months. Not only did classroom instruction cover elementary aerodynamics and the theory of flight, but much time was devoted to the operation and maintenance of power plants as well as to the actual construction and rigging of aircraft. In the practical field, practice flying commenced the same day a new class was convened: after

71

15 hours of instructional flying, a candidate was expected to make his first flight unassisted; on completion of 25 hours airborne, he was required to "solo," and if successful was thereafter qualified "to fly alone." In addition to instruction in heavier-than-air seaplanes and flying boats, commensurate stress was extended to the manipulation of free balloons, a field in which students were likewise required to become proficient. In the beginning it had been contemplated that the Navy would fly seaplanes exclusively, leaving landplanes under the jurisdiction of the Army. It soon became evident that such a tacit delineation would not necessarily be feasible as applied to the Navy's contemplated establishment of Advanced Fleet Bases, and in time it was agreed that some interchange between the two services would have to be effected. By 1917, this had been accomplished by an arrangement permitting Army officers to train in "water flying" at Pensacola in exchange for allowing Navy pilots to use the landplanes at the Army's Signal Corps Aviation School at San Diego, California.

Perhaps the best day-to-day record of Geiger's progress as a pilot under instruction at Pensacola are the brief notations contained in his Aviators Flight Log Books for the pertinent period. With a few exceptions the entries pertaining to his seaplane flights are rather routine. They reveal that from 31 March until 8 June 1916, Roy performed 34 flights in Curtiss "pushers," totaling 16 hours, 30 minutes. On 15 May, after 15 hours of dual instruction, he made his first flight unassisted: Flight No. 31 of 20 minutes duration. Theoretically, he had now soloed successfully; however, with the enforced change-over from Curtiss "pushers" to the newer N-9 "tractors" occasioned by the hurricane in the autumn of that year, all of the students then in training had to requalify in the latter model. Accordingly, Geiger's Log Books show that from 8 September 1916 to 23 March 1917, he made 17 additional flights amounting to 9 hours, 30 minutes air-borne. On 23 March, then having amassed a total of 25 hours in practice flights, he soloed satisfactorily for the second time: Flight No. 51, 30 minutes aloft. He was thereupon notified officially that he had been "qualified to fly alone."

It is readily evident from the aforementioned records that it required almost a year's time for Geiger to meet the minimum demands of a qualified pilot. In this respect, the time span in his case was neither appreciably greater nor less than his contemporaries. He was regarded as an excellent student, although as his instructor, Captain Evans, was frank to admit, Geiger had a tendency towards stubbornness: he learned to fly "the hard way." By the same token Geiger frequently complained that his tutor made him nervous: in one instance he felt so harrassed he actually asked Evans to get out of the aircraft and to let him fly it alone. Notwithstanding their differences of opinion the two officers got along very well together, and remained fast friends throughout their careers. In fact, although Geiger did not plan it that way, he got a chance to even the score with his mentor by an unforseen dunking in Pensacola Bay. The first time Geiger took over the controls of his *N-9* trainer, he attempted a practice landing in the harbor. Aware that this type of seaplane had a reputation for "porpoising," Geiger took unusual pains to make a perfect descent and landing. To his consternation, just as he was about to set the pontoon on the water, he noticed directly beneath him a small submarine in the act of surfacing. To avoid an air-to-water collision with the rising submersible, he effected a radical change of course which threw the plane far over to one side, and terminated the maneuver by nose-diving into the water. Although the flying machine was completely wrecked, both of the occupants received only minor cuts and bruises to the extent that neither thought it necessary to report to Sick Bay for treatment.

Undeterred by this incident, Evans proceeded shortly thereafter to make his renowned flight in which he double-looped a seaplane; meanwhile, Geiger, equally undisturbed, continued with his training as if nothing irregular had transpired. During the period 28 March–9 June 1917, he performed, flying alone, 54 flights of 43 hours, 30 minutes duration. On 4 and again on 9 June he was given his final tests, which he easily passed. With a total of some 69 hours of flying time (of which at least 50 saw him at the controls, unassisted and alone) to his credit, he had finally earned his wings in the heavier-than-air category.

As for the lighter-than-air phase of the training program, instruction in free ballooning progressed concurrently with the seaplane flights. Unlike many of the student pilots who profoundly despised, and in some instances, feared, this aspect of their aeronautical indoctrination, Geiger enjoyed it thoroughly. He was fascinated by it, and from the very beginning he believed in "ballooning for fun." Long after balloons had lost much of their practical value, for they were soon outmoded by the development of high-performance aircraft, he remained an avid balloonist, and as will be subsequently related, he continued to make lighter-than-air "flights" well into the 1920's at Quantico.

It was indeed fortunate that he took to ballooning from the start. The swaying basket of a free balloon was no place for a pessimist or a chronic worrier: its peculiar lateral motion not to mention a sudden climb or a precipitous drop was quite sufficient to make even the hardiest deathly airsick. From a navigational point of view, the manner of its control was simplicity in the extreme. In theory, if one wished to descend, one valved or discharged hydrogen from the massive bag; to climb, one threw overside ballast usually in the form of small sand bags. In practice, however, it required endless hours of experimentation and very skillful manipulation to obtain the precise degree of change desired, quite aside from the fact that the balloon's passengers for the most part were at the mercy of the winds and the air currents, subject to extreme fluctuation occasioned by changes in atmospheric temperatures. As for the landings, no two were ever exactly alike, and until almost the very last moment it was relatively impossible to predict with any real degree of accuracy not only where or when they would be made but also how they would be accomplished.

An inspection of Geiger's Balloon Log Books while at Pensacola discloses that during the interval 17 November 1916—29 June 1917, he made 14 free balloon ascents (and landings) in *BF-1*, totaling 28 hours, 45 minutes. His initial flights locally were conducted under the guidance of Lieutenant Commander Frank R. McCrary, USN; most of his later, so-called long-distance flights were made accompanied by Ensign Ralph G. Pennoyer, USN, who had joined the station also as a student pilot in December 1916. Despite the passage of some forty-five years, the details of several of his flights with Geiger are still quite fresh in Captain Pennoyer's mind, today, so irregular were certain of the events.

The most spectacular "rides" took place in the early spring of 1917. With the sea breeze blowing in strongly from the Gulf of Mexico, it was expected that the wind would carry the gas-filled bag due north and to a distance of some fifty miles inland from the shores of Pensacola Bay. This was uniformly achieved without difficulty, but the subsequent descent and actual landing somewhere in the vicinity of either Brewton or Tyson, Alabama, always posed a problem. Geiger invariably preferred to stay aloft until the very last minute—until such time as the balloon was positively limp from loss of hydrogen—hence he was not particularly concerned with the location or condition of the landing site provided he had traversed a greater distance and had remained air-borne longer than his associates. Nor was he at any time bothered by the state of the weather, the degree of visibility, or the time of day or night. When it was time to go down, down he went regardless of the overcast, trusting to luck.

Frequently the dangling drag ropes managed to entangle themselves in the branches of trees or in fence posts, summarily ending that particular flight, then and there. Just as regularly, the descending carrier or basket toppled over sheds, tore up barn roofs, or cut a swath through a farmer's stockyard, stampeding the cattle and horses, knocking down fences, and uprooting vegetable gardens and flower beds with utter abandon. In at least one instance, Roy was forced to let down, after dark, in a cemetery. The spectacle of the balloon's two occupants attempting to extricate themselves from the maze of ropes and the cloud of canvas that threatened to engulf them, tripping over the tombstones in the darkness, shouting back and forth to one another, was a sight the local citizenry was not prone to forget for months to come. The latter had assembled to conduct an impromptu, candlelight revival and prayer meeting in the vicinity of the graveyard, and the unscheduled arrival in their midst of two young men "from out of the clouds" was not unnaturally interpreted by certain of the more enraptured hymn singers as a Visitation from On High.

Fortunately, such irregular landings as these and others in the backwoods' regions of Alabama were made without injury. Perhaps Geiger's closest shave was a near altercation with an enraged farmer. Having selected a likely cornfield for a landing site, Roy commenced to unload his ballast to decrease his "landing speed" and to ease the shock on contact. Unknowingly, he dropped a sand bag right through the roof of an outhouse. Scared half out of his wits, the startled occupant hurriedly emerged from the privy to see hovering over his head a free balloon. Shaking his fists at Geiger, the farmer proceeded to pick up his shotgun, and discharged one or more rounds aimed at the basket. Realizing that

75

discretion was the better part of valor, Roy tossed overboard his last remaining sand bag, thereby permitting the balloon to rise just sufficiently to clear the barn yard (and to get out of buckshot range), and to coast along over the countryside a mile or two further where it landed in an undefended pasture.

As far as Geiger was concerned, landing was half the fun of free ballooning. Other than a few practice jumps, from balloons and under supervision, included in the training agenda at Pensacola, there is no record that Geiger throughout his subsequent career as an aviator resorted to a parachute landing. He was a staunch exponent of that school which championed the concept that a pilot never deserted his plane in flight. As a balloonist was expected to stick by his craft until it returned to earth, so, too, was the pilot of an aeroplane required to "ride his ship down," remaining at the controls (or what was left of them) until the undercarriage or underside of the fuselage finally touched land or water. This was not a matter of sentiment or stubbornness. In the Merchant Marine or the Navy it has always been traditional that the officer in command will stick by his ship to the very last moment. Similarly, naval aviation saw no good reason to change a time-tested custom. It reasoned that a pilot was equally responsible for his airship, and that by remaining in the cockpit he alone retains a chance—no matter how slim—of regaining control of a damaged or burning aeroplane. Aside from the moral obligation to refrain from deserting his fighter or bomber, was the element of safety: parachutes do not always open; sometimes their shrouds become caught in the tail section of the abandoned aeroplane; and of the choice of two desperate alternatives, frequently the best chance of survival is to hang on tightly and hope for the best rather than "hitting the silk."

In the same fashion, early in his aviation career, Geiger developed a few strong convictions on the subject of weather conditions. To his mind, they were largely incidental. If a flight were scheduled or a mission involving aircraft assigned, unfavorable weather was cause neither for delay nor for cancellation: if you were caught in a storm, you tried to climb over, under or around it—if you had time. If you did not, you went through it regardless of its intensity. As for local weather conditions at the anticipated landing site, the mere fact that they might be most unpleasant did not call for any change of plan. He relied unreservedly on his instruments and his skill as a navigator: when it was time to descend, a descent was made through pea-soup fog, a blinding rainstorm, or heavy cloud cover. In his opinion, every cloud "had a hole in it," and any pilot worth his wings had to find that hole. In the early days when instruments were far from reliable and navigation confined in the main to "contact" tempered by dead-reckoning, it was sheer determination that enabled him to fly and to land on schedule. Later, when proper navigational aids became commonplace, he trained himself to become a skilled instrument pilot, a field in which he pioneered and persevered without interruption in his quest for perfection. Obviously, Geiger's pronounced opinions on these and other matters pertaining to the piloting of aircraft quickly earned him a reputation. Fearless in his approach he spurned the more cautious and the timid: were any member of his command afraid to follow their leader in aerial flight, it was wisest to apply for a transfer rather than await the inevitable forced change of station which their commander would demand.

Having fulfilled all of the requirements at the Navy Flying School—in the classroom, in the cockpit, and in the balloon basket—Geiger at long last was awarded his ticket. On 9 June 1917, he was formally designated a "Naval Aviator," at that time the forty-ninth naval pilot to win his wings, the fifth officer of the Marine Corps to be so honored. Some five months later, in November, the Aero Club of America with headquarters at New York City, similarly presented him with a Balloon Certificate, No. 174. During the remainder of the month of June, although he performed no ascents, his Aviators Log Book records that he completed five additional seaplane flights of some three and one-half hours' duration. Therefore, from start to finish at Pensacola, in the heavier-than-air department, Roy had engaged in a total of 107 flights, and had amassed an aggregate of 73 hours of flying time.

Meanwhile, recognition and advacement had been forthcoming in other fields. In September 1916, he had been promoted to the rank of Captain (with effective date of rank, 29 August). Convinced that his future looked bright and reinforced by a substantial increase in pay, Geiger saw no good reason why he should not at least investigate the possibilities of matrimony. Notwithstanding the large numbers of hours which pilot-officer candidates had to devote daily to classroom study and to practice flights, life at Pensacola by no means was a matter of all work and no play, and there were ample opportunities for the young fledglings to engage in recreational sports and to take part in many of the local social activities. Although the total fatalities resulting from instructional and solo flights were fortunately low in number, the incidence of accidents and minor injuries sustained was correspondingly rather high. As a result the training program was occasionally brought to a standstill by acute personnel and materiel shortages: while unlucky instructors and instructees retired temporarily to the hospital to lick their wounds, mechanics and riggers worked around the clock to recreate operational seaplanes out of twisted masses of splintered woodwork and shredded fabric. Pending completion of repairs—corporal and material—for the remainder of the student body it was "class dismissed until further notice," whereupon those who felt so inclined took off for the beaches or got out their fishing tackle.

Government quarters for single officers at the Flying School being notably meager, Roy elected to live off the naval reservation in a downtown boarding house at Pensacola operated by a Mrs. Thornton. Among other aspirant fliers residing there were two of his close friends, Lieutenants Harry Cecil and Paul Peyton of the Navy. Taking into account the fact that all three of these young gentlemen in time were to achieve positions of considerable responsibility in their respective branches of the naval service, such a prediction during their early careers as budding pilots could not have been taken too seriously, if their youthful antics and high-spirited escapades at Pensacola were to be regarded as the sole criteria of their future progress.

Styling themselves "The Three Whiskyteers" these gay young bachelors soon established quite a daring reputation, and their combined presence at any gathering was more than enough to guarantee its success. One of their better known trade marks was the manner employed to secure advance table reservations at one of the city's more popular restaurants. This consisted of swooping in low at telephone pole height over the establishment, and dropping from the cockpit of the aeroplane a penciled note wrapped around a bit of board or a flat stone bearing such terse instructions as: "Steak for 3 at 7." On one occasion a midnight snack at a downtown cafe turned out to be a costly affair. One of the members of the trio suddenly decided that a stained glass window had no business being in such a place. In his opinion it was sacrilegious albeit the design in question was nothing more than a cluster of purple grapes. So upset did he become, he picked up his chair and threw it at the window. His two companions, seeking to oblige, promptly heaved their seats at the target, completely demolishing it, frame and all. Presented with a bill for $75.00—and this time, by chance, it was Geiger's turn to pay for the communal wreckage—the reparations made quite a dent in his wallet. However, in due course he was able to recoup his loss at the card table. Rabid poker enthusiasts, the inseparable trio were incessantly involved in a series of seemingly endless games which came close to setting a new endurance record. A consistent winner at cards, Geiger finally brought one lengthy session to a close by agreeing to accept exclusive title to a battered Chevrolet *Grand* in lieu of a cash payment, which otherwise would have forced the losers into total bankruptcy.

It was still an era when horseback riding and carriage driving were very much in vogue in spite of the common acceptance of motor vehicles, and it was customary on week-ends for mixed couples of riders on private or rented mounts to trot around the countryside. At selected sites they were joined by chaperones in their surreys, loaded down with bulging picnic baskets containing the sandwiches and bottles of cold beer. And it was at one of these informal outings that Roy was introduced to his future bride by Lieutenant Cecil.

His new acquaintance, Miss Eunice Renshaw Thompson, was a young lady of markedly diverse interests and talents. As a child she had been taught to ride horseback, to care for horses, and to train them for competitive performance in the show ring. Keenly observant and with a profound affection for animals of all sorts, a desire to express their movements and their conformation through the medium of art was consequently engendered in her formative years. The fusion of this basic interest with an education which laid strong accent on the classics, literature, and the fine arts not unnaturally impelled her in time to undertake professional courses of instruction in the latter fields. Not only did she become proficient with brush and canvas, but also with pen and paper, and with the passage of time she became a painter, an author, and a poetess of no little distinction.

The only child of the late Louis Edward Thompson and Florence Renshaw (Thompson), in the summer of 1916 Eunice was living with her widowed mother in a spacious country residence some eight miles north of the town of Pensacola. Fronting Cove de Loro on Escambia Bay the main house stood on a high bank overlooking the right of way and the celebrated trestle of the Louisville and Nashville Railroad extending eastward to far distant Jacksonville. Her father, a Canadian born at Montreal, had come to Pensacola as a civil engineer, and had engaged in the construction of the Pensacola Branch of the aforementioned railway in the 1890's. On completion of the line, Mr. Thompson, his wife, and their three-year-old daughter, Eunice, returned to Canada. Leaving his family at Montreal, Thompson joined the Alaskan Gold Rush of 1898, but he did not prosper financially, and his health gave way under the rigors of the pack trail and the rugged existence of mining camp life. In search of a more equitable climate, the Thompson family thereafter moved to New Orleans, Louisiana. Following Mr. Thompson's death there, in 1906 Eunice and her mother returned to Pensacola after a ten year's absence where they purchased the home of a former timber merchant and saw mill owner.

To complement the Scots-Canadian ancestry of the Thompsons was the combination of the Spanish, French, and English lineage of the Renshaws. Born at Pensacola, Eunice' mother was the daughter of a Lieutenant of the United States Navy, stationed at the old Navy Yard there; later, a Commodore of the Confederate naval forces. A descendent through intermarriage on the part of her ancestors of one of the oldest and most respected families of the region, Mrs. Thompson could trace her family tree in Florida as far back as Dr. Eugenio Antonio del Sierra, the Surgeon-General of the Spanish Fleet (wherein he held the rank of Captain), which had accompanied General de Gálvez in the Campaign of 1781 at the time of Pensacola's capture from its British defenders.

A participant in many of the social functions and riding parties at Pensacola, it was only a question of time until Eunice Thompson made the acquaintance of young Army officers serving at Fort Barrancas and their naval counterparts undergoing training at the nearby Navy Flying School. Now in possession of an automobile, and with the necessary ground work accomplished thanks to Lieutenant Cecil's timely introduction of Captain Geiger to Miss Thompson, Roy soon discovered that he was devoting more and more of his off duty hours on the dirt highway leading out to the house on Escambia Bay. In fact, so accustomed did the neighbors become to the rattling across the old wooden bridge of Roy's Chevrolet on Saturday nights, when he was returning his date to her residence, they could set their clocks by the sound with the same regularity normally associated with the midnight whistle of the northbound freight, blowing to alert the keeper of the swing span on the railroad causeway. In time the old Chevrolet could no longer stand the bumps or the ruts nor the strain of keeping such late hours, for it gave up the ghost and had to be replaced. Fortified by his steady winnings at poker not to mention his flight pay, Roy thought he could afford a more respectable vehicle. Seeking to impress his date with the degree of financial affluence so recently attained, he decided to invest in a Buick Roadster. Rather than have the dealer deliver the automobile, Roy bought it, cash on the line, right in the showroom, and insisted on driving his shiny new purchase directly off the floor into the street once the papers had been signed.

Never known to vacillate, what commenced as casual dating soon progressed to a determined romance, so intent was Roy to win the lady's hand in marriage. Mrs. Thompson, meanwhile, wisely decided to apply the brakes, for the prospect of her daughter's matrimony with a daring and rather headstrong young aviator was not entirely to her liking. She was well aware of some of Roy's more spectacular feats and his rather wild capers as a gay young blade, for she had asked certain of her relatives to investigate his reputation at the air station. Despite his charm and his winning ways, she regarded some of his outbursts of zeal with reservation. Additionally, she was concerned with the future of her only child and daughter and of her potential son-in-law were the couple to wed. Eunice was eight years Roy's junior, and as the bride of a Marine officer she could look forward to an unsettled life of continual transfers and changes of station, quite aside from the far from remote possibility that as the wife of a naval aviator her husband's career—and his life—could figuratively be snuffed out like a candle in the event of an unforseen accident. Consequently, she advised caution, and warned her daughter against making an important decision she might have cause later to regret.

By late spring of 1917, however, having won his wings and with an almost unlimited future before him, so buoyant was his optimism, Roy was determined to get married. To him the war clouds on the horizon were considerably less frightening than the danger of losing his bride-to-be, for she had other suitors and mounting competition was indicated. In characteristic fashion, so confident was he that Eunice would accept his offer of marriage, he thought it unnecessary to propose formally to the young lady. Instead, he casually asked Mrs. Thompson one evening "if he could take Eunice out." Mrs. Thompson was thus taken somewhat by surprise, for she had never objected to the couple's dating, and she thought Geiger merely was asking permission to escort her daughter to a dance. Belatedly realizing what he was trying to convey, she immediately replied that if Roy wanted an answer to that question he should ask Eunice directly. She also stated that as far as she was concerned, she would not oppose the marriage if her daughter accepted his proposal. Accordingly, Roy asked Eunice to become his bride. After discussing the matter between themselves at considerable length, the couple came to the conclusion that the most sensible, if not the most satisfactory, solution to their personal problem was an indefinite postponement of their marriage plans. Neither of the two wished to terminate the romance, but it was tacitly agreed that no final decision would be forthcoming on Eunice' part until such time as Roy's future assignment and location of duty station could be more positively determined.

As events transpired, the conclusion to hold their plans in abeyance turned out to be less unpropitious than had at first been anticipated. With the declaration of war against Germany on 6 April 1917, the tempo of naval aviation training was appreciably accelerated, and from that moment onwards no pilot's time was exclusively his own. Within a few weeks the Marine Aviation Section at Pensacola was split into two sections to provide the necessary fliers and ground personnel for the activation of a Marine Aeronautic Company, designed to serve as a component of the Advanced Base Force already in training at Philadelphia Navy Yard. By this time Captain Cunningham had been detached and assigned to duty in connection with the selection of sites for naval air stations, which were to be constructed along the Atlantic seaboard. With the immediate transfer of McIlvain and Evans to Philadelphia, it was clearly understood that Geiger, Brewster, and McCaughtry would ultimately follow their former instructors north to fly seaplanes from coastal bases, just as fast as they could be designated qualified pilots on completion of their training in Florida.

On 2 July, less than a month after his certification as a pilot, Geiger received his orders to report to Philadelphia. From Pensacola he proceeded by rail to Jacksonville, where it would seem the combination of the festive spirit of Independence Day and his forced separation from his fiancee impelled him to make a long-distance telephone call. The upshot of the conversation was the resolve on the part of the two principals to get married before Roy continued one mile farther north. Instructed to pack up and to join him without further delay, Eunice and Mrs. Thompson took the very next train out of town bound for Florida's East Coast. A little frantic telegraphing on Roy's part and an understanding Adjutant at Headquarters resulted in his being granted ten days' delay in reporting to his new station, to be charged as leave. Other problems had arisen in the meantime, which for the moment defied prompt solution: Eunice was a Roman Catholic whereas Roy had no professed faith. Fundamentally deeply religious, he was candid to admit that he never knew to which Church he belonged, considering himself in his own terms, "a religious vagabond."

Introduced to clerical authorities at Jacksonville, he was able to dispel any determined effort on their part to dissuade him from his marital intentions. As for Eunice, she found herself the innocent victim of geographic abnormality: Pensacola's Catholics fell within the jurisdiction of an Alabama Diocese, and it required the permission of the Bishop at Mobile to wed "outside the Church." Somehow, an arrangement agreeable to all parties was arrived at, and on 12 July 1917, in the Rectory of Jacksonville's Church of The Immaculate Conception, Roy and Eunice were pronounced husband and wife. Of necessity the honeymoon was brief for the Captain's leave was fast running out. The very day the couple was married, they boarded a Pullman for Washington. At Headquarters, Roy delayed only long enough to adjust his accounts with the Paymaster, for by this time he was down to his last $5.00. Continuing northward by rail the bride and groom at length arrived at Philadelphia. Reporting for duty to the Officer of the Day at League Island Navy Yard on the morning of 17 July, Roy fully expected that he would be allowed to remain at the station at least until his foot locker and his professional books had time to catch up with their owner.

Somewhat to his surprise he found awaiting him supplementary orders assigning him without delay to temporary additional duty aboard the battleship, *USS North Carolina,* then at anchor in Chesapeake Bay. Retracing his steps to Norfolk Navy Yard, a steam launch from the *USS Pennsylvania,* Flagship of the Atlantic Fleet, finally brought him alongside the gangway of *North Carolina,* busily loading ammunition at Yorktown, Virginia, prior to putting out to sea. A brief conference with her Commanding Officer, Captain (later, Admiral) Mark L. Bristol, disclosed that Geiger had been especially selected for an exacting mission: that of serving as an aerial observer for the vessel while engaged in trans-Atlantic convoy operations. Fitted with a makeshift landing platform and a plane launching catapult activated by compressed air, it was possible for the ship to land or to launch reconnaissance aircraft in port or at sea. Additionally, the battleship was provided with an $R-6$ Curtiss seaplane (a twin-float tractor designed to carry a torpedo), which could be recovered and hoisted aboard by the use of ship's cranes. To round out the picture, *North Carolina* had been supplied with a kite or captive balloon with a special winch mounted on her after deck.

If flight operations while underway were difficult, the prospect of sending a captive balloon aloft with an observer to an altitude of some 1,000 feet above the parent vessel (and maintaining that elevation) could be considered wholly hazardous. In any sort of a seaway and with a brisk wind blowing across her decks, *North Carolina* could naturally be expected to pitch and toss. Aside from the discomfort of the ship's motion transmitted to the occupant of the balloon basket, was the acute danger of the fouling of the towing cable, or its entanglement in one of the ship's funnels or prominent cage masts, particularly at times of ascent or recovery. Were the thin wire to snap under tension, the observer and his hydrogen-filled bag would be left to the mercy of wind and wave: his only resource in case of such event was to valve the gas from the balloon and to make an unscheduled descent into the sea, with a slim chance of being picked up by an attendant destroyer or one of the convoy escorts.

Undaunted by the perilous nature of his duties (for he had never before flown in a captive balloon), Geiger at once applied himself to learning all the tricks of his new trade. During the period 21 July–12 October 1917, Roy served continuously aboard *North Carolina* as an aerial lookout, scanning the seas for telltale signs of German submarines, while engaged in convoy duty. Although no periscopes nor onrushing enemy torpedoes were sighted, he had no difficulty attaining the required number of monthly "flying hours" entitling him to his extra pay. On the New York to Havre convoy run, the passage out and back normally consumed ten days each way, the remaining ten days of the month being spent in port for refueling and provisioning.

Whereas the records do not indicate that Geiger took part in any seaplane flights while *North Carolina* steamed back and forth across the Atlantic, he is shown as having performed 24 flights of 7 hours' duration at various times during the month of September, while his ship was at anchor in New York's Hudson River. With regard to his ballon ascents, all 11 totaling 9 hours air-borne were made at sea under conditions of combat readiness in late September and early October. Fortunately, no accidents nor emergencies marred his record.

In one respect, nevertheless, his service aboard *North Carolina* was marked by the occurrence of an unfortunate incident despite the fact that it was not his fault. One of three officers assigned additional duties as Communications Watch Officers, a safe containing highly classified cipher materials was inadvertently left open. Some of its contents were lost or were removed by parties unknown. A Board of Investigation was hastily convened, and although Geiger was absolved of blame for the security violation, an entire cryptographic channel had to be scrapped overnight lest it become compromised, and its subsequent replacement throughout the naval service involved considerable trouble and expense. This affair was very disturbing to Geiger, for although he was in the clear, the burden of proof of his innocence in such a serious matter rested on him, and he worried over the possible damaging effect to his future career occasioned by the incident for months to come.

In other respects his interlude of temporary duty aboard *North Carolina* was highly profitable, and was made doubly enjoyable by his opportunities to be with his wife while the vessel was in port. By this time he had been able to find suitable hotel accommodations at New York, and throughout the summer of 1917, whenever he was not otherwise concerned with his official duties aboard ship, he lived ashore with Eunice at the Hotel Hargrave, conveniently located near the Fleet Landing Piers at West 96th Street. With the advent of the fall season and the threat of winter gales in the offing which would preclude further balloon flights, his service with the *North Carolina* was terminated in mid-October, at which time he returned to Philadelphia to rejoin the Advanced Base Force.

During his absence the Marine Aeronautic Company had gradually been increased to a strength of 34 officers and 330 enlisted men. It was woefully deficient in flying machines,being limited to two *R−6* Curtiss seaplanes, two Curtiss pusher "land aeroplanes" with tricycle landing gear, one old Farman biplane used as a trainer, and two kite balloons. On 12 October, this organization was severed into two parts, thereafter designated the 1st Marine Aeronautic Company and the 1st Aviation Aquadron. The former, to which Evans and Brewster had been posted, was then transferred to Cape May, New Jersey, for seaplane training exclusively. In January 1918, having by that time attained a strength of 12 officers and 130 enlisted, it sailed from the United States for the Azores where it engaged in anti-submarine patrols. The latter unit, to which McIlvain and Geiger had been assigned, and which was composed of 24 officers and 240 enlisted, simultaneously was moved from Philadelphia to Hazelhurst (later, Roosevelt) Field, at Mineola, Long Island. It was the intention of the authorities to train its personnel in land-based aircraft, hence it was attached to a recently established Army Aviation School at the new site.

Once again Geiger was denied the opportunity to serve with a heavier-than-air aviation command. By October 1917, he was generally conceded to be the Marine Corps' (if not the Navy's) No. 1 "ballon expert," having had more hours of practical experience in lighter-than-air flight than any other naval aviator. The Navy being anxious to observe and to compare the progress of its sister service in this field, it was decided that Roy should serve as its representative at one or more of the Army's training sites. Initially, he was sent to St. Louis to attend a course in free ballooning sponsored by the Missouri Aeronautical Society. There, he took part in 7 cross-country flights of 15 hours' duration. Immediately following, he proceeded to the Army's Balloon School at Fort Omaha, Nebraska, where he made numerous ascents during the month of November in captive balloons. Now thoroughly cognizant of comparable developments in the armed services, he wound up his tour of temporary additional duty (which, after some six months was gradually assuming a permanent aspect) by reporting his findings to the Major General Commandant and to the forerunner of the Navy's future Bureau of Aeronautics.

Free at last of his special assignments, he was detached from Headquarters at Washington, and reassigned to aviation duty at Philadelphia. At the time of his joining, in December, the Navy Yard was practically devoid of aviators and aircraft: McIlvain's 1st Aviation Squadron at Mineola had almost swept the hangars clean, and the few antiquated seaplanes remaining were poorly adapted to making water landings on the now ice-filled Delaware River, for their thin pontoons would have been slashed to ribbons. The only resort was to request a small allotment of land-based aircraft for the training of a few recent graduates of Pensacola's Flying School awaiting assignment to operational commands.

In spite of the fact that Geiger had never before taken off nor landed in a "land aeroplane," to his mind this oversight was merely incidental: the day the first aircraft arrived, he climbed into its cockpit, taxied out on the strip, took-off, circled the Navy Yard and the flying field, and landed as if he had done it countless times before. Throughout the winter of 1917-18—and it was a bitterly cold one—he made regular, brief flights regardless of the weather along that part of the Atlantic seaboard extending from New York to Washington. On at least one occasion his wife occupied the rear cockpit. On her first flight, he decided to treat her to a bird's-eye view of downtown Philadelphia with emphasis on certain of the more historic buildings. So close did he circle the City Father's statue atop City Hall, the snow was blown from William Penn's hat; so low was his elevation over Independence Hall, the pedestrians thought he was trying to make a landing on the Mall. Back at the field, Mrs. Geiger was asked if she had seen the Liberty Bell, to which she replied that so frightened was she during her introductory venture into the third dimension, all she could observe during the flight was the back of her husband's head in the forward seat.

By February 1918, a sufficient number of aviation personnel had been assembled at Philadelphia to warrant their transfer to a larger training site, and Geiger was ordered to move his detachment south to the Naval Air Station at Coconut Grove, Florida. Among the officers who accompanied Roy to the new duty station were Lieutenants Douglas B. Roben and Arthur H. Page. A troop train consisting of a mixed lot of coaches and box cars was provided by the local Quartermaster. Notwithstanding the Spartan prospects of the pending four-day rail trip, Mrs. Geiger and Mrs. Page saw no valid reasons why their respective husbands should be exclusively entitled to the warmth of Florida's sun, and at the last moment announced their intention of boarding the train. On a technicality the means at hand actually constituted "first available government transportation" on a permanent change-of-duty-station, and the opportunity was too favorable to be dismissed. By all account, the rail movement was not one likely to be forgotten. One of the young officers of the detachment was the son of a prominent Philadelphia family of substantial means. At the depot he was presented a number of *Bon Voyage* baskets by his admiring relatives and friends. Their cubic content and the nature of their wares were such that the Lieutenant in question was better prepared for a trip around the world on a very slow boat rather than a mere railroad passage to Florida. As a consequence, this unforseen and ample stock of rare delicacies and exotic foods was at once commandeered to supplement the meager supply of rock-bottom Government rations, and for the duration of the ride officers and enlisted men alike enjoyed a menu, which if not a gastronomic treat, was assuredly a bold, new venture in eating.

On arrival at Coconut Grove, Roy's detachment was placed under the jurisdiction of the Commanding Officer of the Naval Air Station, Lieutenant Marc A. Mitscher, USN. This officer had taken his preliminary flight training with Geiger the preceding year at Pensacola. Mitscher insisted that all of the Marine pilots first qualify in seaplanes, to which Geiger readily acquiesced, but with the understanding that if and when land-based aircraft could be procured the aviators would receive commensurate instruction. Despairing of the arrival of the latter, Geiger began to comb the area in his search for land aeroplanes. On a sandy field near the edge of the Everglades, he discovered a flying school operated by Curtiss engineers flying *JN–4D's,* the celebrated *Jennies* of World War I fame. Forthwith,at every opportunity, Geiger would drive out to the Curtiss field with one or more of his student fliers, and in this fashion he managed to "check-out" his pilots in the operation of these land-based trainers.

Employing the "fly it or smash it" technique an ever increasing number of Marine officers won their wings at Coconut Grove. Among them was a Lieutenant Ford O. ("Tex") Rogers. Asked one day by Geiger if he had learned to fly, Rogers replied that his flight instructor had not given him the chance. Impressed by his eagerness, Roy ordered the young trainee to climb into the first aeroplane they encountered on the flying field, and the pair took off. While in flight Geiger successively switched off the ignition, and, jammed the throttle, to test the younger pilot's response to emergencies. Rogers in turn promptly took correspondingly corrective measures, and quite unperturbed, carried on as if nothing had transpired. Back at the field, Geiger left the aircraft, and instructed the Lieutenant to take off again, alone. Shortly thereafter, Rogers' regular flight instructor complained to Geiger that his trainee was not prepared to solo, having but two hours flight time. By way of reply, Geiger pointed to Rogers circling far overhead, with the poignant remark that regardless of his instructor's views, Rogers seemed "to be doing a pretty good job of it."

Ultimately, almost one year to the day after the entrance of the United States into the first world conflict, Marine Corps Aviation came into its own: during the first week of April 1918 the Naval Air Station, Coconut Grove, was redesignated the Marine Corps Flying Field, Miami. At the termination of three months intensive training in Curtiss *JN–4D's* at the Army's Gerstner Field at Lake Charles, Louisiana, Captain McIlvain's 1st Aviation Squadron was brought eastward to Miami, where it joined forces with Geiger's detachment. Commanded by Major Cunningham, the combined strength of the two units amounted to 90 officers and 825 enlisted men, and as will be subsequently related, this air component, soon to be officially termed the 1st Marine Aviation Force, was destined by early summer to embark for the war zones of the Western Front.

Chapter V

France and the Flying Coffins

By mid-May 1918 the 1st Marine Aviation Force at Miami was more than ever anxious to shake the sand out of its collective shoes and to get to France as rapidly as possible. By that date the 1st Marine Aeronautic Company was operationally employed in the Azores flying anti-submarine patrols; the Marine (Fourth) Brigade of the Second Division, American Expeditionary Force, was already in the trenches near Chaumont-en-Vixen, soon to be rushed to Château-Thierry in time to repel General Ludendorff's third offensive down the valley of the Marne toward Paris. Composed of four tactical squadrons, Captain Geiger as senior officer present commanded not only Squadron A, but also the entire group inasmuch as its nominal leader, Major Cunningham, found it necessary to make frequent trips to Headquarters at Washington. The latter's task was a difficult one, for despite the fact that his command had been trained to the best of its ability in such types of land-based aircraft as could be obtained locally and was prepared for immediate deployment to the fighting zones, two basic problems had not yet been resolved. The mission of the Force and the specific manner of its employment remained to be determined; moreover, it was still awaiting the arrival of combat-type aeroplanes.

In substance, naval aviation had been assigned the comprehensive task of wiping out the German U-boat menace to Allied shipping. It had been agreed upon that such a mission could best be accomplished by stationing seaplanes at friendly bases in the Calais-Dunkerque area, from which bombing runs could be made against German submarine pens to the northeast at Oostende, Zeebrugge, and Brugge. The United States Navy had a supply of seaplanes on hand for such duty; however, their bomb load was quite limited, and their speed so slow that without fighter escort they were little better than "sitting ducks," extremely vulnerable to hostile aerial counter-attack. Almost in desperation the Navy turned to the Army requesting the loan of land-based bombers (which were to be flown by naval personnel) and requisite numbers of fighters to be provided and manned by the Army Air Corps. To this suggestion the latter turned a deaf ear on the logical grounds that it needed every plane, pilot, rigger, and mechanic it could get its hands on to back up the Army's combat infantrymen, fighting for their lives far to the south along the main battle lines of the Western Front.

Thanks in large part to Major Cunningham's foresight and powers of persuasion such an impasse in time was successfully bridged. Appearing before the General Board, he fostered the notion that fast, around-the-clock scout-bombers might suffice to kill the two birds with one stone. He readily conceded that his Marine Aviation Force at Miami would need additional time to familiarize its personnel with the suggested type of combat aircraft—when and if they could be delivered in quantity—but there was no question in his mind but that his Marine pilots could do the job and do it well. Impressed with his eagerness and the feasibility of his project, the Navy at once voiced its approval, and the Northern Bombing Group thereafter became a tactical reality rather than a strategical concept.

Commanded by Captain David G. Hanrahan, USN, the Northern Bombing Group was made up of two elements: the Day Wing, Cunningham's four squadrons of the 1st Marine Aviation Force; and its counterpart, the identically organized Night Wing, manned by the Navy's pilots. The operational assignment and the organizational structure of the Bombing Group having been settled, there remained what appeared to be an almost unsurmountable barrier—the acquisition of sufficient numbers of suitable combat aircraft for the selected task. After some three years of experimentation, British aeroplane manufacturers by 1918 had gotten into production their celebrated DeHavilland *(DH)* two-place, light bombers. Considered reasonably efficient by the Royal Air Force, United States authorities decided to construct near duplicates of the basic English design, with the result that contracts were let out to a number of American firms.

Known as *DH-4's* and powered with American-built Liberty engines with double the horsepower of the British Siddley's, it was expected that the new flying machines would roll off the production and assembly lines in quantity within the space of a few months. Such was not to be the case for the rush nature of the construction order was far beyond both physical and technical capabilities of the manufacturing establishments. Not until May 1918 could even token deliveries be made, and the few machines that found their way to naval air stations left much to be desired so serious were their defects. Almost without exception every aeroplane required a major overhaul: wings were badly warped and control wires were too short. As for their power plants, so haphazard was their assembly and so inferior the caliber of their workmanship, even the essential parts had to be rebuilt. So marked were the structural and mechanical deficiencies of the new scout-bombers, the entire wartime aviation effort of the Navy as well as of the Army was notably impaired and needlessly handicapped from the very outset. By mid-summer of 1918 this sorry state of affairs had gradually assumed the aspect of a national scandal, and it took many months and a substantial outlay of Federal funds before the production bottleneck in the manufacture of aircraft could be cleared.

Considering that the *DH-4* eventually became the standard American combat plane not only for the First World War but for practically a decade after its termination, mention of some of its more important characteristics would seem indicated. A two-seater biplane, the *DH-4's* fuel capacity permitted it to remain airborne for some four hours. With a rated ceiling of 15,000 feet and a rate of climb calculated as 10,000 feet within 15 minutes, it could carry a load slightly in excess of one half a ton. At full power it could attain a speed of 120 miles-per-hour at 2,200 revolutions-per-minute. Sustained operational speed was set at 90 miles-per-hour; landing speed at 60. Its forward-firing armament consisted of fixed, twin 30-caliber Vickers Machine Guns, synchronized with the camshaft of the plane's engine to permit firing through the interstices or intervals of the rotating propeller blades; the rear cockpit was fitted with dual .30-caliber Lewis Machine Guns mounted on a scarff ring affording a 360-degree traverse. Racks for general purpose or fragmentation bombs of 25, 50, or even 100-pound size were attached to the underside of the lower wing, and could be released by either the pilot or the free gunner from their respective cockpits.

All too appropriately referred to as *Flaming Coffins,* this gruesome nickname was directly attributed to a peculiarity of the *DH–4's* design. With pilot and rear gunner seated in tandem, separated only by a large unarmored gasoline tank, not to mention the overhead gravity feed, a 30-gallon auxiliary fuel container, installed in the upper wing above the pilot's head, fire was a constant dread. The exhaust manifolds from the twin-six Liberty trailed aft from the engine mounting along both sides of the fuselage. Once these became red-hot, a mere teaspoon of what then sufficed for aviation gasoline spilled upon them would instantaneously ignite the mixture, in turn setting fire to the highly inflammable, doped fabric of the plane's main shell or outer covering. Even a nasty jolt on landing was sufficient to touch off a conflagration. One well aimed burst of hostile tracers or incendiary bullets into the main fuel tank could literally explode a plane in flight; a sudden dip or turn performed during an aerial dog fight could cause the gravity feed to slop over or spill some of its lethal contents with equally disastrous results. Were the pilot miraculously to survive the intial heat and shock blast occasioned by the explosion and fire, his chances of extricating himself from his cockpit were indeed slim. Bundled up to his ears in his flight clothing and further restricted by the harness of his seat-pack parachute, he had almost to become a contortionist either to get into or to get out of his compartment, for he was stationed under the central portion of the upper wing with but a minimum of clearance. In time this grave defect was corrected in the later model *DH-4B,* wherein the main fuel tank was positioned in front of the pilot rather than behind him, and the trailing edge of the upper overhanging wing was partially cut away to permit greater ease of access to the forward cockpit; however, such modifications were not made to any appreciable degree until long after the Armistice had been signed.

If the pilot of a *DH–4* suffered from claustrophobia, his rear gunner-observer conversely had equal cause to complain of overexposure. To man his free guns, he folded up his jumpseat, and stood erect with his feet on the floor boards of his cockpit. Lashed more or less securely to the ring mount by leather straps, he was at liberty to rotate his weapons in any direction he chose.

Generally speaking, his situation was analogous to a man standing upright in a full gale in a waist-high wash tub, trying to maintain his balance on the one hand, and on the other to drawing a bead on a fleeting target of opportunity. Once the actual dog fight got under way, and the plane began to swerve, climb, or dive with alarming rapidity, he was in acute danger of being tossed right out of his machine. Like the bucking bronc rider, were his lashings to snap under the strain, forthwith he could expect to be hurled into the "wide blue yonder." On one occasion, in aerial combat over Belgium in September 1918, Gunnery Sergeant Harry Wershiner "riding shotgun" in a *DH−4* piloted by First Lieutenant Everett Brewer, not only was pitched bodily overside, but incredibly managed to land on the plane's tail assembly, from which he clawed his way inch-by-inch back into his rear cockpit. Seriously wounded and in the face of overwhelming odds—for no less than fifteen German *Fokkers* had gotten into the act—the Lieutenant of Marines turned the tables by gunning down two of his opponents and simultaneously retrieving his far-flung gunner, a feat neither of the two American airmen had any great desire to attempt a second time. In essence, taking into consideration the number of built-in hazards associated with the *DH−4's,* the marvel was not so much that the planes would fly, but rather that men could be found who would volunteer to fly the machines in combat.

It was not until May 1918 that the Marine aviators at Miami received their initial consignment of *DH−4's,* and then only four arrived. With four squadrons each with a quota of eighteen aircraft, the prospect of ever attaining the full, theoretical wartime complement of seventy-two scout-bombers seemed remote. Furthermore, to compound their problems was increasing pressure brought to bear by the Navy to transfer the 1st Marine Aviation Force, lock-stock-and-barrel, ready-or-not, to France at earliest possible opportunity, regardless of the degree of its combat readiness or of existing deficiencies of operational aeroplanes. By early June it was evident that the Force was as combat ready as it were ever going to be, and on the 23rd of that month, Captains Geiger, McIlvain, and Roben, the commanders of Squadrons A, B, and C, respectively, and 75 enlisted men left Miami by rail for New York with the expectation of proceeding to Europe without further delay. This party, the advance echelon, boarded the *USS Siboney* at Hoboken, New Jersey, on 30 June, and sailed the same day for France. Twelve days later the group disembarked at Brest, and continued on to Paris, where in due course it reported to the Commanding Officer, United States Naval Aviation Force. Pending the arrival of the main body of the 1st-Marine Aviation Force in France, the advance party under Geiger's leadership was attached for training purposes and combat indoctrination for some three weeks to Group 5, Royal Air Force, then at Dunkerque. Early in August, after crossing the Atlantic aboard the *USS DeKalb* and the greater part of northern France jammed into boxcars, Cunningham's group arrived at the scene—a body of 97 officers and 657 enlisted men, the Headquarters Detachment and the flight personnel of Squadrons A, B, and C. They had no aircraft of their own; nevertheless, they proceeded to erect two or more airdromes in the general Calais-Dunkerque area. Squadrons A and B were spotted at Oye, Squadron C was based at La Frêne, and Headquarters was established at Bois-en-Ardres. With Major Cunningham in command of the Day Wing, Geiger resumed his normal duties as leader of Squadron A, and by October, with the arrival of the fourth and final element, Squadron D, 40 officers and 190 enlisted Marines under command of Captain Russell A. Presley, the transshipment and regroupment of the entire organization had been successfully effected.

As the Day Wing of the Northern Bombing Group the Squadron designations were officially changed from A, B, C, and D to 7, 8, 9, and 10. Supply bases were set up at Paulliac and at Eastleigh, England, and to Squadron 10 at La Frêne was assigned the task of repair and maintenance for the Day Wing. The command was later reinforced by the 88th Company, First Marine Regiment, a searchlight detachment of 2 officers and 100 enlisted, furnished by the Advanced Base Force from far distant Philadelphia. As finally constituted the Day Wing, including attached U. S. Navy Medical Personnel, was brought up to an aggregate strength of 165 commissioned officers and approximately 1,000 rank-and-file. The number of its aircraft was far less impressive: not until late September did the Day Wing receive its first *DH-4*, and by mid-October it had only taken delivery of seventeen of which not more than eight could be considered fully capable of flight. Rather than delay any longer, the first raid in force by the Northern Bombing Group was conducted on 14 October using those eight machines of Major

Roben's Squadron 9, at which time a ton of bombs was dropped on the railway junction at Thielt from a height of 15,000 feet.

Despairing of ever obtaining their assigned quota of aeroplanes, the young Marine pilots sought assignment to British flight commands. Members of Royal Air Force Squadrons 213, 217, and 218, they flew in any machine that would fly, the *Sopwith Camel Scout,* or "1 and ½ strutter," being one of their favorites. Operating with Group 5, Royal Air Force, the Day Wing of the Northern Bombing Group blew up enemy held canals and railroad lines, German supply dumps and airfields. By late fall, their initial objective, the German submarine pens in Belgium, held a relatively low priority, for the Kaiser's highly vaunted undersea fleet had long since shot its wad, and its morale had plummeted to a dead low in the face of ever mounting losses at sea incurred by contacts with American and British destroyers, not to mention the effectiveness of the North Sea Mine Barrage. Although air-to-air combat was not their primary mission, for the Marines flew no fighter aircraft, the Day Wing managed to shoot down at least half a dozen enemy aeroplanes in airborne operations; its own casualties numbering four Marine officers killed in combat or in crashes in France and Belgium. On the whole the Wing was most fortunate in that respect, for although at elevations above 5,000 feet anti-aircraft fire was not particularly effective, on low-level bombing runs or on reconnaissance flights every rifleman on the ground opened up with a vengeance, and for a solitary plane to make a head-on approach attack on a sand-bagged nest of heavy machine guns was almost suicidal. As for the Wing's bombing strikes, some 14 tons of high explosive were dumped on enemy installations during the autumn of 1918; moreover, on one occasion a flight of three aeroplanes from the Day Wing, flying at an extremely low altitude, dropped much needed rations to a French regiment, besieged and isolated in a forward salient, and completely cut off from friendly replenishment sources.

In spite of the fact that the majority of the bombing missions was carried out by Roben's Squadron, the pilots of the participating aircraft were drawn from the entire command. Undoubtedly, the plight of a Squadron Leader in France with no aeroplanes to fly in combat was a frustrating experience. This was noticeably applicable in Geiger's case, for second only to Cunningham he had worked harder than any other member of the

Day Wing to make his command fully operational. Much of his time perforce had to be devoted to administrative affairs and to supervising the re-assembly of the few machines that were delivered. Many hours had to be spent scouring the countryside, trying to beg, borrow, or steal aircraft from neighboring French or British air components in order to get his own pilots airborne. As a result, he was a difficult man to pin down at any precise moment, and notification of the birth of his first child, a daughter, born at Pensacola, Florida, on 18 July, did not reach him until some three months after the event, during which interval his wife's cable announcing the tidings chased him in vain throughout much of northern France. He had far better luck with official correspondence proclaiming his promotion to the rank of Major (on a temporary basis), for the papers caught up with him on one of his field trips, and his advancement became effective on 28 August.

Early in October he had succeeded in getting his hands on a *DH–9A* (Navy Number E-8472), which had just been flown across the English Channel from the Group's Supply Depot at Eastleigh. Geiger wanted to try out the recent acquisition himself before turning it over to one of his squadron pilots, and on the spur of the moment decided to make a lone plane strike on an enemy railway center at Loos, Belgium. The aircraft had arrived with its forward-firing Vickers installed but lacked its free guns. To make good this deficiency and to load up with bombs, the Armament Officer of the Northern Bombing Group, Lieutenant Commander Harold B. Grow, USN, suggested that Geiger fly the brand-new machine to a nearby Aviation Ordnance Supply Dump maintained by a Major Welsh of the Royal Air Force. Having had little opportunity to fly in combat, Grow asked Geiger if he could accompany him on the flight as co-pilot and tail-gunner, a request which was granted with enthusiasm.

On arrival at the British field, the Lewis machine guns were quickly mounted, and four 100-pound bombs were clipped to the racks beneath the plane's wings. With a number of English pilots looking on, Geiger was especially anxious to depart in grand style; in fact, so eminently spectacular was the nature of his take-off, the details of the undertaking are still crystal clear in the mind of Captain Grow, today, some forty-five years after the incident. Having taxied out on to the airstrip, the Major lined up his machine, advanced the throttle to full power, and took off with a deafening roar. The moment his wheels cleared the surface, he pulled back hard on the stick, and forced his aeroplane into a steep, climbing flipper turn, momentarily forgetting the all important fact that the *DH* was a good 500 pounds heavier with its additional armament and bomb load. At the top of the turn and at an elevation not exceeding 350 feet, his machine commenced to slip rapidly. Belatedly realizing what had transpired, Geiger managed to level off his scout-bomber just before it hit the ground at an air speed calculated of at least 200 miles-per-hour. At the moment of impact the *DH* bounced high off the sod, leaving behind the entire landing gear assembly, the two lower wing sections with their respective bombs, and both wooden blades of the propeller. Soaring through space for another 100 yards with two drooping top wings, and an engine—on fire—spinning a propeller hub at the rate of more than 2,000 revolutions-per-minute, the scout-bomber hit the turf a second time, right side up, and skidded to a stop on the underside of its fuselage. "The Marines Have Landed!" was now a certainty, no longer a slogan. A little shaken but otherwise unhurt, the Major and the Commander unfastened their seat belts, and sheepishly stepped over the cockpit cowlings onto the ground. Within seconds an ambulance crew and a crash truck pulled up alongside the blazing aircraft, somewhat disappointed that their services could now only be utilized to give the grounded airmen a free ride back to the hangar. Deposited in front of the Officers' Mess, the pair made their way directly to the bar, and in rather studied nonchalance (for no one thought it necessary to comment on the performance) downed a brace of double Scotch-and-Soda's, meanwhile Major Welsh obligingly made arrangements to loan thèm an automobile with a Royal Air Force driver to ensure their returning safe and sound to their own flying field.

In view of the fact that the now irreparable *DH* had arrived in France at 0930, and had been smashed to bits and set afire at 1430 the very same day, the Operations Officer of the Northern Bombing Group was not at all amused. As for the Commanding Officer, rather than waste time congratulating the two occupants of the wrecked plane for having been able to walk away from the debris unassisted, Captain Hanrahan summarily "grounded" both Geiger and Grow for ten days for "unauthorized flight." In the air or on the ground there were many operational matters which required the Major's constant attention from dawn until dusk, and as the Germans gradually retreated from western Belgium, the Wing correspondingly moved forward in echelon: by 1 November McIlvain's Squadron had pushed eastward as far as an abandoned enemy station at Knessalare. By that date, however, the war had but ten more days to run its course; in the meantime, the Wing had fallen afoul of another menace—an epidemic of influenza of alarming severity and scope which swept through the Group from top to bottom, invaliding scores of men and causing more than a dozen deaths.

Three of the four Marine Squadrons were hard hit by the "flu" and lost several of their number, Major Roben being among those who succumbed to this dreaded malady. Geiger's Squadron had relatively few admissions to the hospital. Realizing that the best defense against contracting this infectious disease was the maintenance of good health, he had wisely insisted on a strenuous physical conditioning program for all members of his unit, and and every morning at daybreak personally set the example by engaging in half an hour of calisthenics, followed by a run around the flying field, a cold shower, and a hearty breakfast. Despite all his precautions, in his case they seemed to be ineffective, and with a raging fever and so weak he could barely stand, an ambulance eventually carted him off to the Wing Sick Bay.

Overworked and understaffed, and at that date comparatively powerless to combat this little known virus, there was not much the doctors and hospital corpsmen could do to assist the afflicted: bed rest, aspirin in large doses, and whisky being the sole remedies which showed any evidence of making even the slightest impression. There were never enough cots to handle the number of applicants, and if the supply of pills were unlimited, the average patient, so long as he remained conscious, generally took the attitude that he was being cheated out of his rightful share of the liquor. No exception to the rule, Geiger promptly tossed his pills under his bunk, and somehow managed to persuade a Pharmacist's Mate to step up his spirit ration. So successful was he that notwithstanding a temperature of 105 degrees, he struggled back into his uniform, and crept unobserved out of the ward into the hospital courtyard.

There he spied an official vehicle, a large Cadillac sedan,

engine running, and driver patiently waiting at the wheel. Without further ado Geiger opened one of its rear doors and slid upon the seat, and after ordering the Marine chauffeur, a Corporal Shields, to turn on his driving lights (dusk had fallen and a black-out invariably in effect), instructed him to head at maximum speed for the front lines, then distant to the east about ten miles. Somewhat startled by the nature of his directive, not to mention the demeanor of his unexpected passenger, Shields nevertheless complied with alacrity, for he definitely was in no position to question the authority of a Marine Officer wearing gold oak leaves on his shoulder straps. The Major, of course, had it all planned: deprived of an opportunity to meet his adversary face-to-face—in the air, on land, or sea—he was going to get into the scrap by some means even if it entailed starting a personal feud with the Kaiser himself in the latter's backyard. After some fifteen minutes of hard driving, for the roads were badly rutted and pock-marked with shell holes, it became evident that figuratively speaking, the Allied Main Line of Resistance must now be located in the immediately adjacent vicinity. The battle ravaged landscape was periodically brilliantly illuminated by flares and gunfire flashes, and it was patently obvious from the continual din of small arms fire and the screeching of artillery missiles overhead that the scene of actual strife was very near at hand.

The roads had long since given way to narrow lanes, which in turn degenerated into a slough of mud, and by this time the automobile's rate of advance had progressively slowed down to a crawl. This was precisely the situation Geiger's pursuers had been anticipating. Directly behind the Cadillac—with its engine now stalled—a field ambulance and motorcycle with sidecar drew up, whereupon several individuals hurriedly dismounted, ran forward, and climbed on the running boards of the sedan. The rear compartment had been locked from within, but in order to see better Geiger had lowered both of its side windows. Aware that its occupant must have been half out of his mind with a high fever, the breathless Lieutenant of the Navy Medical Corps decided that the end justified the means: every moment counted now and shell splinters were beginning to rattle on the roof of the motionless Cadillac. Reaching inside the vehicle, he seized one of Geiger's arms into which he plunged a hypodermic syringe with sufficient force to penetrate the Major's coat and shirt sleeves before its tip reached his skin and flesh. As for Corporal Shields, he turned his head just in time to stare right down the business end of the barrel of a Colt .45-caliber automatic pistol, thrust into the driver's compartment by a burly Military Policeman, who, in addition to certain other remarks, told the frightened chauffeur to switch off the sedan's lights at once.

The sedative took effect almost instantaneously, for the Major had been given a jolt strong enough to topple over a horse. After some difficulty another member of the "posse", a Hospital Corpsman, succeeded in releasing the catch securing one of the sedan's rear doors. Leaving a couple of Military Policemen behind to help Shields extricate his bogged-down car, the doctor and his assistant somehow managed to half-steer, half-load, Geiger into the field ambulance; forthwith, the latter party cleared the area as rapidly as possible. Amazingly, none of the group was scratched (discounting the hole in the Major's epidermis made by the needle); however, both vehicles visibly bore the marks of the incident, the battered Cadillac having to be dead-lined for several days in the repair shop before it could again be considered reasonably presentable. Readmitted to Sick Quarters, the authorities took no chances of losing their prize patient a second time. They took all of Geiger's clothing away from him, and after he had regained strength to sit up in bed, assigned him an orderly with explicit instructions to keep his eyes on the Major day and night

In about a week's time Geiger was restored to full duty. For all the good it did him he might more profitably have remained in a convalescent leave status, for he shortly became involved in a verbal altercation with his immediate superior, and as a consequence, on 8 November, he was suspended from duty for ten days. For quite some time prior to the blow-up there had been many indications of Geiger's differences of opinion with Major Cunningham. That a run-in between the two individuals was inevitable, sooner or later, was almost taken for granted primarily as the result of their contrasting temperaments. Throughout the Day Wing, Cunningham was the subject of no little criticism for which he was in large part directly responsible. Conscientious to a fault and inclined to take himself too seriously, Cunningham had progressively developed a trend toward over-paternalism in his dealings with his subordinates. Nicknamed "Ma" or "Mother,"

101

Cunningham had earned these terms of endearment because of his tendencies to shelter if not over-protect his flock to a degree which some of the younger squadron pilots found rather annoying. On one occasion, for example, "Ma" felt called upon to station himself in front of a line of planes waiting to take off on a raid, and then dropped his white handkerchief as the signal to "give 'er the gun." To pilots and observers about to risk their necks in combat such a gesture seemed a bit incongruous, and this sort of display, along with other of Cunningham's peculiar mannerisms, in time was bound to engender resentment on the part of youths who overnight had grown up to become men.

Although Geiger throughout his career was known as a strict disciplinarian, he was eminently capable of expressing himself freely and in a rough and ready manner, being particularly outspoken in his denunciation of timidity and overcautiousness. Doubtless, some of the policies and opinions of the Day Wing Commander were not to Geiger's liking, and occasionally he was known to have rebelled openly against certain of his superior's decisions as well as the latter's inability to arrive at a positive course of action. Cunningham, not unnaturally, considered Geiger overly brash and aggressive, and to curb his junior's proclivity to "talk back", he took appropriate disciplinary action.

Placed under suspension, relieved of all duties in connection with his squadron, and restricted to the limits of camp for ten days "for making disparaging remarks about your superior officer", Geiger chafed under the terms of his enforced inactivity. He never served out his full sentence: on 11 November, Armistice Day, he was officially informed that the remainder of his suspension had been cancelled and that he had been restored to duty, kind of a general amnesty measure, it would appear, in keeping with the tenor of the international situation and the temporary agreement to "bury the hatchet."

The end of hostilities with the Central Powers was not accompanied by any decrease in the administrative work-load of the Northern Bombing Group. On the contrary, a number of housekeeping problems and disciplinary matters had arisen, which, with the passage of time had snowballed into a mass of such sizable proportions it threatened to engulf the entire staff. Ironically, in his new role Major Geiger discovered that his position had become totally reversed: the erst-while "prisoner" and victim of a personality clash had now been recast as a lawyer and a judge. Initially a Member, and subsequently the Judge Advocate of a Naval Court of Inquiry, convened at Autingues, France, under the guidance of Captain David F. Boyd, USN, Geiger was detached from Group Headquarters in late November in order to devote full time to the investigation of a touchy situation replete with international complications. Herein, one of the Group, a Lieutenant Chamberlain of the Marines, allegedly made certain false claims concerning his exploits in combat, and it required many weeks of interrogating witnesses and collecting pertinent evidence before the Court could arrive at its decision. The scope of the fact-finding board was such that Geiger spent most of December engaged in continual travel in northern France as well as in southern England, and it was not until January 1919 that he was finally relieved of his subsidiary legal duties.

Ultimately, on 10 January, he received orders from Headquarters, U. S. Naval Forces in Europe, then at London, to proceed from that place to Liverpool to await transportation back to America. Two days later he boarded the *SS Haverford* bound for Philadelphia, and on the last day of that month the troop ship steamed up the ice filled Delaware to discharge its passengers at League Island Navy Yard. For Major Geiger, the European War of 1917-18 was over and done with. Regardless of the comparatively limited achievements of the Day Wing in combat overseas, recognition of what had been accomplished in the face of adversity was not to be denied those who had done their best under discouraging conditions, and Geiger along with Cunningham and McIlvain in time was awarded the Navy Cross "for distinguished service in the line of his profession." As of the moment, however, he had several other matters of a more personal nature on his mind, and before reporting to his newly assigned duty station at Miami, he applied for and was granted a month's leave to spend with his wife and infant daughter (whom he had not yet seen) in Pensacola.

*   *   *   *   *   *   *   *   *

The coming year witnessed many changes—confronted with drastic budgetary cuts and chronic personnel shortages, Marine Corps Aviation commenced a long struggle for survival, and its reorganization and regroupment was no easy task. The 1st Marine Aviation Force had been disbanded overseas, less than a month after the Armistice, while the 1st Marine Aeronautic Company sailed for home from the Azores in January 1919. The remnants of those two units were reassembled at Miami on their return to the United States, and to them were added a number of individuals who had not served abroad, but had nevertheless been retained on active duty until the expiration of their enlistment contracts. With two Marine Brigades then actively engaged in field operations for the suppression of banditry and the restoration of law and order in two Caribbean Republics, plans were immediately initiated to reinforce the conventional ground forces there with aviation components. With three flying fields now at its disposal—at Quantico, Parris Island, and San Diego—Marine Corps Aviation likewise had to spread thin its meager complement of men and material to permit the sustained maintenance and operation of its recently acquired aeronautical facilities in the United States. Reduced from its wartime peak of some 2,400 officers .and enlisted men to a figure of approximately 1,000 Marines *in toto,* the adjusted allotment of aviation personnel was barely sufficient to man and operate five tactical squadrons, of which at least two were considerably understrength.

At home, two Squadrons, A and C, were assigned to the Marine Barracks at Quantico for duty with the Advanced Base Force, while Squadron B (including balloons) was detailed to Parris Island. Abroad, the 1st Division (6 land planes) of Squadron D was sent to San Pedro de Macoris in the Dominican Republic, in February 1919, to serve with the Second Marine Brigade. Its counterpart, the 1st Division (6 flying boats and 6 land aircraft) of Squadron E, was posted to Port-au-Prince, Haiti, about one month later, and attached to the First Brigade. In theory, each of the two Squadrons in the Caribbean was so organized and equipped as to be considered completely self-sustaining units; in actual practice it took near miracles on the part of their respective quartermasters and engineering officers to feed, clothe, and house the personnel and to keep their antiquated Curtiss *Jennies* and seaplanes from falling apart. With a small caretaking detachment and a training cadre at San Diego, and half a dozen officers on duty at Headquarters serving with Major Cunningham, the Officer-in-charge, Marine Aviation, it is quite apparent that by late spring of 1919 the Corps' air arm was fully committed in more ways than one.

In March of that year, at the time of his joining the composite group termed the Marine Aviation Section, at Miami, Geiger was still technically a Major. As senior officer present, he was designated the Section Commander. Similar to the majority of the Corps' officers, his temporary wartime rank was shortly to be terminated, and while on duty there awaiting transfer to an operational command overseas, he played a leading role in the game of "Musical Chairs." In July his commission as a Major was revoked, and he reverted to his permanent grade of Captain with date of rank, as before, going all the way back to 29 August 1916. On notification of his forced reduction in grade, command forthwith passed to the next ranking officer, in this case, Major McIlvain. Two weeks later McIlvain in turn was officially informed that he, too, had been "busted," whereupon Major Brewster became the new commanding officer. Hardly had Brewster assumed his new position but that word arrived of his reversion to his permanent rank of Captain. There being only those three officers present at Miami, and the cycle having run its course, Captain Geiger once again became the officer in charge with the same duties and responsibilities as before but now accompanied by a sizable decrease in pay and allowances.

By no means was his "demotion" any cause to slacken his manner of living. If anything it merely served to accelerate the pace of Geiger's progress, at least as far as his personal habits were concerned. Now the proud owner of a large and very powerful motor car, to while away his off-duty hours he took great delight in racing up and down southern Florida's highways at a high rate of speed. So fast did he operate his vehicle, the City of Miami's motorcycle policemen had to admit that short of setting up road blocks they were licked: at 80 miles-per-hour none of their machines could catch Captain Gieger streaking north on the open road from Opa-Locka to Daytona Beach early on a Sunday morning. On the few occasions werein they manged to flag him down, they considered it more appropriate to write him a ticket not for driving an automobile too fast but rather for "flying one too low." The Florida interlude could not last forever, and following a few month's service at Miami and several weeks at Quantico, in the late autumn of 1919 Geiger was detached and ordered to proceed overseas for duty with the First Provisional Brigade in Haiti.

Having boarded the *USS Kittery* at Charleston Navy Yard, a week's steady steaming brought that vessel to Port-au-Prince. Disembarking there, Gieger reported to Brigade Headquarters and to its Commander, Colonel John H. Russell, and was assigned to Squadron E as the relief for Captain Harvey B. Mims. The organization to which he had been posted was not particularly impressive: a dozen-odd flying boats and land-based aircraft operating from the Haitian Navy Yard at Bizoton, about three miles east of the capital. So primitive were the landing strips in the interior of the Republic, pending their development most of the Squadron's flying activities were confined to strictly water operations along the Haitian Coast. Shortly after Geiger's assumption of command at Bizoton, he was able to make a very favorable impression on a group of economy-minded Congressmen from Washington who had occasion to inspect his Squadron. Having no funds for an office or for an operations control center, Geiger had makeshift structures fashioned locally by Squadron personnel at no cost to the Government: a Shantytown of abandoned aircraft shipping crates shingled and roofed with flattened kerosene tins.

Joined by his wife and daughter at Port-au-Prince a few weeks after his arrival in the Republic, the Geiger family set up housekeeping in a rented residence, "Villa Keitel," on Rue Bois Verna up the hill from the National Palace. An incurable romantic at heart, the Squadron Commander succumbed to inner temptation soon after they moved in. Late one evening he deliberagely threw his mattress out of the window and on to the patio directly beneath the balcony of their second-story bedroom. The next morning when Port-au-Prince' roosters loudly proclaimed the arrival of dawn, great was Mrs. Geiger's amazement to observe her husband slumbering peacefully, in full uniform on the missing bed pad. Asked for an explanation, the Captain promptly replied that he set great store of sentimentality in marriage; that he had always wanted to sleep "under his wife's window;" and that the opportunity was too good to let pass unused. Just to make the scene complete, the mattress had fallen close to a rose bush, and after plucking one of its buds and handing it to his wife, Gieger walked over to the Government Ford touring car parked in the driveway, cranked up its engine and got it started, and took off for a day's work at Bizoton.

By no means was Geiger's first tour of duty in Haiti a blissful sojourn in a sun-caressed Caribbean isle. The situation throughout the Republic in general and at Port-au-Prince in particular in early 1920 was extremely critical, and the "Call to Arms" for those residing at the capital was an ever present contingency. It should not be forgotten that as far as the Marine Corps was concerned, the cease fire arrangement with Germany in November 1918 did not mean that the former's battles in other parts of the world were simultaneously terminated. On the contrary, the Corps still had two private "shooting wars" of its own going full blast in the West Indies, in which Marine riflemen and aviators could be killed just as dead by bandit bullets or by being hacked to bits by guerrilla machetes, as they could be mowed down by machine guns or put out of action permanently by having been gassed on the Western Front. Parenthetically, it is also pertinent to note that between the First and Second World Wars Marine pilots and gunners were the only aviation personnel of any of the nation's armed services to experience combat duty, serving with ground elements of Marine Brigades in the Dominican Republic, Haiti, and Nicaragua.

Applied to Haiti, although as far back as 1916 a material degree of law and order had been restored after two years of strenuous field campaigning by the Marine Forces of Occupation, brigandage and pillage had only been suppressed superficially, especially in the more remote regions of the country. Thus, the embers of resentment and revolt were still smoldering, waiting only to burst anew into flame. Despite the creation of the Marine trained and officered *Gendarmerie d'Haiti,* or Native Constabulary, to assist the First Brigade in its untiring efforts to police the land and to insure the introduction of some semblance of a legally constituted, democratic government, a return to the political and financial anarchy and chaos which had existed prior to the American intervention was far from a distant possibility. Until such time as the last remaining bandit group and its nominal commander could be wiped out, the future of Haiti hung in the balance.

Holed up in their mountain lairs and momentarily beaten into a state of sullen submission, the *Cacos* remained a threat to the Republic. They were not patriots but rather organized bands of professional thugs, ready to support any revolutionary movement willing to hire their services, led by irresponsible leaders

107

who knew no other trade nor occupation than murder and thievery, out for personal gain. Feared and hated by law-abiding Haitians, these outlaws were formidable adversaries. To curb their depredations, it was deemed essential to rebuild the nation's roads (which had fallen into complete disrepair), in order to permit the *Gendarmerie* and the Marine Brigade to patrol the internal areas of the Republic. This was accomplished by resorting to the institution of the *corvee,* the employment of enforced free labor on public highways. Opposition to the improvement and extension of the country's transportation network based on such a concept was not long in manifesting itself. If the *Cacos* were alarmed at the prospect of losing the security of their rural fastness, no less indignant were apathetic Haitain peasants at the idea of being made to work. Additionally, in some instances the *corvee* was all too closely associated with abuses and bribes thereby losing much of its effectiveness. Realizing that a tailor-made source of discontentment with great popular appeal was free for the taking, several dissatisfied politicians and guerrilla gang leaders readily seized the *corvee* as their whipping boy, and were consequently enabled to foment a full-scale insurrection against the Federal Government.

Among their number was Charlemagne Peralte, a *Caco* chieftan who had been captured by the *Gendarmerie* and forced to work on the roads. Subsequently managing to escape he took to the hills, and having attracted a following of several thousand malcontents, in the fall of 1918 he launched a year-long campaign of violence throughout much of northern Haiti. His avowed aim being the overthrow of the Administration currently in office, as well as the driving into the sea of the Marine Forces of Occupation, he gradually worked his way south. Some of his followers attacked Port-au-Prince in October 1919, but warned of their designs, the bandits were dispersed by the *Gendarmerie* and the Marines. Thereafter, a relentless pursuit of Peralte was undertaken, which finally culminated in his being shot to death later that month by *Gendarmerie* Captain Herman Hanneken, in a particularly hair-raising encounter near Grande Riviere du Nord.

Although the removal of Peralte from the scene brought about a notable decline in outlawry in northern Haiti, banditry and other guerrilla activities continued to flourish in the mountainous region east of Port-au-Prince. Led by Benoit

Batraville more than 2,500 *Cacos* laid much of central Haiti waste, and by January 1920 a band of his adherents felt bold enough to attack the capital. In this engagement the *Gendarmerie* and the Marine Brigade for a second time proved more than a match for the rebels; nevertheless, it was obvious that the mere passive defense of Port-au-Prince fell far short of ridding the Republic for once and for all of the *Caco* threat to its security.

The solution to the problem was the decision by the Brigade Commander to carry the war into the heart of the bandit areas. Commencing in early 1920, the Brigade (which now numbered 1,200) and the Native Constabulary (with a strength of some 2,600) took to the field, and for the ensuing six months in a series of intensive drives kept the *Cacos* on the run. Steady pressure against the outlaws was accomplished by maintaining relays of fresh patrols on their trail, which denied the bandits rest and prevented their obtaining reinforcements or supplies. Such aggressive measures in time wore down the *Caco* will to resist: divided and scattered into small groups and constantly harassed, those who had not been killed in skirmishes or already captured gradually began to surrender in increasing numbers. With the shooting of Batraville by a Marine Captain near Las Cahobas in June 1920, the comparatively few *Cacos* still at large lost heart in their cause. By mid-summer of that year so improved were general conditions in the Republic, the majority of the troops in the field were returned to garrison duties in the principal towns and to routine police patrolling in the adjacent countryside.

Aviation's role in the successful conclusion of the *Caco Revolt* was of paramount inportance, especially in the mopping-up phase. Operating in close conjunction with the mobile ground forces, Squadron E's services in rendering direct fire and logistical support were invaluable. Besides flying countless numbers of reconnaissance missions and acting as aerial observers, Squadron pilots engaged in aerial photography and map-making, delivered mail and messages to the troops in the field, dropped supplies including medicines, and in some cases were able to evacuate the sick and the wounded. Although air-to-air combat, World War I style, did not take place, if for no other reason than that the outlaws had no air force, the technique of what later came to be termed close air support was progressively refined to a marked degree. Once Squadron E was able to replace its obsolete and worn-out *Jennies* with war surplus stocks of *DeHavilland* scout-bombers, air-to-ground strafing runs and bombing strikes became commonplace types of air attack, and were effectively employed against bandit columns, defensive positions, and ambush sites. Meanwhile, utilizing gangs of captured outlaws and convicts, landing strips suitable for those aircraft were concurrently cleared in close proximity to many of the more important garrison outposts. With air support now at their beck and call, the task of locating and rounding up the few remaining, isolated rebel bands was made far less time consuming for the patrol leaders and their weary foot troops in the bush.

As Squadron Commander of the Brigade's solitary aviation component, Captain Geiger thrived in his new assignment. No two days were ever exactly alike, and in contrast to his frustrating experiences in France, he now had ample opportunity to fly to his heart's content with but minimum interference from higher authority. Among the seven pilots of Squadron E was a young Marine Lieutenant, Lawson H. M. Sanderson. To this officer may be attributed in large part the development of a new concept of aerial attack: that of glide bombing. Whether or not he exclusively *invented* the technique is subject to debate; that he actually *pioneered* in its application is well substantiated fact. Aware that horizontal bombing of enemy targets in the jungles or in mountainous terrain could endanger friendly ground forces, he sought a more accurate method of delivering a bomb load on a selected objective. Resort to out-and-out dive bombing was ruled impracticable, for in 1919 aircraft were still so flimsy a steep angle of descent (in excess of 45 degrees) at maximum velocity could easily rip the plane's wings from its fuselage. Equally disturbing was the fact that were a pilot able to pull his machine out of its abrupt plunge in time to escape the blast effect of its own bomb drop on the target, on recovery his engine was quite likely to stall, or to "hang on its propeller," with equally calamitous results.

Sanderson's answer to the problem was a compromise between the flat approach run and the vertical nose dive. Using a homemade bomb rack incorporating a canvas mail sack attached to the underside of his plane's fuselage, tied at the mouth by sash cords leading to the pilot's cockpit, and a rifle barrel for a bomb sight, the Lieutenant discovered that if he lined up his machine with the target, and released his load of 20-pound bombs after diving to a level of about 250 feet above the ground, at an angle between 30 and 45 degrees, an unusually high degree of accuracy could be attained. So satisfactory were his glide bombing attacks on *Caco* camps near Mirebalais, Haiti, which he and his observer, Lieutenant Lewis B. Puller of the *Gendarmerie,* conducted in the autumn of 1919, other officers immediately became interested in this new technique of aerial assault. No one was more enthusiastic than Captain Geiger. He instructed that all Squadron pilots be trained in its application, and once generally adopted, the new tactic was uniformly employed against the bandits throughout the duration of the Haitian Campaign.

An inspection of Geiger's Aviators Flight Log Book for the year 1920 reveals that he was a very busy Squadron Leader. Much of his time was devoted to aerial reconnaissance pertaining to the selection of future landing fields. Additionally, he flew numerous rescue missions: delivering a surgeon on a rush call to this outpost, bringing back from that one a gravely injured Marine for further treatment at the Brigade Hospital at Port-au-Prince. Lieutenant Colonel Louis McC. Little, Commanding Officer of the Eighth Regiment, or Central Haiti Field Force with Headquarters at Mirebalais, particularly desired Captain Geiger's services. Flying as the Colonel's personal pilot, sometimes in a *Jenny,* more frequently in a *DH–4,* the Squadron Leader traversed much of the eastern section of the Republic, stopping here and there at such places as Hinche and Thomonde to permit his passenger to make visits and to conduct inspections, or proceeding with him as rapidly as possible to the scene of reported bandit activity to get an on-the-spot estimate of the situation from the patrol leader or the nearest outpost commander. When not otherwise engaged, the Commanding Officer of Squadron E was regularly called upon to fly the mail between Brigade Headquarters at the capital and those of the Garrison Commander at Cap-Haitien on the northern coast.

Three of Geiger's flights were of significant interest, all of them round trips from Haiti to the neighboring Dominican Republic. In mid-August, piloting *DH–4B* (No. A–5813) and carrying dispatches for the Major General Commandant of the Marine Corps (then on an official tour of inspection), he landed at Santiago in the Dominican Republic, following a non-stop flight of roughly two hours from Port-au-Prince. This was the first time an aeroplane of that type had touched down on that Dominican flying field. Geiger returned with his machine to Haiti the next day, but within a week's time he was back again in the Dominican Republic, this time having flown the same plane, also with dispatches, from Port-au-Prince to Santo Domingo City. As before his flying time was two hours, and to clear the central mountain range he had been forced to climb to 14,000 feet, almost the maximum ceiling for his machine. Intent on finding a pass through the barren range, he made a second flight to Santo Domingo City in December. On that occasion, flying *DH–4B* (No. A-5811) he slid over the crest at 12,000 feet. Strong headwinds kept him from reducing his flying time on the eastbound run, but on the return leg with the aid of the favorable Trades, the duration of his flight was trimmed down to one hour and one half aloft.

For a lone pilot to fly any one of the six segments of those three round-trip flights was no mean feat. Had a forced landing been necessary at any time, Geiger's plight would have been very serious. The possibility of finding a cleared plot of ground in such rugged terrain which could suffice as an emergency landing strip was very slender. Moreover, even if by a stroke of luck the aeroplane could be safely landed and its pilot uninjured in the process, his troubles would only have just commenced. Unless the descent had been observed (and located) by a friendly ground patrol, close enough to the landing site to reach it within a few hours at the most, the pilot in all probability could expect to be summarily overwhelmed by hostile natives. To bandits in the bush the sudden and unexpected arrival of an American Marine aviator complete with his plane into their midst would have been a veritable bonanza. He would have been slaughtered on the spot for his side arms, his binoculars, and his personal possessions, while the salvaged machine guns, ammunition, and bombs from his downed aircraft would have been considered worth their weight in gold. Bearing in mind the fact that bandit gangs at large in the Dominican Republic in 1920 were just as unruly and anti-American as the *Cacos* of Haiti, a forced landing far from help anywhere along Geiger's route in either direction could well have been his last.

Considering the many risks encountered in flight during his first tour of duty in Haiti, Geiger was most fortunate to have escaped injury. During the period he commanded Squadron E, there was but one fatality among its commissioned ranks. In

August 1920, Second Lieutenant James G. Bowen lost his life in a bad plane crash at Mirebalais. At a later date, after the landing strip at Port-au-Prince had been considerably enlarged, and the Squadron transferred there from Bizoton, the renovated installation was named Bowen Field in his memory. As for Geiger's personal affairs with one tragic exception the gains far outweighed the losses. In addition to Geiger's official mount, his wife maintained a private horse for recreational riding. Both of those animals were stabled along with some forty Government horses at a site on the northern outskirts of Port-au-Prince adjacent to the landing strip. During the height of the emergency at the capital in the spring of 1920, there was a great deal of rioting throughout the city. An outbreak of violence afforded the opportunity for one or more Haitians to gain entrance to the Post Stables, and while the guards were absent every one of the horses was hamstrung. The motive behind this cruel act was the Haitian belief that the Americans would need their steeds to make good their escape from the capital, when and if the *Cacos* took it over. The fact that they chose to disregard the presence of numerous motor trucks and automobiles, which could better be used to transport the dependents of Marine officers and other American civilians in the event of such a dire predicament, served only to indicate the unrealistic and childishly naive attitude displayed by the average, uneducated Haitian peasant. Hopelessly crippled and with slim chance of recovery due to infection of their wounds (inflicted by machetes), all of the horses subsequently had to be put out their misery by veterinarians, much to the dismay of the owners of the mounts.

To counterbalance this loss there was other news of a more favorable nature in store for the Geiger family. In September 1920, the Captain was notified that for the second time in his career he had been temporarily promoted to the rank of Major. The restoration of the increased pay and allowances accompanying Geiger's advancement, which had been curtailed only the year previously, was doubly welcome for Eunice had informed her husband that an addition to the household was to be expected during the coming winter season. Neither parent having any great desire to have their second child born outside the United States, the Major's wife and daughter sailed from Port-au-Prince for Florida in early December. The prognostication proved most

113

accurate, for somewhat in the nature of a slightly belated Christmas present, on the 26th day of that month Geiger received a cable from Pensacola apprising him of the birth of his son at the Naval Station Hospital.

The Major, meanwhile, had his hands full attending to some unfinished business and tying up a few loose ends in Haiti prior to his departure for his next duty station. On 1 January 1921, the 1st Division, Squadron E, ceased to exist. Henceforth (and until March 1923), that organization became known as Flights G and H, 4th Air Squadron. The scope and value of its water operations and flying boat activities having progressively diminished, as the interior of the Republic was opened to and prepared for land-based aircraft, one of the Squadron's Flights was transferred from the seaplane base at Bizoton to the new landing field at Port-au-Prince. Now in receipt of his detachment orders, on 21 January Geiger relinquished command of the 4th Air Squadron to his designated relief, Captain Arthur H. Page. Flying to Cap-Haitien he boarded the transport *USS Hancock,* and a week later arrived at Hampton Roads, Virginia, with instructions to proceed with twenty days' delay to count as leave to the Marine Barracks at Quantico.

Looking back on his first tour of duty in Haiti, Geiger found much that was profitable despite the comparatively short period of his assignment there. The experience gained as a Squadron Leader had been invaluable from an administrative as well as from an operational point of view. Secondly, he had made the acquaintance of several officers serving with the First Brigade, or attached to the *Gendarmerie d'Haiti,* who had come to regard highly the abilities of the senior Marine aviator present, and as time went on were in a position to further his advancement, one of their number at length becoming the Major General Commandant of the Marine Corps. Finally, there had come the realization that given the opportunity, the pilot in his plane could work in close harmony with his counterpart on the ground, the rifleman and the machine gunner, for their mutual benefit. To develop this idea and to interest others in it became one of Geiger's basic aims, and with it the awareness that intensive study in the classroom and related discussion in conference groups perforce would be necessary, to achieve that end. Although in January 1921 Geiger had no way of knowing it, his initial service in Haiti was not destined to be his one and only duty tour in that unpredictable land. To the contrary, so fascinated was be by that country and its people, within four years' time he was back once more in Port-au-Prince commanding the Marine Brigade's aviation unit, and throughout the decade of the 1930's he made repeated visits to the Republic in connection with Fleet maneuvers in the Caribbean.

Chapter VI

Cross-Country and Classroom

Among the essential attributes of leadership are a man's abilities to produce the desired results and to inspire his subordinates to follow him under adverse or extremely demanding conditions. Given an equitable climate, reasonable competition, ample time, and adequate means—the manpower and materials, the funds and technical skills-even a mediocre executive can turn in a satisfactory performance in production and sales. Under such favorable circumstances it is not overly difficult for an individual to lead or to impose his will on others. If, however, the person in a position of responsibility finds that his resources are drastically curtailed, the opposition relentless, and the future doubtful, it will draw on all of his self-confidence and determination to keep on moving in the proper direction while continuing to retain the undivided support of his juniors.

This was the general situation confronting the leaders of naval aviation in the early 1920's. To Rear Admiral William A. Moffett, Chief of the Navy's Bureau of Aeronautics, and to Lieutenant Colonel Thomas C. Turner, Officer-in-Charge, Marine Corps Aviation (1920-25), were allotted challenging tasks. They were expected to make efficient flying organizations out of such personnel and materiel as could be provided by an austerity-minded Congress, war-weary and intent on disarmament. As a consequence, the aviation authorities had to do the best they could with what they had on hand, not with what they desired. Moreover, to cloud the issue were restrictions placed on their freedom of action by constant wrangling between as well as within the armed services as to the assigned roles and missions of aviation with relation to the over-all framework of the Army and the Navy. To the so-called "Battleship Admirals" the prospect of diverting funds for the purchase of new aeroplanes or for the building of future aircraft carriers was not wholly to their liking. They would have much preferred to utilize their limited naval appropriations primarily for dreadnought and cruiser construction. Already faced with the prospect of scrapping a sizable portion of the Navy—ships in commission as well as those on the building ways—to meet the terms of the Washington Conference, their problems were further aggravated by the bitter controversy between the relative merits of land-based aircraft as opposed to ship-mounted ordnance, a heated dispute in which the Army's Air Corps bombing exponents threatened to overwhelm them.

Applied specifically to the Marine Corps, its tiny air arm soon became the outright stepchild if not the poor relation of naval aviation, despite the fact that somewhat ironically, of all of the nation's air components, it was destined to be the only one to engage in actual armed combat in the 1920's and 1930's. Although since their adoption in 1916, the Marine Corps had consistently regarded its aeroplanes not as a separate arm or branch (with a special role), but rather as tactical weapons fully integrated for use with the conventional artillery of its landing forces and expeditionary troops, certain clarifications and refinements of the manner of their employment and extent remained to be resolved.

In Congress, considerable doubt was expressed concerning the Marine Corps' basic justification for operating aircraft. For example, in 1922 the Corps' stock of effectual aeroplanes was down to forty-two, of which all but a few were war-surplus machines transferred from the Army and Navy. To meet its operational commitments in the field a request was made for $720,000.00, the estimated cost of twenty-four replacements: twelve fighter-pursuit ships, and a dozen observation-scout, light bombers. The reaction to this modest entreaty was typical of the times. The Chairman of the Subcommittee of the House Committee of Appropriations, Mr. Patrick H. Kelley, at once brought up the vital question of where and for what purpose were such aircraft to be employed. Testifying before a Committee Hearing, Admiral Moffett forthwith enlightened its members of the contemplated mission of the aeroplanes in no uncertain terms by his terse explanation: "They (i.e., Marine pilots) are using them right now in Santo Domingo and in the Republic of Haiti. I believe the Marines there are doing more in land aviation than any one in the world, except, perhaps, the commercial aviation between Paris and London. But the military purpose of the airplanes is so that the Marines will have aviation just as they have other branches."

As for the tactical commanders—the squadron leaders at home and overseas—they were expected to work wonders with poorly fabricated, obsolete equipment. Progressively cut back to a strength of 46 commissioned officers and 730 enlisted men, Marine aviation personnel was visibly straining at its collective seams trying to keep air-borne its meager complement of trainers and combat aircraft. Not more than five squadrons could be maintained in anything approaching a fully operational status. Two of them, totaling 24 machines, were operating at two thirds normal strength: VF—1M and VO—3M, both at Quantico, each consisting of two active divisions of 6 aircraft. The other three units, amounting to 18 aeroplanes, were reduced to but one active division apiece: VO—1M (Santo Domingo), VO—2M (Haiti), and VS—1M (Guam). In addition funds and manpower had to be sufficiently stretched to permit the maintenance of a single division of 3 kite balloons, ZK—1M, hangared at Quantico and reserved for aerial spotting in conjunction with field artillery components of the Third Marine Brigade.

A heterogeneous assortment of out-moded and worn-out aeroplanes held together largely by bailing wire and paint, better suited for a museum than for aerial maneuvers, Marine aviation's flying equipment of the early post-war era almost defies description. The lone Fighter Squadron, VF—1M, flew *Thomas-Morse MB—3's;* the three Observation Squadrons, VO—1M, VO—2M, and VO—3M, were composed of a mixture of *DeHavilland DH—4B's* and *Vought VE—7's,* while the remaining element, VS—1M, was supplied with *Naval Aircraft Factory F—5—L* flying boats. Backing up those machines and held in reserve were a dozen-odd *Jennies,* most of which had been reconstructed from the ground up, at least twice, and from spare parts and remnants salvaged from scrapped or wrecked aircraft. To round out the picture, there were additionally present for duty several former German fighters and trainers, *Fokker D—7's* and *C—1's* which had been turned over to the Marine Corps, and a few experimental ships, the *Elias EM—1* and *EM—2* "Marine

Expeditionary Scouts."

The most distinguishing feature of all of those aeroplanes was the non-interchangeability of their basic parts. They had been torn apart and rebuilt so often and for so long, each machine and its particular engine was an entity unto itself. Standardization of components had thus given way to hand-wrought, custom alteration and on-the-spot improvisation to the degree that no two planes of the same design were exactly alike, regardless of the fact that originally they might have been identical models produced by the same manufacturer. Each airship having its own peculiar characteristics, aviators perforce had to be checked out on an individual-machine basis because of built-in idiosyncracies accompanying each unit. With regard to a ship's power plant, normally its performance was so diverse, its pilot similarly had almost to become its respective mechanic. Once assigned a specific plane, he took care to insure that no one else tinkered with its motor without his express approval and knowledge. However, in one minor respect there was unanimity: by the early 1920's service pilots and commercial fliers had generally agreed that on this side of the Atlantic Ocean, flying machines of the heavier-than-air category henceforth would be called and spelled *airplanes* in place of the former British term, *aeroplanes.*

Fresh from the wilds of Haiti, such a confused state of affairs was of relative unconcern to the new Commanding Officer of Quantico's 1st Aviation Group, Major Geiger. Aside from his service in France, his recent tour in the tropics had afforded him abundant opportunity to produce results with the means available, and he had learned through experience that a "makee-do" attitude went far to surmounting the obstacles confronting Marine aviation activites. Rather than idling about his headquarters in some hangar, wasting his energies bemoaning the uncertainties of the future, or, worse yet, bombarding higher echelon with numerous letters of complaint, decrying the lack of this item or the unsuitability of that, he concluded that his wisest course of action was to do everything in his power to "sell" the potential value of the Marine air arm to those among his seniors who were in a position to do something about it.

Fortunately for him, his immediate superior, Brigadier General Smedley D. Butler, commanding the East Coast Expeditionary Force, the Third Marine Brigade at Quantico, was not only Geiger's close friend but also a person of remarkably similar temperament. Butler quickly decided that if nothing else his Brigade would be kept busy in the field, not sitting around in barracks. When his Marines were not actively engaged in tactical exercises and maneuvers in nearby Virginia wastelands, they were put to work reconstructing and enlarging the post, converting it to a permanent installation. In time, the troops managed to build a large athletic stadium from salvaged materials procured from the general area; moreover, they were able to field a series of formidable football teams.

Not to be outdone, the Aviation Group Commander turned out his forces to erect a new flying field and seaplane base within the main reservation as a replacement for the small landing strip at Reid, south of Quantico. In June 1921, Major Geiger received a Letter of Commendation for the project, and when completed the following year, Brown Field (named in honor of a young Marine Lieutenant who had lost his life in an aviation accident) with its land plane hangars and machine shops, warehouses and seaplane ramps along the Potomac, became an important adjunct to the Corps' largest East Coast Base.

By no means were the activities of the 1st Aviation Group exclusively confined to their labors with pick and shovel. The 20 commissioned officers and 370 enlisted men comprising Geiger's command accounted for roughly one half the total strength of Marine Corps Aviation, and their concurrent flight training and gunnery practice programs were quite as rigorous as their aircraft maintenance and base construction endeavors. High on the agenda were their services as aerial photographers and map makers. Of equal importance was their employment to determine the most feasible, all-weather flight paths and air routes, and sites for future landing fields, all along the Atlantic Coast from Rhode Island south to Georgia, as far west and inland as the Allegheny Mountains. Their most significant assignment was their joint participation in large-scale field problems with ground troops, with emphasis not only on the development of constant and reliable radio communication between the two elements (as well as among themselves), but also on their ability to deliver effective, close air support utilizing machine gun fire and glide bombing drops on designated ground targets. Cross-country hops of varying duration for familiarization, formation flying, free and fixed-gun firing practice, and many hours devoted to bombing runs against land as well as water objectives rounded out their busy program of comprehensive aviation training.

The last mentioned function was particularly noteworthy. During the spring of 1921, the entire group spent at least two months concentrating on bombing practice at Quantico and at Hampton's Langley Field against terrain outline-plans and mock-ups of simulated battleships supplied with real searchlights and anti-aircraft batteries firing blank ammunition against the attacking aircraft. During June and July of that year, a selected division of the 1st Aviation Group, led by Geiger and flying *DH—4B's* in conjunction with Navy air squadrons, played a major role in the actual bombing of the obsolete battleships, *USS Iowa* and the former German *Ostfriesland,* at anchor off the Virginia Capes. Following the destruction of those stationary vessels was a prolonged period of night flying instruction at Quantico in preparation for the forthcoming autumn Brigade maneuvers. As previously related in an earlier Chapter, it was during this interlude that Captain John Minnis closed out his flying career by his precipitous plunge into the Potomac. For Geiger's part in the recovery of the unfortunate pilot's body, he received well earned Letters of Commendation from both the Brigade Commander and the Major General Commandant, John A. Lejeune.

Geiger's performance of duty throughout the 1921 tactical exercises was typical of the man. A partial re enactment of the Wilderness Campaign of the Civil War, the Major outdid himself in his tireless efforts to provide the closest possible liaison between air and ground units acting as a common team. Observed by President Harding and high-ranking officers of the Navy, his group put on such a splendid show in support of General Butler's troops, he was later the recipient of several congratulatory letters from the Chief of the Navy's Bureau of Aeronautics and General Lejeune, both of whom had been most favorably impressed with Geiger's skill as an aviator and with the efficient teamwork demonstrated by his Squadron pilots. Having been given the opportunity to display his wares, the Major correspondingly distinguished himself on numerous occasions by making landings and take-offs to deliver messages on any parcel of cleared ground which could accommodate his airplane, Additionally, he served as General Butler's personal pilot, and regardless of the condition of the weather or the suitability of the terrain, could always be depended upon to fly the Brigade Commander to any spot he desired throughout the duration of the maneuvers.

During the winter of 1921–22, Geiger, accompanied by his crew chief, First Sergeant Belcher, made several flights from Quantico to Tampa and Pensacola. Normally, he stopped both ways for fuel at the Army's Fort Bragg at Fayetteville and at the Marine Corps Flying Field at Parris Island. Some idea of his flying time may be ascertained from the flight logs of his *DH–4B*. Southbound from Quantico to Pensacola required 10 hours and 15 minutes, actual time aloft. The return trip as a rule necessitated an additional hour air-borne. Compared with the earlier two-plane flight of Colonel Turner and Lieutenant Sanderson, in April 1921, from Washington (Anacostia) to Santo Domingo City and return, a 4,850-mile round trip of 46 hours, 20 minutes flying time, Geiger's runs to Florida, entirely over land, were not nearly as spectacular nor as hazardous. On the other hand, his unguarded, solitary plane trips, at that time, were very much in the nature of pioneer flights, and if nothing else served to demonstrate conclusively that the commanding officer of the 1st Aviation Group was doing his level best to extend the range of his flying excursions to the limit of his ability.

For Quantico's aviators, 1922 was inclined to be almost a repetition of the year before; however, the scope of their activities was notably enlarged. To prove that the personnel of his observation and fighter squadrons were as proficient on the ground as they were in the air, the Major consolidated his fliers and mechanics, clerks and cooks, into a battalion of infantry, and so well did they drill in competition with rifle and artillery units of the Third Brigade, their detachment commander was extended another Letter of Commendation from the Major General Commandant. Simultaneously, favorable mention was made of the excellent condition of Quantico's flying field, its aircraft, and its base maintenance and repair facilities. As for the 1922 Brigade field exercises, the 1st Aviation Group managed to get all 24 of its airplanes and its 3 kite balloons aloft for the maneuvers, held that year at Gettysburg, of which the most impressive feature was a reproduction of Pickett's Charge. As before, Geiger's services were in great demand: this time he was detailed to fly the Assistant Secretary of the Navy, Theodore Roosevelt, Jr., over the rolling fields of southeastern Pennsylvania. By the time the show was over, the Major's group had flown a total of 38,500 miles, achieving some 500 hours of flying time in the process.

Much to Geiger's personal satisfaction, in July 1922 his assignment to flight duty was extended for another two years. Detailed exclusively to aviation since June 1917, in the normal course of events as decreed by Marine Corps General Order No. 8. of 1921, he could have expected a return to line duty on completion of five years' continuous service as a pilot. Thereafter, he would be required to put in three years of troop duty before he could be reassigned to an aviation billet. Nevertheless, there was a specific provision of that General Order which permitted the retention of certain individuals beyond the usual limits, not to exceed two years, and Geiger fortunately found himself included in that select category.

During the fall and winter of that year he commenced the advance planning and preparation of his crew for a contemplated transcontinental flight. At that period the Army Air Corps at San Diego's North Island Aviation Station decided they had a surplus of *Martin*, twin-*Liberty* heavy bombers, and they were perfectly willing to relinquish four of their total stock of ten to the Marine Corps. One of the conditions of the transfer obliged the new owners to accept delivery at the spot where the planes were currently hangared. Faced with the prospect of paying out $20,000.00, representing freight charges to ship the four ponderous *MBT's* by rail from California to Virginia, the Officer-in-Charge, Marine Corps Aviation, came to the conclusion that the cheapest way to bring his new acquisitions back to the East Coast was to have them flown back under their own power by Marine pilots. Accordingly, Major Geiger at Quantico was selected to lead the team which would ferry the four planes across the United States.

The nature of his unique assignment posed a variety of operational and administrative problems. To begin with, no member of the 1st Aviation Group was more than generally familiar with either the basic characteristics or the behavior in flight of dual-engine heavy bombers, and there were no other aircraft of that type readily available for instructional purposes. Secondly, careful consideration had to be given to the selection of a suitable air route, bearing in mind that fueling points and maintenance facilities (even for minor repairs), especially in the more remote regions of the southwest and at various locales in Texas, then left a great deal to be desired. Thirdly, was the navigational aspect including the state of the weather, for the pilots would have to fly contact, restricting them to daytime operations, at a time of year when flying conditions were far from ideal, always subject to radical change. Last and by no means an unimportant matter, was the choice of determining which of the personnel were best fitted to meet the demands of a grueling, 2,800-mile flight across the continent in open planes.

Geiger solved the first part of the problem by reporting in person to the Air Station at North Island accompanied by a team of 20-odd pilots and mechanics. During the last week of March and the first two weeks of April 1923, he and his crew undertook a number of familiarization and practice flights in the newly acquired *MBT's* to the degree that all of the 8 commissioned officers became thoroughly acquainted with the machines, and were individually checked out on their assigned planes. As for the route, the Rocky Mountains were by-passed by flying far to the south, and the flight path was eventually decided upon as follows: San Diego–Yuma–Tucson–El Paso–Marfa–Del Rio–San Antonio–Dallas–Tulsa–Kansas City–St. Louis–Indianapolis–Dayton–Moundsville–Washington–Quantico. For proper control and guidance, Geiger insisted that the aircraft remain in formation throughout the long flight. As finally determined, the 13 officers and enlisted Marines selected to fly the four planes were respectively apportioned: No. 1., Major Geiger, Captain Francis Mulcahy, and Gunnery Sergeant Pounders; No. 2., Captain James Davis, Captain Russell Presley, First Sergeant Karns, and Sergeant Groves; No. 3., Captain Louis Woods, Lieutenant Walter Hallenberg, and Gunnery Sergeant Alcorn; No. 4., Captain Arthur Page, Lieutenant Guy Hall, and First Sergeant Blackwell.

Taking off from North Island on 19 April 1923, the four airplanes arrived at Quantico, safe and sound, eleven days later, thus completing the longest flight hitherto attempted by such a formation without mishap, serious accident, or damage. The greatest period of time aloft was the hop between Dallas and Tulsa–three and one half hours. The shortest time air-borne was the brief one half hour run from Anacostia to Brown Field. Merely to observe that the flight was an unqualified success would not only be an understatement, but would also be a denial of the deserved credit accruing to the participants, which reflected most favorably on their individual as well as their joint skills. If nothing else, the cross-country aerial venture represented more nearly a profound triumph over adversity and exposure.

Equipped with but the simplest of navigational aids and an equally primitive system of manual controls, pilots literally had to strain to keep their fragile machines aloft. Cold or wet weather continually plagued the airmen of the era of the open cockpit. When it rained, or, worse yet, snowed or hailed, aviators were soon soaked to the skin from the waist up in spite of their jackets. Under extreme conditions a man's shoulders, his flight goggles, and helmet could become coated with a thin sheet of ice. Having to fly contact, he had usually to restrict his altitude to 2,000 feet unless the visibility was remarkably good. Were it poor due to fog or mist, frequently he was forced to fly at even lower altitudes. Cruising along so close to the ground at a sustained operating speed of some 90 miles per hour subjected the aircraft to violent down-drafts and other atmospheric disturbances, conditions which could often cause even the most rugged individual to become desperately air sick.

Even when the sun shone brightly there were problems—the combination of the heat, the glare, the air currents, and the slip stream could half bake a man's face, so minor was the protection offered by the thin mica or isinglass windshield. Another hazard of the period was the ever present danger of being struck by other flying objects, and more than one aviator and his plane were known to have been put out of action peremptorily through inadvertently making contact in flight with a flock of buzzards. Forced landings, of course, were to be expected on short notice—clogged fuel lines, overheated bearings, cracked exhaust manifolds, and cooling system failures could ground a plane just as surely as a broken control cable, a snapped guy wire, or a splintered wooden strut. Taking all of the aforementioned factors into consideration, the 38 hours flying time required by Geiger's plane to travel from coast to coast were far more indicative of his mastery of the elements than a carefree, springtime joy ride in the "wild blue yonder." Under the circumstances, the subsequent bestowal of a Letter of Commendation from General Lejeune for

Geiger's leadership and perseverance had been more than justly earned in this instance.

Back at Quantico and fortified with the experience gained from his long ferry hop, Geiger was tempted to undertake a further aerial venture of even greater proportions. He believed that it was eminently possible for a lone airplane to circle the globe. After discussing the matter at considerable length with Captain Page (who had agreed to serve as Geiger's co-pilot), he had decided that a Navy torpedo bomber, a *Douglas DT—2,* subject to certain alterations, could do the job. Stripped of its ordnance to provide for an increased fuel capacity, he estimated that at a cruising speed of approximately 70 miles per hour, the aircraft could remain aloft for 20 hours at a stretch. Selecting 15 May 1923 as his tentative date of departure, Geiger was of the opinion that utilizing the late spring and early summer months, he could complete the encirclement of the world in 90 days from start to finish. He intended to fly westward, and set up the following itinerary: Washington—San Diego—Aleutian Islands—Japan—Philippines—Bombay—Gibraltar—Azores.

He realized that a destroyer escort in mid-Pacific would be highly desirable in the event of a forced landing at sea. He was also aware that replacement parts would have to be sent out in advance to selected stops along his route: 4 complete, new *Liberty* engines and 4 new wooden propellers, to be spotted at an Alaskan base, at Manila, Bombay, and Gibraltar. So convinced was the Major that Page and he could ultimately succeed in the achievement of his aim, he typed an official letter to the Major General Commandant through the normal chain of command, outlining his plans and listing his requirements, and even enclosing a comprehensive summary of weather conditions prepared by a Navy aerologist. Oddly enough, for rarely was Geiger dissuaded by contrary opinion, his letter apparently was never signed nor submitted, although a copy may be found today in his personal correspondence file.

It has been claimed that Geiger was talked out of his proposal, almost at the last moment, for a variety of reasons. Undoubtedly, his project might well have been regarded in certain official circles more as an unwarranted stunt than anything else, quite aside from the fact that the mere preparations and arrangements for such an unprecedented flight of necessity would have been highly complicated and correspondingly costly. Whether or not the Navy could then have maintained a flotilla of destroyers, strung out like a chain of beads across the Pacific, is open to question. Furthermore, the prospect of losing the services of two experienced pilots from their regular assigned duties for at least three months—if not forever—might indeed have struck a discordant note at Headquarters. Transcending those objections was the paramount issue that the wives of the two officers concerned were far from happy with the proposition. Not only did they view unfavorably such a lengthy, enforced separation from their respective mates, they also felt that so slim were their chances of future reunion with their husbands based on an undertaking which was purely voluntary, as distinct from falling within the bounds of their expected flying commitments, the two Marine aviators might just as well take off for another planet—and remain there. Dauntless against the physical forces of nature, Geiger was nevertheless forced to admit that his wife had voiced an objection to which he could not supply a logical explanation, whereupon his contemplated round-the-world jaunt was shelved indefinitely.

Seeking some other form of release for his pent-up energies, the Major soon discovered that he had a challenge much closer at hand. Besides the three kite balloons at Quantico, somebody came across a free balloon, left over from the European War, now stored in one of the warehouses at Brown Field. Other than their commanding officer few if any of the group pilots had ever flown in free balloons, and to them the apparatus seemed somewhat of an anachronism, an obsolete and unwieldy novelty of questionable value which was otherwise taking up much needed storage space. Geiger listened to their jibes until he could stand them no longer. Determined to disprove their contentions that free balloons were unreliable and well-nigh impossible to control, he ordered the object of their derision wheeled out on the field and inflated. Selecting at random four candidates for a demonstration—Captain Woods, Lieutenant Holderby, Gunner Eurton, and Corporal Paczkiewicz—the group piled into the basket on a sunny morning in August 1923. Under Geiger's tutelage an ascent was made followed by a free flight of some two hours' duration in the general vicinity of Quantico. To the passenger's astonishment (and possibly Geiger's) their pilot managed to land the basket not in the

Potomac nor in some distant cow pasture, but precisely on the very spot from which they had previously ascended. A little chastened but still muttering that it was sheer luck that their pilot had been able to make such an auspicious landing, it was obvious that the airmen were only half convinced that free ballooning was of any use.

Disdainful of their remarks and resolved to refute the allegations of the scoffers that the Major couldn't repeat the performance even if he tried all the rest of the summer, Geiger at once announced that he could do it all over again, in the same fashion, any time he liked. To prove his claim, he picked a second crew—Captain Presley, Gunner Eurton, and Corporal Dowling—and forthwith made a second ascent. By this time everyone not occupied with more pressing business hung around the field to watch the fun. One hour and fifty minutes later Geiger gently valved the remaining hydrogen from the balloon's now shrunken bag, and lowered the gently swaying basket right back on the center of Brown Field. Wide-eyed with amazement at his feat, the balloon's occupants slunk off out of sight without saying a word. As of that moment there was no doubt in the minds of any of the members of the 1st Aviation Group that if the *Old Man* were so inclined, he could drop a free balloon down a factory chimney, and for the duration of Geiger's tour of duty as their commanding officer, there were no further derogatory remarks on the topic of free ballooning.

For the 1st Aviation Group, the remainder of the year closely followed the pattern of the two previous ones. Some of the officers took part in the Air Races at Cleveland and Detroit, others entered the Pulitzer Trophy Contest at St. Louis, Geiger attending all. Parenthetically, it is pertinent to note that such racing meets as these and others (the Schneider Trophy for seaplanes being one of the more publicized) wherein America's most highly skilled civilian and service pilots competed for cash awards, did much to stimulate the technological progress of the nation's growing aviation industry. Admittedly, these air pageants capitalized on the natural rivalries of the fliers and their respective services. Immense crowds were attracted to observe the formation flying and the maneuvers not to mention the aerial acrobatics and the outright stunts. But despite the carnival atmosphere surrounding the running of many of the events, and the tendency to glamorize certain of the individual contestants, these meets did serve a beneficial purpose. Indirectly, they spurred the imagination of aeronautical designers and engineers to produce faster and better planes with more reliable motors burning new fuels, and they attributed in no little part to the development of streamlining including the innovation of retractable landing gear.

Following the annual bombing and gunnery practice at Hampton Roads (and for the second year in a row, VO—3M won the coveted Navy "E" for excellence in gunnery, thereby entitling Geiger to a Letter of Commendation from the Secretary of the Navy), the 1st Aviation Group turned out in full force for the usual Brigade exercises. Held in the Shenandoah Valley and incorporating a representation of the Civil War engagement at Newmarket, Major Geiger once again was kept busy flying General Butler from one site to another.

By the close of 1923, Quantico's aviation detachment had conclusively proved its ability to meet all of the many demands made upon it, and had established an enviable reputation for dependability and versatility. During the winter of 1923—24 the authorities decided to employ its fighting and observation squadrons in support of the ground components of the East Coast Expeditionary Force in large-scale ship-to-shore training exercises in the Caribbean. Operating in conjunction with other aircraft from the Navy's Scouting and Battle Forces, the 1st Aviation Group took an active part in Fleet Problems No. 3 and No. 4, staged at Panama and at the Island of Culebra, respectively. Although the landing operations and the simulated naval bombardments were later the subject of considerable debate—for certain grave errors had been made clearly apparent—there was relatively little criticism of aviation's tactical conduct beyond the fact that insufficient numbers of planes had been provided for the assault forces at the Culebra phase of the maneuvers.

Back once more at its Quantico base, the Group girded its loins in preparation for the Brigade's annual field training, scheduled to be held in the summmmer of 1924 in the vicinity of Sharpsburg, Maryland. As for Major Geiger, not only was his tour of duty rapidly drawing to a close, but also his two-year extension to aviation, granted in 1922, had now about run its course. A review of Geiger's flight record for the seven-year period terminating in March 1924 is of more than passing interest.

Excluding his flight time aloft as a passenger or while serving as co-pilot, since March 1917, he had racked up a total of 739 hours, 30 minutes, *solo* time. This figure included slightly more than 100 hours in free and captive balloons. More than one half of his air-borne hours at the controls and been made in *DH–4's,* some 73 hours in *VE–7's,* and 63 in *JN's.* He had flown in eighteen distinctive types and models of seaplanes, flying boats, and land-based aircraft, from basic trainers to heavy bombers, of American, British, and even German manufacture (4½ hours in a *Fokker D–7*). During that seven-year span, he had managed to maintain more than 100 hours, average annual flight time (solo), or approximately 8 1/3 hours per month aloft. Considering that an individual assigned to flight duty was required to fly a minimum of 4 hours monthly to qualify for his flight pay, Geiger had obviously doubled his quota.

During the period 1917–24, he had witnessed Marine Corps Aviation expand from a mere handful of planes and young pilots to a Wing in France and Belgium, and to an operational force of five squadrons in time of nominal peace. Likewise, he had not only observed but had also played a singular part in the progressive development of the Marines' air arm to a point where it had demonstrated its worth in no uncertain terms. For by 1924, in spite of numerous drawbacks Marine Aviation had definitely manifested its capacity to deliver the goods in the following fields: reconnaissance, scouting, and patrolling; artillery spotting; photography and map making; transportation of personnel and supplies, including the evacuation of wounded; aerial glide bombing and gunnery—close air support in offensive combat against marching columns and pack trains, as well as against men in trenches and in beach defense emplacements.

Turning to the other side of the coin, Geiger was additionally aware of the evolution of another related phenomenon: the compilation of the casualty rate. Throughout the 1920's the figures were pretty depressing by any set of standards: specifically, from 1922–27, they were rated at 25%. Discounting the accidents to pilot-trainees at Pensacola, among the actual operating squadrons the average annual number of plane crashes came to 25. From these smashes evolved almost a uniform average of 5 total fatalities, and 5 seriously injured, of whom the majority had to be removed permanently from a flight status. Translated into other terms, these statistics meant that even if Marine Aviation were fortunate enough to qualify 1 new pilot per month, per annum (which it was seldom able to do), the total number of its flight personnel could be increased by 7 rather than by 12. As a consequence, the aggregate strength of Marine Aviation remained relatively constant throughout the decade under discussion: somewhere between 50 and 60, the number of its aircraft similarly averaging about 55. Although the definition of what constitutes "pilot failure" has traditionally been a debatable issue, it would appear that most of the plane crashes were then caused either by mechanical failure in flight (thus resulting in a forced landing), or by accidents on landing or take-off (usually brought on by reduced or very poor visibility). Whatever the reason, it is apparent from the dismal accounting above that applied to Marine fliers what is generally now referred to as "job-security," was then practically non-existent; however, by no means did this factor deter the more adventurous from pursuing a career as a flying Marine.

Relegated to line duty, Geiger might well have been posted to an infantry or an artillery unit as a Battalion Commander, or he could have been detailed to the staff of a Regiment or a Brigade. Furthermore, he was eligible for assignment to advanced instruction either as a student at the Marine Corps Schools or at an Army or Navy educational center, in some course commensurate with his present rank (his permanent commission as a Major having long since been reinstituted). As events transpired, he eventually wound up in a school billet to which he had been nominated by General Butler, his former Brigade Commander, now serving as Philadelphia's Director of Public Safety on a two-year leave of absence.

Rather than enter the Field Officers' Course at Quantico, Geiger had made up his mind, that given the chance, he would prefer to attend the Army's Command and General Staff Course at Fort Leavenworth, Kansas. The prerequisites for the latter, particularly in the case of a Marine officer, were difficult, for not more than four Marines of field grade could be selected annually for entrance to that ten-month course. Geiger hesitated to apply for he sought no special favors. His wife knew that her husband had long had his heart set on attending Leavenworth, and she discreetly asked General Butler if he would care to nominate Roy for the next course, scheduled to commence in August 1924. To this the General responded with enthusiasm, heartily endorsing the idea, and submitting the Major's name to the Commandant for consideration. This, of itself, was an out of the ordinary thing for Butler to do, for he was an outspoken member of the faction that believed that schooling for Marine officers was of small value. To him, the notion of sitting in a classroom being taught "how to soldier" was of little account, inasmuch as he thought the one and only place for an up-and-coming Marine officer to increase his professional knowledge was to get out there (and stay there) in the field with the troops, and to learn "by doing it." At a loss to understand why Geiger had chosen formal schooling out in Kansas in lieu of troop duty under canvas at Quantico or Parris Island, Butler, nevertheless, was determined to back up his good friend to the limit. With the nomination approved by General Lejeune, the way was clear for Geiger to head west, and as will be subsequently related, neither of the two Generals had cause to regret their decisions for Geiger was soon to demonstrate his complete ability to master his new assignment.

In late August, and with his flight duty now revoked, the Major was detached from Quantico, and with his family in tow reported under orders to the General Service School at Fort Leavenworth. Of the 260-odd officers under instruction there, Geiger was one of four Marines, the others being Lieutenant Colonel Thomas Holcomb (who had established quite a name for himself in France as a Battalion Commander of the Sixth Marines), Major William Upshur (just back from Haiti following a tour as Chief of Staff of the First Marine Brigade), and Major Oliver Floyd. Under command of Brigadier General H.A. Smith, USA, Leavenworth's Class of 1924—25 included in its student roster the names of several officers who in time were to become extremely well known. Among them were Lieutenant Colonel Benjamin Foulois, one of the Army's more celebrated aviators, who had early cut his teeth in the flying game as the commander of the First Aero Squadron attached to General Pershing's Expeditionary Force in Mexico, 1916—17; subsequently, a Chief of the Army Air force. Four of the Infantry Majors, Hodges, Patch, Simpson, and Buckner, during the Second World War all rose to the rank of Lieutenant General, and served, respectively, as the commanders of the United States First, Seventh, Ninth, and Tenth Armies.

Major Devers, a Field Artilleryman, and Major Crittenberger of the Cavalry, as future Lieutenant Generals, correspondingly commanded the Sixth Army Group and an Armored Corps in Europe. With regard to the Marines, Holcomb became the Corps' Seventeenth Commandant, Upshur as a Major General and Geiger as a Lieutenant General were to hold positions of great responsibility in the Pacific Campaigns, while Major Floyd shortly went on to gain fame in the Second Nicaraguan Intervention of the late 1920's.

Perhaps the best way to describe the Army's Command and General Staff Course would be to remark that it was a steady ten-month-long grind, a period of intensive concentration which demanded every moment of the students' undivided attention six-plus days (and nights) a week. A combination of map problems and practical terrain exercises, it was deliberately designed to separate the men from the boys, and for the unfortunate few who fell by the wayside in the process, their careers were usually washed-up, once and for all, then and there. In some respects, Geiger was at a decided disadvantage from the very start. With a few exceptions all of his Army Classmates were West Point graduates, a majority having likewise attended previous courses of instruction in the various Schools of application representing their particular branch of the service, such as the Infantry School at Fort Benning, the Cavalry School at Fort Riley, or the Field Artillery School at Fort Sill. Several officers were Engineers and there was a large contingent of Coast Artillerymen, well qualified and highly trained technicians, the cream of the crop. By contrast, Geiger was practically in a class by himself. As far as his formal, professional instruction was concerned, all he could resort to was what he had been taught years before at the Marine Officers' School of Application and at Pensacola's Flight School, back in the pre-War era. Beyond that, all he had to offer was some fifteen years of practical experience, at home and abroad, during which time he had marched or ridden horseback hundreds of miles, and had flown hundreds of hours. Otherwise, he had been too busy attending to his duties as a Squadron or an Aviation Group Commander to take time out to increase his theoretical military schooling.

On the other hand, he had two predominant assets. To begin with, he was intellectually curious, eager to learn, and with a born aptitude to be an outstanding pupil. As Geiger was to state repeatedly, he much preferred being a student than acting as an instructor; hence, he enjoyed his tours of duty under instruction at all of the various service schools he attended. In brief, he welcomed the opportunity to examine new concepts and doctrines, and to adopt new techniques. Of equal importance was his ability not to "fight the problem." Obstacles did not easily dishearten him, and by temperament, once he had started some project, he was inclined to see it through it its logical conclusion. Thus, with a mind like a freshly wrung-out sponge, receptive to new ideas and ready to absorb any and everything which he thought could be useful, he was content to buckle down to work, concentrating on the problem at hand, and with the assurance that he could reason things out and come up with a workable solution.

It was well that early in the game Geiger had tuned in his mental attitude to the proper frequency for the coming ordeal. During the sweltering heat of the summer and the chilly blasts of a sub-arctic winter he worked like a galley slave, poring over estimates and summaries, formulating schemes of maneuver, writing formal operation and administrative orders, and drawing up pertinent annexes. Introduced to countless Tables of Organization and Equipment, in time he became thoroughly acquainted with the detailed contents of Staff Manuals. Loaded atop all these were terrain studies, map and aerial mosaics, and much practical field sketching. By no means were his lengthy studies confined to the limits of the classroom and the lecture hall. At frequent intervals the student body turned out booted and spurred, *au cheval,* for tactical exercises with the School Troops and for extended, mounted reconnaissance rides, welcome changes from the desk and the draftsman's table, and at least, opportunities to keep in reasonably decent physical condition despite the long hours indoors.

Assigned government quarters in converted barracks known locally as the "Beehive" because of the scores of small children of officers' families in residence, Geiger had meager time for domestic affairs. Nevertheless, he did his best to devote what few free moments he felt he could spare to be with his wife and children. As for Eunice, she was a pillar of strength, for she helped him in innumerable ways with the preparation of his maps and his special papers, and often read to him until the wee hours of the morning when his eyes were so tired he could no longer bear to glance at the texts.

Such perseverance and conscientious attention to duty paid off handsome dividends after almost a year of unbroken, strenuous mental gymnastics. Along with Colonel Holcomb and Major Floyd, Geiger was one of thirty-nine Distinguished Graduates of the Command and General Staff Course, standing well up in the top quarter of his class. Such an accomplishment was not passed over unobserved or unheralded. In due course he was to receive a Letter of Commendation from General Lejeune, complimenting the Major on his demonstrated ability as evidenced by his outstanding record at Leavenworth. General Butler, equally an interested party, wrote Geiger a personal letter of congratulations and reiterated his desire that his friend return to flight duty, stating in his own words: "I have not been up since you left aviation, and will not risk it until you are available to run the show," a compliment, indeed, from a General Officer who was never known to praise a man without adequate cause.

There were other compensating factors derived from Geiger's tour at Leavenworth. Paramount among them had been the unique chance for him to become acquainted with many of the Army's more brilliant field officers destined to play important future roles in wartime. For it was during Geiger's attendance at the School that he struck up a lasting friendship with (and admiration for) Major Simon Bolivar Buckner, Jr., and it was more than plain happenstance that on the occasion of General Buckner's demise in action at Okinawa, twenty years later, that General Geiger, commanding the III (Marine) Amphibious Corps, succeeded to the position of Commanding General, Tenth Army. Conversely, many Army officers slated for high-level command positions had been given the opportunity to meet not just a Marine, but a Marine aviator, and were to profit by the revelation that the Corps' reputation for versatility was far more than an idle boast.

On graduation from Leavenworth in June 1925, Geiger ordinarily could have expected to have been posted to troop duty in the field or to the staff of the Marine Corps Schools as an instructor. Inwardly, he wanted to return to aviation duty at the earliest possible date, so he was noticeably elated to receive detaching orders assigning him to the Marine Barracks at Pensacola's Naval Air Station, with ten days' delay to count as leave in reporting. Moreover, on receipt of those orders he was again (and for the third time in his career) detailed to flight status, which he was to retain, uninterruped, for the duration of his active service. The new Officer-in-Charge, Marine Corps Aviation, Major Edward Brainard (who had replaced Lieutenant Colonel Turner at Headquarters in March 1925), was of the opinion that Geiger's services could be best utilized as an instructor at Pensacola; additionally, it would afford him a fine opportunity to catch up on recent developments in naval aviation, including the chance to fly some of the newer planes then undergoing tests prior to adoption by the tactical units. This arrangement was more than agreeable to Geiger, for at that time the commanding officer's billets of the air squadrons at both Quantico and San Diego were filled by aviators senior to him (Turner and Major Ross Rowell, respectively), and he was not then due for another tour of foreign service until the following year.

Geiger's short stay at Pensacola from July through October 1925 was comparatively uneventful. A welcome breather after the strain of Fort Leavenworth, his so-called refresher course in aviation was largely spent flying more or less as he pleased, from morning until night. With its facilities greatly enlarged since he had last been stationed there in 1917—for flying at the base was no longer exclusively restricted to seaplanes—Geiger concentrated for the most part on familiarizing himself with several of the newer models of land-based fighters including the *Boeing FB−1's,* powered with *Curtiss D−12,* water-cooled engines.

By the time autumn had rolled around, he was more than ever anxious to return to a tactical command, preferably on foreign duty. At this point in Geiger's career it was high time that he looked to his laurels. Although two of the Marine aviators senior to him in rank, Lieutenant Colonel Cunningham and Major Evans, were not then serving in a flight status, several other officers commissioned prior to him had transferred from the line to aviation, and could thereby out-rank him at the few Marine bases in the United States which were assigned flight organizations. Having no great desire to play Second Fiddle if he could get a command of his own elsewhere, he commenced to look around for an appropriate billet. Being too senior to command the Scouting Squadron at Guam, all that remained was VO-2M at Port-au-Prince, Haiti. Without further delay he applied for assignment to the latter organization, and in October 1925 his request was approved, and he was alerted to stand by for transfer in the near future from Pensacola to the First Marine Brigade in the Haitian Republic.

Chapter VII

Training for Higher Command

From the very outset Major Geiger's second tour of duty in Haiti appeared at least superficially to be destined to become almost an exact duplication of his first. In early November 1925, practically six years to the day following his previous departure from the United States, in the same vessel, *USS Kittery,* and from the same port, Charleston Navy Yard, he sailed for Port-au-Prince to rejoin the First Marine Brigade. To complete the sequence of similar events, he was likewise detailed to an identical billet, commanding officer of the Brigade's solitary observation squadron, VO-2M, as a relief for Captain Louis M. Bourne, who was under orders to report to Langley Field. After making his official call on the Brigade Commander, Colonel John T. Myers, Geiger forthwith drove out to Bowen Field, where he found that as before his command consisted of 7 Commissioned Marine pilots, 1 Warrant Officer, 100 enlisted men, and 1 attached officer of the Navy Medical Corps. As for the aircraft such changes as had been made were negligible. There were 12 airplanes of which two-thirds were considered fully operational, the remaining units being kept in reserve: 8 *02B-1's* (*Boeing*-built modernizations of *DH-4-B's* with metal fuselages), 3 *DH-4-B-1's* (remodeled versions of the old *DeHavillands* with larger fuel tanks and heavier landing wheels), and 1 lone *JN.* Considering that the entire operating and maintenance budget for that particular squadron for the Fiscal Year ending 30 June 1926 had been set at $88,500.00, this comparatively small allowance at the disposal of the squadron commander and his engineering officer posed a considerable challenge to their ingenuity to keep the unit airborne and its

138

aircraft sufficiently gassed and lubricated.

On the other hand, in marked contrast to conditions which had prevailed thoughout the Republic during Geiger's earlier period of service there, no combat operations or active field campaigning on the part of the Brigade were momentarily indicated. By 1926 President Joseph Louis Borno had settled down to commence his second term in office, and with the *Gendarmerie d'Haiti* established to the degree that banditry in the hinterlands no longer was a menace, an era of uninterrupted peace and material progress seemed about to unfold. As for the Marine Brigade, one of its two Regiments, the Eighth, had been disbanded, and the strength of the other, the Second, had been progressively reduced to less than 1,000. Restricted to garrison duties in the principal coastal towns, the Brigade's paramount function was one of remaining quietly in the background as a reserve, a force in readiness to support the native constabulary only in case of some unforeseen emergency. With public works and road building projects under way, the American High Commisioner, Brigadier General John H. Russell, formerly in command of the Marine Brigade, had little to do other than to provide customary diplomatic representation and to direct the adjustment of the Republic's long-standing indebtedness, under American supervision, according to previous (1915) treaty stipulations between the United States and Haiti.

Under such circumstances the personnel of the Brigade could look forward to a rather unhurried, leisurely type of existence. Discounting those on Guard Duty, drills and formations invariably ceased at midday, and the afternoons could be devoted to sporting and athletic activities, including horseback riding and polo playing. With regard to the commissioned officers and their ladies, especially at Port-au-Prince, off-duty hours from garrison routine generally assumed the aspect of a pattern of daily living somewhat akin to Rudyard Kipling's legendary tales of cantonment life among British Regiments serving at hill stations along India's famed North West Frontier in the 1880's and 1890's. With a crowded schedule of social entertainment, for those who were so inclined and could stand the pace there was no dearth of evening parties and dances. Once the American Club closed its doors at midnight, it was a relatively simple matter to pack up the band and its instruments along with the waiters and the guests, and to repair uptown to the nearest, conveniently located private residence where the ball went on unabated until the roosters crowed. Arranging for an unexpected dinner party of sizeable proportions was never a problem: by pooling the community's entire stock of dishes and glassware, table linens and silver service, not to mention the household servants, any determined hostess could lay out a repast of restaurant-size dimensions given an hour's advance warning.

Nor was the aspect of a never ending, week-end house party confined exclusively to the elders, for Port-au-Prince was equally a tropical paradise for American children. Not only were there picnics, swimming and riding parties, but in addition most of the youngsters were allowed to keep as many pets as they chose to adopt. No exception to the rule, the Geiger household soon became a menagerie of dogs and cats, goats and chickens, peacocks and parrots. Two of the last mentioned have long been remembered, by name *Jacko* and *Macker Babb*. Parenthetically, the second parrot owed his title to that of a Colonel commanding the Second Regiment, for it would appear that as far as the Geiger children were concerned, both their bird and Colonel Babb down on the parade ground had several similar, distinctive characteristics: protuberant eye sockets, an abrupt raucous manner of expression, a bandy-legged strut, and a pronounced tendency to preen themselves.

Primarily to amuse the youngsters Eunice thought it would be fun if the parrots could be made to talk rather than merely to squawk. Selecting *Jacko* as the more promising candidate, she concentrated on him for weeks, and in due course the bird was able to say: "Hello There!" The Major discovered what his wife was up to after making discreet inquiries from the houseboy, and decided, unbeknownst to her, that he would work on the other parrot. Whenever he could persuade Eunice to leave the house, he would open the cage and take *Macker Babb* out to the relative seclusion of a small kiosk in the garden of their residence on Rue Toujours. After more than a month of patient coaching he was finally able to get his bird to master what his mentor considered an appropriate interjection: "Go to Hell!" The inevitable day of awakening was not long in coming. One evening as the Major and his wife were enjoying their after dinner coffee in the living room, several callers from the Brigade dropped by to pay their respects.

Hardly had they stepped inside the screen door but that *Jacko* from his perch delivered his friendly term of greeting, whereupon *Macker Babb* not to be outshone, let loose full blast with his treasured epithet. Caught between two contrasting poles as it were the Geiger's guests were somewhat nonplussed if not thoroughly embarrassed, but the Major's outburst of hearty laughter, echoed by the children who had been quietly listening in an adjacent room, quickly put everyone present at ease. Thereafter, and for the duration of the Geiger's tour of duty at Port-au-Prince, the two outspoken parrots became very much of a conversation piece; however, whenever Colonel Babb and his wife showed up for a party, both of the birds were speedily transferred for the time being to the darkness of the gardener's shed.

For all of its picturesqueness and its air of the exotic—the Victorian gingerbread-cooky and cardboard-cake frosting of the frontings of its ramshackle frame houses, the aroma of burning charcoal from the cooking fires of native squatters spread up and down the slopes of its purple-hued mountain backdrop, the crowing cocks, braying donkeys, and barking dogs at the first crack of dawn—Port-au-Prince was not free from many hidden dangers. If its Iron Market and its waterfront with their strange sights and sounds were interesting to visit, there was nothing quaint about their over-powering smells. With the prevalence of abject poverty and accompanying disease and filth ever close at hand, foreigners walked with care, always mindful of the fact that they were a distinct minority of the privileged in the midst of a seething mass of humanity, incredibly ignorant and uneducated, and steeped in African superstition. By no means could an alien Force of Occupation in a single decade erase the lingering aftereffects of a tragic heritage of slavery, followed by almost an unbroken century of rebellion and oppression, exploitation and violence, and the savagery of the surrounding jungle and the beat of the voodoo drums were but a stone's throw from the town's squalid limits.

For the Gieger children there was one unpleasant episode neither they nor their parents were to forget for months to come. Invited to an evening reception at the National Palace the Major and his wife left their eight-year-old daughter Joyce and their son, Roy Junior, then six years of age, with a trusted Haitian nurse, and drove down the hill in their Hudson touring car. When the couple returned some two hours later to their residence, they were startled to observe that there was not a light burning in the house; moreover, all of the doors and windows had been shut and fastened securely. From within all they could hear was a low moaning noise. Breaking the lock on the front door, Geiger at length gained entrance, and in the gloom was able to discern lying on the floor and whimpering like a beaten animal the panic-stricken nurse. Turning on the lights he rushed into the children's bedroom to find them huddled together in a corner, wide-eyed with fear, but apparently unharmed. The native girl was so distraught she was unable to express herself in either French or English; similarly, the children were too frightened to talk coherently.

After inspecting the house and the grounds—and finding no one—Geiger immediately sent for the police and telephoned the Officer of the Guard at Brigade Headquarters. Questioned by a Gendarme the Haitian girl pulled herself sufficiently together to make it plain that the house had been molested during the Major's absence; other than that she would not—or could not—go into greater detail. Taken to the American Legation for further interrogation, one of the Secretaries present there who had made a study of acquiring a familiarity with Haitian creole, or native *patois,* finally got her to relate the entire story. Shortly after Roy and Eunice had left the house the children thought they heard something whining and scratching near the front door. Thinking it possible that one of the dogs had been inadvertently left outside, the nurse naturally opened the door, and to her consternation saw what appeared to be a human being, practically naked and bent over on all-fours, trying to climb up the steps to the front porch. Her first reaction was that it was a drunken native prowler, but the expression on his tortured face and the weird contortions of his body soon convinced her that whatever or whomever was outside trying to get inside was suffering from something far more potent than an overdose of *clairin.* Slamming the door shut and bolting it—but not before the children had been given the opportunity to view the strange apparition—she forthwith ran through the interior of the building closing and securing all of the shutters (there were no glass panes). In the hope that the intruder would lose interest and wander away elsewhere, she had enough presence of mind to extinguish the lights.

At this juncture the "thing" on the porch—man or beast—began to howl—pitifully and loudly—and having no success pounding on the front door tried to break into the residence by prying loose the wooden blinds. By this time it had dawned on the Haitian nurse that their nocturnal visitor was an insane person, probably a victim of a bite transmitted by a dog infected with rabies, for there had been recent cases of that dreadful affliction reported in Port-au-Prince, and bands of semi-wild and often diseased dogs were known to roam the streets at night in the poorer sections of the town, searching aimlessly for food. Terror-struck at the thought of what might transpire if the hydrophobic creature burst into their midst, the nurse succumbed to a state of shock. The two little children, left to their own devices, knew that something was terribly wrong and instinctively sensed the grave danger of the situation, but there was little if anything they could do about it other than to remain quiet and to hope that the fastenings on the doors and shutters held tightly. Fortunately, the timely return of their parents, the noise of the automobile's motor and the glare of its headlights, frightened the intruder away in the nick of time.

As a consequence of this incident, whenever the Major and his wife had future occasion to leave the house together after dark, they took measures to leave behind a security force capable of coping with most any emergency. The reception committee in this instance was provided in the form of one of the Squadron's non-commissioned officers, who was paid to mount guard until the parents' return. This arrangement was perfectly agreeable to the children for they were always delighted to have as their "baby-sitter" a six-foot-two, Polish-American Corporal or Sergeant with tattooed forearms, who liked to smoke cigars and to tell tales of his aviation exploits in his own brand of broken-English, meanwhile he sat in a rocking chair with a double-barreled 12-gauge shotgun loaded with buckshot across his knees, ready, willing, and able to repel boarders.

When not otherwise engaged in his routine activities in command of his squadron, Geiger made many independent flights throughout the length and breadth of Haiti. He particularly enjoyed his runs up to the north coast, inspecting improvements to landing strips and ferrying back and forth Brigade and *Gendarmerie* officials from Port-au-Prince to Cap-Haitien and Fort

Liberté. Based on his prior flying experience in the Republic, whenever possible a second airplane accompanied him to act as a pick-up man in case of an accident or a forced landing, for it was still rather a risky business for a pilot to be compelled to set his aircraft down, alone, in the more remote sections of the interior. On the other hand, were Geiger to spy something interesting or out of the ordinary taking place below on the ground, he seldom hesitated to make a landing on any likely patch of reasonable level terrain, so that he could walk over and get a closer look at the situation. In later years one of his former Sergeant Crew Chiefs related that he never dared go aloft with the Major unless he had brought along his emergency repair kit. This consisted of a generous supply of extra fabric, dope, sewing needles, pack thread, and a roll of wire cable to make on-the-spot, temporary restorations of broken gear, for Geiger, it would appear, frequently would elect to make a landing in any goat pasture or banana clearing which looked large enough to accommodate his plane, regardless of the presence of stray rocks, tree stumps, or irrigation ditches.

Eunice went along for the ride on at least one of his north-bound hops, seated behind her husband in the rear cockpit, thereby affording the necessary ballast which otherwise would have been provided by the addition of one or more filled sand bags. In this fashion she was able to visit King Henri Christophe's legendary fortress and castle, *La Citadelle La Ferriere,* on the summit of Bonnet-a-l'Eveque, some 15 miles south of Cap-Haitien, as well as the ruins of that long-deceased monarch's equally fabulous palace and regal court, *Sans Souci,* near the little town of Milot. In this respect it should not be overlooked that in 1926-27, Haitian roads other than the main arteries of transportation, were better suited to mounted patrols on muleback rather than to motor vehicles on pneumatic tires; hence, the ability to fly to and to land in the nearby vicinity of any desired locale reduced the travel time from days to hours. Even so, to climb on foot up the steep winding rails leading to *La Ferriere* was far more strenuous than a simple afternoon's hike through the woods, and so primitive were conditions there, it was not until November 1929 that an official post of the by then renamed *Guarde d'Haiti* could be established at that isolated spot.

With regard to the Major's operational flying, so efficiently did his squadron perform in its annual gunnery and bombing exercises, its commanding officer was warmly commended by both the American High Commissioner and the Major General Commandant. Likewise, so favorable was the impression made on the visiting representatives of the Adjutant and Inspector's Division by the excellent discipline of Geiger's unit, the turn-out of its personnel, and the condition of VO-2M's aircraft and repair shops, the Major was again in line for formal congratulations. As events worked out it was well that so much time and effort had been devoted to the squadron's training, for within a matter of a few months the majority of its pilots, radio operators, and flight mechanics found themselves fully committed to field operations in Nicaragua as well as China.

Commencing in the early months of 1927 and continuing on through the better part of the ensuing six years without a break, the Marine Corps—on land and sea as well as in the air—had to extend itself to its utmost to dispatch simultaneously two Expeditionary Forces to two widely separated parts of the globe; meanwhile, the First Brigade had to be maintained in Haiti (until 1934), and seagoing Marine detachments had to be furnished for ships of the Battle Fleet in the Pacific, of the Asiatic Squadron in the Far East, of the Scouting Force in the Atlantic, and of the Special Service Squadron in the Caribbean.

That the Corps was able to meet its extraordinary commitments under unrelenting pressure for such an extended period reflected great credit on the part of both the Major General Commandant, General Lejeune, and the Officer-in-Charge, Marine Corps Aviation, Major Brainard. By October 1927, some 435 commissioned officers and 6,600 enlisted men were serving on Expeditionary Duty in Nicaragua, China, and Haiti. By July 1928, 11,500 Marines or two thirds of the entire Corps was stationed outside the continental limits of the United States: 9,150 on Expeditionary Duty and Legation Guards; 1,550 on Sea Duty; 300 on Aviation Duty, overseas; and 500 in transit to or from foreign service. Considering that the actual, appropriated strength of the Corps was then 17,400 (despite the fact that as far back as 1919 Congress had set its authorized enlisted total at 27,400), it meant that the Commandant had to maintain the administrative, training, and security forces at home (such as the Navy Yard Guards) with the remaining 33% of the Corps, and at the same time meet the replacement drafts and the loss through wastage of the 66% on sea or foreign field service, a most difficult undertaking by any set of standards.

Bearing in mind its small size (and the advanced age of its aircraft), the role of Marine Corps Aviation for the period under discussion was significantly noteworthy. During the first year (1926) of Geiger's Haitian tour, the Marines' air arm consisted of 68 officers and naval aviation pilots, of whom 60 were in an active flight status, and roughly 800 enlisted men. Major Brainard had requested authority and the funds to operate 8 tactical squadrons, 1 balloon squadron, and 1 service squadron. With a peace strength set at one-third the theoretical wartime complement, each of the tactical squadrons was allowed 1 active division of 6 aircraft, plus an allotment of 3 spares per squadron as a reserve. Thus, 48 airplanes were to be considered fully operational, with 24 additional on a stand-by status, bringing the total number to 72. Personnel were assigned on the basis of 9 pilots, 1 ground officer (the Squadron Quartermaster) and 80 enlisted men to each tactical squadron; however, in the case of independent organizations such as were stationed in Haiti and Guam, the latter contingent could be increased to 100. Four of the squadrons were observation (2 at Quantico, 1 each at San Diego and Haiti), three were classed as fighters (2 at Quantico, 1 at San Diego), and one was nominally designated a scouting unit (Guam). In actual practice, the Marines had 74 planes on hand: 40 at Quantico, including 4 bombers; 14 at San Diego (6 observation-scouts, 6 fighters, and 2 bombers); 12 at Port-au-Prince, Haiti; and 8 at Guam. Other than at the last mentioned station, which was supplied with *Curtiss* flying boats, the aircraft were predominantly a mixture of *DH-4-B's, O2B-1's* and *VE-7's.* It is relevant to state that at that time Major Brainard had no other recourse than to use maintenance funds for the rebuilding of his ancient flying machines, for the allowance for the purchase of new aircraft was so paltry as to be negligible: thirty Privates or the equivalent of a platoon of Marine Riflemen could be maintained for one year for the price of a factory-fresh $30,000.00 combat airplane (which might be smashed to bits within a week of its delivery), and in 1926, literally, every single body counted.

By mid-summer of Geiger's second year of duty at Port-au-Prince, although the total number of Marine Corps aircraft

146

remained unchanged (74), not only had replacement planes entered the picture; principally, *Curtiss Hawks* and *Falcons, Loeing* amphibians, and *Boeing FB-1* fighters, but also one additional squadron had been activated. By that date Major Rowell's VO-7M was engaged in actual combat flying in Nicaragua as part of General Logan Feland's Second Marine Brigade, while far away in North China, Lieutenant Colonel Turner and Major Evans with VO-10M and VF-10M, were attempting to set up air bases from which they could operate in conjunction with General Smedley Butler's Third Marine Brigade.

With Haiti clearly in the backwash, for already a battalion of the Second Regiment had been sent to Nicaragua to reinforce the Marine Expeditionary Force there in its efforts to suppress a civil war, and with VO-9M (as of 1 July 1927, VO-2M was so redesignated) gradually losing one after another of its best young pilots for assignment to a combat command, it was high time for Major Geiger to pick up his hat and coat and leave the party before it was too late. In brief, there were then far too many significant developments taking place in aviation, civil as well as military, to miss the golden opportunity of getting in on the ground floor, and pleasant though the duty was at Port-au-Prince, if Geiger wanted to stay abreast of the new trends he had best depart from his tropical oasis, and the sooner the better.

In this connection, it is pertinent to mention that Captain Charles A. Lindbergh's historic trans-Atlantic flight of May 1927 had not only focused attention on his skill and determination as a pilot, but what was of greater consequence, the spotlight on his *Ryan* monoplane had provided a much needed impetus to the advancement of American aviation by arousing notable public interest. Applied to the military side, Major Rowell and certain of his squadron pilots, among them First Lieutenant Hayne D. Boyden and Marine Gunner Michael Wodarczyk, were progressively refining the techniques of low-level glide bombing and strafing in close-air support missions to the degree they were scoring striking successes in their aerial combat sorties against Augusto "Cesar" Sandino and his fellow insurrectionists, deep in the mountain areas of Nicaragua. And by no means a minor consideration was the gradual introduction of new and far more powerful aircraft for Marine aviation, planes such as the *Vought* two-seat fighters, *02U-1's,* with radial, air-cooled engines and metal propellers, which could perform evolutions impossible in the old *DH-4's,* and the *Atlantic TA-1/2's,* tri-motored transports with all-aluminum wings and fuselages, durable landing gear, and improved radio sets.

Convinced that the time had arrived for him to get back in harness once more, attuned to the steady stream of innovations and improvements which were profoundly affecting the aviation world, Geiger eagerly welcomed the arrival of his detachment orders. On 7 July 1927, the Major turned over his squadron to his second-in-command, Captain Russell Presley, and taking the well-worn track back to Quantico via Hampton Roads on the venerable *USS Kittery,* reported for duty there toward the end of that month. Two noticeable changes, however, differentiated the conclusion of his second tour in Haiti from his first. This time he brought back no medals, whereas in 1921 he had been awarded two for his expeditionary duty in that Republic, and on his return to Quantico, his good friend and admirer, General Butler, was no longer in command, being absent with his brigade far across the Pacific at North China's Tientsin.

Despite the transfer of several of its elements to the Orient and to Central America, the new commanding officer of Aircraft Squadrons, East Coast Expeditionary Force, found that Quantico's hangars had not been swept completely bare: two fighting squadrons were still present, flying *Hawks* and *Falcons,* and the utility outfit had everything in the cupboard, so to speak, from trainers and scouts to amphibians and bombers. More important yet, Geigers's pilots included such experienced aviators as Major Bourne, Captains Davis and Mulcahy. This was most fortunate for although nominally in charge of Quantico's air base, Geiger was assigned additional duty on the staff of the Marine Corps Schools, as an instructor and technical adviser. He was not overjoyed at this arrangement, but at any rate, he could still fly whenever he could get time off from his educational pursuits, and it permitted him to retain his flight status along with aviation pay. Actually, he had little cause for complaint, for had he been sent instead to San Diego, he would have found nothing of any consequence at its air station other than a half a dozen decaying *DeHavillands,* everything else of any real value having long before been shipped out to the Far East, quite aside from the fact that being a dyed-in-the-wool champion of his home state, to Geiger

Southern California had nothing in the way of climate or bathing beaches which could even approach what Florida had to offer along those lines.

Nevertheless, his teaching assignment with the Schools did succeed in preventing Geiger from taking part in two important, long distance flights. In December 1927, the first of the *Fokker (Atlantic)* transports was flown from Washington to Managua, Nicaragua, via Miami by Major Brainard, accompanied by Gunnery Sergeant Morris Shephard and Sergeant Nero Winchester. This was said to be the first flight westward across the Caribbean, and was a trail-blazer for the initial Pan American Airways seaplane runs from Florida to Central and South America, a service which commenced the following year. For the same reason, he could not participate in the January 1928 flight of two additional *Fokker* tri-motors, piloted by Major Bourne and First Lieutenant Jacob Plachta, which flew non-stop from Miami to Managua, 1,200 miles in 12 hours. All in all, Marine Corps Aviation was making its mark: throughout 1927 its pilots flew some 19,000 hours or 1,600,000 air miles in 70 planes. Their record was marred by only 8 crashes with no fatalities until October of that year, at which time an aircraft flying a combat reconnaissance patrol incurred a forced landing near Quilali, Nicaragua, and although the pilot (Lieutenant Thomas) and his observer (Sergeant Dowdell) were seen to leave the wreckage unharmed, both men were subsequently tracked down, captured, and slain by native bandits.

By the late spring of 1928 Geiger was relieved at Quantico by Major Charles A. Lutz, and was forthwith ordered to Headquarters for duty as Acting Officer-in-Charge of the Aviation Section of the Division of Operations and Training. As Major Brainard's assistant (and still in a flight status) Geiger was able to assume some of the mounting burden which had fallen on his superior's shoulders occasioned by the scope of Marine aviation's activities overseas. To maintain two observation and two fighting squadrons in Nicaragua and China, totaling some 33 pilots and 300 enlisted men flying 38 aircraft, or about one-half its stock of operational airplanes, put the Corps' air arm under considerable strain to make both ends meet. Besides, there was no way of knowing what might transpire elsewhere, especially in Haiti, and somehow, more aircraft had to be procured and more pilots had to be forthcoming. Major Brainard was particularly concerned with the problem of ensuring that his aviators and their planes would be on hand, ready for action, when they were needed. As he was to testify in the Hearings for the Navy Department's Appropriation Bill for the Fiscal Year 1929, when Colonel Turner's squadrons went out to Shanghai in 1927 they were of no use to the Brigade Commander at the time of landing, for their planes had to be brought on later in "follow-up shipping." Furthermore, Turner had first to establish a land base and flying fields on foreign soil. To prevent the reoccurrence of this undesirable predicament in the future, Brainard strongly urged the Navy to furnish the Marine Corps with one or more small escort carriers, specifically designed and equipped to accompany an amphibious expeditionary force. His pleas and his foresight went unheeded for some sixteen years, for in 1928 Congress was economy-minded, and as for the Navy Department, its officials were primarily concerned with keeping their new construction programs within the tonnage limitations of the Geneva Naval Conference; moreover, they had not yet been given time to correct all of the kinks in their two recently commissioned, fleet aircraft carriers, the USS *Saratoga* and the USS *Lexington*.

Geiger's sojourn at Headquarters turned out to be one of short duration, for on 1 Sepatember 1928 he was detached and ordered to the Army War College at Fort Humphreys on the Potomac as a student officer under instruction. Having successfully completed the Command and Staff Course at Fort Leavenworth, he decided that he might as well go the whole way in his efforts to increase his professional education; besides, he was interested to find out what, if anything, the Army Air Corps was doing to integrate its air arm with the operations of ground forces in the field. There being three vacancies open to Marine officers for the coming school year at the War College, he applied along with Colonel Charles B. Taylor and Lieutenant Colonel Walter N. Hill, and was delighted to be informed that General Lejeune had honored his request for admission. In preparation for his contemplated ten-months residency in Washington, he rented a house in Cleveland Park for himself and his family, for there were no government quarters for students at Fort Humphreys.

With Major General William D. Connor, USA, as its Commandant, the War College as the senior institution within the Army's education system (for the National War College at

Washington was not established until 1946) was definitely no place for a novice or for an individual seeking a respite from troop duty. Far from being a rest cure its course of instruction in the art and science of land warfare was undeniably difficult. Its curriculum was correspondingly elaborate, much stress being laid on the maneuvering of large tactical groups such as divisions, corps, and even field armies. With respect to strategy, its scope encompassed everything from a review of the basic fundamentals to a study of the concepts and doctrines for the operational employment of all arms of the service, and its comprehensive coverage included such advanced topics as detailed area studies and strategical war planning on a national scale. Much independent work was expected of the students with emphasis on special projects and the submission of lengthy written reports.

Unlike the Command and Staff Course, the War College had far fewer students. Some forty-odd officers of the Regular Army along with the three Marines and two line officers of the Navy formed the student body, each of whom had twenty years or more of active service in his respective branch. It was a very select, potentially star-spangled group, for the great majority of those under instruction were to attain general or flag officer rank prior to or during the Second World War. Although superficially the competition may have been less pronounced than it was at Fort Leavenworth, the students at the War College nevertheless sought perfection, for a certificate of satisfactory completion of the course with a favorable endorsement signed by its Commandant was invariably regarded by the Army recipients as a sure-fire ticket to a future, top-level command billet, and a high standing in the class was a keenly sought goal.

Again as at Fort Leavenworth Geiger applied himself without stint to his studies, and devoted much attention and industry to his special assignments. Unquestionably, through practical experience and formal instruction his knowledge of aviation techniques was far superior to that of most of his associates, and as such his presence at the War College was a material contribution to the better understanding of the related role between air and ground components in combat. So strongly did he feel the need to impress others with the capabilities of aviation, working not as a separate arm or service, but rather as a working partner and co-equal team member of closely integrated air, land, and water fighting elements, he requested permission to concentrate his supplementary studies on that vital topic.

This was approved and from November until the following May, Geiger burned the midnight oil preparing his written report. This special study, entitled "Relation of the Army and Navy Air Components in Joint Operations," was an extremely carefully prepared and thoroughly documented paper. It was also bound to invite comment, for Geiger touched on several highly controversial matters. As a lead-off, he made it crystal clear that a separate Air Force was not the solution, for in his considered opinion, a bomb dropped from a plane was just another weapon—another means of delivering the counterpart of an artillery projectile—hence, aviation could not justifiably lay claim to having a detached role, an independent mission or function, apart from the soldiers in their trenches or the seamen-gunners in their turrets. To Geiger's mind, an attack plane or a bomber merely served to increase the range of action of land or sea based forces. Naturally, in the eyes of certain of those students who were members of the Army Air Corps, such views by a fellow aviator (even though he was a Marine) smacked of heresy. In fact, he was almost a traitor to his own class, for even in 1929 there were factions within the Air Corps which championed the notion of a separate Air Force, cut loose from Army domination, and they expected that Geiger would follow the party line. Herein, they failed to convert Geiger, for he was always a staunch advocate of the close bond between the Marine Corps and the Navy, and he saw no reason to draw up a bill of divorcement to sever naval aviation from the Marines on a beach or from the sailors in their battleships or cruisers.

He dwelt at length on this theme in the body of his report, stipulating that in an assault landing, aircraft take the place of the landing force's artillery. Not only did the planes support naval gunfire, but they were also available for the close air support of the attacking ground elements. As for the wrap-up, he signed off with the recommendation that a Joint Air Staff School be inaugurated and that Joint Air Maneuvers be conducted annually to educate and to train all aviators—Army, Navy, and Marine—as to their proper function as team members working together with the doughboys and blue-jackets toward a common aim.

On the theory that a man gains from a course of instruction in direct proportion to that which he puts into it, Geiger's "term paper" was the *grand finale* of his labors at the Army War College. This report was significant in more ways than one, for Geiger, a future Director of Marine Aviation, laid it on the line, clearly and concisely, just where he stood on the critical issue of the desired relationship between aviation and the land and sea forces. Never a Billy Mitchell fan, throughout his career Geiger was strongly opposed to a unified air force. His experiences as an aviator and as a line officer in the Second World War served only to confirm and to strengthen the convictions he had expressed in 1929, and as will be subsequently related, his testimony before the Senate Committee on Military Affairs, on 7 December 1945, as the Commanding General, Fleet Marine Force, Pacific, was in essence a re-iteration and a re-affirmation of his battle-tested views concerning aviation's proper role.

As if to prove that he was far more than an air-chair theorist, Geiger entered the practical realm of aviation's abilities by participating in several aerial ventures while still a student at the War College. During the month of June 1929, accompanied by Major Charles A. Meyer, a Coast Artilleryman, the pair made an extensive air reconnaissance of the State of Maine. A large number of aerial photographs were taken, which were made available to the College for school purposes and reconnaissance exercises, and for his part in the project he was given an official Letter of Commendation by General Connor. By the time July 1929 rolled around, it was graduation day, and with certificate (with honors) in hand, he drove out the Main Gate for the last time, looking forward to thirty days' well-earned leave at Pensacola before returning once again to his old stamping ground at Quantico's Brown Field.

On his return to Quantico in August, Geiger and his family moved back into their old Quarters, No. 18, on the hill overlooking the Barracks and the Brigade Offices. While Eunice yet another time struggled with the crates, unpacked the cups and saucers, and rehung the curtains, the children looked about the Post in search of former acquaintances, and enjoyed the last of the summer's fun before the Post Schools opened their doors. Geiger, too, was among old friends, for by that date General Butler had returned with his Brigade to Quantico following its expeditionary service in China, and he was more than happy to have the Major around to serve as his personal pilot. Up at Headquarters in

Washington, Colonel Turner was now the Officer-in-Charge, Marine Corps Aviation, having taken over that assignment from Major Brainard, who had resigned in order to enter private enterprise. And out at the flying field, Geiger as Commanding Officer, Air Squadrons, East Coast Expeditionary Force, was reunited with many pilots and mechanics with whom he had flown for many years.

Gone to the scrap heap were the old *DH–4'ss* for the two fighting squadrons were now supplied with *Corsairs* and *Hawks, Falcons* and *SeaHawks* (*F7C–1's,* carrier versions of earlier models). As for the balloon squadron, ZKO–1M, its days were numbered: in the interest of economy and because observation-type aircraft had proved superior for artillery spotting, the "gas bag outfit" was to be disbanded in December 1929. The most significant event of the year were the improvements to Brown Field, for thanks to Colonel Turner's prodding and his insistence that the newer planes demanded longer landing strips, he had gotten an appropriation for $500,000.00 to enlarge the air base.

Flight operations consisted in the main of the usual bombing and gunnery practice, night and formation flying, and participation in such showy events as the National Air Races at Cleveland in the autumn and at the All American Race Meets at Miami in the winter. Acrobatic and dive-bombing exhibitions (the newer planes with their increased strength and power could now make steeper descents) were the main features of those affairs. On the more prosaic side, any number of rescue and emergency flights were conducted on an on-call basis, ranging from bringing in supplies for flood stricken victims of the Ohio and Mississippi Rivers to forest-fire patrols along the Atlantic slopes of the Alleghenies and the Appalachians. Much attention was devoted to the intermediate and advanced training of young pilots, fresh from Pensacola, for the Marines in Nicaragua, notably Major Mitchell's fighter-observation and utility squadrons, were still at it hammer-and-tongs with the bandits in the northern and eastern regions of that strife torn land, and filling replacement quotas for flight personnel was one of the essential functions of Geiger's command at Quantico.

With the recent experience gained at the Army War College Geiger was frequently called upon to lecture before the student body at the Marine Corps Schools. His subject matter invariably stressed the need for establishing a training center for joint air-ground operations and an aerial observer's course for all line and aviation officers. Additionally, Geiger, echoing Major Brainard's earlier entreaties, strongly advocated that Marine pilots be assigned to escort carriers for use with the amphibious troops in assault landings. Another service which he performed was that of acting in an advisory capacity to Colonel Turner in formulating plans for the future employment of Marine Aviation including the preparation of related estimates and budgets.

Through no fault of his own Geiger became indirectly involved in the running feud between his immediate superior, General Butler, and President Hoover's Secretary of the Navy, Mr. Charles Francis Adams. Taciturn and inclined to be somewhat of an introvert, Mr. Adams' temperament and demeanor were diametrically opposed to Butler's outspokenness and showmanship, and there was clearly no love lost between the two parties. Furthermore, the Secretary, who had a deep interest in maritime affairs and was an avid yachtsman, was noticeably partial to the Navy at the expense of the Marine Corps, and was very intolerant of some of the latter's activities on the grounds that they were a waste of money. He was especially critical of Marine Aviation which he regarded as an unnecessary duplication, and he did not hesitate to state that the Navy could do any flying which the Marine Corps wanted. On one of his visits to Quantico, in July 1930, Mr. Adams provoked Butler, and embarrassed Geiger, at an inspection of the air squadrons, immediately following an impressive aerial display and formation flight staged for his benefit. Picking up a single blade of grass, Mr. Adams wandered about among the parked planes until he found a minuscule hole in the fabric wing of one of them, into which he plunged the green sliver accompanied with a sharp admonition to the General that the latter had been lax in his attention to the state of his command. To make a critical situation even more desperate, Secretary Adams then proceeded to berate Butler, again in Geiger's presence, for the expenses incurred in the enlargement of Brown Field, seemingly oblivious of the well established fact that one of the reason for the extension advanced by the Navy's Civil Engineer Corps had been expressly designed to fill in some of Quantico's swamp lands, which otherwise afforded a magnificent breeding ground for the Post's countless mosquitoes.

Aware that the powder train leading to the central magazine had commenced to smoulder and that the eventual blow-up was only a matter of time, Geiger resolved that given half a chance he would stand clear of the blast by making his presence scarce. He got his opportunity sooner than he had expected, for early in September a tropical hurricane of violent intensity struck the eastern section of the Island of Hispaniola, killing some 2,000 Dominicans and leveling most of the ancient City of Santo Domingo. The holocaust overnight also propelled into the driver's seat the erstwhile commander of the Republic's Marine trained *Policia Nacional Dominicana,* Rafael Leonidas Trujillo Molina. Having but a few days previously taken over the position of the country's Chief Executive after a bloodless revolution, the new incumbent had been given a most fortuitous chance to bring order out of chaos. The American Red Cross and other agencies promised speedy relief, and Marine Aviation was selected as the means to transport medical supplies, clothing, and food from the United States to Santo Domingo.

Assigned the responsibility for the aerial delivery of the relief materials, Geiger flew from Hampton Roads to Santo Domingo in a heavily laden *Ford* tri-motor (A–8273) accompanied by two Navy transport aircraft, arriving at his destination on 13 September. An incident of the particular flight provided the basis of an anecdote relating to Geiger's imperturbability. Flying over the Caribbean, the formation ran into a severe tropical storm. One of the Navy pilots, fearful of the ominous black clouds, nervously radioed back to the flight leader: "What about the storm?" Never known to concern himself unduly with unfavorable weather conditions, Geiger's instantaneous response was typical of the man: "Well, what about it?" he spat back into the intercom, and not one whit dismayed by the approaching squalls, kept straight on without varying his course a single degree.

After delivering his initial load at Santo Domingo's devastated capital, Geiger flew back to Port-au-Prince. There, he set up an advance base and field depot at Bowen Field, and drawing upon the services of Major Evans' VO–9M proceeded to inaugurate an air shuttle service between Haiti and the Dominican Republic to deliver further stocks of emergency supplies which had been brought to Port-au-Prince via ship from Charleston and

Guantanamo Bay. This turned out to be a very satisfactory arrangement, and in due course Geiger received Letters of Commendation from both the Secretary of the Navy and the American Red Cross for his skillful handling of the situation. Ever mindful of the value of good public relations—especially with the United States—President Trujillo outdid the American authorities by means of an Executive Decree conferring the award of the Dominican Medal of Military Merit on Major Geiger for "valuable and self-sacrificing services, piloting the first rescue aircraft, and for generous contribution to rescue work." Having evidenced a strong liking for the Republic's heady brand of cigars, Geiger unexpectedly found himself the recipient of not just one free box, but a standing offer on the part of Santo Domingo's President to insure that in future the Major's stock did not run dry, and for the rest of his life Geiger was more than amply supplied with samples of Trujillo's personal selection, complete with the latter's portrait embossed on the band.

Less than six months later, a set of near similar circumstances in Nicaragua furnished Geiger with another occasion to prove to Secretary Adams that the Marines' air arm could deliver the goods on an on-call basis. In March 1931 Managua was shaken to bits by a violent earthquake. This was followed by an uncontrolled fire of such proportions that the few city edifices which had managed to survive the initial tremors were summarily burnt to the ground. The Brigade Commander, Brigadier General Frederick Bradman, at once sent out a call for assistance, and for a second time Quantico's air squadrons were handed a relief mission. Departing from Brown Field on 5 April, Geiger piloted a *Fokker* transport (A–8018) to Hampton Roads to load badly needed medical supplies, and three days later arrived without incident at Managua, stops having been made en route for fueling in Cuba and Honduras.

Assigned temporary additional duty with Major Mitchell's VO–7M, Geiger pitched in along with other Marine officials present at the capital to assist in the setting up of first-aid and food distribution centers for the needy. After several weeks the situation calmed down to the extent he felt free to request return to Quantico. This was granted, but before his departure he flew north to Jinotega in mid-April in a *Corsair* in order to acquaint himself with some of the conditions Marine pilots had to face in their patrolling and supply operations in support of the Brigade in the field. Leaving the *Fokker* at Managua to reinforce the transport group stationed there, Geiger boarded the train and took passage to Corinto, thus duplicating the same trip he had taken over the line eighteen years before as a Lieutenant during the First Nicaraguan Intervention. At that port he embarked in the *USAT Grant,* and after landing at Brooklyn, New York, on 20 April, reported to Quantico's Brigade Commander the following day. Again as in Santo Domingo, his rescue mission did not pass unrewarded: at the next session of the Nicaraguan Congress, the Chief Executive, General Jose Moncada, signed a Presidential Decree granting Geiger the award of the Nicaraguan Medal of Distinction for his mercy flight to the Republic's devastated capital.

Notwithstanding the favorable light which Geiger had directed upon Marine Aviation as the result of his two emergency flights to the Caribbean and Central America, it was doubly fortunate for him personally that he had perforce been absent from Quantico during part of General Butler's final tenure of office as its Post Commander. By the time Geiger had resumed his normal duties at Brown Field in April 1931, General Butler's long drawn-out quarrel with Secretary Adams was all over but the shouting. Incensed by some of Butler's public utterances, Adams had so lost patience he had ordered the General relieved of duty and placed under arrest, to await trial by General Court-Martial. Although Butler was able to quash the disciplinary proceedings, and was restored to duty, his future value to the Corps was so diminished he had no other alternative but to request retirement. This was accordingly conceded, but it is significant to note that one of his last acts while in command at Quantico was to write Geiger a Letter of Commendation, congratulating the Major for his outstanding services as the Commanding Officer, Air Squadrons, East Coast Expeditionary Force. Never known to be overly free with the conferring of awards, Butler was nevertheless always loyal to his subordinates, and as for Geiger, until the very last moment Butler remained in command at Quantico, there was no other officer on the Post more faithful or devoted to his immediate superior than was the Major to his lifelong friend and benefactor.

Inwardly disturbed by the chain of events culminating in General Butler's retirement from active duty, Geiger decided that the best cure for his worries was to keep himself fully occupied, and during the late spring and summer of 1931 he spent much time as an official observer at certain of the Army Air Corps' exercises and demonstrations at Dayton's Wright Field. If Butler's removal from the scene had upset him, it was only surpassed by the news of Colonel Turner's untimely death on 28 October. Having flown to Gonaives, Haiti, to inspect a landing field, Turner, on dismounting from his *Sikorsky* amphibian had the misfortune to walk inadvertently into the tip of one of the plane's still revolving propeller blades. Horribly injured, he had somehow managed to cling onto life for three days after the accident, succumbing at length to shock and loss of blood as a patient in the Brigade Hospital at Port-au-Prince.

Although on a technicality Geiger was not then by virtue of date of rank the senior aviator of the Corps, being junior to Major Rowell in command of Air Squadrons, West Coast Expeditionary Force, at San Diego, he was nevertheless the Corps' most experienced pilot, then in an active flight status. Herein, he had originally won his wings in June 1917, whereas Rowell had not become an aviator until November 1922. At any rate, there was no doubt in the mind of the Major General Commandant as to Geiger's fitness for a position of responsibility; consequently, on 31 October the Major received orders transferring him from Quantico to Headquarters for assignment as the Officer-in-Charge, Marine Corps Aviation, to fill the billet brought about by Colonel Turner's demise.

Chapter VIII

Commanding Officer, Air One

The position and duties of the Officer-in-Charge, Marine Aviation, having been progressively enlarged during the 1920's, some amplification of the nature and inherent responsibilities of Major Geiger's newly assigned billet at Headquarters would seem indicated. By January 1932 it had become quite evident that the Chief of the Marines' air arm was serving in a dual if not a triple capacity. Fundamentally charged with administration, training, and operations of Marine Aviation, his office as such constituted a division of Headquarters (it was not made an independent section until 1935), besides being attached to the Navy's Bureau of Aeronautics. The Officer-in-Charge consequently served as an adviser to the Major General Commandant on all aviation matters with additional duties as the liaison officer between the Marine Corps and the Bureau of Aeronautics as well as the Bureaus of Engineering, Ordnance, and Supplies and Accounts. Two of his assistants worked under his direct supervision: the Personnel Officer, and the Officer-in-Charge, Marine Aviation Reserve. Two other officials, the Materiel Officer and the Plans Officer, occupied office space in the adjacent Bureau of Aeronautics. Although the control of aviation personnel and actual command was vested in the Commandant, the number of officers and enlisted men assigned to aviation duty, their aircraft (including radio and ordnance), and their training remained the primary responsibility of the Bureau of Aeronautics, Marine Aviation along with the Marine Corps as a whole being controlled by the policies of the Navy, and employed as directed by the Chief of Naval Operations.

By 1932 it had become firmly established that the basic

function of Marine Aviation was that of an adjunct of an advance base force in connection with naval operations; i.e., to support landing forces in amphibious assaults designed to seize and to defend advance naval bases for the fleet, as well as for the support of related troop activities in the field incident to such operations. It was not contemplated that Marine Aviation would operate from naval vessels but rather from shore bases, although it was readily conceded that under certain conditions—such as long-range expeditionary missions—Marine pilots and planes would of necessity have to serve aboard Navy carriers, having none of their own. Accordingly, Marine Aviation had as its secondary role that of providing replacement squadrons for carrier-based, naval aircraft.

To implement this subsidiary mission, commencing in November 1931 and continuing through November 1934 (by which date the Fleet Marine Force had become a functional reality), two Marine squadrons were attached to fleet carriers on a rotational basis: VS—14M, initially commanded by Captain William J. Wallace, aboard *USS Saratoga,* and VS—15M, originally led by First Lieutenant William O. Brice, in *USS Lexington.* Each squadron was composed of 8 pilot officers and 36 enlisted mechanics and radio operators, and was equipped with a 6—plane division of *Vought Corsairs (02U—2's),* later replaced by *SU—1/2/3's.* During its three-year assignment to carrier duty it is pertinent to mention that almost two thirds of Marine Aviation's entire stock of naval aviators served aboard one or the other of the two aforementioned carriers. Despite the fact that there were no Marine bombardment, torpedo, or attack squadrons, its observation and fighting groups were trained to conduct light bombardment missions besides attack or ground strafing. As for Major Geiger, it was characteristic of him to have requested instruction in carrier operations and techniques including landings and take-offs, and to have successfully qualified as a carrier pilot at Norfolk and at Hampton Roads in 1931 prior to detailing junior Marine aviators to seagoing billets. In the same fashion he had additionally performed several familiarization flights aboard Navy dirigibles at Lakehurst's Naval Air Station to keep in touch with contemporary lighter-than-air developments, following the disestablishment of the Marines' one and only balloon squadron at Quantico.

161

It was singularly fortunate that both the Major General Commandant, Ben H. Fuller, and his recently appointed Chief of Aviation were capable individuals, for by 1932 the effects of the National Economic Depression were making their presence felt in numerous ways, several of which were closely allied to the future of the Marine Corps. If the armed services in general were likely targets for budget cuts, the Marine Corps in particular seemingly enjoyed the dubious distinction of being especially singled out to bear the main brunt of the Chief Executive's and Congress' economy axe. Granted that General Fuller had been able to obtain sufficient funds to maintain the Corps' enlisted strength at 17,500 for the Fiscal Year ending 30 June 1932, he was informed that for the ensuing twelve months he would somehow have to carry on with a reduced complement of 15,343. To make the bitter pill all the more difficult to swallow, President Hoover in December 1932 strongly suggested a further decrease to 13,600. To this dire implication General Fuller forthwith replied that such a 22% forced reduction in the size of the Corps would entail the closing of the East Coast Recruit Depot at Parris Island, and would ultimately result in the extinction of the already far under-strength expeditionary forces. Faced with the prospect of withdrawing all Marines, ground and air, from Haiti, Nicaragua, and China (regardless of the fact that their services had been at a premium to restore order and to maintain the peace in those countries), and having the Corps shorn of all of its functions other than to provide ships' detachments and to stand guard over Navy Yards at home and overseas, there would therefore be no further requirement for Marine Aviation inasmuch as there would no longer be expeditionary troops for it to support. Mr. Hoover, however, underestimated the power of the press and the influence of Congress which combined to vote down his proposed cut in early 1933, and restored the Corps' strength to the 15,343 figure, but it had been a very near thing, and the fate of the Marine Corps was to remain an uncertain issue for at least another year.

Under the circumstances Geiger's position at Headquarters as General Fuller's principal counselor on aviation affairs became all the more important, one of the Major's more significant tasks being the preparation of aviation estimates and his appearance to testify in their behalf in the Hearings for the Navy Department's annual Appropriation Bills. As an example, the Appropriation Act

1914 – Rifle Team, Legation Guard, Peking, China
Lieutenant Geiger, third from right

1916 – Naval Air Station,
Pensacola, Florida

Lieutenant Geiger
student naval aviator

1916 — Curtiss Training Seaplane Pensacola
Lieutenant Geiger about to solo

1918 — Naval Station,
Miami, Florida

Captain Geiger
prior to departure for France

1920 — Landing Strip, Santo Domingo, Dominican Republic
Arrival of first military aircraft, Major Geiger, pilot

1923 — Autumn Maneuvers with the 3rd Marine Brigade
Forced landing in a Virginia tree, Captain Davis, pilot.

1923 – Marine Corps Air Station, Quantico, Virginia.
Major Geiger, C.O. 1st Aviation Group, son and daughter

1923 – 1st Marine Aviation Group
East Coast Expeditionary
Force, Quantico

Major Geiger, C.O. 1st
Marine Aviation Group

1923 – Marine Corps Air Station, Quantico, Virginia
Termination of cross-country Bomber flight, Major Geiger, center.

1927 – Port-au-Prince, Haiti
Major Geiger, C.O.,
VO-9M, with parrott pets

1936 — Marine Corps Air Station
Quantico, Virginia

Colonel Geiger, C.O. Aircraft One
Fleet Marine Force, Quantico

1937 — Winter Maneuvers
Culebra, West Indies

Colonel Geiger, C.O. Aircraft One
Fleet Marine Force, Quantico

1941 – Marine Corps Air Station
Quantico, Virginia

Brigadier General Geiger
Commanding 1st Marine
Air Wing, FMF

1943
Headquarters U.S. Marine Corps
Washington, D.C.

Major General Geiger
Director, Marine Corps Aviation

1943 – Operation CHERRYBLOSSOM (Bougainville)
Major General Geiger, Commanding I Marine Amphibious Corps
Admiral Halsey, second from left

1944
Operation STEVEDORE (Guam)
Major General Geiger
Commanding III Marine
Amphibious Corps, with "Bozo"

1945 – Operation ICEBERG (Okinawa)
Major General Geiger, Commanding III Marine Amphibious Corps
at Forward Observation Post, 3 miles north of Naha

1945
Operation ICEBERG (Okinawa)
Lieutenant General Geiger
Commanding U.S. TENTH ARMY

1945 – Tokyo, Japan, prior to official surrender. Lieutenant General Geiger, Commanding General, Fleet Marine Force, Pacific, "collecting the bet"

1958
Marine Corps Education Center
Quantico, Virginia

Dedication Geiger Hall
Brigadier General Krulak
and Mrs. Geiger

for Fiscal Year 1932 restricted the amount of pay "for making aerial flights" to $138,148.00, thereby practically freezing the number of Marine pilots entitled to draw flight pay. During that accounting period a total of 130 aviators could be maintained, but for the next Fiscal Year it had dropped to 124 (representing 4 fatalities, 1 death from disease, and 1 officer discharged for violation of flying regulations). For Fiscal 1934, no increase could be provided and only 1 promotion could be effected. With regard to Marine aircraft, the number of operational squadrons had been reduced to eight, not counting the two serving in *Saratoga* and *Lexington;* meanwhile, the total number of planes was held to 90 and enlisted strength kept at approximately 900. After December 1932 flight operations ceased in Nicaragua, permitting the return of the two squadrons which had served there to Quantico. The following year the squadron at Port-au-Prince was disbanded along with the First Marine Brigade. The scouting squadron formerly stationed at Guam having long since been withdrawn as an economy measure, Marine Aviation in time became about equally consolidated at Quantico and San Diego, thus making possible further economies and a stricter husbanding of its curtailed resources.

Having no desire to devote all of his energies to pencil-pushing and paper-shuffling at Headquarters, Geiger felt that he could be of far greater value out in the field with the operational forces. Whenever possible he engaged in long distance flights, visiting all of the existing airfields and installations at home and abroad. His inspection tours took him to Nicaragua in late 1932, immediately prior to the departure of the Second Marine Brigade, and to Haiti in 1933, for the purpose of arranging the wind-up of VO–9M's affairs in the latter Republic. Keenly aware of the favorable publicity to the Corps as a whole which could be rendered by Marine aviation, Geiger favored maximum participation by squadron pilots in all of the many scheduled aerial pageants and parades from Montreal to Miami and from Cleveland to Los Angeles. Flying *Curtiss Helldivers (02C–1's), Boeing* light bombers *(F4B–3's)* and speedy fighters *(F4B–4's),* Marine aces on their return from the tropics thrilled the crowds in the grandstands with their skillful acrobatics and tight formation flights (the plane wing tips frequently being tied together), along with the intricate evolutions of the "Lufberry Circle," and their breath-taking demonstrations of glide and dive-bombing at full power. The opening of nearly every civilian airport of any consequence was marked by their colorful presence, and their performance at the inauguration of an air meet or a speed contest was invariably one of the more spectacular features on the program of events.

It was well that Geiger had made the decision not to be confined to a mahogany desk in an office, for notwithstanding his attempts to keep his weight in check by a rigorous course of daily calisthenics, it was difficult for him to remain slim and trim. Standing 5' 8" he was a stocky 198-pounder in his mid-40's, and he required fresh air and outdoor exercise to keep in shape. According to the records of his Flight Physical Examination, administered on 24 December 1931, he was found "overweight, 31 pounds," and with "defective hearing, each ear." The Medical Officer, however, realized that Geiger was doing everything possible to take care of himself as evidenced by the notation: "It is the opinion of this Bureau (i.e., Medicine and Surgery) that these defects in the present degree are not disqualifying, at the present time." Nevertheless he had been given fair warning, and for the rest of his life he labored with might and main—on the golf course and in the hand and volley ball courts—to maintain himself in decent physical condition.

Constantly on the go from morning to night, and frequently out of town over week-ends—for Geiger always seemed to do his best when there was lots of work to be done—he had scant opportunities to be with his family. At the time of his transfer from Quantico to Headquarters, he had decided that rather than pay Washington's high rentals it would be wiser for him to purchase a residence. With this idea in mind he bought a small house on 44th Street, N.W., in Foxhall Village, which, with the passage of time turned out to be a very astute investment. With both children now away at school all day, Eunice had time on her hands, and it was at this period that following the precedent established by Mrs. Hoover, she commenced to take a very active part in the Girl Scout Movement as well as the American Red Cross. About the only chance her husband could be reunited with his family was during periods of leave, which, no thanks to the Economy Act of 1933, meant that he was deprived of his pay for those intervals. Despite this temporary curtailment of his only source of income, whenever affairs quieted down to the extent he could take two week's leave, Geiger would pack up the family in their automobile, and they would drive south to Pensacola where they could all swim and ride horseback to their hearts content.

On one of those occasions there occurred an incident which even thirty years after the event is clearly remembered by his wife and family. Shortly after their arrival at the old homestead overlooking Escambia Bay, one of Roy's local friends and immediate neighbors dropped by one evening to pay his respects, and brought along as a sample a 5-gallon cask of what he claimed was very fine Bourbon Whisky. At that time although the provisions of the Volstead Act had been relaxed to the degree that light wines and so-called 3.2 beer were considered reasonably fit for consumption by the adult American public, anything more lethal was regarded with a very jaundiced eye and was fair game for Federal Revenue Agents. In spite of his friend's insistence that the liquor had been properly aged, Geiger decided that another week or two of mellowing in the wooden keg would do it no harm, and rather than draw the bung there and then, he persuaded its co-owner that it would be more prudent to let it ripen before sampling its contents.

Sitting out on the front porch one late afternoon, rocking the treasured cask back and forth on his knees, Geiger was startled out of his lethargy by the ringing of the telephone. The call was a long-distance communication from Headquarters requesting his return and peremptorily cancelling the remainder of his leave. While the family rushed around hurriedly packing up their clothing and loading the car, Geiger remained immobile trying to figure out what should be done with the whisky. In desperation (for his friend was out of town on business), he finally came to the conclusion that rather than transport the keg back to Washington, the smartest thing to do was to hide it, and thus preserve it intact until some future period of leave. Calling to his son, Roy Junior, he instructed him to run down the way to fetch a young colored boy, who helped maintain the grounds, and to bring back on his return a pick and shovel from the tool shed.

Quite unperturbed by his wife and daughter, now dressed for the pending motor trip and seated in the car fuming at the unexpected delay, Geiger proceeded to look about for a likely spot in the front yard to serve as a cache for the Bourbon. At length he selected a site, and after carefully pacing off the distances and taking the bearings from such reference points as the front steps, the bird bath, and a few prominent trees, transferred the data to a scrap of paper taken from his wallet. With the arrival of his two assistants he grasped the spade and started to dig. Young Roy naturally thought that a shallow hole or trench, perhaps a foot or more in depth covered by a flat rock, would suffice, but he soon found that he had woefully underestimated his father's prowess as an excavator. After an hour of steady digging—and by this time it was getting dark—the lad peered over the edge of the pit, which was so deep he could look right down on top of his father's head. After gently lowering the cask to the bottom of what appeared to be a 6-foot chasm, the two boys helped Geiger climb out of the abyss of his own making, and the trio pitched in together to shovel back the earth.

Both of the lads thought the matter was over and done with, but to their surprise Geiger announced that the job was far from completed. Forthwith, under his direction they cut pine boughs to serve as rakes and brooms and gathered baskets of dry leaves and grass cuttings. As young Roy was to state many years later, that night he learned more about the practical art and science of hasty entrenchments, concealment, and camouflage than he was to acquire until his plebe year course in military engineering and field fortifications at West Point. It required almost another hour of steady labor until his father was thoroughly satisfied that all traces of the subterranean hiding place had been adequately screened from prying eyes. Then and only then could he be prevailed upon to change his clothes and to commence the long hot drive back to Washington.

The incident, of course, had the usual sequence. Geiger soon lost or otherwise mislaid the vital bit of paper with its cryptic calculations, and with its disappearance guesswork had to take over the job of mathematical triangulation. On his next trip back to Pensacola Geiger tried in vain to remember the location of his underground treasure trove. Thereafter, and for the ensuing fifteen years one of his favorite forms of outdoor diversion during leaves at Pensacola was to probe about with an iron rod and to dig up various portions of the front yard; on occasion the lawn and the shrubbery looked like a miniature reproduction of a portion of the Western Front much to his wife's disgust and the gardener's utter despair. He was never successful in his endless quest, and to the best of the knowledge of all parties concerned who survived him, somewhere, 6-feet deep under the greensward there reposes to this day what by all rights should be a rare treat to a connoisseur of 30-plus-year old, 100 proof, aged corn whisky.

If his first two years as the Chief of Marine Aviation had been busy ones, the remaining two were equally stimulating, involving considerable flying about the country. Luckily, there were no accidents or narrow escapes similar to the situation which had transpired in early April 1933. Invited by Admiral William Moffett and his old friend of Pensacola's flying school days, Harry Cecil, now as Commander, to make an extended test hop in the new dirigible, *USS Akron,* Geiger had accepted the invitation with alacrity, and had made plans to fly in his own plane from Anacostia to Lakehurst where the *Akron* was hangared. At the very last moment he had to back out due to other more pressing matters at Headquarters, and was thus spared the fate of those 73 members of the dirigible's complement, who perished in a violent storm over the Jersey Coast in one of the greatest peacetime disasters suffered by Naval Aviation.

Throughout 1934 there was plenty of work to keep him busily occupied at Washington and at Quantico for the new concept of the Fleet Marine Force had recently been adopted, thereby placing the majority of the Corps' operating forces, land and air, under the direct tactical command of the Commander-in-Chief U.S. Fleet, and now included in the Fleet organization as one of its integral parts. In spite of the fact that the units assigned to the new Force (which replaced the former East and West Coast Expeditionary Forces) were largely skeletonized because of lack of sufficient funds for the first two years of its existence, the foundations for a true force-in-readiness, composed of balanced arms, had been well established, and Marine Aviation's role had been clearly delineated. To insure that the aerial components reached a satisfactory condition of operational alertness for their closely integrated role under the new framework, Geiger undertook a series of cross-country flights commencing in April 1934. The senior member of the Aviation Board of Inspection for Regular as well as Reserve air units and station facilities, he first visited Air Two, now a part of the Second Marine Brigade, FMF, at San Diego, and from there proceeded northward to Long Beach, Oakland, and Seattle, with a brief stop at Minneapolis on his way home.

By the time autumn had rolled around the provisions of the much discussed Selection (Personnel) Bill enacted the preceding May had begun to take effect. To his delight—and after thirteen and one half years in grade—the Major turned in his pair of gold oak leaves for a Lieutenant Colonel's set of silver ones, on 31 October (with date of rank 29 May 1934). Of even greater significance was the subsequent abolition of the Economy Act, which restored the 15% pay cut which had been imposed on all Federal employees for two years, thereby immeasurably boosting the morale of all members of the armed services after an enforced period of austerity existence.

Aside from his participation as an observer at Fleet Landing Exercise No. 1. held at Culebra in January and February 1935, wherein one of Quantico's observation squadrons had taken an active part along with the First Marine Brigade and fleet units of the Navy's Scouting Force, Geiger devoted much of his attention to formulating plans designed to remove Marine Aviation from the Division of Operations and Training at Headquarters with the intention of making it an independent section under the Major General Commandant. With the gradual increase in the number of its pilots and planes and the extension of the scope of its activities, Geiger was convinced that Marine Aviation was eminently worthy of a more exalted level within the organizational structure and framework of the Corps' hierarchy of command. By no means was his conviction a thinly-veiled plot to advance the mere lineal position of the Officer-in-Charge, but rather was predicated on his firm belief that aviation had earned the right to have a greater say in the conduct of its affairs, and should be correspondingly represented at Headquarters. In this respect Geiger was also remarkably prescient of coming events: to him it was essential that the correct groundwork be laid well in advance lest Marine Aviation at some future date find itself hamstrung with an archaic command arrangement wildly out of date with contemplated developments. Herein, he had just cause for concern, for before the passage of the Vinson-Trammel Act (the Naval Parity Bill of 27 March 1934) the Navy was limited to 1,000 aircraft and the Marine Corps to 100, but it was now estimated that the Navy would need 1,910 planes and Marine Aviation about 175. To man the latter's scout bombers and fighters the appropriations for Fiscal Year 1935 called for 128 Marine pilots, while the number for Fiscal 1936 had been tentatively set at 140. If and when the Marine Air Program were to be fully implemented, 185 aviators would be required for the expected 175-plane air force.

Therefore, he recommended the creation of an Assistant to the Major General Commandant to be entrusted with all pertinent aviation matters, the incumbent to be an aviator with the permanent rank of either Lieutenant Colonel or Colonel, but with temporary rank while in office as a Brigadier General. It was intended that this official should serve for a period of four years, and that his appointment by the President would be subject to the advice and recommendation of the Major General Commandant, and to confirmation by the Senate. To a degree Geiger's foresight and powers of persuasion were shortly to be realized: within a week of his relinquishing command to his designated relief, Marine Aviation was reconstituted as an independent section, and the following year the title of Officer-in-Charge was altered to Director of Aviation with division status as a part of the Bureau of Aeronautics. With regard to his suggested increase in rank for that officer, it took the onset of a second world conflict to bring that to pass, by which time the Marines' air arm was counting its numbers in terms of Groups rather than Squadrons. A final bit of legislation on Capitol Hill in which Geiger was notably concerned was that pertaining to the revitalization of the Reserve Pilot Program, and he was more than gratified to note the passage of the Naval Aviation Cadet Act of 1935, which made provision for extended periods of active duty with Regular components by aspirant fliers drawn from civil life.

After some three and one half years of duty at Headquarters it was high time for Geiger to spring himself loose from his plate glass enclosure in Washington's "Main Navy" at 19th Street and Constitution Avenue, and to seek a welcome change from the smoke-filled chambers of the Senate Naval Affairs Committee in the form of an open-air cockpit. Much as he had enjoyed his tour of duty at the very seat of the Corps' command, he was anxious to depart and to become a more active participant in the expanding aviation orgaizations which he had helped to create. With orders to proceed to Quantico to assume command of its newly designated Aviation Group attached to the First Marine Brigade, FMF—Air

One—on 1 June 1935 he was relieved by Lieutenant Colonel Ross E. Rowell, and departed without further delay for Turner Field. Hardly had he been given time to conduct more than a cursory inspection of his Group but that Geiger took off with VF—9M for Toronto to take part in the Canadian National Air Pageant held at the City Race Track and Exhibition Grounds. The lead plane in a formation of 19 *Boeing* fighters arranged in two V—shaped echelons, each of 9 aircraft, the Squadron Leader put on a particularly impressive air show and demonstration of 40 minutes' duration, resulting in much favorable publicity and comment on both sides of the Border. Later that summer—just to keep his hand in—Geiger performed at least two long-distance flights from Quantico on a temporary additional duty basis, flying to Pensacola in a *Vought Corsair* and to Montgomery's Maxwell Field in a *Curtiss Helldiver.*

By early autumn, in preparation for the forthcoming winter maneuvers, a gradual transition was commenced at Air One. One of its two Observation Squadrons (VO—9M) was converted into a dive-bomber unit (VB—6M), replacing its *Vought* scouts with the newly adopted *Great Lakes (BG—1)* bombers, while the Utility Squadron (VJ—6M) was provided with two of the all-metal, twin-engine fast monoplane transports, *Douglas R2D—1's,* in lieu of the now outmoded *Curtiss Condors.* Two of the first of a long line of versatile amphibians, the *Grumman JF—1's,* were introduced, and among the aircraft assigned ·to the Service Squadron were two *BG—1's* (A—9220 and A—9854), especially fitted as command planes for the Group Leader. With its complement of some 64 operational aircraft Air One represented 56% of the total stock of Marine Aviation's 114 planes, and under Geiger's dynamic leadership soon became a powerful adjunct to the Brigade's striking force.

Back in his chosen element the Group Leader thrived in his new assignment. Long interested in the development and perfection of aerial navigation, throughout the fall and early winter Geiger pioneered in the adoption of instrument flying for his pilots, regardless of the fact that at that time training in the use of mechanical, directional aids or synthetic devices was regarded with considerable skepticism by all but a very few of the Navy and Army Air Corps aviators. Setting up a small-scale instrument indoctrination and training program in one of the hangars at

Turner Field, Geiger led the pack of an ever increasing number of converts in the manipulation of radio direction finders, and stimulated interest in the subsequent installation of Link trainers. In the air he delighted to coat the canopy of his *Great Lakes* dive-bomber with *Bon Ami* soap solution, and to prove that a pilot could "fly blind," on instruments alone, by making a series of runs without observation from Quantico to New York's Lake Placid. Using instruments on every possible occasion in preference to flying contact, within a very short space of time he built up a creditable number of hours air-borne, flying exclusively on navigational appliances, and he soon achieved the well deserved reputation of becoming known as one of the most highly skilled instrument pilot-navigators among the ranks of both military as well as naval aviators.

With the arrival of 1936 Air One was amply prepared to demonstrate its worth. During the months of January and February it performed a stellar role in Fleet Landing Exercise No. 2. Leading a mass flight of fifty planes from Quantico to Culebra (via San Juan, Puerto Rico), Geiger brought his Group south to the maneuver area without accident or delay to mar the 2,150-mile hop over land and water. With Group Headquarters and two squadrons based at San Juan's Isla Grande Airport, and one each at landing strips at Culebra and at St. Thomas in the Virgin Islands, the entire unit participated daily for several weeks with the attack and landing force elements in simulated assaults against Culebra's defenders. Making live machine gun and bombing runs against selected beach targets, the various squadrons conducted innumerable daytime sorties and air strikes, and in addition to laying smoke over the beaches to screen the boat landings, spotted for ships' gunfire, and flew reconnaissance and photographic missions on call. The net result of the extensive maneuvers was to prove that the procedures set down in the *Tentative Manual for Landing Operations (1934)* were fundamentally sound, although it was noticeably apparent that in an actual operation specially designed attack aircraft mounting heavier armament and capable of delivering larger bomb loads would be far preferable to the fighter-observation planes with which the Group had been supplied.

On the return of Air One to Turner Field there seemed little more to which its Group Leader could aspire. Now at age 51 he was still in his prime, and with 29 years of prior service, of which 19 had been devoted to aviation duty, he seemed completely capable of surmounting any challenge which came his way in the foreseeable future. With more than 2,500 hours of flight time to his credit Geiger was by far the most experienced Marine aviator then in an active flight status, and was only surpassed in rank by Colonel Rowell, the Director of Aviation. In the process Geiger had become somewhat of a living legend thanks to some of his aerial feats, and in the eyes of his associates no other Marine pilot was more respected for his demonstrated fearlessness or more admired for his proven ability as a leader. Assuredly he was not found wanting by his superiors, for in December 1936 he was selected for the grade of Colonel, and the following March his appointment was confirmed and his promotion effected.

For the moment, Geiger had the rare opportunity to catch his breath and to find enjoyment in his non-flying hours watching his children attain maturity; meanwhile, he was still active enough to enjoy riding at the Post Stables and polo on the artillery drill grounds. Besides, he was determined to improve his golf score, and unless it were raining in torrents, Saturday afternoons were spent on Quantico's golf course. These lengthy sessions were a never ending source of wonder and amazement to the more venturesome who dared to stand on the sidelines, so to speak, and to watch the proceedings. The charter member of a staunch and relentless foursome, Geiger was invariably accompanied on his rounds by Colonel Edward Osterman, then the Chief of Staff at the Marine Barracks, by Major William McKittrick, one of Squadron Leaders of Air One, and by some junior member from the Staff of the Brigade Commander, more or less detailed to the job for the afternoon similar to an Officer of the Day. With an unofficial slogan patterned after the defenders of the Verdun Forts—"They Shall Not Pass"—the quartet became a formidable obstacle to any other more rapidly moving groups—foursomes or twosomes—should those players have the temerity to even suggest that they be allowed to pass through the road-block. And woe betide the fate of any young Lieutenant or Captain who had the misfortune to drive up the fairway behind Geiger and his party and to shout "Fore!"

According to his son who occasionally played golf with his father, the latter was deadly with his approach shots. Around the green with mashie or niblick Geiger was very accurate, and he seldom failed to hole his ball (provided it still retained a reasonable facsimile of its original, spherical shape) in two putts. On the tee or in the fairway it was quite a different story. If he could control his irons with uncanny accuracy the reverse was true of his wooden clubs: for all the good they did him, he might just as well have swung a croquet mallet. With a tendency to drop his right shoulder on the forward part of his drives, all too frequently he would strike the ground several inches behind the teed-up ball, thereby cutting up the sod and driving the ball barely more than 25 yards. To compensate for this irregularity he would sometimes lower the club head a little too late, with the result that he would either "top" the ball or drive it so hard into the turf that it would have to be dug out before he could take another shot.

On one occasion which General McKittrick can clearly recall to this day, Geiger took a vicious swipe at the ball with his driver which threw up a shovelful of dirt but otherwise failed to move the ball further toward the pin than the edge of the tee. Staring fixedly at his handiwork for a good thirty seconds, Geiger eventually raised his head and with a grin turned to his partner and stated: "My God, Mac, I hit it hard enough to start a train!" A true sportsman to the very core such setbacks failed to discourage his enthusiasm, and he never gave up trying to improve his medal score. As for Quantico's links, on Monday mornings the grounds-keeper could easily trace the blow-by-blow trail of the foursome's week-end foray, for although Geiger was always careful to replace his divots on the fairways (and some of them were as large as pie pans), there wasn't much he could do to resurface the tees, many of which appeared to have been grazed by a ricocheting 6 in. artillery projectile.

With respect to his son and daughter, both now in their 'teens, if some of his mannerisms seemed a bit peculiar to them, no less was their father bewildered by many of their antics. They had come to regard "Daddy" as kind of a gruff but nevertheless good-natured bear who growled every now and then, and stood up on his haunches when he got ruffled. Cornered or pushed too far with bristles fully erect he was a rugged opponent, and any adversary would think twice before getting within range of his big paws. Over the years the children had learned to divine certain of his moods, and they could predict within reasonable limits their father's reaction to various situations by the tenor of his remarks. When "Daddy" said, "I *can't understand* why you want to do such-and-such," Roy and Joyce knew that he was annoyed, but that it was quite safe to continue with their entreaties. When the situation had developed to the second stage, "Daddy's" observation, "I *can't conceive,*" meant that they had at best no more than a fifty-fifty chance of bringing their father around to see their side of the argument. And when "Daddy" turned to his wife and barked, "Hon, it's *beyond my comprehension* why these children insist on doing this-and-that," it was patently obvious that the next best move was to break off the engagement as quickly as possible, and to look around for a suitable spot to serve as a cordon defense perimeter, preferably in sight and sound defilade, until the roaring died down. But it was always great sport and lots of fun to bait *Poppa Bear* in his den, and the children adored their father all the more for his outbursts of zeal within the family circle.

Likewise, it was during this tour of duty at Quantico that Geiger came into daily contact with some of the more outstanding non-commissioned officers and enlisted men assigned to aviation duty at Air One. One of those persons, who was very definitely "a character," was the crew chief selected to care for his command plane. In addition to serving as the machine's mechanic and radio operator, Staff Sergeant (in time, Master Technical Sergeant) John Donato gradually assumed supplementary duties more or less as the Colonel's "Man Friday." He was extremely versatile, and being possessed of a very engaging personality and a tendency to be quite outspoken was literally cut out for the particular job. He was a man after the Colonel's heart, for he, too, had started at the very bottom, and had overcome no little adversity to make his way in the world.

Of Italian descent and born in one of Philadelphia's more depressed districts, Donato by the use of his fists and his wits had managed to rise above the squalor of his Oregon Avenue and South Broad Street environment by the simple expedient of enlisting in the Marine Corps in the mid-1920's. Requesting foreign duty he was forthwith packed off to Haiti to fill an aviation billet, and thus embarked on a rather fantastic career of more than twenty years' service with Marine Aviation, eventually receiving a commission during the Second World War. A member of Geiger's squadron at Port-au-Prince in 1927 (and an avid polo player), as a Corporal he soon proved himself to be a master mechanic and an expert rigger, and with such qualifications mixed with his ready wit and an almost overbearing self-confidence, he found himself, ten years later at Quantico, as the most likely candidate to fill the exacting demands required of the *Old Man's* rear-cockpit assistant and maintenance chief.

On his lengthy aerial flights with his superior up and down the Atlantic seaboard or back and forth across the Caribbean on maneuvers, there was comparatively little to occupy Donato's time and attention other than to man the plane's radio apparatus and to view the scenery. Equipped with dual receivers and transmitting keys, it was customary to leave both front and rear cockpit circuits open so that either pilot or radio operator could listen or communicate at will. According to Donato the Colonel had developed a harmless yet annoying trait of fingering the Morse sending key while in flight; meanwhile, he hummed snatches of tunes which happened to cross his mind, and kept time with the rhythm of the melody by tapping on the knob of the transmitting lever. Realizing that the Colonel was indulging in a little day-dreaming brought about by the monotonous hum of the plane's engine, Donato deemed it prudent not to disturb Geiger's blissful reverie. On the other hand, every time the *Old Man* tapped the knob, Donato got the full blast of the key clicks in both his ears. Rather than switch off his radio set he decided to put up with the distraction, fearing that if he closed down his circuit he might miss some important incoming message.

After several hours of this treatment Donato's patience became exhausted. More than a trifle upset he picked up the microphone of the plane's intercom, and having dialed the volume control to its maximum, bellowed into Geiger's earphones: "God damn it, Colonel, get your big mitts off that transmitter; you're driving me nuts back here!" Quick as a flash came back the pilot's retort: "OK, OK, Donato, keep your shirt on!" whereupon Geiger turned around in his seat and sheepishly grinned at his harassed companion. Back at the field on the completion of the flight, Geiger readily admitted that he had been at fault, and Donato, never known to apologize to anybody for anything, let the matter drop but not before he had gotten in the last word: "Hell, I just wanted you to know what was going on, Colonel, so I thought I'd better tell you, that's all." In later years Donato delighted to relate this little incident, which with the passage of time in the countless re-tellings was to become somewhat elaborated upon, but similar to other "tales" (such as the beer can spectacles with the cut-out railroad tracks presented to another pilot who always felt safer flying contact with the Florida East Coast Railway as his guide) became classic stories of Marine Aviation, part and parcel of its fabled lore. Parenthetically, Donato's verbal altercation with his superior was illustrative of the mutual respect the two parties had for one another. Donato knew that Geiger was at fault, and the best way to get him to admit it was to lay it on the line. The Colonel, in turn, in accepting the censure—not to mention the manner and the tone in which it had been delivered—showed that he could "take it" as well as "dish it out," for there were very few persons, regardless of rank or position, who ever dared to address Geiger in such fashion as his crew chief had employed.

At the conclusion of the first half of his four-year tour of duty as the commanding officer of Quantico's Air One, a comprehensive review of the changes and developments which had taken place in aviation since Lindbergh had completed his historic trans-Atlantic hop some ten years before was almost startling to contemplate. Gone was the old pull-through or "Armstrong System" for cranking a plane's motor. Even the elastic shock cord with the boot had given way to the inertia wind-up; the shotgun-shell starter had been introduced, and the push-button, electrical impulse starting gear was only a matter of time. Planes now had brakes—and even flaps—to reduce landing speed. Streamlined housings with covered controls, and sleek all-metal fuselages were taken for granted. Retractable landing gear had entered the picture, and folding wings to conserve storage space on carriers had proven feasible. Metal propellers with variable pitch were supplanting the old wooden "props," and the former water-cooled, block engines had long since been replaced by air-cooled radial motors of far greater power and reliability. Monoplanes were gradually displacing the obsolescent biplanes with their exposed struts and bracing wires, thus decreasing the effects of drag and permitting superior air speeds in the new models, while better radio communications and improved instruments respectively facilitated control and navigation, regardless of the state of the weather or the degree of visibility.

As for Geiger's career as an aviator of some twenty years' service, if the first decade had been basically a period of learning and experimentation—a time of improvisation and trial—the second had been one of progressive development and marked refinement. By 1937 Marine Aviation had put aside its short pants and had shifted into long trousers. Its mission as an essential component of the Fleet Marine Force had become concisely defined, and with the provision of increasing numbers of properly designed and powered high-performance aircraft and well trained pilots to fly those new machines, it had truly come of age. For the first time in its checkered career it figuratively had the stuff to deliver the punch, and as events transpired it was indeed fortunate that Marine Aviation had kept abreast of the changing times, for within the space of but five years it was going to be put to the test in the far reaches of the South Pacific. With regard to Colonel Geiger, he had correspondingly taken an active part in the forging of the Marines' aerial striking force, and when the time came for action, to nobody's surprise, he was the right man, at the right place, at the right time.

Chapter IX

The War Clouds Gather

Outwardly the second half of Geiger's four-year tour of duty as the commanding officer of Quantico's Air One seemed merely an undisturbed continuation of his previous activities in that capacity. However, there were certain differences for not only had the scope of his responsibilities and the area of his operations been considerably enlarged, but in addition the progressive introduction and adoption of technological refinements in aircraft and their equipment had vastly increased the capabilities of his Aviation Group. Generally speaking the period January 1937–June 1939 witnessed the gradual replacement of earlier models of *Curtiss* and *Vought* scout-bombers with newer and faster versions, meanwhile the recently accepted *Grumman* fighters, principally the *F3F–2's*, began to displace the older *Boeing* machines. In the field of communications the changes were most significant. By 1937 short wave radio had been perfected to the degree where it could be installed in high-performance aircraft. The paramount feature of this innovation was twofold. Air-to-air communications between the squadron leaders and their flight units permitted more rapid and efficient tactical control, while air-to-ground interchange provided the vital ingredient for the air-ground, united team concept which created the all important link between the Marine pilot in the air and his counterpart, the Marine rifleman on the ground. Consequently, ground troops assaulting enemy defenses either on a beach or on a battlefield could now literally "talk" the aviators onto selected targets as opposed to prior methods of visual signaling, heretofore restricted to laying out ground panels or employing smoke or pyrotechnical devices.

Admittedly this important break-through in communications techniques was not to be fully exploited for several years to come. Initially the system was far from fool-proof; installations were notably limited and were not uniform. It required time to educate and to train operators to achieve maximum benefits; nevertheless, it was decidedly a forward step in the right direction. As for the introduction of instrument flying Geiger's pioneering efforts had not been in vain. Increasing numbers of pilots were attracted to its use, and once aware of its inestimable value and boundless potentialities, the resistance of many of those who had been inclined to regard the innovation more as a practice of one of the "black arts" started to diminish.

As events transpired it was well that these and other related transformations had at least been initiated for commencing in the winter of 1937 Air One was to undertake a series of annual, major training exercises with ground components of the Fleet Marine Force, destined to continue more or less unbroken for the ensuing four years. The first of these operations, Fleet Landing Exercise No. 3, far surpassed in magnitude the earlier maneuvers of 1935 and 1936. Held on San Clemente Island off the Pacific Coast near San Diego, it was the first time the Second Marine Brigade on the west coast was provided the opportunity to share in landing exercises; moreover, a reinforced regiment from the Fourth Army was included among the participating troop units. Thus, the inclusion of the two Marine Brigades with their attached aviation elements, Air One and Air Two, combined with the provisional Army force, all operating in unison with the Training Squadron of the United States Fleet, made the undertaking very definitely a joint enterprise. Despite the heavy surf encountered and the complete inability of ordinary ships' motor launches to cope with the situation, the landing exercises were generally considered satisfactory, if for no other reason that certain outstanding deficiencies, especially in the ship-to-shore phase of the operations, were laid bare.

Geiger's role in the maneuvers was a prominent one. Sweeping Quantico's hangars almost clean, he led a mass formation flight of fifty-four aircraft (and fifty-nine pilots) cross-country westward to San Diego without incident en route. There, he was assigned duties as Commander, Force Aircraft, assuming titular and tactical control of both Air One and Air Two, the latter Group being commanded by Lieutenant Colonel Ralph J. Mitchell. Throughout the months of January and February Geiger's five-squadron Wing of eighty-four scout-bombers and fighters flew designated attack missions in support of numerous troop landings, conducted reconnaissance and general observation flights on call, and laid smoke on assigned beach areas. Air spot for naval gunfire, however, was flown by naval aircraft, catapulted from the decks of the five heavy cruisers and the six battleships of the Attack Force. At the subsequent critique Geiger pointed out the necessity of providing Force Aircraft with modern attack planes with the capabilities of destroying and neutralizing beach defenses; furthermore, he again stressed the advisability of Marine Aviation being supplied with escort carriers of its own to insure its primary mission in amphibious operations. Lack of sufficient funds, of course, precluded positive action on both recommendations, but his foresight and his aggressive leadership had not been passed over without favorable comment by his superiors. Back at Quantico's Turner Field with his Group intact by mid-March, Colonel Geiger found awaiting him a Letter of Commendation extended by the Major General Commandant, Thomas Holcomb, complimenting the recipient for the high degree of efficiency displayed by Air One during the recent landing exercises and congratulating the commander for there having incurred neither injuries nor accidents to the Group's personnel and aircraft.

The remainder of Geiger's stay at Quantico was practically a rubber stamp reproduction of the former months: frequent instrument flights from Quantico to Lake Placid and to Floyd Bennett Field as well as to Parris Island, and participation in aerial pageants and máneuvers at Miami. During the winter of 1938, Air One took part in Fleet Landing Exercise No. 4 at Culebra in the Caribbean; the following year it similarly engaged in Fleet Landing Exercise No. 5, also conducted east of Puerto Rico. Just as regularly the Group's commanding officer came in for his fair share of the honors. Typical of the comments were those made by Rear Admiral A.W. Johnson, flying his flag in *USS New York,* dated 14 March 1938: "The work of Air One in these fields of activity (i.e., as part of the Attack Force) under the able leadership of Colonel Geiger is deserving of the highest commendation. His organization is completely integrated into that of the Fleet Marine Force; his operations characterized by thoroughness of preparation, resourcefulness, and skill in execution." Herein, Geiger had just cause to be pleased with himself, for the Admiral commanding the Training Detachment was known to be exceedingly chary when it came to passing out compliments for a job well done.

The 1939 maneuvers at Culebra closely followed the pattern established by its predecessor although the number of troops, vessels, and aircraft taking part was appreciably greater. By that date the feasibility of close air support had become increasingly apparent. Some doubt still existed in the minds of the more conservative numbers as to its practicability in actual usage as contrasted with the simulated conditions and artificialities imposed by mock warfare. They argued that it was too dangerous and not necessarily effective: there was much debate as to how "close" to troops could close air support be safely employed; there was similarly considerable deliberation as to its alleged superiority over conventional field artillery or naval gunfire. To Geiger there was no question in his mind as to its effectiveness: he went on record as stating that: "The primary reason for the Marine Corps' having airplanes is their use in close support of ground units." He elaborated on the theme by proposing that close air support be regarded as a supplementary arm to be used in coordination with artillery and naval gunfire against enemy troops and defensive installations in the immediate vicinity of the assaulting riflemen, and he felt that as far as his aviators were concerned, they were perfectly willing to drop their bombs or to fire their machine guns just as "close" to the advancing infantry as the latter's leaders desired.

As for the exercises as a whole, there were times when he was visibly bored by the monotony of what had now become almost a routine performance on the part of Air One. With patience strained to the utmost on at least one occasion the Group Commander felt so frustrated he detached one of his squadrons from the landing exercises, and on his own responsibility led it over an extensive reconnaissance flight across the length and breadth of the Virgin Islands. In February 1939 he piloted one of the two *Douglas* transports (assigned to VMJ—1) across the Mona Passage from San Juan to Ciudad Trujillo to take part as one of the official representatives of the Marine Corps in the dedication ceremonies of "Avenida United States Marine Corps" at Generalissimo Trujillo's now rebuilt capital. The only other incident of note during his Caribbean sojourn was his involvement in a serious automobile accident one evening in San Juan while driving back to the flying field at Isla Grande. Falling asleep at the wheel his enlisted driver unfortunately drove head-on into the concrete support of an overhead bridge, and Geiger was bodily thrown forward against the windshield of his vehicle with such force that the glass was shattered, thereby incurring a deep cut in his forehead which left a prominent scar.

With the advent of spring his prolonged tour of duty at Quantico was fast drawing to a close. It was time for a change for a variety of reasons. With the war clouds now gathering over Western Europe and the Balkans, Geiger was convinced that sooner or later diplomacy and bickering would give way to outright force of arms. Desirous of furthering his formal schooling not to mention brushing up on current concepts in the art and science of warfare while he yet had the opportunity, he applied for admission to the next session of the Senior Course at Newport's Naval War College, scheduled to convene in late June. Besides, with his daughter engaged to be married to a First Lieutenant of Marines and his son a cadet at the United States Military Academy at West Point on the Hudson, his house seemed unusually quiet. Even his trusted crew chief had deserted the fold: in May Technical Sergeant Donato had been transferred from Quantico to Bogotá, Colombia, and was now maintaining the *Grumman Duck (J2F–4)* assigned to the Naval Attaché at the American Legation, in the northern Andes. On 8 June Geiger made his final flight in his *Great Lakes* command plane (A–9854), and the succeeding week, in anticipation of his pending transfer and his desire to scout out in advance the locale of his future duty station, he made a solo hop to Newport and the general Narragansett Bay region in a *Grumman* fighter.

His request for reassignment having been approved by Headquarters, on 20 June Geiger was detached from Air One, and following a period of ten days' leave reported to the Naval War College under orders as a student officer with his flight status confirmed for the duration of the period of instruction. One of seven Marine officers admitted to the ten-month Senior Course along with forty-two naval officers of the line, the curriculum which he was about to undertake was a difficult assignment for a non-Naval Academy graduate. At that time one of the main criticisms leveled at the Naval War College was that it had been unduly slow—if not deliberately adverse—to accept the concept of education, as contrasted with training. In substance, the Navy as a whole was inclined to regard education as basically a substitute for actual experience: the Naval War College was thus primarily concerned with the development of the professional competence of officers in operational planning and the exercise of operational command. With its interests essentially directed to strategy, tactics, and logistics, only marginal concern was devoted to non-technical matters. Familiarity with the broader aspects of history—naval, military, and diplomatic—fell more within the exclusive purview of the related Advanced Course, which likewise dealt extensively with international relations and international law.

Be that as it may, to Geiger the Senior Course of itself was a decided challenge, and to keep abreast of his classmates his only recourse was to spend long hours in the College Library when he was not otherwise attending classes or lectures in Luce and Mahan Halls. Whereas, unlike the majority of his associates, he had never commanded a cruiser nor spent countless hours on a destroyer's navigating bridge, he was notwithstanding somewhat familiar with nautical affairs, having served two consecutive tours of sea duty aboard battleships not to mention his participation in joint operations with fleet units, including carriers, in more recent years. By relentless application he was able to maintain a standing in the upper one third of his group, but he admitted that it was no easy task. He had only the barest opportunity to fly, especially during the winter months, but throughout his first year at Newport Geiger somehow managed to average some eight hours per month airborne. Flying an $O3U-3$ (A–9143) he made frequent runs back and forth from the landing strip at the Torpedo Station to New York's Floyd Bennett Field.

Whenever he had the opportunity he would borrow an automobile from someone at the flying field on Long Island, and would motor into Manhattan to take the train for a brief visit with his son at West Point. Occasionally, Eunice would drive over in the family car from Newport to the Hudson, and at the Hotel Thayer the trio would be reunited. At one of those meetings, Geiger questioned his son as to his intentions upon graduation from the Military Academy. There was considerable discussion concerning the particular branch of the service. He agreed with young Roy that something more stimulating than the Infantry would be desirable, and the choice eventually narrowed down to either the Cavalry or the Artillery. The former then being in a state of flux—mechanization and motorization were gradually supplanting horsepower—the Colonel was of the considered opinion that the cannoneers had a far brighter future. He cautioned his son against the Coast Artillery on the grounds that in any future conflict it seemed most unlikely that any aggressor would venture to bring its fleet units within effective range of the United States' formidable series of permanent shore batteries and harbor forts; hence, the Coast Artillery Corps for the most part would have nothing more to do than to stare out of its concrete emplacements upon a barren horizon.

As for the Corps' antiaircraft branch, speaking strictly as a combat aviator, he had never been overly impressed with the effectiveness of ground artillery shelling of high-performance airplanes, and he advised Roy Junior against entering what he believed was an unrewarding and rather frustrating assignment. There was no doubt in the father's mind but that the Field Artillery was *the* combatant arm with which to be associated, and he strongly urged the cadet to apply for a commission within its ranks, with the certainty that as the Infantry's main combat support weapon, in due course any Field Artilleryman would see plenty of action. Convinced that his father's reasoning was sound, young Roy in time applied for and was granted a commission as a Second Lieutenant of Field Artillery, thereby commencing a brilliant career in that branch of the service which he has never since had the slightest cause to regret.

With regard to Eunice, throughout the duration of her husband's protracted stay at the Naval War college she found plenty to keep her active mind and her busy fingers occupied. With her mate with his head in a pile of papers and technical manuals from dawn until midnight not less than five days per week, she seldom saw him during daylight hours, but she did her best to assist him in the preparation of his independent reports and staff studies in the late evenings. Living in a small rented cottage across the street from Newport's celebrated

Muenchner-King Hotel, she opened up an impromptu art studio in conjunction with her painting lessons given by a local resident. Working in oils the culmination of many months of labor was a half-length portrait of the Colonel in his blue uniform, complete with medals, a striking likeness of the man, which to this day remains prominently hung over his mahogany desk in a corner of the living room at his wife's Pensacola residence. Additionally, she wrote poetry, attended auctions, played some golf, and rode horseback on occasion, and otherwise entered fully into the round of social entertainment which went on unabated among the numerous wives of the student officers and the instructors at the War College and their counterparts, the ladies of the Army officers forming the garrison at nearby Fort Adams.

On completion of the Senior Course in mid-May of 1940, Geiger was awarded his diploma by the President of the College, Rear Admiral E.C. Kalbfus, who took the opportunity to congratulate the recipient for standing so well in his class. Immediately after the close of the graduation exercises Roy and Eunice loaded up the car and drove south to Florida for a well earned thirty days' leave. Much as Geiger enjoyed the surf bathing at Newport even in mid-summer the water temperatures at Bailey's Beach could not compare with those of Florida's Gulf, and he far preferred the long sandy stretches of Jacksonville's and Daytona's waterfronts to the rocky inlets and tidal coves common to Narragansett Bay. Another reason for his return to his home State was to receive honors from his Alma Mater. On 3 June 1940 (while the remnant of Britain's Expeditionary Force was struggling to clear the beaches at Dunkerque), Stetson University conferred on Colonel Geiger the honorary degree of Doctor of Laws. Seated in the front row of the platform at Deland with cap and gown, compared to his similarly attired associates Geiger was definitely not the professional type as far as appearances were concerned, and so cramped was the space allotted to one of his size and stature, the ceremonial exercises were more in the nature of an ordeal. Nevertheless, despite the lack of elbow room and sufficient place to set his feet, he was quite proud of the accolade which had been bestowed upon him, and he was equally elated that some thirty years after his admission to the Bar; his State and Law School thought enough of his achievements in the service of his country to extend suitable recognition for his untiring efforts to excel in his chosen profession.

Returning to the War College later that month he at once buckled down to his new responsibilities as one of five officers (two Navy, two Marine Corps, and one Army) selected to take the Advanced Course at that institution of learning. This supplementary session of eight months' duration was definitely more comprehensive than the Senior Course, and its subject matter was far more interesting to Geiger than his former preoccupation with the maneuvering of tactical naval units. With his legal background it was only natural that the emphasis laid on maritime (admiralty) and international law had great appeal. With regard to the seminars in international relations and current events these were particularly timely bearing in mind the rapid kaleidoscope of foreign and domestic affairs taking place during the summer and autumn of 1940. Despite his heavy work-load Geiger did not neglect his flying. In June he made his first flight in a naval patrol bomber, a six-hour familiarization run and check out in a *PBY-2* attached to Navy Patrol Squadron 54 operating from the Newport Naval Training Station. In August he made his second flight in a *Consolidated Catalina,* a *PBY-3* (No. 0850) assigned to the Naval Air Detail at the Torpedo Station. In other respects he confined his flying activities to piloting single-engine *Vought* Navy fighters along the Atlantic Seaboard from Cape Cod south to Sandy Hook.

As for his studies, between the Battle of Britain, the Italian invasion of Egypt from Libya, and the destroyer-naval base exchange agreement between the United States and England, there were ample topics for lively discusion, while on the home front President Roosevelt's decision to commence an unparalleled expansion of naval tonnage and the creation of a two-ocean Navy was obviously a heady stimulant to the entire War College. To Geiger the latter development was most significant and worthy of close attention, for with Congressional approval of the Navy's 10,000-plane program, the Marine Corps' portion would amount to more than 1,100 aircraft, and it was anticipated that ten Marine Air Groups each of four or more Squadrons would in time be activated as a direct result of this unprecedented increase. With the subsequent passage of the Selective Service Act and the federalization of the Army's National Guard and the Organized Reserves of the Navy and Marine Corps, the student body and the instructors alike at the War College felt it was high time to vacate the classrooms and to return to duty posthaste with the operating forces. It was therefore with a pronounced feeling of relief that the Advanced Course was terminated in March 1941, and once the diplomas were issued, the graduates could hardly wait to pick up their transfer orders assigning them to their new duty stations.

On completion of his sojourn at the Naval War College Geiger's position was momentarily rather obscure for it was difficult to find him an appropriate billet in the spring of 1941. At that date he was unquestionably one of the best educated officers of his rank in the Corps, not only among its aviators but also of the line, and by rights he could expect to be employed in a manner which could make full use of his varied talents and his accumulated command experience. On the other hand, applied to Marine Aviation in either an operational or staff capacity for the moment "the boat was loaded." Its Director, Colonel Mitchell, was junior to him in grade. Moreover, Geiger was then too senior for assignment to either of the two, presently existing Marine Air Groups at Quantico and San Diego. Until such time as their status was respectively raised to the First and Second Marine Air Wing (which was ultimately accomplished in July), Geiger was figuratively "on the beach," unassigned and awaiting a command commensurate with his rank.

A way out of this embarrassing situation was soon discovered. There being an acute need for officers with unusual qualifications, the authorities at Headquarters selected Geiger as their most promising candidate for a special mission, and he was summoned from Newport to report without further delay to Washington. Assigned to aviation duty within the Office of the Chief of Naval Intelligence, he was alerted for posting overseas to the Mediterranean for temporary duty, to observe British naval and aerial operations from Gibraltar east to the Suez Canal as well as those conducted by the military ground forces in the Western Desert area. On 25 March he received his orders from the Acting Secretary of the Navy, Mr. James Forrestal, directing him to proceed by commercial air from the United States to Europe. Taking passage in a Pan America Clipper, Geiger left New York a week later, arriving at Lisbon, Portugal, on 1 April. There, he reported by dispatch to the American Embassy at London, whereupon his supplementary orders, placing him on aviation duty with diplomatic status as an Assistant Naval Attaché carried on the rolls of the London office, became effective.

The Naval Attaché, Captain C.A. Lockwood, Jr., forthwith instructed his assistant to continue to Gibraltar. Accompanied by a British Intelligence Officer, Geiger sailed from Lisbon on a Swedish collier *(SS Milos)*, and on his arrival at that Crown Colony on 7 April, he first called on its Governor and then reported to the Admiral Commanding the North Atlantic with offices ashore at the Dockyard. Following a detailed tour of "The Rock" and its elaborate defenses, he was assigned as an observer to Group 200, Royal Air Force, which operated under the direction of the Admiral Commanding the Station. During his three-week tour at Gibraltar the Colonel took part in all of the Group's diverse activities which ranged from patrolling the sea approaches to protecting convoys and flying anti-submarine attack missions. Not content to sit passively in one of the participating seaplanes watching the conduct of operations as a mere spectator, Geiger chose to assume a more positive role. On 10 April he took over the controls of a *Saunders-Roe London* twin-engine flying boat, and for eight and one half hours engaged in an anti-submarine patrol over the Straits of Gibraltar. For the most part he was not overly impressed with the Group's performance. As he was to state later in his formal report: "The operations conducted were very mediocre considering the importance of Gibraltar, and the maintenance of material appeared to be inexcusably poor." In spite of his crowded daily schedule he managed to find time to correspond with his family. For those who maintain that Geiger was not especially close to his children, one of his letters mailed from "The Rock" addressed to his daughter, now the wife of a young Marine aviator, should serve to disprove such an opinion. Written in a friendly informal vein its contents reveal great warmth and affection, and illustrate a side of the man which was outwardly covered over by his gruff and forceful manner of expression.

The next spot on his agenda of places to visit was Malta. To circumvent roving Italian and German fighters and dive bombers the flight eastward from Gibraltar was made at night in a fully armed *Short Sunderland,* arriving at its destination at dawn. During his five-day stay at that heavily bombed island base, he was the guest of the Governor at San Antonio Palace. Malta then being in grave danger of being literally blasted to bits (for the Axis airbases in Italy and Sicily were but sixty miles distant), to be followed by a full-scale airborne invasion, Geiger's visit to Britain's "unsinkable aircraft carrier" came at a tense moment. A combination of the British Army's anti-aircraft batteries and the Royal Air Force' *Hurricane* fighters managed to hold the enemy at bay, but hostile air raids directed at Valetta were common-place throughout the duration of his brief stay.

On the night of 3–4 May the *Sunderland* took off for Alexandria, Egypt, where Geiger joined *HMS Formidable,* one of the Royal Navy's newest carriers operating in the Eastern Mediterranean. A unit of Admiral Cunningham's Task Force, *Formidable* accompanied by three battleships and several cruisers and destroyers was assigned the mission of escorting an important convoy of tanks and other vital military equipment sent out from the United Kingdom for that part of the run from Malta eastward to Alexandria. Geiger remained in the ship for twelve days (during the British retirement from Greece), disembarking on 15 May at Alexandria where he took the train for Cairo.

At that place he made arrangements with officials at Headquarters, Royal Air Force, Middle East, to visit Group 202, at Bagush about two hundred and fifty miles west of Cairo in the Western Desert. He made this Group his field headquarters from 17 May until 3 June. At that time air operations were being conducted against Libya and Greece, and in support of the British defense of Crete. The very first day he arrived "under his own steam" piloting a *Lockheed Hudson* (a twin-engine reconnaissance bomber) from Cairo. Two days later he motored to Qasaba where he climbed aboard a *Westland Lysander,* for a four-hour familiarization flight to make a survey of the general area and to observe Royal Air Force operations in support of ground troops. His opinions of the capabilities of the lumbering single-engine *Lysander* were perhaps most aptly described by his statement: "The Royal Air Force had no dive bombers or other planes built for Army support with the exception of the *Lysander,* an observation plane which could not be operated near the front without being immediately shot down." To complete the picture he went on to relate: "Observation and ground strafing were done by *Hawker Hurricane* fighters. Distant observation was carried out by *Bristol Blenheim* and *Martin Maryland* light bombers."

About five miles away from Bagush (and Fuka airdrome) were located the Headquarters of the British Commander of the Army Forces in the Western Desert; hence, Geiger had unlimited opportunity to obtain a comprehensive view of joint operations in combat including those incident to the subsequent evacuation of Crete. Having been present at Intelligence Briefings and wishing to form an opinion concerning the degree of co-operation between the Royal Air Force and the Army from the latter's viewpoint, he requested permission to visit the troops in the desert as well as the besieged garrison at Tobruk, invested on the land side by units of General Rommel's *Afrika Korps.* This was granted without delay, and he drove to Matruh where he boarded a trawler, *HMS(AS) Southern Isles,* which, after an all night, blacked-out coastal run, deposited its American passenger within the Australian lines at the port of Tobruk. Geiger remained inside the perimeter for two days inspecting its defenses. The *Luftwaffe* having undisputed mastery of the air (aircraft alarms were continuous), and there being a chronic shortage of drinking water and rations, his stay could not exactly be described as pleasant or uneventful although it is readily conceded it was highly informative. Embarking in a destroyer, *HMS Harrow,* he returned to Matruh without incident, and drove back in due course in a Royal Air Force vehicle to his base at Bagush.

Characteristically, Geiger delayed there only long enough to catch up with a few missed meals and a little lost sleep, and to change his clothing. On 30 May he left for the actual front about one hundred and fifty miles to the westward near Sidi Baranni. By that date Rommel's two-month offensive had about run its course (from lack of fuel), and for the moment there was a comparative lull in the fighting. Reporting to the Headquarters of General Gott's Mechanized Division, he proceeded to the British front lines in the vicinity of Halfaya Pass just east of Salum. Under General Gott's guidance he made the rounds of the British defensive positions, and inspected tanks and reconnaissance cars including captured or abandoned enemy vehicles. At the conclusion of his two-day tour, he piloted his *Lysander* from Gabush to Cairo, and during the first week of June divided his time between observing Balloon Barrage Squadrons protecting the fleet anchorage at Alexandria and visiting Fighter Wing 252 to observe the operations of its filter and sector control rooms.

On 8 June Geiger took off for Cyprus at the controls of a *Lockheed Hudson.* He paid visits to its three main airdromes, and spent considerable time talking with New Zealand Officers who had survived the German airborne assault on Crete, and had been purposely sent to Cyprus to advise the authorities there what they could in all likelihood expect in the event of a future landing by parachutists and glider troops. Providentially, such a development was indefinitely postponed by Hitler's decision to hurl the might of the *Wehrmacht* and the *Luftwaffe* against the Soviet's western front later that month, but the opportunity to meet and to converse with men who had experienced the attack on Crete was a rare one for a transient American observer.

By mid-June the Middle East phase of Geiger's mission had been completed, and it was now time for him to shift his attentions to other areas. Leaving Cairo on 16 June aboard a British commercial transport, the Colonel retraced his steps to Lisbon in rather a roundabout fashion: across the Soudan and Nigeria to Sierra Leone and Gambia, and from thence to the Iberian Peninsula, with stops at Khartoum, El Fasher (where an epidemic of yellow fever was flourishing), Fort Lamy, Lagos, Freetown, and Bathurst. Continuing on from Portugal, his twelve-day flight at last terminated at Poole, England. Pausing briefly to consult with the Naval Attaché at London, Geiger thereafter entrained for Liverpool to observe parachute training at Ringway, the Joint Headquarters of the Naval and Air Force Commanders guarding the waters of the western approaches to the British Isles.

At Ringway on 1 July, Geiger made what is believed to be his first flight in a glider. Climbing into a *Whitney* machine, he remained airborne for approximately two hours. Satisfied with its performance, he landed without difficulty, and then proceeded to inspect Ballon Barrage Groups stationed in the Liverpool area. Two days afterwards he flew north in a borrowed *Hudson* from Liverpool to Glasgow, Scotland. Across Lock Fyne at Inveraray he had a chance to visit its training center for joint Army-Navy operations, and on the evening of the Fourth of July he took the night train back to London.

With his European-Mediterranean-United Kingdom "Grand Tour" now completed, Geiger had to select a westbound course to the United States in the same indirect fashion employed on his passage eastward. Taking off from Bristol, England, on 9 July, he continued on by air to Lisbon, where he had to delay for several days until space could be arranged on a homeward bound Clipper. By the sixteenth of the month he was back once more at New York City, and the following morning, bright and early, he reported for duty at Washington's "Main Navy" with a bulging briefcase containing his notes and a parachute bag crammed to overflowing with not less than three weeks' supply of laundry badly in need of a wash.

The next two weeks were spent with the Office of Naval Intelligence. His period of "de-briefing" was a strenuous one: innumerable conferences with interested parties, and the preparation of his formal report which proved to be no light task. The original of what is believed to be the first draft of this lengthy document came to some twenty-five typewritten pages. Highly detailed it was likewise equally critical of some of the procedures witnessed, for Geiger realized the significance of what he had observed, and with his legal background was determined to submit an unvarnished report, as objective as he could make it but with no attempt to conceal facts nor to spare reputations. In a way his Intelligence Estimate was a masterpiece of concise reporting and restraint, although from time to time the personality of the writer and the subjectivity of his views could not be completely submerged by the mass of technical detail recounted. In the light of hindsight many of his criticisms were entirely justified, and it is to his credit that many of his predictions subsequently came to pass, and that many of his specific recommendations in time were to be acted upon.

In substance, Geiger was of the considered opinion that whereas the degree of cooperation existing between the Royal Navy and the British Army in the conduct of their respective operations appeared to be satisfactory, the same could not be said with regard to their relations with the Royal Air Force. He deplored the tendency of the Royal Air Force to go its own way, unquestionably the unfortunate result of its autonomy as a separate service. He was most critical of its seeming indifference, as well as its apparent inability, to render close, effective air support to the other arms. Herein, he claimed that not only had there not been formulated doctrines or techniques for this vital mission, but that additionally, the entire concept of air support had never been thoroughly investigated. By way of example, he cited the case of *Formidable* struck by a bomb during the evacuation of Crete. Requesting immediate air support, the Admiral had been sent two fighters to form a protective umbrella over his fleet with the expectation that two others would be dispatched later. In Geiger's opinion this was a classic example of "too little, too late"—planes should have been airborne and not on the ground at Bagush (he had been in its Air Operations Office at the time of the emergency), and two squadrons should have been sent out, not two planes. Bearing in mind that in December 1941 *HMS Prince of Wales* and *Repulse,* denied air cover by the Royal Air Force, fell easy prey to torpedo-carrying, land-based aircraft flown by Japanese pilots, in the waters north of Singapore, Geiger's predictions of dire things to come made some five months before the fateful event were eminently worthy of attention and related corrective action.

As for cooperation between the Army and the Royal Air Force in North Africa, it was said to be virtually non-existent, or, to state it in Geiger's own terms: "No British planes were to be seen around Tobruk. An occasional *Hurricane* on reconnaissance appeared in the Western Desert. The ground troops during the fighting had no means of communicating with RAF planes. They had no doctrines of air support, and were occasionally attacked by their own aircraft. At times *Hurricanes* attempted to render support similar to that given by German dive-bombers, but with little success because of lack of prior training and preparation." To the American observer it was asking too much of British infantrymen armed with rifles and *Bren* guns, and dependent on trucks for transportation, to stand up and slug it out against the combined onslaught of swarms of *Stuka* dive-bombers backing up fleets of armored *(Panzer)* divisions. Proof of this contention applied to future operations was not long in coming: in January 1942, Rommel launched his second offensive which demonstrated clearly what air power and mechanized forces could do when handled skillfully as a team—in June Tobruk fell suddenly after a powerful coordinated attack of the *Afrika Korps* supported by dive-bombers and artillery, and by July the Eighth Army had been chased all the way back eastward to El Alamein, but sixty miles distant from Alexandria.

Geiger readily acknowledged his awareness of the sacrifices

which the British had already made at Dunkerque and in the Aegean; of the effects of the Battle of Britain; and of the consequent shortages of crucial military equipment and supplies despite the arrival of American materiel. However, in his mind the crux of the situation was the evident neglect of adequate air support to ground units: without the closest teamwork of all arms the British would continue to lose battles if not entire campaigns regardless of locale. As he stated in his Estimate, in July 1941, the implications of such neglect portended a bleak future: "It is time that the British Navy realize that airplanes can and will sink its ships; that the British Army realize that it cannot win battles without complete and intelligent air support, and that the Royal Air Force realize that its demand for independent action is losing the war for the British Empire."

Understandably, the controversial nature of some of Geiger's conclusions raised a few eyebrows at the Navy Department (notably among the Anglophiles), but he had been asked for an unbiased appraisal of the situation, and he saw no reason to mince words. Attributing in large part the failure of Britain's war effort to the disinterest and self-concern of one of its principal combat arms, he resolved then and there that given the opportunity he would put into practice what he had preached, and as will be subsequently related, throughout the ensuing Pacific operations, he strove to develop maximum cooperation between air, ground, and sea elements comprising his commands. Long a foe of the movement in the United States to divorce aviation from the control of the Army and Navy, Geiger's recent experiences as an official observer attached to British forces in combat merely served to strengthen his deep-seated conviction that a separate air force would be decidedly inadvisable.

Still nominally carried on the rolls at Headquarters, on 24 July he flew to Parris Island with Major Sanderson in a *Lockheed* transport assigned to VMJ−1. The purpose of this flight from Quantico was to inspect a glider group and a barrage balloon unit then in the process of being organized at Page Field as well as to take a look at a portion of the First Marine Air Wing (1st MAW), FMF, following its return from Guantanamo Bay on completion of extensive maneuvers and landing exercises in the Caribbean with the First Marine Division. Returning to Washington, on 1 August Geiger was finally detached from the Office of the Chief of

Naval Operations with orders to report to Quantico on termination of twenty days leave.

Assigned duties as the Commanding Officer of 1st MAW, its newly designated leader was overjoyed to be back in harness again with the operating forces of the Corps. During his two-year absence at Newport and in Europe the Marines' air arm had practically doubled the number of its pilots and tripled the total number of personnel serving with aviation. Applied to his new command, by mid-summer of 1941 only one Group (MAG—11) of six Squadrons had been activated, but it consisted of more than one half of the Corps' entire stock of 220 aircraft. By that date 2nd MAW's MAG—21 was already in the Pacific (mostly at Ewa on the island of Oahu)—some 90 planes—while the remainder—VMS—3's eight amphibians—were stationed overseas in the Virgin Islands at St. Thomas. Considering that earlier that year after Fleet Landing Exercise No. 7, the Commanding General, Amphibious Corps, Atlantic Fleet (Major General Holland M. Smith), had come to the conclusion that a single Marine division making an amphibious landing required 12 fighter, 8 dive-bomber, 2 observation, and 4 utility squadrons for proper air support, it was obvious that any such contemplated expansion of Marine Aviation—to some 450 aircraft—would entail an increase which seemed almost astronomical to those of its senior pilots who remembered only too well the lean 1920's and 1930's.

Pending the arrival of more planes and trained aviators to fly them MAG—11 went about its business as best it could with what it had on hand. Throughout the late summer and early fall of 1941 at least three of its squadrons were actively engaged in maneuvers with the First Marine Division (and Army components) at Onslow Beach in North Carolina's New River area and at Cherry Point, nearby, along the banks of the Neuse. Meanwhile, the Commanding Officer of the 1st MAW performed repeated flights from Quantico to New Bern, North Carolina, to Parris Island, and to the Army Air Corps' Maxwell Field, at Montgomery, Alabama, checking on the training and supervising the construction of new air facilities. Promoted at long last to the rank of Brigadier General (with date of rank, 1 October 1941), Geiger and his twin-engine *Beechcraft* (No. 4723) sporting a single star on its cowl could be expected to drop out of the sky at any moment at any one of half a dozen airfields spread up and down the southern Atlantic Coast.

In spite of determined efforts on the part of the Director of Aviation (Colonel Mitchell) and the Wing Commanders of both 1st and 2nd (General Rowell) MAW's to bring the actual strength of their respective commands up to authorized levels, time was running strongly against them. On the eve of the Japanese attack on Pearl Harbor and Wake Island, there was still only one Group in each Wing (Lieutenant Colonel Campbell's MAG–11 and Lieutenant Colonel Larkin's MAG–21), the entire aviation organization comprising 13 Squadrons and 250 planes of various types. With all but one of MAG–21's forty-eight aircraft at Ewa destroyed in the holocaust (not to mention seven *Grumman Wildcats* of VMF–211's slender stock of twelve, shot to bits on the ground on Wake on 8 December), it was most expedient for Quantico's 1st MAW and its MAG–11 to pull up stakes and to head for the Pacific at flank speed. Although three of its squadrons were temporarily absent on maneuvers at New Bern, within forty-eight hours the vanguard of Geiger's 1st MAW was packed-up, gassed-up, and ready for take-off, and on 9 December the command picked up its wheels and started the long grind across the United States for the West Coast.

On 14 December Geiger's *JRB–2* touched down on the runway at San Diego's Naval Air Station on North Island, and by the 24th the 1st MAW was reunited in Southern California. Initially assigned the mission of air-defense group for the San Diego area, MAG–11 momentarily awaited transfer to Hawaii in early January. However, its hopes were dashed for the orders were cancelled, and under the directive for its reorganization, issued in March 1942, MAG–11 was instructed to undergo instead a four-way split to create MAG's 12, 13, 14, and 15. Parenthetically, the 2nd MAW's battle-depleted MAG–21 was similarly augmented at the same time by the creation of four additional Groups—MAG's 22, 23, 24, and 25. Organized at hastily erected Camp Kearney near San Diego, the four new Groups of Geiger's Wing struggled to build themselves into combat ready units. One of them, MAG–13, was given only a week, whereupon its forward echelon departed for Tutuila, shortly followed by the main body, to undertake the air-defense of American Samoa. As for the Wing Commander and his Chief of Staff, General Geiger and Colonel Woods flew up and down the Pacific Coast from San Diego to Oakland and Seattle, endeavoring to procure planes from the Navy with which to equip the Wing's new components, and scoured the desert areas east of California along the Arizona and Nevada borders for likely sites for bombing ranges and gunnery practice.

Called back to the East Coast for a conference at Headquarters (as a result of the Battle of Midway), Geiger flew cross-country in late June 1942, and again the following month for high-level briefings and operational planning relative to the rapidly changing situation in the South and Southwest Pacific areas. By the time August rolled around it had become increasingly evident that the 1st MAW's hectic training period was fast drawing to a close, and that transfer to New Zealand, New Caledonia, or the New Hebrides was shortly indicated. By that time the transport pilots of MAG–25's VMF–253 had completed their "crash" course in aerial (celestial) navigation, given by Captain Weems of the Navy at far off Annapolis, and thanks to the instruction the original six officer-trainees had been able to impart to their associates, their "graduates" felt fully capable of navigating the 5,200-mile over-water stretch from San Diego all the way to Tontouta, New Caledonia. Every evening the wives of many of the Wing's senior pilots, who had motored across the United States from Quantico to San Diego and had taken up temporary residence there, watched their husbands' planes take off after dark, never knowing whether or not they would see them again the next morning. And one evening during the final week of August, the aircraft departed from North Island and did not return: the First Marine Air Wing had taken off for Hawaii as the first leg on its long flight to Guadalcanal in the Solomons to support the hard-pressed First Marine Division (Reinforced), fighting for its life to maintain its defensive perimeter around a partially completed air strip, built by the Japanese on what had once been a Lever Brothers coconut palm-oil plantation.

Chapter X

In the Air, on Land, and Sea

Precipitative though the unheralded departure of the First Marine Air Wing (1st MAW) from California for the South Pacific may have been to most of its pilots and maintenance crews (for striot security measures naturally prevailed), by no means was the move unexpected by the Wing Commander and his Chief of Staff. The Battle of Midway in early June had been quickly appraised by the Joint Chiefs of Staff (JCS) as a vital turning point in the war against Japan. Not only had the immediate threat to Hawaii and the West Coast of the United States been eliminated, but of greater significance, the Japanese had momentarily been thrown off balance and had lost the power to take the initiative at will; meanwhile, the American forces felt sufficiently encouraged to undertake a limited offensive in the Solomon Islands designed to block further enemy advance to the south in that general area. Granted that the decision involved considerable risk—for the means available were limited in number, time for adequate training and rehearsals was at a premium, and the all-important command relationships and responsibilities at that juncture left a great deal to be desired—the fleeting opportunity had to be seized. By July aerial reconnaissance had disclosed that the Japanese had commenced to build an airstrip on the north coast of the Island of Guadalcanal, and it was at once recognized by the JCS that if the Japanese were permitted to complete that installation, enemy dive-bombers based at Rabaul in New Britain and fighters from Buin on Bougainville (the northernmost Island of the Solomons group), would forthwith be supplied advanced landing platforms or aerial springboards for continued offensive operations throughout the South and Southwest Pacific Areas.

To forestall such a dire contingency the JCS, at the insistence of Admiral Ernest J. King, thereupon decreed the mounting of a joint–if not a combined–operation involving a naval movement northward through the Solomons and the Bismarcks in conjunction with an army thrust up the Papuan Peninsula of New Guinea which would ultimately lead to the capture of the Japanese bastion of Rabaul. Guadalcanal along with nearby Tulagi (on the north side of Sealark Channel and the nominal Headquarters of the British Solomon Islands' Protectorate) was selected as the initial target for the amphibious assault. It was generally understood that whichever force, American or Japanese, which could first put the airstrip on Guadalcanal's Lunga Point into operation would be the winner of the entire campaign. To General Douglas MacArthur, Commander-in-Chief of the United States Army Forces in the Far East, was allocated the responsibility for planning and coordinating the advance, and the command of all of its future phases after Guadalcanal had been secured by elements of the Navy and its Marine amphibious troops. To permit the lower Solomons (including Guadalcanal) to be placed under the sole operational jurisdiction of Admiral Chester W. Nimitz, Commander-in-Chief of the Pacific Fleet and of the Pacific Ocean Areas (who would furnish all of the vessels and most of the assault troops), the arbitrary boundary line between the subsectors of MacArthur's Southwest Pacific and Nimitz's South Pacific Areas was shifted one degree westward to 159 Degrees, East Longitude. Given the code name WATCHTOWER (in time more aptly dubbed Operation SHOESTRING) and the mission to seize and hold Guadalcanal's partially completed landing strip, Vice Admiral Robert L. Ghormley, Commander, South Pacific (ComSoPac), was designated the over-all strategic commander of the contemplated amphibious landings in the Solomons. In preparation for the coming operation he transferred his flagship from Aukland, New Zealand, to the harbor of Nouméa, New Caledonia, where he established a floating advanced base headquarters.

Appointed tactical commander of the Expeditionary Force (Task Force–61) was Vice Admiral Frank J. Fletcher, while Rear Admiral Richmond K. Turner served as commander of the Amphibious Force, the Naval Attack element (Task Force–62).

Besides bombardment and escort vessels Turner's organization included the First Marine Division (1st MarDiv) under the command of Major General Alexander A. Vandegrift, serving as the Landing Force Commander. To complete the picture, beyond carrier-based aviation aboard Fletcher's three large flattops, *Saratoga, Enterprise,* and *Wasp,* were land-based airplanes (Army, Navy, Marine Corps, and Royal New Zealand Air Force) under the control of Rear Admiral John S. McCain, Commander, Aircraft, South Pacific (ComAirSoPac). From Samoa, Tongatabu, and the Fiji Islands McCain had been progressively readying airstrips westward across the South Pacific, and by the end of July he had made operational additional fields at Efate (Vila), New Hebrides, at Nouméa (Tontouta), and at Espíritu Santo, also in the New Hebrides, gradually extending his flight path nearer and nearer to the objective area, although it should be noted that the last-mentioned was still some 560 miles away from Guadalcanal, across open water. Interestingly enough, and by way of comparison, the main Japanese air base at Rabaul was exactly the same distance northwest of Guadalcanal; however, their aerial route to the objective could be made across intervening islands already under their military control.

The net result of this factor was the restriction that when the 1st MarDiv made its initial landings in the Solomons the ground forces were beyond the effective flight range of Marine fighters and dive-bombers. Thus, such combat air support as was available for the Guadalcanal-Tulagi assaults and for the defense of the beachhead areas once ashore had to be provided not by elements of the 1st MAW but rather by carrier-based Navy planes and long-range Army bombers. Admitted that at the time of the landings there were two Marine Squadrons in the South Pacific, the 2nd MAW's VMF—212 from MAG—23 and VMO-251 from MAG—25, their fighters based respectively at Efate and at Espíritu Santo were still too far distant to furnish direct air support for the Guadalcanal-Tulagi operation.

This serious handicap must be fully realized in order to obtain a clear understanding of the unique employment of Marine aviation in the early months of the Pacific campaigns. Denied escort carriers (CVE's) of their own and tied-down to nearby, short-range land bases or to captured enemy airfields within actual objective areas, Marine aircraft for months to come had to be committed on a catch-as-can basis, shuttled-in piecemeal as circumstances would permit, usually being brought within flying range of the selected objective aboard Navy carriers. Such a concept was at distinct variance with the expected manner of usage if not the fundamental role of Marine aviation. Although the employment of all available air components, regardless of whether or not such utilization was consistent with the express purposes and training of those forces, was not in accord with accepted Marine aviation doctrine, Marine pilots, nevertheless, rapidly adjusted themselves to the peculiar conditions then existent. On occasion, to state it mildly, both airmen and ground troops felt frustrated. To cite a concrete example: direct air support in the form of Marine aviation could not be supplied to the Landing Force Commander at Guadalcanal until thirteen days after the primary, successful landing; meanwhile, the almost desperate 1st MarDiv, struggling against heavy odds to hold its defensive perimeter encircling the beachhead and the air strip, had to get along as best it could without benefit of air cover. To cite another case: during the early phases of the Guadalcanal campaign, command over all aviation units regardless of particular service (or even nationality) of necessity had to be performed by the senior Marine aviator, present and on the spot, and this stopgap, unified air "command," commonly referred to as the CACTUS Air Force (Cactus being Guadalcanal's code name) went without formal recognition for some six months after the initial assault. In time, as will be subsequently related, Marine Air Wings working closely together with their respective numerical Marine Divisions as integrated air and ground force teams came into their rightful place, but generally speaking, such an arrangement was not achieved until after the termination of the original Guadalcanal campaign.

On 7 August 1942 as much of the civilized world was soon to discover-within a week's time Guadalcanal had become a household word throughout the United States and in many parts of Australia and NewZealand–after an introductory bombardment by naval fire support vessels, the assault waves of General Vandegrift's 1st MarDiv climbed down the nets from their transports into waiting landing craft and sped ashore to both Guadalcanal and Tulagi. Thereafter, and for several ensuing bitterly embattled months they were to pursue a brilliant "offensive-defensive" campaign in the lower Solomons which became a classic in the annals of amphibious warfare. Although enemy opposition on Tulagi was marked (it took the Marines three days to secure that objective), the landing on Guadalcanal was not contested on D-Day, the principal hindrances to the Marine advance rather being the jungle and the kunai grass plus the vicious climate which was especially hard on men not yet physically conditioned to tropical temperatures and high humidity. By dusk on 7 August the Marines had dug in in defensive positions just short of the landing strip, and until that moment had yet to engage in hand-to-hand combat with Japanese ground troops.

Not that the latter had been caught completely napping—there were other surprises in store, and they were not long in making their presence felt. Hostile reaction came from the skies and from the seas. As a warm-up on D-Day afternoon, Japanese bombers began to drop their loads on American shipping in the transport area, and daily for months to come made bombing or strafing runs on any and all American vessels which happened to be present off the beaches not to mention devoting their undivided attentions on the 1st MarDiv's precariously held beachhead and defensive perimeter. Except when inclement weather intervened to postpone hostile air strikes, Japanese aviation superiority was such for at least the first two weeks following the American landings that it was definitely a one-sided affair in the former's favor from dawn to dusk. If the days were harrowing in the extreme, the nights were equally hideous. For the Japanese Navy, similar to its naval air arm, originally held local mastery of the sea areas and water approaches to the Solomons, and from dusk until dawn literally plastered the Marines ashore with every projectile Japanese battleships, heavy and light cruisers, destroyers, and even surfaced submarines could lob into the Lunga Point region of Guadalcanal. Meanwhile, fleet units of the assembled American and Australian Navies, lacking room to maneuver in confined waters, hopelessly outgunned and outnumbered (and frequently outwitted) were either sunk or heavily damaged with alarming regularity. So pronounced were the effects of superior Japanese torpedoes and gunfire at the Naval Battle of Savo Island (off the northern tip of Guadalcanal Island) on the night of 8-9 August, not only Admiral Turner's Naval Attack Force but also Admiral Fletcher's Screening Group decided to pull out (after heavy losses) in an effort to seek safety in having greater sea room than could be found in the cramped and crowded waters of the lower Solomons.

The peremptory withdrawal of the American transports, cargo vessels, (prior to completion of their unloading) and gunfire support ships at this critical stage left General Vandegrift woefully short of rations, ammunition, and other essential supplies and engineering equipment in addition to the loss of nearly 1,400 badly needed Marines serving with ships' unloading parties or still embarked but earmarked as reserves to back up the riflemen already committed ashore. Left to its meager resources with grave manpower and logistical shortages, a line of communications and a supply route (across exposed water) to rear areas dangling on a thread, and now bereft of naval surface and air support, the 1st MarDiv indeed faced a grim future. The Landing Force Commander had no other alternative but to build up a perimeter defense area with its base extending along some 5,000 yards of the coast between Alligator Creek on the east and Kukum village to the west, and along an arc inland which encircled the airfield site south of Lunga Point. With his troops dug in around the limits of this curve, Vandgrift turned his 1st Engineer Battalion loose inside the perimeter to complete the airstrip the Japanese had begun. Working like beavers around the clock the engineers (with very limited means) managed to level it sufficiently so that on 12 August a Navy *PBY* was able to land on the strip soon to be named Henderson Field (in honor of Major Lofton R. Henderson, killed in action leading the Marine dive-bombers at the Battle of Midway). Three days later a quartet of destroyer transports (APD's) dashed inshore bringing some stocks of aviation gasoline and lubricants in drums, bombs and ammunition, and other critical aviation spare parts and gear, and by 18 August Guadalcanal was ready to receive land-based dive-bombers and fighters. However, the strip was shortly knocked out of operation by a hostile bombing raid, and it was not until 20 August that Henderson Field finally obtained its long sought and sorely needed Marine air support.

This welcome supplement was forthcoming in the timely arrival of two Marine Air Squadrons, the advance echelon of Colonel William J. Wallace's MAG–23 (originally part of 2nd MAW, but now assigned to 1st MAW) which flew in from the sea having been catapulted from the flight deck of the escort carrier,

USS Long Island, about 200 miles southeast of Guadalcanal. Composed of Major Richard Mangrum's VMSB–232 and Captain John Smith's VMF–223, the 12 *Douglas Dauntless (SBD–3)* dive-bombers and the 19 *Grumman Wildcat (F4F–4)* fighters could not have shown up at a more opportune moment. Within five hours of their landing on Henderson Field there occurred the first of four determined Japanese attempts to recapture Guadalcanal by ground elements of their Seventeenth Army (from Rabaul) in coordination with both land-based and carrier-borne aircraft. Coincident with those operations ashore were no less than six major fleet engagements in the general Solomon's area designed to dislodge the 1st MarDiv from its bare toe-hold on Guadalcanal, extending from early August until December.

Herein, Japanese basic strategy was formulated on the concept of an all-out utilization of their naval superiority to isolate Guadalcanal by taking command of its encircling waters, simultaneously with the employment of Japanese landing forces on its shores with the intent of overwhelming the Marine ground and air defenders in order to regain control of the No. 1. prize, Henderson Field. Having almost uncontested use of "The Slot," the Japanese dominated waterway between Bougainville and the lower Solomons, the infamous "Tokyo Express," as the nightly forays of armed and escorted amphibious task groups bringing down units of Lieutenant General Hyakutake's Seventeenth Army from Rabaul to Guadalcanal in transports and sampans came to be called, very nearly accomplished that desired aim. It would have met with success, it is true, particularly in the early stages of the Guadalcanal campaign, if Hyakutake had landed sizeable reinforcements. But he persisted in underestimating his opponents, and committed his landing forces in driblets, sending battalions when he should have employed regiments, and brigades instead of divisions, and in the end he paid the price for his stubbornness and his inability to evaluate properly the actual situation. By the time Hyakutake finally got around to seeing the error of his ways it was far too late, for the Marines ashore and in the air at Guadalcanal had been given time to build up enough marginal superiority of force to withstand repeated Japanese thrusts; meantime, the American Navy and its air arm had sunk the enemy's best ships, and had practically written off the books what little remained of Japan's rapidly diminishing stock of experienced naval pilots.

At all events, Mangrum's and Smith's squadrons got their first taste of air combat in short order. After midnight of 20-21 August the first Japanese land counterattack let go full blast on the eastern side of the 1st MarDiv's defense perimeter. About 3,000 yards east of Henderson Field, Colonel Ichiki's Battalion was cut to bits by Marine riflemen and machine gunners in the Battle of Alligator Creek (erroneously termed Tenaru River), Marine aviation getting into the act by making strafing runs on the beach from which the Japanese were attacking, and otherwise assisted in the mop-up. A day later this self-conceived and self-styled CACTUS Air Force was increased by five (later augmented to a total of twelve) Army *P–400's* (export version of the *P–39 Air-Cobra*) of Captain Dale Brannon's 67th Fighter Squadron which had somehow managed to fly up under its own steam from bases in New Caledonia. The ensuing naval engagement of 22-25 August, the Battle of the Eastern Solomons, afforded the Marine pilots unlimited opportunity to tangle with the much vaunted *Zeros*—and to discredit summarily the alleged invincibility of Japanese fighters. During that three-day contest both Marine dive-bombers and fighters flying side by side with naval aviators from Fletcher's *Saratoga* and *Enterprise* tore into Rear Admiral Tanaka's Expeditionary Force (supported by the entire Japanese Combined Fleet from Truk, including three battleships and a trio of carriers), seeking to land reinforcements for their ground forces battling without success to overrun the 1st MarDiv's defense perimeter.

Although this naval battle, principally a contest between opposing carrier task forces, was adjudged another Japanese tactical victory (as applied to the loss of fleet units), Henderson Field's aviators raised such havoc with Tanaka's transport group that Hyakutake's landing force was badly shot up. The outcome of this naval engagement also paid an unexpected dividend. Thrice struck by enemy bombs and with her flight deck holed, the remnants of *Enterprise'* Scouting-5 and Bombing-6 decided that being low on fuel Henderson Field appeared the lesser of two evils as opposed to attemting to roost on the shattered planks of their damaged mother ship. Known as Flight-300 under command of Lieutenant Turner Caldwell, USN, these 11 dive-bombers *(SBD's)* signed up with CACTUS Air Force, and were to remain at Guadalcanal for another month, performing invaluable service throughout the duration of their "temporary additional duty, ashore" on the Island. It was ironically stated that this expedient and the after effects of subsequent carrier casualties were crucial factors in "saving" Guadalcanal: in mid-September 24 *F4F−4's* of Lieutenant Commander Leroy Simpler's Fighting-5, which had been off-loaded at Espíritu Santo since 31 August after their floating hangar, *Saratoga,* had received a Japanese torpedo in her hull, flew in to swell CACTUS Air Force' now battle depleted ranks, and were a decisive factor in stemming the Japanese tide which threatened to engulf General Vandegrift's weary troops.

Be that as it may, by the close of August the arrival of additional Marine, Navy, and Army Air Force planes at Henderson Field, staged through the New Hebrides, flown in from carriers, or brought in by cargo shipping, served to make good in part the mounting figure of CACTUS' aircraft and pilot attrition after ten days of strenuous combat activity. Considering that the success of Operation WATCHTOWER was predicated on the concept that aircraft would form part of the defending force, and in time would provide the means to extend the American push right up the Solomons chain to Japanese outposts to the north, CACTUS Air Force had just as high a priority as the 1st MarDiv. If the mission of General Vandegrift's ground forces was to defend Henderson Field, no less important was the task of the assembled joint aviation component to prevent Japanese reinforcements from pushing the 1st MarDiv back into the sea.

Little by little CACTUS Air Force grew in size while at the same time American troop strength was similarly increased. On 29 August MAG−23's foreward-echelon equipment and ground personnel were brought in by vessel. On 30 August Colonel Wallace, the Group commander, led in its two remaining squadrons, 19 *F4F−4's* of VMF−224 (Major Robert Galer) and 12 *SBD−3's* of VMSB−231 (Major Leo Smith), fortuitously, right in the middle of a hostile air raid. Taking stock of its surviving operational aircraft on that date it was ascertained that Guadalcanal could produce 64 planes on the flight line at Henderson Field. Of that total number, 3 were Army (all that were left out of the 12 *P−400's*), and 10 were Navy from Flight−300. A couple of days afterwards the 6th Naval Construction ("Seabee") Battalion showed up for duty, whereupon its contingent of some 5 officer and 385 enlisted specialists got down to business with their two bulldozers in an attempt to make an airfield out of Henderson rather than a mere landing and take-off strip. They also began to clear a grass covered rectangular plot about a mile to the east to form another strip known as Fighter 1. Despite their best efforts Henderson Field was considered too risky for the landing of Army $B-17$ bombers except in emergencies, the runways being too restricted aside from the fact that there was seemingly never anywhere near enough aviation gasoline to fuel them, such slender stocks as were available being reserved for the fighters and dive-bombers of CACTUS' struggling little air command. As for his pilots, Colonel Wallace was in relatively good shape: he had on hand 86 to man his 64 remaining flyable aircraft. With regard to his logistical back-up, there were shortages of everything, and there was a crisis every hour on the hour, night and day, in what then passed for the aircraft maintenance section, striving to keep in operation four depleted air squadrons with an absolute minimum of essential replacement spare parts.

Such then, in a very comprehensive way, was a partial picture of the situation at Guadalcanal at the beginning of September 1942. It was to CACTUS' battered air force that General Geiger was posted as its commanding officer, and at which he arrived during the first week of that month, having but scant knowledge of the actual conditions which he was going to have confront him, and to surmount, beyond the sketchy reports which had gradually filtered through to the rear areas in the form of hastily written communiques from the battlelines of Guadalcanal to ComSoPac's Headquarters at Nouméa.

*   *   *   *   *   *   *   *   *

Shortly after darkness on 3 September the first land transport plane to lower its wheels on Henderson Field, an $R4D-1$ piloted by Lieutenant Colonel Perry K. Smith of MAG-25, braked to a sudden stop, and in the dim glare of a jeep's headlights the assembled observers watched three officers jump from the open door to the ground. Smith's passengers were none other than General Geiger, commanding the 1st MAW, his Chief of Staff, Colonel Woods, and his Intelligence Officer (A-2), Lieutenant Colonel John C. Munn. Aside from the physical presence on the scene of "The Old Man," which was a welcome shot-in-the-arm to the flight personnel of Colonel Wallace's over-extended MAG-23, the news the trio brought was equally stimulating: that 1st MAW's MAG–14 (Lieutenant Colonel Albert D. Cooley) with service, fighter, and dive-bomber squadrons (some 100 officers and 1,100 enlisted men) was already en route to the South Pacific from the West Coast to bolster CACTUS Air Force.

As for Geiger, his arrival in the combat area marked the culmination of months of preparation terminated by a 6,000-mile flight across open water from California. On 21 August, Major General Rowell, Commander, Marine Air Wings, Pacific (ComMAWPac), then at San Diego, handed Geiger his sailing orders directing him to report to ComSoPac and to ComAirSoPac, and containing explicit instructions that "he was to have general command of all Marine Corps aircraft or other such organizations as may be placed at your disposal by higher authority." It is of interest to note as evidence of the almost continuous fighting then taking place that it was not until ten days after Geiger's arrival on Guadalcanal that General Vandegrift could find the time to sit at his field desk to sign the endorsement: "having reported on 3 September and now in command of the 1st MAW, you are assigned additional duty as Commander, Aircraft, Guadalcanal (ComAirCACTUS)." In any event, in accordance with his basic directive, on 1 September Geiger flew from San Diego to Hawaii, continuing his flight southwestward via Palmyra and the Samoan Islands first to Tontouta, New Caledonia, and from thence to Espíritu Santo in the New Hebrides, finally arriving at his ultimate destination, Henderson Field, some fifty hours distant by air from his point of departure in the United States.

With direct personal control of all of its combat operations now vested in Geiger's experienced hands, AirCACTUS' indomitable fighting spirit, which, out of sheer exhaustion on the part of its flight personnel was beginning to show the effects of creeping fatigue, at once was restored and thereafter soared to even greater heights. In their respective spheres Geiger and Woods were to the 1st MAW what General Vandegrift and his Operations Officer (subsequently, his Chief of Staff), Colonel Gerald C. Thomas, were to the 1st MarDiv: personification of unshaken faith and self-confidence, resolution to maintain and to extend the spirit of the offensive despite overwhelming odds, and determination that come what may the Marines in the air and on the ground under no circumstances would allow the Japanese invaders uncontested advantage of the initiative. With "The Old Man" aboard there were no longer doubts in the minds of AirCACTUS' pilots as to the eventual outcome of the campaign, and although it was readily recognized that the worst was yet to come, Geiger's buoyant optimism soon pervaded even the more skeptical members of his joint command.

ComAirCACTUS on his part was serving under no illusions as to the near desperate conditions to which his pilots and maintenance personnel had been reduced. Quickly acquainting himself with the situation from his improvised Command Post at the "Pagoda" (a Japanese built wooden shack 200 yards from the landing strip), Geiger realized that his primary task was to establish some semblance of order to a command which taken at a glance appeared to be fast approaching the end of its tether. Naturally, there were limits to which he could resort, factors over which momentarily he seemed powerless of control. The condition of Henderson Field, for example, called for immediate action. It was a nightmare to construction engineer and pilot alike, for only 1,000 feet of runway had been matted, and the remainder was deeply rutted and pock-marked from enemy air bombing and naval gunfire. Some improvements had to be summarily effected lest AirCACTUS become permanently grounded as the result of accidents incident to landing and take-offs. Henderson Field seemed to waver between two highly undesirable extremities related to the climate quite aside from the effect of hostile bombardment. When the sun shone the strip became a maelstrom of black dust which worked its way into the carburetors of aircraft engines; when it rained in torrents the field just as rapidly was rendered a slough of sticky thick mud, thereby making it well nigh impossible for a heavily armed and fueled dive-bomber to work up enough speed to clear the end of the runway.

There being no gasoline trucks, refueling consisted of hand-pumping fluid from 55-gallon drums. There being neither bomb dollies nor hoists, re-arming was confined to the "Armstrong System." Devoid of loading machines, belted 50-caliber machine-gun ammunition also became a hand-manipulated operation. Air-to-ground radio communications were far from satisfactory due to makeshift installations and restricted ranges; the little radar gear which was available was primitive and unreliable.

The lot of the pilots and aircraft crews was truly appalling, living conditions having been ground down to the irreducible minimum. Wracked with dysentery and fungus infections and with malaria daily making increased inroads, the general health of the command regardless of rank or rating was far below normal. Cut to a maximum of two meals per day built around *Spam* or cold hash fortified by beans or captured Japanese rice, the totally inadequate diet and improper food afforded another hazard for airmen dependent on high protein intake to enable them to fly effectively at high altitudes on a never ending schedule. Anything approaching reasonable rest let alone undisturbed sleep was an unknown luxury. Throughout the nights single-engine Japanese float planes hovered constantly overhead: with illumination in the form of flares *Louie the Louse* lit up the defense perimeter; meanwhile, his mate *Washing Machine Charlie* dropped impact-fused bombs with utter abandon on the dazed defenders, hopelessly trying to snatch forty winks in an ever deepening foxhole or struggling to stay alive, half-drowned in rain water along the bottom of a slit trench. As a result, the First Marine Division (Reinforced), rifleman and cannoneer, aviator and plane mechanic, birds of a feather suffered together the misery of continual harassment from the skies after dark, and on frequent occasion, just to vary the treatment, found themselves additionally on the receiving end of interdiction fires in the shape of high-trajectory shells tossed into their midst from offlying Japanese naval vessels.

Equally precarious was the aircraft situation. By the time Geiger arrived a Guadalcanal AirCACTUS' pilots had long before learned by bitter experience not to get mixed up in dogfights with the speedier *Zeros.* Aware that the Japanese fighters could outclimb and outrun with comparative ease the far more durable and heavier armed *Wildcats,* Marine aviators early in the game had to devise suitable countermeasures. One of the tactical innovations adopted was the two-plane reciprocally supporting flight section, designed to permit the wingman to shoot the *Zero* off the tail of the leading American fighter. Among AirCACTUS' personnel it had become gradually accepted as Gospel that if one *Zero* were matched against one *Wildcat,* the *F4F−4* was destined a dead duck; by the same token two *Grummans* employing a mutually protective flight formation were eminently capable of engaging four or even five *Zeros.* Proof of the pudding was the eating: the scoreboard showed that utilizing such aerial tactics AirCACTUS shot down considerably more than twice its weight and number of enemy planes, the statisticians in time arriving at the figure that for every CACTUS aircraft lost in airborne combat, the Japanese suffered threefold attrition.

It was fortunate that the scales tipped notably in the American's favor for ComAirCACTUS' biggest headache was trying to maintain not less than 60 flyable aircraft in the face of operational losses resulting from crack-up's during take-off or landing, not to mention the steady stream of plane casualties from actual combat. When Geiger first set up his shop on 3 September, Wallace's 64 aircraft (as of 30 August) had been progressively reduced to 42. During Geiger's first week on Guadalcanal 8 of the latter number succumbed to operational accidents, and although 2 could be salvaged, the remaining 6 were worth no more than the value of their cannibalized spare parts. By 10 September his meager stock of airplanes hit a dead low of 36: 11 *Wildcats* (out of 38 flown in), 22 *Dauntless,* and the 3 *P–400's,* roughly a half-strength Marine Air Group of one fighter and one dive-bomber squadron, badly mauled but somehow patched together and flying by the skin of its teeth on the proverbial "Wing and a Prayer." His luck held out, for ComSoPac was finally prevailed upon to release "grounded" carrier planes, and the following day ComAir CACTUS gained 24 additional *Wildcats* with the arrival of *Saratoga's* Fighting-5 from Espíritu Santo. Granted that the Wing Commander now on paper had a scratch Air Group at his control (as of 8 September his promotion to Major General became effective), he was still operating at a tremendous handicap in consideration of the fact that for every replacement aircraft Geiger obtained, his Japanese counterpart, the commander of the Eleventh Naval Air Fleet at Rabaul, could lay hands on twice that number. Personnelwise, Geiger was doing the best he could with what he had been provided: by mid-September his entire complement of aviation personnel amounted to slightly more than 1,000, of which some 30 were Army Air Force and 60 from the Navy.

It did not take Geiger very long to get shaken down to his assignment. If dehydrated potatoes and tinned corn beef, wet rice and canned fish were all that was in the larder, now was as good a time as any to start working on the waistline. Although he was never one to make a fetish of paperwork, he realized that some records were critical and must be maintained, and that at least the formalities of staff work should be undertaken if order were to be brought out of chaos. Accordingly, he dispatched some of his officers back to Espíritu Santo to set up Wing Headquarters, remaining with his forward echelon and his tactical command group at Henderson Field. Thus, not only could he figuratively keep his finger on all flight operations and current developments, air as well as ground, but of equal importance, he could maintain close personal touch with his immediate superior, General Vandegrift, the Division Commander.

The predicament of the 1st MarDiv (R) at this moment was obvious to all: the Division could hold the perimeter, but other than sending out raiding parties and reconnaissance patrols had not the strength to extend its lines appreciably inland or to its flanks. With the Japanese dominating the seas at night the incursions of the "Tokyo Express" denied the Americans reinforcements and supplies; meantime, the enemy strengthened his combat resources proportionately. For the same reason Japanese aerial strength subjected the American perimeter to intermittent air bombardment. Initial American attempts at glide-bombing after darkness, designed to waylay hostile naval task forces escorting transports and cargo craft, met with sparse success. The Range of CACTUS' aircraft being limited it was correspondingly impossible to intercept the "Tokyo Express" in daylight, far to the northwest. The only recourse left to the Landing Force Commander was to hold on and to wait: to "buy time with blood" with the fond hope that CinCPac, ComSoPac, and ComAirSoPac might be able to scrape a little more from the bottoms of their barrels, and by some hook or crook deliver the goods before Vandegrift's riflemen and cannoneers were swallowed up by the tidal waves of Hyakutake's massed, fanatical assault troops, and before Geiger's worn-out airmen and scrap-pile-bound airplanes collapsed from overwork and plain exhaustion.

As events transpired it was a very near thing. Throughout the last week of August and the first ten days of September substantial Japanese troop arrivals representing the combined strength of a reinforced brigade (about 6,000 men) landed on both sides of the Americans' perimeter. The intention of the Brigade Commander, Major General Kawaguchi, was to coordinate attacks on both flanks with an assault by his main body (advancing through the jungle) against the southern extremity of the Marines' perimeter. Aggressive daily combat patrolling by various elements of the 1st MarDiv (to the limits of its supporting artillery fire) succeeded in delaying Kawaguchi's scheme of maneuver; however, it eventually realized that sooner or latter the Japanese were going to launch an all-out attack simultaneously from three directions, designed to drive the Marines into the waters of Sealark Channel. Fearing the possible arrival of Marine reinforcements (from Samoa), Kawaguchi made plans to commence his attack on the night of 12 September, selecting as his initial objective a ridge dominating Henderson Field, about 1,000 yards south of and inland from that vital installation.

Momentarily braced for just such an eventuality, Vandegrift's concern for his security was further complicated by a most unforeseen development. On the afternoon of 11 September Admiral Turner flew into Henderson Field from Espíritu Santo bringing news, which, to state it mildly, was extremely alarming to the already hard pressed Division Commander. In substance, ComSoPac had arrived at the conclusion that such was the preponderance of Japanese naval strength in the general area, and with every indication that a massive push was about to descend on Guadalcanal, the American naval forces could no longer support the Marines on the Island nor could additional troops be transported there. Left high and dry on the beach, about to be cut off from kith and kin, the tidings which Turner dumped into Vandegrift's lap understandably would have graveled anyone but the most resolute commander. The General took it all calmly and quietly, and proved conclusively what manner of man was he by informing his Operations Officer that the Landing Force would defend the airfield until the troops were physically overrun by the enemy, whereupon, the remnants would take to the hills and conduct guerrilla warfare to the last man. Furthermore, before Turner left, Vandegrift persuaded him to agree to bring in by sea the Seventh Marine Regiment (R), up from Samoa and then in the New Hebrides, whether or not the Navy decided to pull stakes and to retire to let Operation SHOESTRING wither on the vine.

Turning to Geiger, Vandegrift acquainted ComAirCACTUS

with the contents of Turner's recent bombshell, told him that the Division was prepared to make a last ditch stand, and asked his Wing Commander what he proposed to do about the situation. Chomping down a little harder on his frayed cigar, Geiger fanned a few ashes off his shirt and snapped back that as long as AirCACTUS had a plane that would fly, his command would continue to support the Division. He continued to the effect that only if his aircraft could not be used back in the bush would they be flown away from the Island. Geiger then laid it squarely on the line by remarking that come hell or high water he was determined to stay with the Division Commander, and that if he no longer had a plane with which to fight the Japanese, he'd pick up the first rifle and bayonet handy, and plunge into the scrap.

This bit of business having been attended to both officers proceeded to devote their attention to more pressing affairs then taking place in their joint front yard, for enemy exploratory attacks into the perimeter had already commenced, naval shelling was mounting at a steady rate, and hostile air raids repeatedly bore down on Henderson Field. If the night of 12 September was marked by intermittent fighting, the ensuing twenty-four hours was warfare at its bloodiest. This engagement, the second battle for Henderson Field, was termed the Battle of Edson's (Bloody) Ridge, and reached its crescendo on the night of 13–14 September. In the face of everything Kawaguchi's brigade could hurl at the defenders, the Marines in front of the airfield held fast, although at one point in the fighting a few Japanese managed to squeeze through only to be slaughtered outright by members of Vandegrift's headquarters staff between the Ridge and the Field.

In an attempt to replenish his fast diminishing supply of aircraft ComAirCACTUS sent out an urgent call for help. ComSoPac obliged to the best of his ability by sweeping clean surplus planes from carriers: naval aviators from *Hornet* and *Wasp* rushed in 18 extra *Wildcats* to make good losses in VMF—223 and VMF—224. Over at Espíritu Santo 12 dive-bombers of Scouting-3 and 6 torpedo planes of Torpedo-8, formerly attached to the damaged *Saratoga,* were released to join the fray. These 36 planes plus the 24 Simpler previously had brought to Guadalcanal saved the day for CACTUS Air Force: on 13 September Geiger's outfit lost 6 aircraft in combat but managed to maintain the scoreboard in its favor by shooting down 11 Japanese.

For a brief interlude after the defeat of Kawaguchi's brigade there was a comparative lull in the fighting ashore. At sea, on the other hand, the situation became even more grave: on 15 September while escorting the Marine reinforcements promised by Turner to Guadalcanal, *Wasp* was torpedoed (thereby reducing the Navy's operational carrier strength in the entire South Pacific to exactly one solitary unit, *Hornet*); moreover, in the engagement other Japanese torpedoes found targets in battleship *North Carolina* and in destroyer *O'Brien.* True to his word, Turner got the five transports and two cargo vessels intact to the waters off Lunga, and with the arrival of the Seventh Marines (R) with their tanks, artillery, combat service support personnel, aviation ground crews, and communications gear on 18 September, the Division Commander felt that his chances of survival had been significantly increased. With some engineering equipment now available—notably barbed wire and sand bags—the strengthening of his defenses went on at a steady pace, and despite the ominous threat of future Japanese thrusts of even greater magnitude, General Vandegrift felt strong enough to commence a series of spoiling operations to keep the enemy disorganized and under unrelenting pressure.

As for ComAirCACTUS it was "business as usual," a never ending struggle to perform miracles to keep his squadrons reasonably effective (and supplied with gasoline). As an indication of how busy Geiger had been to keep his command from falling apart, he had had no opportunity to fly himself until the third week of September. Other than his arrival entry on 3 September, the only other notation in his flight log for that month is listed: 22 September, *SBD–3,* (No. 03296), 1.2 hours duration, Pilot—Geiger, Passenger—Van Kirch, Combat Mission. There are two or more versions of the circumstances surrounding this particular flight. One—the more probable—would have it that Geiger was simply interested in getting into the scrap. The other relates to a morale factor: one of AirCACTUS' recently joined pilots, evidently dismayed by the horrible condition of the surface of Henderson Field (after an unusually severe naval gunfire bombardment), quietly stated his opinion that he did not consider it feasible for landings or take-off's pending some repair. Realizing that whereas the complaint might be valid its implications were alarming lest the defeatism spread, Geiger decided to take

215

immediate action. This consisted of walking down the strip to the first *SBD* handy, spotted on an apron, checking to see that it was fueled and that the controls had not been shot away, and ascertaining that the dive-bomber had been armed.

Revving up the machine, Geiger tried to dodge the worst of the shell holes as he taxied down the runway, and finally took off without benefit of fighter escort. Once airborne he headed his plane northward, and when over what he believed to be a concentration of Japanese troops including an antiaircraft battery in the Visale area, yanked the release cable and dumped his 1,000-pound bomb into their midst. Without further fanfare, he reversed course and landed safely half an hour later, again weaving his way in between bomb craters and rain gutted areas to return to the same spot from which he had previously departed. Without making a single remark ComAir CACTUS, aged 57 years and displaying not the slightest trace of emotion other than his customary stare, glared at the little group of youthful aviators who had witnessed his feat and had gathered around his *Dauntless,* almost inviting challenge with his unspoken retort: "So you didn't think I could do it, did you? Well, I just showed you. From here on it's up to you."

Back at the "Pagoda" for the usual "de-briefing," without bothering to explain whether he was referring to fainthearted pilots or his Japanese adversaries, Geiger grinned as he remarked to his Chief of Staff and to his Operations Officer: "Oh, I guess I just did it for spite." In any event, such a demonstration as this performance (and others allied to it) provided proof positive that he expected nothing from men that he was not first willing to attempt himself, not to mention the boost it gave morale: no matter how bad the situation appeared, "The Old Man" would find a way to lead his flock safely out of the mess.

Notwithstanding the apparent gloom which hung over Guadalcanal's defenders—for the signs were patently clear to all that the Japanese thrusts of September were building up to bigger and worse things to come in October—AirCACTUS was beginning to accumulate a tiny reserve. In early September MAG—25 had commenced its operations on a modest scale by flying in a few luxuries and flying out with the wounded, gradually increasing the scope of its activities to the point where South Pacific Combat Air Transport (SCAT), as MAG—25's transport pilots collectively came to be called, became generally regarded as another of the crucial factors in saving Guadalcanal because of its ability to deliver supplies and personnel regardless of the weather or Japanese attempts to shoot down its unarmed and unarmored planes flying over vast expanses of the ocean. Even better news were developments during the final week of September: the arrival of MAG–14's commanding officer, Lieutenant Colonel Cooley, with the long awaited combat elements of VMF–121 and VMSB–141 which trickled in bit by bit, 5 or 6 pilots on one day, half a dozen or more planes ferried in the next. Caldwell's Flight-300, or more specifically, its few surviving pilots and gunners, left the Island to return to their parent carrier. To compensate for this decrease AirCACTUS gained 6 *SBD's* from Lieutenant Commander John Eldridge's Scouting-71, backed up by 4 more *TBF's* from Torpedo-8. In addition, Lieutenant Colonel Bauer's VMF–212 from Efate and Lieutenant Colonel Hart's VMO–251 (flying fighters, not observation aircraft) from Espíritu remained as before on an "on call basis" to fill in gaps in depleted formations. As a consequence, the combination of this intermittent stream of reinforcements and the Herculean efforts of Geiger's maintenance crews to bind up the gaping wounds of AirCACTUS' crippled aircraft permitted its commander to hang on to between 50 and 70 operational planes in early October. On the 9th of that month the rest of VMF–121's machines at long last arrived at Henderson Field, raising the number of *F4F–4's* from 26 to 46, and bringing AirCACTUS' grand total of all types to 80.

With this impressive force at his disposal Geiger made several improvisations. Based on his experience at Guadalcanal the employment of the usual composite Marine Air Group organization was far from satisfactory. According to the book such a unit was set up to be self-sustaining for 90 days with its headquarters, service, and air warning squadrons accompanying its tactical elements, two squadrons each of fighters and dive-bombers. On Guadalcanal, however, the splendid organization on paper fell apart in practice, due to the intermingling of squadrons from various Marine Air Groups, the physical separation—in many instances, hundreds of miles, spread over different islands—between the tactical elements of any particular squadron and its respective ground echelon and normal source of

217

supply and replacement, plus the unalterable fact that as a result of extraordinarily heavy combat casualties and operational fatalities, the notion of being able to maintain intact 18 or 20 pilots (for more than a week) within any squadron was quite beyond the realm of possibility. On Guadalcanal when it pertained to bullets, bombs, or aviation gasoline, let alone spare parts, it was strictly a matter of "makee-do" with what limited means might be procurable at any one moment. Consequently, expediency rather than resort to formal supply and service channels ruled the day: by pooling its paltry provisions and doling them out as the situation warranted, AirCACTUS could just barely keep from going under.

Geiger's solution to the matter of command and control was equally simple. With the better part of two Marine Air Groups making up his Air Wing, augmented by several other squadrons drawn from neighboring island commands, in turn strengthened by the heterogeneous assortment of flying hardware provided by attached Army Air Corps units and Navy flights "borrowed" from carriers or loaned from ComAirSoPac, the only resort was to initiate Type Commands. Using this system all planes of one type, used for the same purpose, were placed under the control of a single Group Commander. Geiger's plan of regroupment consisted of placing Cooley (MAG–14) in charge of all dive-bombers to be known as the Strike Command, with mission of search and attack. To Wallace (MAG–23) was given the Fighter Command with the task of: furnishing escort with his *Wildcats* for Cooley's *SBD's* and *TBF's,* shooting down any Japanese fighters of bombers wherever encountered, providing combat air patrol (CAP) over the defense perimeter, pursuit, low level strafing, and ground support which could be handled by the Army's medium altitude *P–39's.* Continuing to exercise full responsibility for the combined combat performance of Strike and Fighter Commands, ComAirCACTUS now had a tailor-made organization with a command relationship designed to fit the job. Although for administrative purposes, individual numerical Squadron, Group, and Wing designations were retained as before, the flexibility plus the massed striking power of the Type Command structure at once demonstrated its superiority over the limitations of the former composite groupment. Tested and proven on Guadalcanal the new system set the standard pattern not only for the defense of the Island but also for future Marine air operations in the South and Central Pacific.

It was once written of the old Austro-Hungarian Empire in the twilight days of August 1914 that: "The situation is hopeless but not yet critical." Superficially, it might be said that an identical prospect faced the 1st MarDiv (R) on Guadalcanal in October 1942. Having had first a battalion and then a brigade chopped to pieces and hurled back by Guadalcanal's defenders, Hyakutake decided that for his third assault he might as well go the whole hog and send General Maruyama with his 2nd or Sendai Division to wipe the Marines off the map for once and for all. Relying on his dependable "Tokyo Express" Hyakutake intended to land his troops from six destroyers backed up by heavy artillery and tanks carried aboard two seaplane tenders far west of the Marine perimeter, near Tassafaronga, and from whence he would proceed overland eastward toward the mouth of the Matanikau River, picking up other Japanese troops on the way, prior to the launching of his main attack. To insure his arrival reasonably intact he was given as a Covering Force down "The Slot" Rear Admiral Goto's three cruisers and three destroyers, which, along with the usual air cover would blast AirCACTUS' planes and Henderson Field.

On the other side of the fence, so to speak, it had been decided by Admiral Nimitz, a recent visitor at Guadalcanal, that ComSoPac would make available reinforcements to General Vandegrift in the form of Colonel Bryant Moore's One Hundred Sixty-Fourth Infantry Regimental Combat Team (of General Alexander Patch's Americal Division). Taking that unit aboard his transports at Nouméa, Admiral Turner sailed for Guadalcanal on 9 October. His Covering Force consisted of Rear Admiral Scott's Task Force-64, four cruisers and five destroyers. On the night of 11-12 October the two opposing Covering Forces intercepted one another near Savo Island. This, the third major naval engagement of the Guadalcanal Campaign, known as the Battle of Cape Esperance (or Second Savo), was an inconclusive victory for the American Navy. Tactically, Scott won on points (albeit at heavy cost to his larger units), but he did not fully press his advantage. Two of Goto's crippled destroyers fell victim on the 12th to AirCACTUS' dive-bombers and torpedo planes while Scott retired with his damaged ships. But, in the long run, Hyakutake succeeded in his overall mission: his troop reinforcements, heavy artillery, tanks, and supplies got ashore west of the Matanikau while the navies were slugging it out, and the Americans within their perimeter were going to feel the inevitable result.

For almost a week prior to the Battle of Cape Esperance the Japanese had curtailed mass air attacks on Henderson Field—at least during daylight—but by 13 October the enemy had returned to its old routine. On that day as a welcome for Moore's Reinforced Regiment of Infantry, then landing on Guadalcanal, his troops were forthwith subjected to the two heaviest air raids the Island had heretofore experienced. Twice caught unprepared through 'the inability of coastwatchers and radar to alert ComAirCACTUS in sufficient time to get his planes airborne and at a high enough altitude, both Henderson Field and Fighter 1 (a subsidary strip some 2,000 yards to the east, commonly called the "Cow Pasture") were plastered with Japanese bombs. The runways on each field were badly damaged, several of CACTUS' grounded aircraft were hit, and worst of all, 5,000 gallons of precious aviation gasoline went up in a pillar of flame. This was just the prelude to Hyakutake's elaborate plans to retake Guadalcanal: during the next couple of days and nights the Island's defenders in the air as well as on the ground were almost ground to a pulp so determined were the Japanese to put an end to stubborn American opposition.

The succeeding action of 13–15 October, the third concerted Japanese attempt to capture Henderson Field, surpassed in ferocity any of the fighting which had hitherto taken place. During the night of 13–14 October Hyakutake's Seventeenth Army Artillery, consisting of a regiment and three batteries of 150-mm. howitzers, let loose on the western edge of Henderson Field. Given the name *Pistol Pete,* a single gun of this formidable artillery groupment continued its highly destructive interdiction fires without opposition, for its emplacement was far beyond the range of the 1st MarDiv's 105-mm. field artillery pieces of the Eleventh Marines and the 5 in. seacoast guns of the Third Defense Battalion (which could not be trained to bear inland). If the constant harassing fire from Japanese land-based heavy artillery were hard on the nerves, it was relatively minor compared to subsequent enemy shelling from the sea. Early in the morning of 14 October a Japanese naval task force moved close to the Island,

and aided by flares obligingly dropped by *Louis the Louse,* proceeded to paste Henderson Field from one end to the other. For an hour and a quarter battleships *Haruna* and *Kongo* deposited some 900 rounds of 14 in. high explosive projectiles on the airfield—after the first salvos flares were no longer necessary as burning gasoline, supply, and ammunition dumps lit up the general area—meanwhile, such retaliatory measures as the Americans could provide were totally ineffective.

When the "dawn came up like thunder" the next morning, the wreckage defied description: Henderson Field was a twisted ruin; out of 39 dive-bombers only 2 *SBD's* could fly; one half of Fighter Command was out of action, and all of the 24 surviving *F4F's* needed extensive repairs. The "Pagoda" was so badly torn apart Geiger ordered it bulldozed flat (lest it be used as a registration point for Japanese artillery), and moved his Command Post (CP) to the comparatively undamaged "Cow Pasture," which, for the moment was just out of range of *Pistol Pete.* To add insult to injury (out of 60 casualties in AirCACTUS, 40 total fatalities resulted from the bombardment), Japanese bombers in droves flew unchallenged over the perimeter, and up the coast to the westward Hyakutake's destroyers, transports, and supply vessels in an unrelenting stream, practically unopposed, continued to land the necessary personnel and matériel for the projected enemy attack against Vandegrift's perimeter.

While Geiger's ground crews worked themselves to a frazzle trying to put together the remaining aircraft which had not been completely destroyed, "The Old Man, " despite intermittent shell fire, began to lead a frantic search for fuel to make good the losses from the previous bombardments. The tanks of two *B–17's,* wrecked beyond repair, were quickly drained for their contents; fortunately, somebody remembered the existence of about 400 drums of 100-octane gasoline, which had been carefully stashed away in little clumps, in holes and covered pits, several hundred yards from Henderson Field. In the confusion from the recent bombings abetted in part from weariness and strain, Geiger had all but forgotten the presence of this pre-planned fuel reserve for just such an emergency. Colonel Woods had sent Geiger a written memorandum informing him of the cached supply, but the latter had had neither the time nor the inclination to read it what with other urgent matters on his mind. After the "crisis" of mid-October, when Woods came over from Espíritu to confer with ComAirCACTUS on the Island, the memo, still unopened, was found reposing in the pocket of "The Old Man's" combat jacket. At any rate, by scrounging this and digging up that, plus additional drums of fuel either brought in by VMJ—253's transports, 10 containers at a time, or carried aboard escort vessels, YP—boats, and destroyer-sea-plane tenders, ComAirCACTUS was able after a fashion to keep what little was left of his air force supplied with enough gasoline to resume limited combat operations.

The night of 14—15 October was merely a repetition of its predecessor, perhaps in a slightly minor key. Again Henderson Field took it on the chin, this time from Eighth Fleet heavy cruisers, *Chokai* and *Kinugasa,* which proceeded to pump more than 750 8 in. high explosive and incendiary projectiles onto the strip; meantime, the landing of additional Japanese troops and supplies in the Tassafaronga area begun during the hours of darkness continued unabated in broad daylight, so powerless were American air or naval forces to intercede. Such United States naval task forces as were then present in the South Pacific theater were either in port trying to effect "running repairs," or too distant from the scene of operations to intercept the "Tokyo Express" in time to be of any value. With regard to Geiger's air force daybreak on 15 October revealed he had only 3 *SBD's* able to fly. One of them slipped into a shell hole while trying to get to the runway; the second cracked-up on take-off; the third somehow managed to make it.

Realizing that single plane strikes were of no earthly use, Geiger brought them to a halt until such time as his mechanics (those who had miraculously survivied the shellings were half dead on their feet from lack of sleep) could patch up a dozen-odd crippled machines. Pending the completion of their endeavors, Geiger's personal pilot and aide-de-camp, Major Jack Cram, requested permission to undertake what appeared to be a forlorn hope. Having returned from a ferry run to Espíritu in Geiger's "Blue Goose" (*PBY—5A,* No. 08030) with two 2,000-pound torpedoes attached under each of the amphibian's outstretched wings, Cram asked if he could make a daylight torpedo run against the Japanese transports. Geiger was reluctant to accede for despite his unqualified confidence in the Major's flying abilities, he doubted if the ungainly amphibian could take-off, bearing in mind the condition of Henderson Field, quite aside from the remote possibility of the plane's getting through to the target without first being shot out of the air so great was the preponderance of Japanese aerial superiority. At length he assented (there being no Navy torpedo-planes operational to fly such a mission), but only on condition that Cram would be accompanied by a scratch force of dive-bombers and fighters, not much in the way of support in view of the fact that at least 30 Japanese *Zeros* were known to be over the transport unloading site.

With no co-pilot to assist him, Cram successfully cleared the strip, flew to the selected target area, put his plane into an abrupt dive at a speed almost twice that for which it had been designed (and could withstand), and in the face of heavy Flak from covering Japanese destroyers, released both his torpedoes which slammed into the hull of a beached transport, exploded, and broke the vessel's back. With five *Zeros* on his tail, Cram nevertheless managed to get the "Blue Goose" 12 miles back to Fighter 1. Reporting to Geiger at the strip, ComAirCACTUS took one look at 50-odd holes appearing in the "Goose's" fuselage, tail assembly, and wings, and proceeded to berate Cram for neglect and willful destruction of government property. Having driven that point home, "The Old Man" thereupon walked over to what served as his operations shack and wasted no time writing up a citation recommending Major Cram for a well-deserved Navy Cross.

Three of the Japanese transports having been burnt or sunk by CACTUS' Air Force, and three others so badly hit they had to retire, General Hyakutake had to alter his plans accordingly, although by mid-October practically all of the 2nd (Sendai) Division and even elements of another, the 38th, had been brought to Guadalcanal. More or less to even up the score for this set-back—and to bloody the Americans' nose a little further—the Japanese decided to take another punch at Henderson Field's tired defenders before delivering the final knock-out blow. Under the personal command of Vice Admiral Kondo of the Second Fleet two heavy cruisers, *Maya* and *Mikayo,* and two destroyers stood off Lunga Point on the night of 15-16 October, and at ranges varying from 4 to 5 miles tossed onto the landing field another 1,200 rounds of 8 in. and 5 in. shell in an hour-long naval bombardment. As usual, CACTUS Air Force bore the brunt, and when the firing ceased all that were left were some 30 aircraft, of

223

which one third were fighters, most of them in poor condition, one jump away from the scrap heap.

Once again with his back to the wall Geiger had no other choice but to put out a call for reinforcements. Over at Efate, Bauer gassed up 19 *Wildcats* of his VMF−212, and along with 7 *Dauntless* dive-bombers flew straightway to Guadalcanal. Before that day (16 October) was finished he won the Medal of Honor by taking on a nine-plane squadron of *Val* dive-bombers, four of which he shot down unassisted. As for the fuel situation it was temporarily alleviated by the timely arrival of destroyer-seaplane tender *McFarland,* which, having landed her priceless cargo of drummed aviation gasoline, had the subsequent misfortune of having her stern blown off by enemy dive-bombers.

Following three days of intensive shelling by land and sea it was logically assumed by the Americans that this was but a prelude in the chain of events, a softening up to be shortly followed by Hyakutake's all-out attack on Henderson Field. For a variety of reasons; chiefly, the frightful weather, the jungle, lack of communications and insufficient time to coordinate thoroughly secondary thrusts with the primary assault, the Japanese were denied the advantage of their initial opportunity. Not so ComAirCACTUS, who put the breathing spell to good use by effecting long overdue transfers of several of his battle-worn components. What little was left of Mangrum's VMSB−232 and Smith's VMF−223 had already been relieved on 12 October. By the 16th the survivors of VMSB−231 and VMF−224 were so few, they too were ordered out. With the exception of Bauer's VMF−212 and a few ground personnel MAG−23 closed down its operations on Guadalcanal on that day, Wallace turning over his tactical command to MAG−14 (Cooley). Reviewing its record MAG−23's was most impressive: between 20 August and 16 October the Group plus attached Marine, Navy, and Army Air Corps units shot down 244 planes of Rabaul's Naval Air Fleet, and was credited with having hit some 30 vessels of various categories, 7 of which were actually sunk. On the debit side at least 22 of its fighter pilots were lost in combat; moreover, 33 additional aviators representing the associated squadrons were killed. The total number of its casualties would doubtless have been decidedly greater had it not been for the efficient search and rescue teams, which saved the lives of more than one half the American airmen shot down over or around Guadalcanal.

For MAG–14 there was not a moment's rest. Commencing on the 17th, VMF–121 and VMF–212 were ordered to break up squadrons of hostile bombers and fighters which had begun anew to intensify their raids on Henderson Field as their contribution to Hyakutake's general plan of attack on the American lines. In spite of the relatively small number of aircraft at Geiger's disposal, during daylight hours AirCACTUS was able to hold its own locally, as before, but at night it was powerless to halt the stream of Japanese reinforcements landing west of General Vandegrift's perimeter. As sea, under the personal control of Admiral Yamamoto a large task force of battleships, carriers, and heavy cruisers had already sailed from Truk bound south toward the Santa Cruz Islands, ready to close in for the kill at the propitious moment and to spray Henderson Field with a naval bombardment of even greater intensity than it had heretofore been subjected.

While this was transpiring General Maruyama's division was busily engaged hacking its way through the jungle, endeavoring to position itself on schedule to assault the Americans from the south; meantime, on either flank other Japanese forces were readying themselves for simultaneous drives from east and west. In substance, Hyakutake had devised a plan to encircle and to smash the Americans' perimeter by land attacks from three directions taking place at the same time, and in conjunction with aerial strikes and naval shelling. In theory his course of action appeared to be the perfect "School Solution;" in practice it fell apart because of its inherent complexity rendered even more difficult to execute because of unfavorable weather conditions and a breakdown in effective control measures. Innumerable delays and postponements in the long run proved more confusing to the attackers than to the defenders: it was not until midnight, 24–25 October that the "big push" from the south really got going, and by that date, after four days of Japanese probing around various sectors of the Americans' perimeter, the latter had been given the opportunity to ascertain the nature and direction of Hyakutake's scheme of maneuver. Furthermore, at sea the unexpected Japanese procrastination had enabled the American Navy to bring from as far away as Pearl Harbor a second aircraft carrier and a brand new battleship to reinforce its depleted strength in the Southern Solomons.

When the Japanese at last committed themselves on land and in the air for this, their fourth (and final) massive attempt to capture Henderson Field (22–26 October), it so happened that besides commanding Guadalcanal's Air Force, Geiger found himself acting as the Deputy Commanding General of the American Ground Forces inasmuch as General Vandegrift was temporarily absent at Nouméa during a vital part of the engagement. On 18 October, Vice Admiral William F. Halsey, then on a familiarization tour of the South Pacific area prior to assuming command of a carrier task force, was summarily instructed by Admiral Nimitz to proceed forthwith to Nouméa to relieve Admiral Ghormley as ComSoPac. Having complied with his basic directive, and being unable to obtain a clear-cut picture of the actual situation at Guadalcanal from staff officers at Nouméa, Halsey had no other choice but to request that the principal commander concerned, General Vandegrift, fly to his headquarters to render a personal account of current developments. On the 23rd Vandegrift reported aboard Halsey's flagship, *USS Argonne,* to brief his superior. Among the high ranking naval and military dignitaries present at the conference was Lieutenant General Thomas Holcomb, Commandant of the Marine Corps, who had been visiting with Vandegrift on Guadalcanal at the time the latter received his summons to report to Halsey, and had accompanied Vandegrift on his flight to Nouméa.

The meeting was of transcendental importance, for it was firmly established that Guadalcanal would be held at all costs. Of equal significance was Halsey's realization that Vandegrift needed more active support than he had been receiving from ComSoPac. In reply to the General's request for reinforcements to counter the constant Japanese build-up in the Lower Solomons, Admiral Halsey agreed that his command would furnish the defenders of Guadalcanal with every possible resource within its sphere of operations.

While Vandegrift was making his point at Nouméa, Geiger as his deputy found that affairs within the perimeter as well as at Henderson Field required his undivided attention. Characteristically, he took that additional responsibility in his stride, and proved that he was fully capable of making decisions and seeing to it that once made they were carried out thoroughly. Once it had been determined that Maruyama's main effort was being directed against the southern edge of the Americans' perimeter, Geiger did not hesitate to employ his reserves: the 1st Battalion, Seventh Marines, engaged in a fierce fire fight with their Japanese assailants, was instantly buttressed by soldiers of the 3rd Battalion, One Hundred Sixty-Forth Infantry. Fighting side by side the Marines and infantrymen held firm, and throughout the early morning hours of 25 October threw back the lines of screaming Japanese causing fearful slaughter among the ranks of the attackers.

By continually reorganizing his lines and strengthening his defensive positions as the situation dictated to counter Japanese thrusts at various points along the perimeter's edge, Geiger was able not only to hold the enemy at bay but also to repel Hyakutake's troops with very heavy losses to the invaders. In this manner an even stronger Japanese attack on the night of $25-26$ October was successfully contained. By that time it was becoming evident that the principal Japanese assault was a dismal failure, a victim of piecemeal, uncoordinated commitment of separate units against a determined and skillfully directed defender. For the next two days and nights enemy activity steadily diminished, his attacks becoming progressively weaker, and by the 28th it was apparent that the Japanese had conclusively lost the engagement.

If the incessant rain had hampered enemy movements and troop dispositions on land no less had it affected American air operations which were seriously curtailed when they were most needed. 25 October went down on record as "Dugout" or "Red Sunday," for air support for the hard pressed riflemen could not be delivered until such time as the take-off strips dried up sufficiently to permit AirCACTUS to take to the skies. Pinned down to Fighter 1 by thick mud it was not until the afternoon that Geiger's *Grummans* could put up any opposition to countless hostile air raids. Once the Marine and Navy pilots took off they were almost continuously in the air engaging enemy machines, returning to the field only for refueling and rearming. Reduced to a strength of only 12 *SBD's* even these could not be employed for the mud on Henderson Field had rendered it inoperative. Faced with renewed enemy naval activity in the waters adjacent to Guadalcanal, Geiger had no alternative short of requesting help from the outside. Over at ComAirSoPac's Headquarters at Espíritu, Rear Admiral Aubrey W. Fitch helped out to the limit of his ability. All he could scrape together from the New Hebrides and New Caledonia were 7 fighters and 3 dive-bombers, sent posthaste to assist AirCACTUS. They got there in time, and combined with the aircraft Geiger managed to fly off the fields at Guadalcanal in three separate attacks drove off several menacing destroyers and seriously damaged a light cruiser.

On 26-27 October, as the Japanese land operations to seize Henderson Field foundered to a halt, there was a momentary recrudescence of naval activity on the high seas some 300 miles east of Guadalcanal. In that ocean area Admiral Yamamoto's Combined Fleet consisting of 4 battleships, 4 carriers, 8 heavy cruisers, and 24 destroyers (representing Vice Admiral Kondo's Second and Vice Admiral Magumo's Third Fleet) was cruising about, burning up fuel, impatiently waiting the signal from Hyakutake on Guadalcanal to come forward to take part in the anticipated surrender ceremonies once Henderson Field had been overrun. ComSoPac, of course, was aware of the presence of this large task force, and had taken steps to intercept it. Although the odds were 2:1 against him, Rear Admiral Thomas Kinkaid's tactical command (2 battleships, 2 carriers—*Enterprise* and *Hornet*, 6 heavy cruisers, and 14 destroyers) was determined to give a good account of itself. The Americans drew first blood: a search plane having spotted the enemy task force, a hit was scored on the flight deck of the light carrier *Zuiho*, and the naval Battle of the Santa Cruz Islands got under way with a roar.

Essentially a carrier air engagement, when the shooting died down and the smoke cleared away every indication pointed to another defeat for the American Navy. *Hornet* and two destroyers were sunk; *Enterprise*, battleship *South Dakota*, and cruiser *San Juan* were damaged. The Japanese lost no vessels; however, both heavy cruiser *Shokaku* and light carrier *Zuiho* were torn up severely. The losses of naval aircraft were about equal: the Americans 74, the Japanese 69. But one thing the cold statistics did not reveal was the unalterable fact that attrition of their experienced naval aviators was so high the Japanese were incapable of providing carrier cover for their next attempt to seize Guadalcanal. During the ten-day period which terminated in the Battle of the Santa Cruz Islands, the Japanese Naval Air Arm lost approximately 200 aircraft. These might be made good in time, but the replacement situation pertaining to pilots was quite another matter, destined in the long run to contribute materially to the collapse of the Japanese naval effort in the Pacific Campaigns. For the moment, however, one thing was quite clear. The Japanese had been thrown off balance, and before they could amass further reinforcements to make another attempt to wrest Guadalcanal from the Americans they had lost their chance, for by then the United States Pacific Fleet was in the driver's seat.

Naturally, ComAirCACTUS had no way of knowing the significance of the recently fought naval engagement. His principal concern at that particular moment was finding some way to build up his battle damaged air squadrons, for by the end of October Geiger's air force numbered but 29 combat aircraft. All of them were in poor condition, but the suspension of enemy air raids over Henderson Field for three or four days after the repulse of the Japanese ground troops afforded Geiger's mechanics a heaven-sent opportunity to hammer out a few kinks and to patch up a few holes in the remaining battered *Wildcats* and *Dautless's,* still considered capable of being flown. The best news of all were reports that another Marine Air Group of four squadrons was arriving at New Caledonia, proof that Admiral Halsey was doing everything possible to "deliver the goods."

Bit by bit MAG-11 under the command of Lieutenant Colonel William O. Brice made its way to Henderson Field, moving progressively northwestward from Noumea and Espiritu. By mid November both of its fighter squadrons, VMF-112 and VMF-122, its two dive-bomber components, VMSB-132 and VMSB-142, and the Marines' first torpedo bomber squadron, VMSB-131 (attached to MAG-14), were at ComAirCACTUS' disposal. At that time Guadalcanal's aviation units had risen to a total of 1,748 pilots, gunners, and mechanics, of which 1,557 were Marines. So large was the number of personnel and machines it was decided to construct a supplementary take-off strip west of Henderson Field and the Lunga River. After three days of cutting brush and leveling the terrain, the new addition termed Fighter 2, was ready for use. Compared to the lean days of September and October AirCACTUS was beginning to exhibit definite signs of "growing up."

With regard to its first commanding officer the time seemed ripe for a change of scene. So busy had Geiger been during the month of October for the first, and only, time in his career as a naval aviator his flight log drew a complete blank—not a single entry. It was not a matter of his being ready, willing, and able—which Geiger most assuredly was—but simply that he had not had the opportunity to fly what with the crushing responsibilities of command and control (not to mention the problem of staying alive) for more than sixty days and nights without a break as ComAirCACTUS. The physical and moral courage which he exhibited throughout that trying period, his resourcefulness, personal leadership under hazardous conditions, and the inspiration which he instilled in his command were not passed over unnoticed by his superiors. For his devotion to duty, sound judgement, and bravery he was to be awarded two combat decorations: a Gold Star in lieu of a second Navy Cross and the Distinguished Flying Cross.

On 7 November 1942 his former Chief of Staff, Louis Woods, now a Brigadier General, flew in to relieve Geiger as ComAirCACTUS. Both Vandegrift and Geiger opposed the latter's transfer, but ComSoPac was insistent that he be pulled back to Espíritu so that he could work closely with Admiral Fitch's Headquarters. Still Commanding General of the 1st MAW, Geiger consoled himself with the thought that he might as well make a trip over to the New Hebrides on general principles to see what his Headquarters looked like, having not been given the chance since he set up his tactical CP at Henderson Field in early September. He remained at Guadalcanal until Admiral Halsey (who had flown up from Nouméa) had personally acquainted himself with the situation on the Island, and on the 8th accompanied by his aide, Major Cram, Geiger flew his "Blue Goose" south to ComSoPac's Headquarters to bring himself up to date on the "big picture" prior to flying back up to Espíritu Santo to resume his new duties at that place.

Chapter XI

The Man with the Twenty-foot Stare

Having reported to Admiral Halsey's Headquarters at Nouméa, Geiger remained there for more than a week participating in numerous briefings and staff conferences, and when opportunity permitted, catching up on some badly needed rest and taking aboard decent rations. He had gotten out of Guadalcanal just in time. Had he remained at Henderson Field a few days longer he would have been treated to another dose of 8 in. shells from hostile cruisers which pounded the Island's aviation facilities on the night of 13-14 November incident to the Naval Battle of Guadalcanal (or Third Savo), the final Japanese attempt to knock out Henderson Field once and for all, from the sea, in a four-day running engagement involving surface vessels and aircraft, which ended disastrously for Admiral Kondo's battleships, Admiral Mikawa's cruisers, and Admiral Tanaka's transports.

Although the threat to Guadalcanal was generally conceded to have been terminated by this American victory at sea, General Hyakutake had no intention of tossing in the towel, ashore, without fighting it out to the bitter end; hence, for the ensuing month both the 1st MarDiv (R) and CACTUS Air Force were to continue their combat activities unabated as before. Operating from his 1st MAW Headquarters at Espíritu Santo as a subsidiary component of ComAirSoPac, Geiger's principal concerns were to ensure that the Marine Corps elements of AirCACTUS were provided with the proper logistical means to carry out their assigned tasks—the beans, bombs, and bullets—and that trained replacement personnel continued to flow westward to Lunga Point to make good combat and operational wastage in the tactical

231

squadrons. Unlike MAG's-14, -23, and -25 which had both their Headquarters and Service Squadrons accompany their fighter and bomber elements to Guadalcanal, only MAG-11's Headquarters Squadron proceeded to the Island. Its Service Squadron was deliberately retained at Espíritu acting as a combination supply and training command for the 1st MAW as a whole, even though, as previously related, its tactical squadrons in part or united ultimately served with AirCACTUS.

To coordinate all the varied activities of the 1st MAW at Guadalcanal as well as in the New Hebrides and in New Caledonia, the Commanding General of necessity had to engage in considerable flying himself throughout the months of November and December. Naturally, this was greatly to Geiger's liking after his enforced abstinence, especially during the month of October. By mid-November, his twin-engine *Beechcraft* (*JRB-2,* No. 4723), which he had not flown since he left San Diego in August, had been brought out to the South Pacific by ship. He could hardly wait for it to be gassed up, whereupon with Lieutenant Colonel Perry Parmelee serving as co-pilot, the pair took off from Nouméa for an inspection tour of Espiritu and Efate. Interesting enough, there is no record of his flying that particular machine west of Espíritu. Whenever Geiger had occasion to make a flight to Guadalcanal, he always employed his trusty "Blue Goose," which, quite aside from the fact that its range was considerably greater than his light command transport, was obviously armed, and being an amphibian could make water or ground landings at will. Besides, although Henderson Field had been appreciably improved since Geiger's detachment, he may have been understandably apprehensive lest the *JRB's* comparatively fragile landing gear be wiped out by a "hard" touchdown on the strip's irregular and uneven surface.

One of Roy Geiger's distinctive characteristics during much of his career as a Marine Officer was a marked tendency to depend little on others. He had his own personal reasons for most everything he did, and those reasons seemed to satisfy him. Doubtless, this trait was developed while still a youth, and whereas many men as they grew older and assumed greater responsibilities often sought professional advice from others, Gieger persisted in keeping his own counsel, playing his cards close to his chest. Regardless of whether he was officiating as the commanding officer of a Squadron, a Group, or a Wing (or even later, of a Marine Amphibious Corps), he preferred to serve as his own Intelligence Officer. It was not so much a matter of his not trusting his technical advisers, but rather a sincere desire on his part to find out what was going on, and of even greater importance, to ascertain what could happen in the future. He wanted to have firsthand knowledge of current and pending operational matters, and he deeply resented what he considered unnecessary and unwarranted interference.

As the Commanding General of the 1st MAW working in close conjunction with Admiral Fitch (ComAirSoPac), Geiger was not satisfied to sit for hours listening to others brief him on enemy activities and capabilities. He just had to find out for himself what was transpiring, for he felt reluctant to issue orders without first knowing all the facts. On several occasions while serving at Espíritu he gratified his whim by simply taking to the air himself to obtain a close-up view of the situation. For example, on 4 December while on a visit to Guadalcanal he learned from the Intelligence and Operations Sections attached to ComAirCACTUS' Headquarters that a Japanese task force was reported coming down "The Slot." Other than the fact that it was known to be composed of destroyers and transports, and was presumed to be trying to bring in supplies to Hyakutake's now retreating troops, the staff officers—at that moment—could furnish no further details concerning its composition or progress.

Taking Major Cram aside, Geiger told him not to tell anyone, but to get the "Blue Goose" ready for take-off inasmuch as the General planned to go aloft and to scout the hostile group that evening. Climbing into a jeep Geiger was driven from Headquarters over to nearby Henderson Field by Colonel Parmelee, whom Geiger had sworn to secrecy lest General Woods try to persuade "Rugged Roy" from making a hazardous, unescorted night flight. Taking off after dark and with Cram at the controls the pair flew back and forth between Guadalcanal and New Georgia for a total of seven and one half hours, returning to Henderson Field after dawn. During that period, at 0200 on 5 December, using the plane's radar they located four enemy destroyers. These were tracked and reported to AirCACTUS' Operations. A second group of seven destroyers and transports were similarly spotted at 0500, and their presence also was duly relayed to Henderson Field. At no time was the fact that Geiger was aboard the "Blue Goose" disclosed. This incident and subsequent flights of the same nature was typical of Geiger: unless he could get into the act himself, he felt that he was not doing his job properly; moreover, not wishing to have somebody else tell him how to do it (or how not to do it), he went about his business quietly, undetected, and with a minimum of fuss and fanfare.

Two days after his reconnaissance flight Geiger was back again at Henderson Field, this time to say good-by to General Vandegrift and his departing 1st MarDiv (R), relieved by General Patch's XIVth United States Army Corps (consisting of the Americal Division, the 25th Infantry Division, and the 2nd MarDiv). AirCACTUS including the forward echelon of Geiger's 1st MAW and MAG's-11, -14, and -25 were to remain as before on the Island, MAG's-12 and -24 likewise maintaining their bases at Efate. By that date Woods' air command numbered more than 100 planes for the first time, and by mid-December the total number of aircraft at his disposal, representing all of the services, reached almost 200 of which about one half were fighters.

The United States Navy having at last achieved naval supremacy in the South Pacific, Guadalcanal was considered past the "critical period," and although at least another two months of constant combat were required to drive the remnants of the Japanese Seventeenth Army from the Island, the eventual conquest of Guadalcanal progressively became a matter of isolating and destroying scattered groups of enemy stragglers, fighting a rear-guard action in the best traditions of guerrilla warfare. Meanwhile, with the ground forces committed to mopping-up operations, AirCACTUS continued its bombing strikes over the "Tokyo Express" in "The Slot," now striving to evacuate what was left of Hyakutake's shattered command to the north.

With the situation in the lower Solomons gradually developing in the American's favor, certain of the amenities of daily living, heretofore denied its defenders, began to creep in. At Espiritu Geiger enjoyed the comparative luxury of tents with wooden flooring and even screens. Long a physical fitness addict he kept in decent shape by playing volley ball, usually before the evening meal. When some member of the staff suggested the idea of constructing a volley ball court, it was originally intended to build it near the Operations tents where the terrain was reasonably level. When Geiger first heard about the project he protested on the grounds that the noise and the shouting would be disturbing to officers on watch in that area. He proposed moving the site further away, down at the other end of the camp, and this was done. So enthusiastic did he become about the game within a week's time he changed his mind, and forthwith had the entire court moved close to his tent so that he could participate in every contest. He soon selected his players with care, and before long his team was willing to challenge any other on the base, As always he hated to lose any match, but he was far more critical of his own mistakes than he he was of the errors of his teammates.

In the field he was perfectly willing to share its hardships, without complaint, but back at the base he felt that there was no sense being uncomfortable when there was no reason for it. Such being the case he ran the best mess possible supplementing the ration issue with little extras paid for out of his own pocket. Frequently he invited the younger and more junior officers of his staff to eat at his table, and although the table conversation at times may have been a little forced (for he had no "small talk"), he went out of his way to try and put his guests at ease.

Technically classed as a rear-area installation this of itself afforded no guarantee that Espíritu Santo was immune from enemy attack. On 21 January 1943, while Secretary of the Navy Frank Knox and Admiral Nimitz were visiting ComAirSoPac's Headquarters, the Japanese Army Air Force livened up their tour—and interrupted the briefing the distinguished guests were receiving from Fitch and Geiger—by sending down a couple of bombers from Rekata Bay which proceeded to drop their loads within the camp area. Even though the only damage incurred was a temporary loss of their composure, the incident nevertheless served to remind all hands present that hostile air raids, even in the backwash of the main battle theaters, were still a force to be reckoned with.

By that date the Japanese authorities had long since decided to abandon their plans for the recapture of Guadalcanal, and had transferred their attentions to building up New Georgia. As far back as December 1942 they had commenced the construction of a concealed and cleverly camouflaged airfield at Munda, some 175 miles northwest of Guadalcanal. With the aid of photographic planes flying out of Henderson Field the presence of this new installation was soon discovered. Thereafter the site became the Number 1 Target for CACTUS Air Force which strafed and bombed both the field and the now re-routed "Tokyo Express" mercilessly, returning in full measure the punishment the Americans had suffered since the preceding August. By February 1943 the withdrawal of the Japanese ground forces from Guadalcanal had been completed. During the six-month period of AirCACTUS' combat operations, 20 August 1942–10 February 1943, the total number of Marine pilots assigned to 15 Marine tactical squadrons amounted to more than 450. Of that figure some 90 were killed or listed as missing in action while more than 170 had to be evacuated as casualties or re-assigned to noncombat flying billets. Turning to the scoreboard, out of more than 2,000 sorties flown by Marine pilots against Japanese aircraft, some 100 American machines were lost in combat, another 30 succumbing to operational disasters. As for the enemy, some 400-odd Japanese planes were either shot down or were blown to bits on the ground by Marine aviators, singular proof of the superiority of the 1st and 2nd MAW's Squadrons over Rabaul's Eleventh Naval Air Fleet.

February 1943 also marked the swan song of the *Wildcats*. On the 12th MAG-11's VMF-124 flew a dozen of the new *Vought Corsairs (F4U-1's)* to Henderson Field from Espíritu, and within six months all of the Marine fighter squadrons in the South Pacific were equipped with these splendid machines. The *Corsairs* could climb and fly faster than the Japanese *Zeros,* and had twice the range of the older *Wildcats.* Along with the proven *SBD's,* the *Corsairs* formed the ideal team for the continuation of the Marines' War in the Pacific—they became the "work horses" for future campaigns. Moreover, the advent of the *F4U's* had a pronounced effect on the general strategy of the Solomons' air operations: with a 1,000-mile range the *Corsairs* could fly fighter escort for Navy *PB4Y,* four-engine heavy bombers (*Consolidated* versions of the Army's celebrated *B-24's*) as far northwest as Bougainville, a run which was far in excess of the scope of the *F4F's.*

The increased radius of operation of the new aircraft fitted in conveniently with the JCS plans. In essence they envisaged a progressive advance up the Solomon's chain with Rabaul the objective. With Rabaul eliminated the way would be clear for

Admiral Nimitz to bring the big guns of his Pacific Fleet to bear on Truk. Accordingly, it was decided that while ComSoPac started up the rungs of the Solomon's ladder, the American and Australian troops under MacArthur's command (CinCSoWesPac) would continue their advance ashore up the coast of New Guinea northward from Port Moresby. The distance from Guadalcanal to Rabaul being 560 miles across intervening water and island masses it was agreed that both New Georgia and Bougainville would have to be taken, employing land-based aviation to knock out existing Japanese air installations on those islands prior to their actual seizure by amphibious forces. ComAirSoPac and ComAirSols (the revised designation for the former ComAirCACTUS) thus were given a specific mission: to intercept hostile shipping in "The Slot" and to escort bombers flying up from Guadalcanal to attack enemy airfields and airdromes at Munda, New Georgia, at Vila near the southern extremity of Kolombangara, and at Kahili on the south coast of Bougainville.

By March the softening up process against Munda was well under way. Desiring to see how things were going on the 4th of that month Geiger and Cram in the "Blue Goose" flew from Espíritu to Guadalcanal. The following afternoon while conferring with Brigadier General Francis P. Mulcahy, commanding the 2nd MAW, and Brigadier General Field Harris on the staff of ComAirSols, Geiger on the spur of the moment decided that he very much wanted to make a flight to Munda to observe the effects of a combined naval shelling and aerial bombardment which had been scheduled. They discussed the operation at some length, and finally, Geiger, said: "I'm going up and watch the show. If you two want to join me, fine." Turning to Cram he ordered: "Jack, get the plane ready. Get all the information on our forces, where they will be, and from what direction they will be attacking. Also, secure an altitude at which we can fly and be out of the anti-aircraft fire and naval gunfire."

After dark the quartet took off, proceeded by a predetermined route to Munda, watched the shelling and the bombing, and had turned to retire when unexpectedly anti-aircraft fire from American vessels opened up on the "Blue Goose." With Cram at the controls the plane dove from 8,000 feet to an altitude of 1,500 feet in a spiral turn. Fortunately, all of the anti-aircraft fire fell behind them. Because of the situation on Guadalcanal when radio contact was again made with Henderson Field they had to fly all night, as the landing facilities on the ground were out of commission. After dawn on the 6th the return and landing at Henderson Field were made without incident, and after dropping off his two companions, Geiger and Cram refueled the machine and flew back to Espiritu.

To Geiger the flight was but a mere incident—a routine entry in his flight log. Apparently it did not occur to him either then or later what a near thing it had been, or what might have been the consequences had the plane been forced to land at Japanese-held Munda, whereupon the enemy at one fell swoop might have bagged the Commanding Generals of two Marine Air Wings, the future ComAirNorSols in the Bougainville Campaign, and the subsequent commanding officer of VMB-612, one of Marine aviation's most successful night-radar, rocket-firing squadrons. Geiger never counted the "misses" or the "near misses"—you either made it, or you did not, and in either case there was no sense crowing about it.

In mid-March after some six month's service with an operational command in combat, his transfer to the United States became effective. His orders signed by Rear Admiral Theodore S. Wilkinson (Deputy Commander, ComSoPac) dated 19 March, were brief and to the point: "When relieved on or about 15 April 1943, you are detached as Commanding General, 1st Marine Air Wing, and will proceed to Pearl Harbor and report to the Commander-in-Chief, United States Pacific Fleet (Admiral Nimitz) for further air transportation to the United States and to Washington, D.C., for duty as the Director, Marine Corps Aviation."

Thoroughly familiar with existing conditions in the Lower Solomons, in the New Hebrides, and in New Caledonia, Geiger asked permission to visit all of CinCSoWesPac's installations and bases prior to his departure from Espiritu, the better to acquaint himself with the general area and the theater of operations of scheduled, future campaigns in New Guinea and the Central Solomons. Admirals Fitch and Halsey readily granted his request, and assigned him to two week's additional duty to accomplish his mission. Departing from Tontouta on 9 April with Captain Richard Pierce as his new aide and pilot in lieu of Major Cram, now with an operational unit, the indefatigable "Blue Goose"

238

ground its way westward across the Coral Sea for seven hours to Brisbane, Australia. From thence the pair continued northward via Townsville to Port Moresby, New Guinea. After a brief call at General MacArthur's Headquarters arrangements were made to fly north to Buna, across the southern tip of Papua, over the Owen Stanley Mountain Range, in an Army *B-17*.

Having viewed the formidable terrain of southeastern New Guinea (and gained an appreciation of the difficulties confronting the Allied forces on land in that region), Geiger boarded his amphibian on his return to Port Moresby, and on the 14th took off destined for Darwin in Northern Australia. Another nine-hour flight carried them on to Exmouth Gulf at the western extremity of that continent. From there their course took a southeasterly direction, across the bleak desert wastes of Western Australia to Kalgoorlie, and on over the Great Australian Bight to Adelaide. Now flying over reasonably populated coastal areas their flight continued easterly to Melbourne, New South Wales. After visiting with General Vandegrift and his 1st MarDiv, now attempting to regain its health after the rigors of Guadalcanal, the "Blue Goose" retraced its steps to Tontouta, via Sydney, and by 21 April Geiger and Pierce had returned to Espíritu Santo with brief cases crammed with maps and extensive notes and with an accumulation of uniforms in dire need of a laundry.

When they touched down at AirSoPac's landing strip, Major General Ralph J. Mitchell, Geiger's relief who had just completed a long tour as the Director, Marine Corps Aviation, was there to meet them. The change of command ceremonies were short, for Geiger climbed aboard the same plane which had brought Mitchell westward from Pearl Harbor and took off that very evening for Admiral Nimitz' Headquarters in Hawaii. Whether or not he was aware of it at that time Geiger had completed his last flight in his beloved "Blue Goose." When he returned later to the South Pacific twin-engine *Catalina's* had been largely replaced by *Douglas Skytrains (R4D-5's)* and *Consolidated Liberators (PB4Y's);* furthermore, by October 1943, Geiger then a Commanding General of a Marine Amphibious Corps at age 58, normally would not have been expected to pilot his own plane. As far back as 1930 he had been officially certified to fly multi-engine aircraft, and undoubtedly, had he so desired he could have easily flown one of the huge four-motor machines of the later war period. Usually, however, his duties were so manifold and time-consuming, he shared the controls with the officer of the moment, selected to serve as his co-pilot.

Following a short visit at CinCPac's Headquarters, Geiger flew eastward across the Pacific from Ewa to El Centro, California. Given seventeen days' leave he forthwith proceeded to his home at Pensacola, Florida, upon the completion of which he reported for duty at Washington on the morning of 13 May. His ensuing five-month tour as the Director of Marine Aviation was a far cry indeed from his previous service in that capacity back in the 1930's. At that time the entire strength of the Marine Corps did not exceed 17,000; whereas, when the Marines landed on Guadalcanal in August 1942 its air arm alone had climbed to that figure, of which 1,350 were pilots. By the summer of 1942 Marine Corps Aviation consisted of two Wings, each of five Groups, bringing the total number of Squadrons to thirty. A year later Marine Aviation had grown to four Wings of sixty Squadrons, and with 60,000 persons assigned to aviation duty with a pilot strength of 5,000. Having doubled the number of Wings and Squadrons in one year, the next six months brought further increases: by 31 December 1943, although the number of Wings remained unchanged at four, Squadrons had jumped from sixty to eighty-eight, total personnel to 87,500, Marine pilots numbering 8,300. And greater expansion was yet to come.

As the official responsible for what was well on its way to becoming a 100,000-man (and-woman) Air Force in the literal sense of the term, Geiger found he had quite a job on his hands, and endless challenge posing a multitude of problems, many of which defied a solution satisfactory to all parties concerned. As an indication of the manifest importance of Marine Corps Aviation, in August 1943 the branch was transferred from the Bureau of Aeronautics to the then newly created office of the Deputy Chief of Naval Operations (Air) in the office of the CNO. Thus, Geiger had a two-fold task: he was in the direct chain of command with the Air section of CNO, and at the same time had additional duty as Assistant to the Commandant of the Marine Corps (General Holcomb) for Aviation. Aside from problems of finding a place to eat and to sleep in war-crowded Washington were the equally perplexing ones of finding ways and means to ensure that Marine Aviation in the Pacific could be employed profitably and assigned missions commensurate with its proven capabilities, often in the face of opposition by the Navy as well as the Army Air Force.

With the campaign for the Central Solomons getting under way Geiger was aware that once it were terminated the Central Pacific phase of operations would be commenced. As long as the Marines remained in the Southern and Central Solomons their ground forces could continue to receive aerial support from Marine Aviation organizations, based at conveniently located, relatively short range, land fields in the chain of islands along the expected northern route of advance up the ladder toward Rabaul. On the other hand, once the emphasis shifted from the South to the Central Pacific, close air support for amphibious troops would have to be provided by carrier-borne planes, *Hellcat (F6F)* fighters flown by Navy pilots, while deep range, heavy bombardment could be delivered by Army Air Force long-legged *Superfortresses (B-29's)*. Having no carriers of its own and with the radius of action of its *Corsairs* and light bombardment airplanes unable to meet the operational requirements of the wide expanses of the Central Pacific, the inevitable result would be that Marine Aviation would find itself without a suitable combat assignment.

The answer lay in procuring escort carriers for the Marines. Geiger and other of his contemporaries had been clamoring for this for more than a decade. In mid-1943 their chances of success seemed even more remote than they had been in the 1930's. Actually, the Navy had on order, under construction, or in commission a sufficient number of CVE's to spare the Marines at least three or four. However, at that moment every keel was jealously guarded by the Navy, worried over the loss of several of its flattops in the Pacific, already committed to an all-out anti-submarine struggle in the Atlantic, and with the prospect of having to provide additional CVE's for the Mediterranean. Understandably, the Navy was in no mood to discuss placing any vessels of that type at the Marines' disposal, despite Geiger's entreaties. To make a bad situation even worse, at the instigation of ComAirPac, carrier-qualification which had hitherto been a definite feature of the training cycle of Marine pilots, was abandoned, and Admiral Nimitz having approved of that recommendation, there was not much Geiger could do but to go along regretfully with the decision of his superiors.

Among other matters requiring his close attention and

241

support were furthering Marine Aviation's attempts to develop (and to deploy to the South Pacific) a night-fighter Group, complete with ground-controlled radar interception gear. To coordinate all of the various components relating to that complex project involved considerable flying on Geiger's part during the summer of 1943: with Major Blackwell at the controls of Geiger's staff and command plane (*Lockheed, R50-4*, No. 12447) the pair flew up and down the Atlantic Coast from Quantico and Anacostia to the Marine Corps Air Station at Cherry Point, North Carolina, and to the Navy's Air Bases at Rhode Island's Quonset Point and at Norfolk.

In spite of the many trials and tribulations of his Washington assignment—and the hectic battle over priorities along the Banks of the Potomac at times seemed to become as heated as the enemy air activity over Henderson Field the previous summer—Geiger did the best he could with the means available. To make both ends meet something had to be disposed of. The glider program was the first to go, followed by the barrage-balloon squadrons, the personnel of the disbanded units quickly being absorbed by other organizations.

On the whole Geiger stood up well under the strain at Headquarters. An inspection of a photograph taken in the summer of 1943 depicts the Director of Marine Aviation his usual cool, calm, collected self. His expression certainly lived up to the inch his image portrayed in such popular news media as *Newsweek* and *Time* Magazines. To the former Geiger's outstanding traits were his fearlessness and his toughness as well as his calmness under great duress. He was described as "normally taciturn and tight-mouthed" but vigorously intolerant of bungling, and by the same token, "equally verbose in praising high achievement." *Time,* not to be outshone and never at a loss for words (particularly the well turned phrase), re-echoed the same desirable characteristics of its hero as had its rival, and made mention of Geiger's being one of the Marines' "most carefully educated officers," a "handy man to have around." Perhaps its estimate of the man was best summed up in its terse statement: "Thickset, poker-faced, chilly-eyed General Geiger is another Marine's Marine."

To many who knew Roy Geiger firsthand this photograph taken at his desk strikingly portayed yet another of his better known qualities: his famous "twenty-foot stare." No owlish glance this, it was a penetrating stab which passed right through any individual standing before "The Old Man" with the General's eyes focused on the bulkhead across the room. Any person who experienced this treatment was not prone to forget it, for invariably the tenor of Geiger's remarks was as piercing as the hard glint in his eyes, and although he confined his comments to the bare minimum, the recipient was never at a loss as to their meaning. More or less mesmerized by Geiger's bellicose stare, an officer or entlisted man making a verbal report had to withstand this unblinking gaze as best he were able. Listening in silence and often giving the impression that his mind was miles away, Geiger frequently would continue to peer intently at the reporter for several minutes after the close of the recital, without comment, or, what was equally unnerving to the individual on the receiving end, Geiger would bluntly request that the conversation be repeated verbatim. This was his habitual custom when issuing verbal orders to make sure that they were thoroughly understood.

As a consequence, many persons who had to brief Geiger on certain matters or had problems to discuss found those sessions more in the nature of an ordeal. They took pains to make sure that they knew all the pertinent facts in the same fashion that a prudent attorney would prepare his case. With his legal background and his analytical mind Geiger was quick to detect any flaws in an argument. And woe betide any individual who resorted to deceit, for when it came to unmasking a fraud or cutting a man down to size "Jiggs" was the acknowledged past master of that field.

A cooperative worker with his peers and an admirer of General Holcomb, Geiger nevertheless fretted at his desk assignment in wartime, and longed for a transfer far away from the customary intrigue and the close in-fighting associated with the Penagon. He had more or less adjusted himself to sweating out a six-month tour at Headquarters, when to his delight he was summarily informed that his presence was required once again in the South Pacific, and the sooner he got back out there, the better. Relieved by General Woods on 15 October, Gieger was detached on that date, and ordered to proceed to the Department of the Pacific, at San Francisco, for duty with the First Marine Amphibious Corps (I MAC), at the express request of General Vandegrift. Without further delay he flew to the West Coast, took the "Clipper" to Pearl Harbor, transferred to a *Lockheed* transport, and on 22 October joined Headquarters Company, Headquarters and Service Battalion, I MAC, then at Guadalcanal, as its Deputy Commander.

Catapulted practically overnight from a mahogany and plate glass foxhole on the Potomac into the Number 2 command billet of a Marine Amphibious Corps on the very eve of its departure for the objective area, and with D-Day for the assault landing set for only two weeks away, many a high echelon commander might well have expressed concern with such heavy responsibilities thrust upon him at short notice by such an out of the ordinary assignment. Add to this the fact that for almost thirty years previously the incumbent by the nature of his trade was primarily considered by his associates as an aviator rather than as a troop leader of ground forces, an observer not fully acquainted with the situation could reasonably question the wisdom of such a precipitative transfer.

But in Geiger's case normal procedures did not apply. Professionally, as a line officer as well as a pilot, he had received the most advanced training to fit him for just such a contingency. Additionally, by his prior conduct in combat in the Solomons as ComAirCACTUS (and as Commanding General, 1st MAW) he had proved conclusively that he was not wanting in tenacity or in sound judgement; hence, his immediate superior, General Vandegrift, maintained his unreserved confidence in Geiger's leadership abilities be they in the air or on the ground. Accordingly, when at almost the eleventh hour the unfortunate death of the individual then in command of the First Marine Amphibious Corps (Major General Charles D. Barrett) for the Bougainville operation, brought General Vandegrift back to the South Pacific posthaste (he had been en route to the United States when he received the unexpected news), there was no question in his mind but that Gleiger was ideally suited to serve as his deputy. Furthermore, so confident was Vandegrift of the successful outcome of the planned Bougainville assault, and so assured was he that Geiger could handle the situation once the landing force made its way ashore, he made preparations in advance to turn full control of the operation over to Geiger at the earliest possible moment so that Vandegrift could continue his recently interrupted journey back to Washington to become the

Marine Corps' eighteenth Commandant.

As he had done before at Guadalcanal and as he was to repeat at a later date (at Peleliu), Geiger in this instance demonstrated that his superior's trust in the capabilities of his selected deputy had not been misplaced: that Geiger was "the right man for the job, at the right place, at the right time." The instant he left the plane at Henderson Field he drove in a jeep to Corps Headquarters at Tetere, where he closeted himself with the Assistant Corps Commander, Brigadier General Alfred H. Noble, and his staff of well qualified Assistants. After poring over maps and charts, aerial photographs and terrain models, and in general absorbing the details of operation orders and annexes for a solid week, Geiger was able to bring himself up to date on the salient features of the pending amphibious assault which had been assigned the code name CHERRYBLOSSOM.

A daring operation and a dangerous one, for it involved executing an attack deep in enemy-held territory, not to mention the fact that the timing of the main assault had to be carefully coordinated with diversionary landings in the Treasury Islands and a raid on the northwest coast of Choiseul, it represented the climax of months of meticulous joint planning on the part of the staffs of the Amphibious Force, Attack Force, and Landing Force Commanders. With the experience already gained at Guadalcanal and the lessons learned at New Georgia, Admiral Wilkinson and General Vandegrift were resolved that the tactical mistakes of the latter operation would not be repeated at Bougainville: that in this instance the Marines would land first; would seize, consolidate, and expand the beachhead; and when the fighting inland developed into extended land warfare, the Army would move in to free the Marine assault troops for other purposes. Likewise, it had been determined that the construction of a fighter runway and a bomber strip would be initiated immediately upon landing, and with the completion of those air facilities expected in time to assist the defense of the beachhead against any resolute Japanese counter-assault either by land or sea.

Intent on striking the enemy where he least expected it and where his defensive strength was believed correspondingly weaker, Cape Torokina on Empress Augusta Bay, midway up the Island on the western coast, was selected as the site for the surprise attack, despite the fact that surf conditions there were far from ideal, and the terrain adjacent and inland from the landing beaches was known to be a region of deep swamps and dense jungle. It was conceded that shipping shortages existed (much of it being reserved for the invasion of the Gilbert Islands), and that reliance would have to be placed on carrier-borne aircraft and land-based planes from other Solomon Islands' bases to protect the Landing Force pending the completion of the airfields within the beachhead; nevertheless, these and other handicaps were eventually overcome, ComSoPac having agreed (at Vandegrift's insistence) to accelerate follow-up shipping shuttle service from Guadalcanal, and arrangements having been made for carrier task force strikes on the northernmost Bougainville airfields on D-Day (1 November) along with simultaneous bombing and strafing of the Cape Torokina target zone by several of AirSols Marine squadrons.

As planned, on D-Day minus 5, 27 October, the Eighth New Zealand Brigade Group (attached to I MAC) landed on Mono and Stirling Islands in the Treasuries, thereby distracting the Japanese from the main objective on Empress Augusta Bay some 65 miles to the northwest. At an even closer range, only 45 miles from the southeast coast of Bougainville, early in the morning of 28 October the Second Marine Parachute Battalion (without parachutes) put its raiding parties ashore near the northwestern extremity of Choiseul Island, a move designed to throw the enemy further off balance and to confuse him with regard to the actual site of the principal American invasion.

Following a rendezvous west of Guadalcanal on 31 October, the Bougainville amphibious assault groups headed for the target area, and after daybreak on 1 November the I MAC—precisely on schedule—landed on the narrow beaches north of Cape Torokina. Its combat elements intially consisted of the Third and Ninth Marines of Major General Allen H. Turnage's Third Marine Division (later augmented by its third rifle regiment, the Twenty-first Marines), the Twelfth Marines (division artillery), the Nineteenth Marines (engineers, pioneers, and CB's), and the Third Defense Battalion. Also attached was the Second Provisional Marine Raider Regiment, one of whose battalions seized Puruata Island, half a mile offshore from the Division landing beaches, while the other was assigned the mission of moving rapidly inland to block Mission Trail, an avenue of approach to the beachhead

246

area considered the most probable route for an enemy counterthrust.

Although the element of surprise had been maintained, fire support in the form of four destroyers and planes from six Marine air squadrons was insufficient to knock out hostile defense installations, a bitter disappointment to I MAC's staff planners who had strongly urged more extensive preparatory naval gunfire bombardment and aerial bombing and strafing. If the intense fire from Japanese bunkers and pillboxes was bad, the surf was worse, raising havoc with landing craft and tank lighters. In spite of sharp enemy resistance and the damage caused by the elements the landing proceeded as planned, the Japanese beach defenders being overrun and killed or forced to flee inland. Notwithstanding a series of enemy air raids, all of which were promptly broken up by fighter cover provided by ComAirSol's planes, unloading of men and supplies continued unabated (in spite of the loss of many boats occasioned by heavy surf). By nightfall all of the assault units had reached their designated primary objectives; meanwhile, the transports and cargo vessels readied themselves to return to Guadalcanal to pick up the Twenty-first Marines and advance elements of supporting Army troops.

Japanese reaction to the landing was not long delayed. Intent on destroying the shipping of the American invaders lying off the beachhead at Cape Torokina, Rear Admiral Omori hastily assembled a small naval task force at Rabaul which put to sea headed south for Empress Augusta Bay. His visions of repeating the Naval Battle of Savo Island and creating another "Ironbottom Sound," this time off the shores of Bougainville, were dashed when his fleet units collided with a near similar sized cruiser-destroyer force commanded by Rear Admiral Aaron Merrill, Task Force-39. In the early morning hours of 2 November, in utter darkness and torrential rain showers, the two opposing groups slugged it out hammer-and-tongs in a hotly contested fleet action known as the Battle of Empress Augusta Bay. Out-maneuvered and out-fought, and with half his command sunk or badly damaged, Omori broke off the action, turned tail, and sped back to Rabaul. Thus, the first air and sea offensive by the Japanese to sever the American supply route between its base on Guadalcanal and its invasion force ashore on Bougainville had been stopped dead in its tracks by the combined action of ComSoPac's aerial and naval surface forces.

The enemy, however, was determined to eject the Marines struggling hard to hold their beachhead and to expand their perimeter in defiance of swamps and jungle, in spite of a lack of beach exits and the absence of an organized shore party to direct and control the orderly flow of supplies over the beachhead, not to mention the totally inadequate road facilities no thanks to the murderous nature of the terrain and the incessant rainfall. On 7 November the Japanese succeeded in a dawn counterlanding by an infantry battalion on the western flank of the Division's perimeter, near the Laruma River. Brought from Rabaul aboard destroyers this Japanese landing force was soundly defeated at the Battle of Koromokina Lagoon, the following day, due in large part to concentrated artillery preparations fired by batteries of the Twelfth Marines, and aggressive action by several rifle battalions, including one of the Twenty-first Marines, recently brought north from Guadalcanal. Thereafter, a series of air strikes controlled by ComAirNorSols (Brigadier General Field Harris) completed the virtual annihilation of the hostile landing party, and with the arrival of the first echelon of Army troops from the Thirty-seventh Infantry Division to bolster the left sector of the beach perimeter the situation—for the moment—seemed well under control.

November the 8th also marked the arrival on the scene of General Geiger, who had embarked two days previously aboard *President Adams* at Guadalcanal. Up to that moment General Turnage had been in command of the 3rd MarDiv (R) and all I MAC troops on the beachhead since D-Day, but after the arrival of the Army troops, I MAC thereupon took up the tactical control and command of all forces ashore. Satisfied that the operation was proceeding as planned and assured that his deputy could continue to keep affairs running smoothly, on 9 November General Vandegrift relinquished command to Geiger. To complete the picture, with the debarkation of the second echelon of the Thirty-seventh Infantry Division four days later, its commander, Major General Robert Beightler, USA, assumed command of the Army or western sector of the perimeter.

It did not take Geiger long to get squared away in his new role. Just because the Americans held local superiority of the air and seas immediately adjacent to the Bougainville beachhead was no cause for complacency: he was aware that with Rabaul

248

approximately 200 miles away, the range was so short enemy air raids would remain a constant threat. Even more significant was the known presence of two Japanese divisions in southern Bougainville, elements of which, sooner or later, could be counted on to make their way northward—regardless of the mountains, the weather, or the jungle—and would doubtless attempt to launch an attack on I MAC's eastern or right flank. At all costs the perimeter had to be deepened as quickly as possible not only to seize critical terrain features dominating the beachhead, but also to prevent the Japanese from emplacing long-range artillery which could shell the contemplated fighter strip near Cape Torokina. After his experiences with the accurate interdiction fires registered by *Pistol Pete* on Henderson Field, Geiger had no intention of putting up with that sort of annoyance, again, on Bougainville.

In substance his defense plan was built around the concept of employing Marine riflemen to secure the commanding higher elevations in the eastern sector of the gradually expanding perimeter, while the Army was given the responsibility of clearing out the western zone. The latter area being the less threatened this arrangement would permit the Thirty-seventh Infantry Division to build up progressively to its normal strength of three rifle regiments and supporting artillery. With regard to the building of the fighter strip, it was necessary for Geiger to divert the engineers and their equipment from hacking out roads and supply trails—much as their services were at a premium—to airfield construction as the completion of that facility was vital to the success not only of the Bougainville landing but also to the continuation of the attack against other Japanese air bases in the northern and southern tips of the Island besides Rabaul itself on New Britain. Therefore, on 10 November work was started in earnest on the Torokina strip. Exactly one month later it was finally declared operational, although on 24 November a successful emergency landing was accomplished on the partially completed field by a Marine dive-bomber, damaged in a raid over Buka.

Fortunately, for a period of about ten days after the initial Bougainville landing the Japanese attempts to bomb the beachhead were poorly coordinated, and the aerial umbrella maintained over it by Marine fighters was so efficient that few intruders were able to penetrate it. Several enemy night raids over

Cape Torokina were experienced; however, the Japanese machines were effectively driven off by Marine planes from VMF(N)—531. On the other hand, with fifteen known hostile airfields within 250 miles of Empress Augusta Bay, Geiger and ComAirNorSols naturally placed a high priority on the completion of landing strips for both fighters and bombers within the American-held perimeter, and Marine and naval construction battalion teams worked unceasingly to finish those critically needed installations.

As for the Marine riflemen, they too had their hands full. The trail and road-block established on D-Day by the Raiders was beginning to feel mounting pressure from Japanese patrols, probing the extreme right flank of the perimeter. By the middle of November what had commenced as a series of fire-fights between opposing skirmishers had developed into first company-size and later battalion-size battles, fiercely fought in mud up to men's waists, and in heavy jungle, officially known as the "Piva Actions." After securing the Piva (or Numa Numa) Trail, Piva Village, and the Coconut Grove (the intended site for the bomber and a second fighter strip), the Marine advance pushed northward, forcing the Japanese inland to the junction of Piva and East-West Trails. Captured enemy documents having indicated that the Japanese 23rd Infantry Regiment was preparing elaborate defense works in that area, labeled Piva Forks, an attack in force was at once launched by the Third Marines. This engagement, which lasted from 19 until 25 November, resulted in the enemy's positions being overrun at great loss to the defenders. As a consequence the only high ground from which the Japanese could threaten or harass the beachhead was now in possession of I MAC's forces, and the seizure of this terrain facilitated effective control of the Marines' sector of the Corps perimeter.

By that date the remaining elements of the Army's Thirty-seventh Infantry Division had landed on Bougainville; there were well over 30,000 American (and New Zealand) troops ashore, and some 25,000 cargo tons of supplies and ammunition had been brought over Cape Torokina's beaches. The final expansion of the Corps beachhead was accomplished in December but not until after three strongly defended and tenaciously held hill masses had been wrestled from the Japanese. Between 6 and 18 December on "Hellzapoppin' Ridge," Hill 600, and Hill 600A, the 23rd Japanese Infantry staged its own version of "Custer's Last Stand."

The capture of "Hellzapoppin' Ridge" was a signal affair in the annals of Marine Corps Aviation. Pinned down by intense rifle and machine gun fire from a carefully prepared, well dug in position along a narrow ridge, the Twenty-first Marines were unable to bring their supporting mortars to bear on the Japanese emplacements; furthermore, because the enemy intrenchments were on the reverse slope of the ridge, in defilade, artillery fire was also ineffective. Under the circumstances Geiger had no other resort than to request ComAirNorSols for direct air support.

Three scout and three torpedo bombers which had just landed on Cape Torokina's newly completed airstrip took off with 100-pound bombs, and made runs on the target area with only partial success. Neither the initial aerial attack made on 13 December nor the strikes conducted on the succeeding two days dislodged the Japanese, primarily because the bombs had been provided with near instantaneous, impact fuses. On 18 December, after shifting to delay-fused bombs, eleven torpedo bombers, flying at times only fifty feet above the ground, dropped their loads on "Hellzapoppin' Ridge" as close as seventy-five yards from the Twenty-first Marines' front lines, thereby all but eliminating hostile opposition. The few Japanese that survived the bombing and strafing found themselves on the receiving end of the Marines' bayonets and grenades. Thus, the combination of a coordinated double envelopment, close air support strikes (controlled from the front lines), and direct artillery fire from 155-mm. howitzers enabled the attackers to gain their objective. With this heretofore impregnable barrier now in I MAC's control, followed by the subsequent capture of the other hill masses, Japanese resistance along the western sector of the perimeter progressively decreased as the survivors drew back east of the Torokina River.

After the consolidation of the final defense line along the recently captured high ground the way was clear to commence the expected relief of the 3rd MarDiv (R). By 15 December more than 45,000 troops and 60,000 tons of cargo had been unloaded, and with additional Army personnel arriving daily it was time for the Marines to pack up and go home—"home" in this instance being Guadalcanal. Effective that date ComSoPac (Admiral Halsey) directed the Army's XIV Corps to assume tactical command of the Bougainville operation, whereupon Geiger turned over the responsibility of the beachhead and the perimeter to his designated relief, Major General Oscar W. Griswold, USA. Beginning on 27 December the Marine units manning perimeter defensive positions in the eastern sector were relieved by elements of Major General John Hodge's Americal Division, and by 16 January 1944, the entire 3rd MarDiv had returned to Guadalcanal, leaving behind the Third Defense Battalion, which remained until June, the solitary remnant of the Marine forces that had participated in the initiatory assault landing on Bougainville.

Its mission completed at a cost of 400 killed and 1,400 wounded contrasted with the estimated loss of 2,500 Japanese during the two-month campaign, I MAC's troops had acquitted themselves extremely well and could look forward to a few months' well deserved rest and refitting before undertaking their next project, the invasion of the Marianas Islands. All of the objectives of the campaign had been completely attained—even before the relief of the 3rd MarDiv, on 17 December, utilizing the new airstrips on Bougainville, AirSols was able to make its first fighter sweep over Rabaul. The only dark spot on the horizon was the future employment of Marine Corps Aviation in the South Pacific. Despite its brilliant display of the effectiveness of close air support at Bougainville—where it had demonstrated beyond doubt that aerial bombardment could be used as close to friendly troops and as accurately as artillery fire—with the exception of limited carrier-borne participation at Peleliu and Iwo Jima, this was destined to be the last time Marine aviators would support Marine riflemen until the terminal campaign, at Okinawa.

For the Commanding General, I MAC, Geiger's handling of the Bougainville operation brought him well deserved recognition: an appreciative "Well Done" from Admiral Halsey on the occasion of Geiger's relinquishing command at Cape Torokina in December, and a letter of congratulations from General Vandegrift the following month. In time he was to be awarded the Navy's Distinguished Service Medal for "exceptionally meritorious" performance of duty ashore at Bougainville, mention likewise being made of Geiger's "skillful planning and daring tactical generalship throughout this hazardous operation."

There was no rest for the weary. While one of I MAC's Marine Divisions, General Turnage's 3rd, started its training cycle anew for its pending invasion of Guam, the other, General Rupertus' 1st, was heavily committed on New Britain following its amphibious landing at Cape Gloucester in late December. Although operational control of the latter was not Geiger's concern—for it was retained by General MacArthur, a part of General Krueger's Sixth United States Army—nominally that Division's administrative control continued to remain under I MAC. Such being the case, after Geiger's return to Guadalcanal he decided in January to make a run up to New Britain to see for himself how things were going in the 1st MarDiv's theater of operations. Flying northward in his *R4D–5* (No. 39072) with Captain Pierce at the controls the plane touched down briefly at Horand field and Finschafen, in New Guinea, before continuing on to Cape Gloucester (the final lap being made aboard PT-boats). Additionally, flights were made in February to the Russells, to Ondonga airfield on New Georgia, and to Vella Lavella to permit Geiger to inspect Marine units stationed at those places.

With planning under way for the various phases of the southern Marianas campaign (scheduled for June) to be followed by amphibious assaults in the Palaus (in September), it was apparent that sooner or later the 1st MarDiv, ear-marked for the latter invasion, would have to be brought back under Admiral Nimitz' command, the Navy having been given exclusive jurisdiction of all Central Pacific operation, This was accomplished on 25 March 1944: I MAC, Corps Troops, 1st and 3rd MarDivs being transferred to CinCPOA's operational command. Assigned Commanding General of all Expeditionary Troops for the combined seizure of Saipan, Tinian, and Guam was Lieutenant General Holland M. Smith, USMC, with Headquarters at Pearl Harbor, Hawaii. Considering that I MAC's 3rd MarDiv and the newly created (as of 22 March) 1st Provisional Marine Brigade were slated to participate in the Guam assault it was imperative that the Corps Commander consult with his superior at the earliest possible opportunity, and it was for that express purpose that Geiger flew from Guadalcanal to Hawaii on 29 March.

Chapter XII

Commanding General, III PHIB Corps

The schedule of the entire Pacific campaign having been appreciably accelerated by the rapid seizure of the Marshall Islands, in the early spring of 1944 the Marianas were thereupon selected as the next logical objective for Vice Admiral Raymond Spruance's Fifth Fleet and the Central Pacific Task Forces. In the opinion of the Joint Chiefs of Staff the possession of the Marianas—principally, Saipan, Tinian, and Guam—was deemed vital in the drive to shorten the war against Japan, for in American hands those islands would provide the means to keep the Japanese homelands under intensive air bombardment and naval blockade. Another primary consideration was the cherished hope that if the United States once broke into the inner ring of Japan's defensive cordon in the Central Pacific, such a move might well precipitate a major naval engagement with the enemy's main fleet. In substance, therefore, the over-all purpose of the Marianas campaign was to secure naval and air bases which would ensure American control of the Central Pacific ocean areas and permit the intiation of lone-range aerial attacks against Japan proper. Saipan being only 1,250 nautical miles from Honshu, American Army Air Force *B-29's* could raid Tokyo and Yokohama from the same fields now used by hostile aircraft, and as for Guam, 100 miles to the south, its capture would enable the American Navy to establish a submarine refueling point in the very heart of Japanese sea lanes. Moreover, Apra Harbor could serve as an advanced naval base, an ideal anchorage for assault shipping, from which further amphibious operations might be launched. Consquently, despite formidable terrain obstacles and enemy beach defenses, encircling barrier reefs, high winds and strong surf, and heavy rains, all of which somehow would have to be overcome by an invader, there was no doubt in the minds of the staff planners, Navy and Marine Corps, at Pearl Harbor but that the value of the prize would be well worth the cost of the pending amphibious attack.

Assigned the code name FORAGER—the consolidated conquest of Saipan, Tinian, and Guam, in succession—and with D-Day for the assault on the first of those three islands set for 15 June, the enterprise by any set of standards was bound to entail a tremendous amount of elaborate preparation and detailed planning with little if any time to spare. To Admiral Spruance's Fifth Fleet was given the comprehensive job of lifting, landing, covering, and supporting a Marine field Force of two Marine Amphibious Corps, the III and the V, consisting of three Marine Divisions, two Army Infantry Divisions, and a reinforced Marine Brigade (plus aviation units). His command, then the largest ever assembled in the Pacific, was made up of more than 800 vessels, which, in addition to providing adequate naval gunfire and air support, had to transport thousands of Expeditionary Troops (and hundreds of thousands of tons of supplies and equipment) to the objective area from Eniwetok and Kwajalein Atolls, some 1,000 and 1,300 miles, respectively, distant in the Marshall Islands.

To V Marine Amphibious Corps under the command of Lieutenant General Holland M. Smith was given the task of seizing Saipan and Tinian. Smith's Corps was designated Northern Troops and Landing Force (NTLF), and was composed mainly of the 2nd and 4th MarDiv's reinforced by the Army's Twenty-seventh Infantry Division in reserve. Besides serving in the capacity as Commander NTLF for the Saipan-Tinian phase of the operation, General Smith was named Commanding General of all Expeditionary Troops including those assigned to Guam. The mission of capturing the latter, identified by the code name STEVEDORE (and with D-Day, 18 June), was allocated to General Geiger. His recently constituted (actually renamed) III Marine Amphibious Corps (formerly, I MAC), which initially consisted of the 3rd MarDiv (R) and the 1st Provisional Marine Brigade, was correspondingly designated Southern Troops and Landing Force (STLF). To complete the picture from the Landing Force aspect, the Army's Seventy-seventh Infantry Division, then in Hawaii, was detailed for use as an Expeditionary Troop reserve in a stand-by status, and later was assigned to III Corps for the Guam attack.

Turning to the naval side of the operation, over-all command of all Central Pacific affairs was vested in Admiral Spruance with command of the Joint Expeditionary Force assaulting the Marianas (Task Force-51) being exercised by Vice Admiral Kelly Turner. His force in turn was separated into a Northern Attack Force for Saipan and Tinian (Task Force–52), over which he retained direct tactical command, and a Southern Attack Force (Task Force–53) for Guam under the leadership of Rear Admiral Richard Conolly.

From the very outset the Conolly-Geiger combination was a most fortunate arrangement, an ideal team. Not only had both the Attack and Landing Force Commanders for STEVEDORE amassed considerable prior experience in amphibious operations—the former in the landings in Sicily, Italy, and Roi-Namur in the Marshalls, the latter in the Solomon Islands at Guadalcanal and Bougainville—but in addition each held his running mate in highest personal and professional esteem, and with the two principals and their respective staffs determined to work together in complete harmony with cooperation the keynote. Writing some twenty years after the Guam campaign Admiral Conolly went on record as stating that he believed the command realationship between the Attack Force and Landing Force Commanders could well serve "as a model for combined operations." Continuing in the same vein Conolly commented on the splendid understanding which existed between Geiger and his III Amphibious Corps with Major General Andrew Bruce's Seventy-seventh Infantry Division, and with specific reference to the Army Commander's loyal adherence and support to Geiger's plans once the reserve had been committed ashore. Transcending those remarks was the Admiral's observation that the success of the entire operation had been predicated on the mutual respect among the commanders which they in turn had transmitted to their staffs and to the troops involved, a marked contrast be it noted, from the turn of events—and misunderstandings—which marred certain phases of the operations.

Be that as it may, Admiral Conolly early in the game set the pattern which distinguished the STLF's participation in Operation FORAGER by flying from Pearl Harbor to Guadalcanal a week after Geiger had returned there so that the two leaders could personally consult on every phase of the detailed joint planning.

Living ashore under canvas at Tetere, Conolly and Geiger and their staffs worked around the clock planning the naval gunfire and aerial bombardments of the target area, the clearing of the beaches and the removal of known underwater obstacles, and all of the intricate details of scheduled training exercises and full-dress rehearsals. By the last week of April Conolly's flagship, the amphibious command vessel *AGC–1, USS Appalachian,* had arrived off Guadalcanal's Lunga Point to take aboard the Attack and Landing Force Commanders and their assistants, and following the rehearsals in the Cape Esperance area, all of III Corps plans had been completed and approved by mid-May.

As far back as the initial conference at Pearl Harbor in April it had been tentatively agreed that the Attack Force for the landing on the west coast of Guam would be subdivided into two parts: the Northern Attack Group under Admiral Conolly, the Southern under Commodore Lawrence Reifsnider. The troops of the Northern Component, Major General Turnage's 3rd MarDiv (R), would land north of Guam's Orote Peninsula on the Asan beaches; those of the southern, Brigadier General Lemuel Shepherd's 1st Provisional Marine Brigade, south of the Peninsula in the vicinity of Agat. Following the landings both units would advance inland and establish the Force Beachhead Line, and having once united would continue the drive to the north to secure the rest of the island. It was clearly evident that were enemy opposition strong enough to contain the beachheads, and thereby prevent the anticipated juncture of the two assault forces on the Force Beachhead Line, the whole enterprise would be doomed from the start. The only way to side-step such an impasse was for Geiger to get his Corps artillery ashore and emplaced as rapidly as possible after the landings to support the Divisional artillery, a thorny problem in this instance involving both control and restrictions imposed by minimum effective range of 155-mm. gun and howitzer field pieces.

With his general knowledge of the employment of Corps Artillery up to that moment being largely based on what he had learned years before as a student at the Army's Command and Staff School at Fort Leavenworth, Geiger's solution was typical of the man. Mention has already been made that Geiger on a previous occasion was not overly inclined to consult with his staff in certain technical areas, such as Intelligence, preferring rather to ascertain for himself what was transpiring. On the other hand, by no means

257

did he disregard the professional advice of his planners in purely Operational matters: if he did not know the answer himself, he knew where or to whom he could turn to find the desired information. In this case he merely sent for the Operations Officer of III Corps Artillery, Lieutenant Colonel Paul Henderson, and requested the latter to furnish him with all pertinent texts and tables pertaining to the manner of use of the medium and general support artillery with which his Corps had been provided for operation STEVEDORE. Henderson in compliance returned to his tent and gathered together about twenty pounds of printed material dealing with that subject, which he carefully indexed, marking appropriate passages for the General's attention. Depositing the bundle on the floor of Geigers's Quonset hut, Henderson briefly made mention of the more important documents, whereupon Geiger thanked the Colonel, informed him in due course he would be consulted further, and dismissed him with a curt nod.

Realizing that the Commanding General had a thousand and one details on his mind concerning the pending assault and only twenty-four hours a day in which to resolve them, Henderson naturally thought that Geiger would not be able to get around to even perusing the collection of detailed statistics and general directives for several days, if then. To his surprise shortly thereafter the General sent around his aide to inform Colonel Henderson that he and the Corps Artillery Officer, Brigadier General Pedro del Valle, were to report at once to the General's Headquarters to discuss the artillery support phase of the future landings.

At that meeting Geiger demonstrated beyond doubt that for an officer usually best known for his abilities as a Marine aviator, he had acquired an unusual familiarity with the concept of employment of Corps artillery. In his artillery planning Geiger decided to land two 155-mm. artillery units in the area assigned to the Southern Attack Group: a 155-mm. Gun Battalion to reinforce the fires of the Twelfth Marines in support of the three infantry regiments of the 3rd MarDiv, and a 155-mm. Howitzer Battalion to assist the two pack howitzer battalions supporting the 1st Provisional Marine Brigade, as well as to protect III Corps exposed southern flank. Later, he was able to add a second 155-mm. Howitzer Battalion to the Southern Landing Group, besides providing Defense Battalions to each of the two principal infantry assault forces, for the antiaircraft defense of their respective zones of action within the Force Beachhead.

Provision was similarly made for the coordination of artillery fires of the Landing Force with air bombardment and naval gunfire support from the Attacking Force, an arrangement which could be achieved just as soon as III Corps Artillery were able to establish its Fire Direction Center (FDC) ashore. This system, the rudimentary forerunner of the later developed and refined Fire Support Coordination Center (FSCC) wherein the three major supporting arms were connected by telephone and radio to a centralized control station, was used extensively and effectively on Guam, and in addition to ensuring the Landing Force of maximum supporting fires for the assault also made provision for the coordinated massing of fires on a single target. This feature of operation STEVEDORE has been dealt with in some detail as it fitted in closely with Admiral Conolly's expressed views on the function of combat support weapons, he having made it crystal clear that ships' batteries and carrier-borne aircraft should and would be available for used as "army artillery." He was aware of the fact that the expenditure of ammunition would be very heavy, reaching as high as 1,000 tons per day; nevertheless, he regarded the cost as a secondary consideration if its effective employment could reduce the duration of the fighting ashore and commensurately lower the casualty rate of the troops comprising the Landing Force.

On 4 June the *Appalachian* departed from Guadalcanal for the staging area at Kwajalein Atoll. With the target date for the landings on Guam but two weeks away every effort (including the use of elaborate terrain models) was made by Conolly's gunnery officer and Geiger's naval gunfire officer to work out the final details to make certain the selected beaches and the adjacent terrain received the heaviest possible preliminary bombardment. As fast as intelligence was received and evaluated, target lists were prepared jointly—nothing was overlooked in the determination of the planners to place naval gunfire where it would do the most damage ashore.

Between 9 and 12 June the various elements of STLF left Kwajalein aboard their assault shipping and cargo vessels, and by the 16th of that month the Southern Attack Force had arrived in the waters of the Southern Marianas. Loaded and locked, impatient to get on with the anticipated touch-down on Guam's western shores two days later, the embarked Marines were startled to receive the news that Admiral Spruance had indefinitely postponed the landings scheduled for the 18th, and had directed Conolly's Task Force-53 to remain off Saipan as a floating reserve. The reason for the cancellation was the direct result of unexpectedly strong enemy resistance on Saipan (causing extremely heavy losses to both 2nd and 4th MarDiv's) which had necessitated the commitment of the Expeditionary Troops (floating) reserve, the Twenty-seventh Army Infantry Division. Furthermore, the threat of Japanese naval forces in the vicinity and the strong possibility of a major naval engagement was so apparent, part of Conolly's support ships, six old battleships, was detailed to act as a covering force west of Saipan while his amphibious shipping withdrew to the east. With Spruance's Fifth Fleet, including Rear Admiral Marc Mitscher's Fast Carrier Task Force (TF-58), free to engage the approaching Japanese Fleet the stage was thus set for the ensuing Battle of the Philippine Sea. In that engagement fought on 19 and 20 June, the Japanese effort to reinforce Saipan was shattered. On the first day a concerted air attack on Spruance's fleet was destroyed by Mitscher's Carrier Task Force off Guam, and on the second the main striking force of the Japanese Navy, Vice Admiral Ozawa's Mobile Fleet, suffered grievous disaster from Mitscher's dive-bombers. Not only did the Japanese incur crippling losses among their naval flight personnel, from which they were never able to recover, but of greater immediate importance, the American Navy had gained undisputed control of the eastern portion of the Philippine Sea which guaranteed that the subsequent landings on Tinian and Guam could be effected without further hostile naval opposition.

With Spruance's victorious Fifth Fleet back at Saipan on 21 June, Conolly's Task Force-53 was released from its duties as a floating reserve. Pending the outcome of the fighting ashore on Saipan which was gradually turning in the American's favor, the Southern Attack Force with STLF still embarked, returned to Eniwetok, to sweat it out until further orders. By 30 June *Appalachian* was back once again at Saipan, and for almost a week Conolly and Geiger and their staffs had the opportunity to visit the front lines to examine firsthand the effects of naval gunfire, air bombardment, and artillery support. A series of conferences were held ashore at General Smith's command post to discuss enemy tactics and to study the terrain (which was quite similar to that of Guam). Impressed by the initial casualties on Saipan, Conolly and Geiger resolved that Guam would receive the most thorough pre-invasion working over, and proceeded to re-vamp their already well planned and programmed schedule of carrier strikes and bombardment from the batteries of attached heavy cruisers and battleships.

On 6 July Admiral Nimitz ordered the Seventy-seventh Army Infantry Divion to act as reserve troops for STLF, and set July 21st as the target date for the beach assault on Guam. As early as 28 June Mitscher's carrier planes had subjected the island to rigorous aerial strikes, and from 8 July until the actual landing Guam was under constant daily gunfire from battleships, cruisers, and destroyers. By 14 July *Appalachian* had reached the waters off Guam whereupon Conolly and Geiger personally took over the supervision of the combined air and surface bombardment of the target area. The net result of this incessant shelling, unprecedented in severity and duration, was a devastating destruction of enemy beach defenses to the degree that underwater demolition teams were able to make their way ashore unimpeded to remove over a thousand obstacles, many of them mines. Although there was later considerable controvery as to the number of Japanese guns which had been positively destroyed or disabled, there was little doubt that the great majority remained silent or deliberately unattended during the critical moments when the troops landed, and there was no question but that in the final analysis, the enemy's general plan of defense had been totally disrupted.

Geiger, who was never willing to pass up a good opportunity to indulge his fondness for swimming, was fascinated by the work of the underwater demolition groups. Somewhat to the consternation of his staff, which was naturally apprehensive of the risks being taken by their Landing Force Commander, the General (as an observer in a "free boat") insisted on accompanying the teams of Navy frogmen and skin divers in their fast launches and rubber floats to the very shoreline. Disdainful of the barbed wire and the spiked obstacles with which the beaches had been liberally sown, on several occasions Geiger took advantage of these daylight forays right under the enemy's nose to see for himself what his troops would have to encounter once they were brought ashore aboard their ampihibian tractors. In his opinion there was nothing reckless or out of place in his actions. He reasoned that the best way for a commander to gain information about the beaches of Guam and its shore defenses was by personal reconnaissance. And he did not feel that he had performed his duty properly until he had convinced himself that everything possible had been done to remove or neutralize the fearsome barrier of Japanese obstructions from the low water mark to the beach limits.

Precisely on schedule and much to the relief of thousands of troops, many of whom had been cooped up aboard their transports like chickens in a crate for almost seven weeks (since their mounting out at Guadalcanal during the first week of June less a brief sojourn ashore at Eniwetok), the STLF touched down on the shores of Guam bright and early at 0830, 21 July 1944. On the northern beaches amphibian tractors landed the 3rd MarDiv with its three infantry regiments abreast against relatively light resistance. Although subjected to hostile artillery and mortar fire from the high ground immediately inshore of the landing sites between Adelup and Asan Points, the attackers pushed ahead slowly toward the southeast. By nightfall not only the Division command post but most of the artillery organic to the Division (the Twelfth Marines) as well as a portion of the Fourteenth Defense Battalion with its anti-aircraft weapons were established ashore. Considering that there were many gaps in General Turnage's lines and that the enemy had yet to be driven from his strong defensive positions along Chonito Cliff, a natural amphitheater dominating the landing zones, the 3rd MarDiv's grip ashore on a beachhead two miles wide and a mile in depth at that moment was far from secure.

As for the assault on the southern beaches at Agat, hostile resistance was comparatively more pronounced, the two rifle regiments of the 1st Provisional Marine Brigade, which had also landed abreast, having first encountered serious damage to their amphibian tractors from antiboat guns and mines, followed by heavy machine gun and mortar fire at the beach. Battling their way yard by yard past those obstacles the Twenty-second and Fourth Marines with the Three Hundred and Fifth Regiment of the Seventy-seventh Army Division in reserve forged inland, and by dark were dug in along the limits of the Brigade beachhead then about 4,500 yards wide and 2,000 yards deep. With General Shepherd ashore and his command post set up on Gaan Point, the Brigade squeezed down a little deeper into its hastily dug entrenchments and foxholes, awaiting the inevitable Japanese counterattack.

Taken as a whole the landings on both beaches were eminently successful, vindicating Admiral Conolly's earlier expressed desire to the effect that if General Geiger informed him what he wanted done in the way of support, the Attack Force Commander would see to it that the troops of the Landing Force "got ashore standing up." Good as his word the shelling of the terrain in the rear of the beaches did not cease with the landing of the troops: Conolly ordered naval gunfire lifted inland and to the flanks in a rolling barrage which continued for an hour and a half. Thereafter, call fires commenced and persisted day and night throughout the operation, deep support fire missions from naval craft being undertaken whenever and wherever possible, and extensive use of star shells being similarly employed for the purpose of interrupting enemy infiltration and spoiling his night counterattacks.

The expected hostile countermeasures took place the night of D-Day against both beachheads; however, the Japanese failed to penetrate the front lines of the 3rd MarDiv, while to the south, after making a temporary breakthrough, the enemy was repelled at considerable loss to himself. The ensuing week witnessed the heaviest fighting of the entire conquest of Guam. The juncture of the two separate landing groups endeavoring to effect a pincer movement could not be accomplished until the 3rd MarDiv broke loose from the restricting confines of the Asan amphitheater; meanwhile, the 1st Marine Provisional Brigade had to overcome the Japanese on Orote Peninsula, which threatened its left flank while pressing its attack toward the north.

For both groups the going was exceedingly rough. Early in the morning of 26 July, the Island Commander, Lieutenant General Takashina, let go the bulk of his 29th Division in a two-regiment frontal attack coordinated with artillery fire against General Turnage's Marines struggling to maintain a tenuous hold along the steep faces of Chonito Cliffs. A fiercely contested night engagement which came near to driving the 3rd MarDiv back into the sea, it was evident by break of day that the Marines had successfully withstood this massive Japanese counterattack, killing some 3,500 of the enemy in the process, and practically eliminating his ability to furnish any further organized defense of Guam. Now free to advance inland to the Force Beachhead Line, the 3rd MarDiv seized the all important hill crests and high ground to the south and at last were in a position to link-up with the 1st Brigade, working its way slowly to the north after its capture of the Orote Peninsula.

The Brigade had had no easy time of it, either. During the night of 25-26 July General Shepherd's Marines had been on the receiving end of a desperate Japanese *banzai* breakout across the neck of Orote Peninsula which they had repulsed in a bitter hand-to-hand struggle, much of the action fought in swamps and dense jungle growth, ably supported by every field piece and howitzer III Corps, 1st Brigade, and Seventy-seventh Division artillery could bring to bear. Following three days of intensive fighting the Peninsula was finally swept clean of Japanese opposition, by which time elements of the Seventy-seventh Division on the Brigade's right flank had made contact with units of the 3rd MarDiv, thus closing the ring around the enemy.

Geiger and Conolly had come ashore on the 24th, and had made their way to General Turnage's command post. At the conclusion of the Japanese counterattacks of 25-26 July they had transferred their attentions to affairs within the Brigade's zone of action, and on the 29th accompanied by Admiral Spruance and General Smith, who had come down aboard ship from Saipan for a conference, the party first made a tour of the front lines, and then took part in the impressive flag-raising ceremonies among the ruins of the former Marine Barracks at Sumay on the shores of Apra Harbor. Later that afternoon they witnessed the arrival of the advance echelon of Colonel Peter Schrider's MAG-21 on the air strip at Orote, an occasion of note marking the reestablishment of Marine Corps aviation on Guam after a lapse of some thirteen years.

With III Amphibious Corps Headquarters set up ashore and with the Force Beachhead reasonably secure as the result of the union of the northern and southern landing groups, the first phase of the capture of Guam had been concluded. The second or pursuit phase—which proved to be far less costly—consisted of a coordinated attack to the north, right across the Island, as the remnants of the enemy, now scattered and disorganized, withdrew hastily to the northeast, presumably intent on making some sort of a last ditch stand in the hilly regions surrounding Mounts Barrigada and Santa Rosa. Given but a day's rest on 31 July the attack was resumed, the 3rd MarDiv on the left and the Seventy-seventh Division on the right, while the 1st Brigade, but recently disengaged from mopping up Orote Peninsula, was assigned Corps reserve. In three days Agana, the capital, was overrun, and within the space of another week (despite heavy rainfall) the Island was progressively cleared to the northward. Against sporadic resistance the advance continued relentlessly, the principal delays being caused by the lack of roads for the movement of supplies rather than by any determined enemy opposition.

A week after the pursuit was launched Geiger decided to commit the 1st Brigade to the left flank of the advancing Corps, for with the Island now fanning out to the westward contact between the Marine and the Army Divisions had become increasingly difficult to maintain, and there was danger of overextending their forward lines. After some five days' concentrated naval gunfire shelling and air strikes against Japanese defensive positions on Mount Santa Rosa, the enemy had no choice but to abandon the site, and the Army troops were able to seize it without a fight on 8 August. By that date the Marines had worked their way to Ritidian Point, Guam's northwestern extremity, and by the 10th the Island's northern shore had been cleared of hostile resistance. To all intents and purposes organized opposition had been terminated; however, by no means did this bring an end to sniping and other guerrilla tactics which went on spasmodically for yet another year and a half: diehard Japanese survivors from caves and jungles made life dangerous for the garrison forces for months to come, and it was not until December 1945 that the last remaining partisan band conceded defeat, by which date the number of Japanese casualties exceeded those killed in the initial capture of the Island.

Throughout the pursuit phase Geiger had remained in the field with III Corps forward echelon. With the Island now officially declared secure and American sovereignty over Guam reestablished, there was little left for him to do other than to write up his action report and pack up his gear. He had more than just cause to be proud of his command and its performance in the campaign. The total casualties on Guam—7,800—were less than half those incurred in the capture of Saipan, whereas the complexity of the defense installations and the number of Japanese defenders on both of those Islands had been nearly identical. It was obvious that the comparatively light casualties and the rapid capture of Guam were the direct result of conscientious preparation, particularly the pre-invasion bombardment, coupled with a prounounced flexibility of both planning and execution on the part of the Landing Force Commander to meet changing circumstances. For his initiative, forceful leadership, and brilliant tactical ability displayed in his conduct of the Guam operation Geiger was to be awarded a Gold Star in lieu of a second Distinguished Service Medal.

As far as Geiger was concerned the only dark spot in the undertaking was his undisguised dissatisfaction with the inferior performance of the Army and Navy in rendering close air support. Annoyed by lengthy delays in executing requested fire missions not to mention lack of proper control of front line air strikes, Geiger voiced anew his long standing request that Marine rather than Navy aviation provide air groups for escort carriers taking part in amphibious assaults so that full advantage might be taken of the troop experience already possessed by many of the Corps' more senior pilots. In this respect General Holland Smith was in complete agreement, and the upshot of their joint recommendations was Admiral Nimitz' subsequent decision to make available four escort carriers with Marine squadrons aboard for future amphibious operations within his theater of command.

His mission completed and the situation on Guam being under control there was no reason for Geiger to remain there longer. Consequently, on 12 August he boarded an *R4D-5* piloted by Captain Pierce, and after a stop at Eniwetok returned to the airfield on Guadalcanal's Koli Point. He had good reason to hurry for the nature of his new assignment gave him scant time to prepare himself—and his staff—for the important role he was destined to play in the forthcoming amphibious assaults on Peleliu and Angaur. The decision to seize the Western Carolines—Ulithi, Yap, and the Palaus—had been agreed upon only after considerable debate, and planning for the operation bearing the code name STALEMATE, which had been commenced as far back as March

266

1944, had been subject to radical changes. Lying southwest of Guam and approximately 450 miles east of Mindanao, the capture of the strongly fortified and garrisoned Palaus was deemed necessary to remove the danger of a hostile flanking attack against General MacArthur's pending invasion of the Southern Philippines. Moreover, in American hands Peleliu's airfields would be of material benefit to assist MacArthur's forces in their northward drive toward Leyte. By the same token the capture of Ulithi Atoll would provide a desirable fleet anchorage for Admiral Halsey's ships.

Having at length decided to by-pass Babelthuap, the main island of the Palau group, Admiral Nimitz set 15 September as the target date for the landings on Peleliu and Angaur, to be followed as the situation permitted by the occupation of Ulithi. Over-all naval command of the operation was given to Admiral Halsey, Commander Third Fleet. Vice Admiral Wilkinson (who had succeeded Turner) was named Commander of the Joint Expeditionary Force for the Western Carolines campaign, while his subordinate charged with direct tactical control at Peleliu and Angaur was Rear Admiral George Fort, the Western Attack Force Commander. As originally conceived Major General Julian C. Smith (of Tarawa fame) was to command all Expeditionary Troops for the Third Fleet, but with the arrival of Geiger at Guadalcanal at the termination of the Guam operation, the latter as the Commanding General, III Amphibious Corps, was forthwith designated Commander, Western Landing Force and Troops.

In addition to Headquarters and III Corps Troops, Geiger's command for what was now referred to as STALEMATE II consisted of Major General William Rupertus' 1st MarDiv and Major General Paul Mueller's Eighty-first Infantry (*Wildcat*) Division. Marine air support for the campaign ultimately was to be furnished by Garrison Air Forces, Western Carolines, under command of Major General James Moore, the principal components being drawn from fighter (including night-fighter), torpedo-bomber, and observation squadrons making up 2nd MAW's MAG-11. Once again as in the Solomons the preceding year, the current target—Peleliu—was too far distant for Marine land-based aircraft to provide effective cover for the actual assault. Furthermore, after the Landing Force had made its way ashore, all air strikes had to be flown exclusively by Navy pilots operating from escort carriers until some ten days after the landing on Peleliu, by which time its captured airfield had been sufficiently repaired and improved to enable VMF-114's *Corsairs* to take over vitally needed close air support for Rupertus' front line ground troops, pinned down by murderous fire from Japanese defenders masked by steep ridges or concealed in caves and tunnels.

From the very outset there was one aspect of Geiger's participation in the Peleliu campaign which bore a close similarity to the position in which he found himself just before the Bougainville invasion. Herein for the second time was the individual responsible for the conduct of the fighting ashore pitched bodily into the operation at almost the last moment possible, and with the time margin immediately prior to the contemplated amphibious attack cut so fine that the Landing Force Commander had practically no other choice but to accept the plan drawn up by the Marine Division slated to make the assault on Peleliu.

Never one to buck the issue Geiger forged right ahead as calmly as if he had been working hard with his staff planners at Pearl Harbor for weeks. Following a brief visit with the Attack Force Commander's Staff at Guadalcanal, on 13 August he flew aboard a *PBY-5A* piloted by Lieutenant Joseph Moss to Banika airstrip in the Russell Islands. At nearby Pavuvu Island where the 1st MarDiv in the face of numerous handicaps was carrying out a rigorous training program, he consulted for two days with General Rupertus and his staff, the upshot of the matter being his approval of the Division's attack plan which was thereupon confirmed as a Corps Order. Outwardly, the situation seemed "well in hand;" nevertheless, there were certain disturbing factors present which could not be glossed over. For all of its previous combat experience the 1st MarDiv's fighting had been largely confined to jungle warfare—as at Guadalcanal and Cape Gloucester. Peleliu, the new target, called for something quite different—ridge and cave fighting against a defender who had been given three months to develop his defenses, painstakingly organized and integrated, in considerable depth, and of even greater strength than those which he had erected at Saipan and at Tarawa. Although captured enemy documents taken at Saipan had enabled Marine intelligence officers to arrive at a remarkably accurate estimate of the total number of Japanese available on Peleliu to resist the American invasion (slightly more than 10,000), by no means did this unexpected bonanza include the engineering plans of the Japanese defense works on the Island.

Lack of proper appreciation of the terrain attributed in no small degree to the attacker's ignorance of the correct nature of the target, further compounded by insufficient aerial photographic coverage and inaccurate maps. What Peleliu was soon to reveal itself was: a small coral atoll with an area of about seven square miles encircled by a submerged barrier reef, and with thick scrub vegetation over much of its northern portion concealing sharp ridges and broken hill masses honey-combed with hundreds of natural caves, which the enemy had laboriously converted by means of interconnecting tunnels and shafts, reinforced concrete and steel, into an intricate mutually supporting undergound fortress of truly formidable proportions.

In spite of the Division's lack of experience in the tactical usage of amphibian tractors and portable flamethrowers, a marked deficiency in engineering equipment, and the fact that but two weeks' time remained to complete its training and to conduct its rehearsals on Guadalcanal prior to mounting out in early September, a distinct air of optimism pervaded its highest command echelon. Beneficial though this cheerful attitude might be, some of it appeared to be unwarranted. The Division Commander, no less, shortly was to express his opinion that although he readily admitted that there would be casualties and that it was only to be expected that the going would be rough, he was, notwithstanding, confident that such rapid progress could be made that the Division objectives could be fully achieved in a matter of some three days. This "walk in and walk over" approach was not necessarily shared by the Assistant Division Commander nor by the Colonels commanding the three Regimental Landing Teams (RLT's) scheduled to spearhead the assault; nor was it endorsed without reservation by the Corps Commander based on the record at Tarawa not to mention what he had observed on Saipan and what he had so recently encountered on Guam. Among other factors Geiger was also concerned with the minute size of the organization set aside to act as the Division Reserve for the Peleliu landing—a sole Rifle Battalion. However, at this stage of the game he was reluctant to interfere and to tell his subordinate how to operate his own show, so despite inner misgivings, he resolved to remain silent.

With regard to the other Division comprising his Corps, the Army's Eighty-first Infantry, for the moment he had no opportunity to check on how it was faring inasmuch as it was located far to the northeast in Hawaii. According to the planning General Mueller's *Wildcats* on D-Day were to make a diversionary feint off Babelthuap, thirty miles to the north of Peleliu; thereafter, the Division would position itself (afloat) to enable it to land on call in support of the 1st MarDiv in the event opposition ashore on Peleliu proved more difficult than General Rupertus had anticipated. Otherwise, once the critical stage on Peleliu had been passed, two of the Eighty-first's Infantry regiments were to land on Angaur, ten miles to the south, while its third regiment was tentatively earmarked for the seizure of Ulithi Atoll, the date to be determined by developments on Peleliu and Angaur. Regardless of what might occur Geiger had no doubt but that the *Wildcats* would render a good account of themselves in battle. Granted that the Eighty-first had yet to participate in combat, it had already undergone many months of arduous field exercises and maneuvers under a variety of climatic conditions, and it was highly regarded. Having established a reputation at Bougainville and at Guam for wholehearted cooperation with his Army colleagues, Geiger saw no reason why this spirit of close interservice relationship should not be maintained in the coming capture and occupation of the Western Carolines, although he was cognizant that General Rupertus evidently did not look with favor on the joint employment of Marine and Army troops in an amphibious operation.

Now, with barely ten days remaining before the 1st MarDiv and its reinforcing elements set sail from five different localities in the Solomons, Russells, and New Hebrides for the objective area, Geiger's principal attentions were devoted to ironing out the final details of the pre-invasion naval gunfire and aerial bombardment of the landing beaches on Peleliu's southwestern coast. There were the usual obstacles with which he and his staff were confronted: shortages of ships, ammunition, and aircraft, aggravated by the unexpected duration of the Guam operation, and of even greater significance, a scarcity of properly qualified fire-control personnel, the most serious omission from the shore bombardment angle being the failure of the 1st MarDiv to appoint a Marine officer as artillery and naval gunfire coordinator to serve on the staff of the Attack Force Commander.

Having attended the final rehearsals at Guadalcanal, on 2 September Geiger boarded Admiral Fort's flagship, the amphibious command vessel *AGC-7, USS Mount McKinley,* and steamed northwestward 2,000 miles distant to Peleliu and Angaur to observe the effects of the preparatory fires laid on the target area by the Navy's carriers and gunfire support ships. During the latter part of August Army *B-24's* had dropped some 600 tons of bombs on the Islands, and commencing the first week of September three groups of Admiral Halsey's fast carriers had taken over the job. After three days of aerial bombardment those vessels were forced to withdraw in order to carry out their assigned missions in the Philippine area. Meanwhile, their escorting cruisers and destroyers had engaged in a little target practice of their own, but at such great range offshore that the results were inconsequential. By 10 September a fourth group of large carriers had shown up to take the place of the departed ships, and this contingent supported by several escort carriers continued the aerial strikes against Peleliu and Angaur right up to the D-Day landings.

If the results of the pre-invasion air assaults were highly questionable, the preliminary naval gunfire on Peleliu turned out to be totally inadequate for the mission. Initially Geiger had requested four days of preparatory fires from Rear Admiral Oldendorf's task group of battleships, cruisers, and destroyers. The Navy had countered with two, but Geiger finally prevailed on his associates to provide three days' fire on Peleliu and five for Angaur. Handicapped by the small size of his staff and with inferior communications facilities aboard his ships not to mention a lack of ability to assess accurately the actual damage sustained by the enemy's defense installations, the fire support group commander's estimate of the situation pertaining to the degree of injury inflicted on known targets was completely unrealistic. Far from having been eliminated and with the defenders themselves underground and relatively untouched in the safety of their deep shelters, the Navy's hurried, hit-or-miss, and poorly controlled preliminary shelling of the target area left much to be desired, and when the Marine assault teams stormed Peleliu's landing beaches

271

they encountered hostile opposition which combined many of the worst features of Tarawa, Saipan, and Guam, now all rolled into one.

These riflemen had not long to wait to discover what was in store for them. After break of day on 15 September to the tune of more than 1,000 tons of naval shells laid on the enemy's defenses within the beachhead area, accompanied by continual strafing runs and bombing strikes carried out by fifty carrier fighter-bombers supplied by the Navy, elements of the 1st MarDiv (R) took their allotted spaces in their amphibian tractors, and headed eastward toward Peleliu's coastline. In calm seas and with little if any surf, the amtracs approached the reef, preceded by rocket and mortar firing gunboats as well as by armored amphibians. The moment the first wave of landing craft crossed the barrier they became the target of intensive and carefully coordinated mortar and artillery fire from hidden blockhouses and other concealed entrenchments. From either flank of the landing beaches was delivered enfilading fire from Japanese antiboat guns which took a heavy toll of the amtracs, and for those who had been lucky enough to survive the initial holocaust, and were yet able to jump overside and wade ashore, the troops were greeted with a withering blast of small-arms fire as well as from machine guns and other automatic weapons. In defiance of this devastating reception which showed no signs of diminishing but rather was marked by an increase in intensity, the survivors with ever mounting casualties somehow managed to make their way across the beaches, their movement inland being further held up by an antitank ditch the Japanese had previously dug along most of the beach front.

With a scheme of maneuver employing three RLT's abreast (from north to south, respectively, the First, Fifth, and Seventh Marines less one BLT) landing on five beaches, it was fundamental for the success of the assault that the primary thrust be conducted as quickly as possible right across the reasonably level ground of the southern portion of the Island, including the capture of its airfield. Once this were accomplished the Marines pivoting on their extreme left flank could then launch an attack against the high ground immediately to the north of the landing strip, which dominated it, and from thence continue the advance northward to secure the crucial terrain feature, the Umurbrogol hill mass and ridge system, the apparent center of enemy resistance amid a nightmare of rocky pinnacles and deep fissures. It was imperative that the Division's organic artillery (the Eleventh Marines) and tanks (the First Tank Battalion) be landed as early as possible in the operation to support the infantry drive inland, and despite bitter opposition this was largely accomplished within a matter of a few hours, some two dozen *Sherman* tanks being most effectively utilized to break up and to halt in its tracks a Japanese tank-infantry counterattack which took place during the afternoon hours of D-Day.

So stubborn was the enemy resistance—and for a change there were no Japanese *banzai* charges, the defenders instead preferring to make maximum use of their concealed firing positions and their meticulously planned defense in depth—the progress of the Marine advance ashore was notably slower than had been anticipated, while at the same time the rate of casualties incurred by the assaulting troops was far greater than had been expected. Other than in the center where the Fifth Marines were able to make some headway, if the Seventh Marines on the right found themselves up against very stiff opposition, the plight of the First on the left flank was well nigh desperate in the face of particularly rugged terrain and point-blank fire from Japanese pillboxes and caves. Notwithstanding the turmoil and the confusion, according to plan the Assistant Division Commander, Brigadier General Oliver P. Smith, had landed about noon on D-Day, and had established a temporary advance command post behind a ten foot sand bank about 100 yards from the beach. In spite of almost unsurmountable communication difficulties, he was able to exercise a fair degree of over-all control considering the circumstances, for at that time the Division beachhead had been extended inland not more than 300 yards from the water's edge.

Although it had been agreed beforehand that the Division Commander and his headquarters group would land an hour after Smith got ashore, so heavy had the losses become among the amtracs because of the accuracy and density of the enemy fire, General Rupertus had to postpone his ship-to-shore movement; in fact, as events transpired he could not boat his headquarters before nightfall, and he himself did not land until the following day. None of this, of course, passed unnoticed by the Commander, Western Landing Forces and Troops, who was understandingly becoming increasingly concerned with the slow rate of progress of the attack ashore quite aside from the fact that the few fragmentary bits of information received back aboard the Attack Force Commander's flagship from the beach were so inconclusive, General Geiger felt that he must somehow get a clearer picture of what was actually taking place within the beachhead. To one of his temperament it would have been asking too much to expect him to remain indefinitely ensconced in the relative security of the *Mount McKinley's* war command compartment, meanwhile all hell had broken loose on the beach, and no one around him at that moment seemed to know how events were faring, and could do little if anything to rectify the situation.

With his patience exhausted by mid-afternoon, Geiger resolved to find out for himself how matters stood. Descending to the foot of the ship's accommodation ladder, he hailed a passing landing craft, and prevailed on its coxswain to give him a lift ashore. Disdainful of the fire-swept beach and the jumbled mass of burning amphibian tractors, he made his way unscathed through a hail of artillery and mortar fire to General Smith's improvised CP. This was about four o'clock in the afternoon, and Smith had not been forewarned of Geiger's impromptu visit—to his surprise he turned his head momentarily from the front, and there hunched down in the sand beside him was none other than his Corps Commander. Smith joking remarked to his senior that according to the book the Western Landing Force Commander was not supposed to be ashore at that time. In reply Geiger barked out above the incessant din of battle that he had landed to ascertain why so many amtracs had been put out of action; moreover, he wanted to see the airfield. The answer to his first query was obvious, for the Japanese antiboat guns were still in commission, as Geiger could readily observe. Smith informed the General that the best way to view the airstrip was to climb the bank immediately to their front from where he could look down on one of its runways which extended to only a few yards from their shelter. Forthwith, Geiger ascended to the top of the sand bank, and at that precise moment the Japanese entertained the visitor by releasing three rounds of rocket fire which screeched over the General's head missing their target by a matter of inches.

Somewhat startled Geiger slid down into the bottom of the ditch behind the dune, his curiosity satisfied on that score. He had not completed his tour of inspection, however, for he stated that he would like to visit all of the three Regimental command posts. After crawling forward to the CP's of the Fifth and Seventh Marines, with which General Smith was able to maintain good communication, Geiger saw no good reason why he should not also pay a visit to that of the First. Using all his powers of persuasion General Smith was finally able to talk Geiger out of undertaking that hazardous mission, for at that stage of the battle there was a gap of some 800 yards between the First and the Fifth Marines, a veritable no man's land, which was no more nor less than sudden death for any individual caught wandering about in the open, shell-swept mass of coral rubble. To add to the confused state of affairs, General Smith could only communicate with that Regiment to a very limited degree; even its exact location was most uncertain.

Visibly disappointed by his inability to establish personal liaison with Colonel Puller's hard-pressed Regiment, Geiger nevertheless decided that his next most profitable employment would be to sit down the General Smith and to draw up together some estimate of the total number of casualties received. Piecing together every available scrap of information which trickled back from the front lines they eventually arrived at a figure which fell considerably short of the mark, for it was subsequently established that the 1st MarDiv's losses by the end of D-Day amounted to 210 killed in action and 900 wounded, the majority in the First Regiment's zone. As for the general situation, it was determined that at least the Division was holding its own. It then held a beachhead about one and one-half miles in length with an average depth of 500 yards. Its center was gradually gaining control of the airfield (which it took the following day). Its right was pushing ahead slowly but surely; however, the advance on its left had been definitely checked by the overwhelming preponderance of hostile firepower from the Umurbrogal hill mass. In brief, the First Marines needed help and they needed it as rapidly as possible. To assist them they were given the Division Reserve, but even with the arrival of the Second Battalion, Seventh Marines, it was clear additional reinforcements would be required to enable the Division's left front to continue its attack to the north.

In substance, the battle of Peleliu can be considered as one of three separate yet related phases. The first, comprising the initial

275

eight days of the attack (15–22 September), encompassed the overrunning of the entire southern portion of the Island, the most singular feature being the aforementioned capture of the airfield, and the seizure and consolidation of sufficient commanding terrain adjacent to it to permit the Division's engineers to develop that installation for the use of land-based Marine observation and attack aircraft. By the close of 18 September fighting on the southern portion of the Island had noticeably diminished: organized opposition had been eliminated and mopping-up had become the order of the day inasmuch as by that date the Fifth Marines had worked their way across the Island to its eastern peninsula, soon to be followed by their capture of that area as well as of several smaller islands off the northeastern coast. Not to be outdone, the Seventh Marines in their zone of action had secured its assigned objectives in the southeastern region of the Island. On the other had, the First Marines even with the help of another battalion of the Seventh, was unable to register any appreciable gains (conducting frontal attacks), so unyielding were the nature of the Japanese defenses and so difficult were the geographical obstacles of the ground it was forced to fight in. By 21 September the First Marines' casualties had mounted to about 1,750. This figure being more than 50% of the Regiment's strength, its combat effectiveness for continued operations was subject to question, and it was apparent that one of two courses lay open: either to relieve the Regiment with fresh troops and evacuate the remnant, or to allow it to batter itself to bits (with even greater casualties) against unequal odds.

The Corps Commander quite naturally was deeply concerned with the plight of the First Marines. Although tactical command of all elements of the 1st MarDiv (R) was manifestly General Rupertus' responsibility, this was an occasion in Geiger's opinion that warranted a measure of direct intervention. After all, there were other means available to bolster the First Marines' combat-depleted riflemen, and there was patently no valid reason to deny them much-needed reinforcements. This force consisted of elements of the Army's Eighty-first Infantry Division, the Three Hundred and Twenty-first and Twenty-second Regimental Combat Teams, which had landed on Angaur two days after the 1st MarDiv (R) had launched its attack on Peleliu. Enemy resistance on Angaur had been generally light to moderate, and after four days of fighting, Japanese opposition had been reduced to the degree one of the two American units present could handle the situation, meanwhile the other could be freed to back up the fighting on Peleliu. Thus, by 21 September the Three Hundred and Twenty-first RCT was readily at hand and within reasonable distance, awaiting only assignment to a supplementary mission.

General Geiger was completely at a loss to understand the seeming reluctance of General Rupertus to take advantage of the presence of combat-indoctrinated and relatively fresh Army troops of the contingent reserve of III Corps, which could be brought into play at a decisive moment, especially in view of the fact that the entire Division reserve had long since been fully committed on Peleliu. Although Geiger felt impelled to intervene, he restrained himself at first. But there were limits to his endurance, and by 20 September his patience gave way to the extent he regarded his stepping into the picture fully justified by the circumstances. With fire in his eye only equalled by the glowing tip of his cigar he made his way to Rupertus' CP. After listening without comment to the latter's far from convincing argument that he could secure the Island in a couple of additional days with the troops currently engaged, in the ensuing discussion Geiger overrode his subordinate's plea that other forces not be introduced. To make his position clear Geiger thereupon directed the Division Commander to draw up plans for the embarkation of the First Marines (or what remained of them) for evacuation, and as a finishing touch informed Rupertus that the Corps Commander without further delay would put in motion the necessary steps to attach one of the Eighty-first Division's RCT's to the 1st MarDiv.

This controversial issue having been lifted out of Rupertus' hands, the Three Hundred and Twenty-first RCT was forthwith transported by sea from Angaur to Peleliu, where it disembarked on 23 September, and was immediately deployed in the zone of action (across the southern edge of the Umurbrogol) in which the First Marines had all but exhausted themselves in the previous week's fighting. The arrival of the Army contingent ushered in the second phase of the conquest of Peleliu. It being essential to isolate the Umurbrogol pocket, the only way for the American troops to outflank it was to move along its western edge, and to proceed up the west coast of the Island in order to gain the approaches from the north. While one force blocked off the northern extremity of the pocket by driving eastward across its upper rim, simultaneously another was given the mission of seizing the eastern coast of the northwest peninsula. This combined Army-Marine Corps advance despite fierce opposition, particularly at the Amiangal hill mass (a smaller scale but none the less lethal obstacle than the Umurbrogol), met with success, and by 28 September the way was now clear for the capture of Ngesebus, a small island 500 yards off the northern tip of Peleliu.

On that date a well-planned and well-coordinated shore-to-shore amphibious assault landing, conducted by a battalion of the Fifth Marines backed up by armored amtracs and tanks, and reinforced by adequate naval and artillery bombardment not to mention highly effective close air support provided by VMF-114's *Corsairs,* resulted in the reduction of that stronghold at negligible cost to the attackers. With its airstrip in American hands the enemy lost its remaining aviation facilities at Peleliu; furthermore, the Japanese were denied a site for some of their artillery which had been a constant source of harassment to the 1st MarDiv. Of even greater significance, the American possession of Ngesebus made it no longer feasible for the Japanese to bring in reinforcements or supplies by sea from the other islands of the Palau group to the north. All that remained now was the annihilation of the surviving Japanese in the by-passed Umurbrogol, holed-up in their caves and armored casemates, determined to fight it out to the last man and the last round of ammunition.

The seizure of this fortified bastion—by this time the pocket had been compressed so that it measured some 900 yards in length by 400 yards in width—witnessed the third and final phase of the Peleliu campaign. A matter of siege warfare and a battle of attrition waged by flamethrowers, demolition teams, and napalm bomb drops by Marine aircraft flying at exceedingly low altitudes on 15-second runs, it commenced on 29 September, and it required almost two months of burning and blasting before the pocket was ultimately overrun by infantrymen of the *Wildcats.*

Hence, by 30 September, fifteen days after the landing on Peleliu, and with only the surrounded Umurbrogol strong-point holding out, Admiral Fort commanding the Western Attack Force considered that for all practical purposes the Island could be regarded as secured. Considerable fighting, it is true, was still in store for the Marines and Army units, but with Peleliu's airfields under American control, with Angaur occupied, and with Ulithi captured by the Three Hundred and Twenty-third RCT of the Eighty-first Division, the mission of III Amphibious Corps had on the whole been essentially achieved. That date also marked the embarkation of most of the survivors of the First Marines; the remainder sailing for their home base at Pavuvu two days later. With regard to the 1st MarDiv's casualties, by the close of September they were slightly in excess of 5,000 of which about one-sixth of the total represented those killed in action, as contrasted with enemy fatalities estimated at more than 8,000.

During the first week of October the Seventh Marines were relieved by the Fifth, and on the 12th of that month General Geiger officially declared the termination of the assault phase of the campaign. Within a few days all of the remaining Marine elements, including the Fifth Regiment, were replaced on the front lines by troops of the Eighty-first Infantry Division. To complete the picture, on 20 October General Mueller formally relieved the 1st MarDiv (R), and assumed command of all combat forces in the Southern Palaus. All that now remained to be done was the evacuation of the Marine Division, which was accomplished by the 30th of that month, its final casualty returns for the entire campaign amounting to approximately 6,500.

Turning to the activities of the Commanding General of the III Amphibious Corps, his participation in the seizure and reduction of Peleliu had been far from passive in nature. No headquarters general in the literal use of the term, Geiger's conduct had shown him to be a field commander who much preferred to position himself right up front where the actual fighting was going on, viewing with his own eyes what was transpiring, and making decisions on the spot as changing circumstances dictated. Pinning himself down far to the rear of the battle lines in the comparative safety and shelter of a conventional Corps Command Post with its telephones and its radios, its situation maps and its files of periodic reports, and with any number of advisers handy to assist him to arrive at a decision, was not to his liking: such an arrangement seemed too detached and too unrealistic for one of his temperament.

Repeatedly throughout the campaign he had exposed himself to hostile fire in order to keep in touch with a moving situation. In this respect he was the despair of his staff, who feared, and not without justification, that their commanding officer was stretching his luck exceedingly thin. Whenever possible he walked erect, disdaining to crawl unless absolutely necessary, and he was not adverse to advancing so far forward, he frequently found himself in the very forefront of an active fire fight. On at least one occasion he incurred the acute displeasure of a Marine rifleman, who, vainly seeking the little protection his shallow foxhole offered in the face of an enemy mortar barrage, turned about and requested in no uncertain terms that the general officer standing alongside his pit take his presence elsewhere on the battlefield, it being the Private's opinion that nice as it might be to have the "Old Man" within spitting distance, the latter was inadvertently offering the Japanese mortarmen a splendid registration point. As far as the trooper was concerned if the Corps Commander wanted to endanger his own skin by conspicuously showing up in the middle of a hotly contested action, it was the latter's affair. But to imperil the being of a member of his command, no matter how lowly, by posing as a drawing card to attract further enemy fire on the Private's own bit of hard-earned real estate, was absolutely inexcusable.

Geiger took it all in his stride well aware that his physical presence on the firing line if nothing else was a boost to morale: proof positive that the "Old Man" wasn't dug-in deeply, two miles to the rear, writing in his diary, or concocting some imaginary press release of the day's doings to pass on to some news-eager war correspondent. After a while the troops became accustomed to having their Corps Commander pop up unexpectedly out of the mass of coral rubble at the most unlikely places and times, and if he did not put in an appearance every now and then, they felt that somehow they had been slighted.

For his services on Peleliu—he took off from its airfield on 20 October after the informal change of command ceremonies, bound for Guadalcanal via Emirau—Geiger was in time to be awarded a second Gold Star for his Distinguished Service Medal. Perhaps the best summarization of what he had tried to do—and how successful he had been in his endeavors—was contained in the following extract from his official citation accompanying his decoration:

"— —Repeatedly disregarding his personal safety, Major

General Geiger kept himself fully appraised of both the enemy situation and that of his own troops, frequently traversing his front lines under merciless blasts of artillery and mortar fire and, by his undaunted valor, tenacious perserverance, and staunch leadership in the face of tremendous odds, constantly inspired his stout-hearted Marines and soldiers to heroic effort during the most critical phases of the fierce battle. His resolute fortitude and decisive conduct through out the entire Palau Campaign reflect highest credit upon Major General Geiger, his gallant command and the United States Naval Service."

Now a veteran of four major Pacific campaigns, first as a Wing Commander, and thrice as an Amphibious Corps Commander, these were but the preliminaries to even more difficult trials, for although he had no premonition of it in October 1944, within a year's time Geiger, then a Lieutenant General, was to command an Army in combat.

Chapter XIII

Tenth Army on Okinawa

Back once more at the old stamping ground on Guadalcanal's north coast Geiger decided that for the moment the best way to unwind after the tensions of the previous month's rugged campaigning was to indulge in his favorite forms of recreation: swimming and volley ball with a little flying thrown in for good measure. During the final week of October someone on his staff brought to his attention that within reasonable flying distance from Koli Point there existed an unusual atoll which might be worth a visit. Known as Sikiana this small island, one of the Stewarts about 100 miles east of Malaita, was said to be a near perfect example of a South Pacific coral atoll completely encircled by an unbroken barrier reef which prevented even the smaller trading schooners from entering within the lagoons. His curiosity aroused by this islet, untouched by the ravages of the Pacific campaigns, and inhabited by natives who were believed to be friendly, Geiger and several members of his staff took off in a *PBY-5A* piloted by Lieutenant Moss on 29 October for a closer view.

Landing inside the circle the party were met by natives who obligingly brought them ashore from the anchored amphibian in their outrigger canoes. With the local chief acting as master of ceremonies Geiger and his group were introduced to what passed for the entire native population of the colony, the distinctive feature of the members of the settlement being that in appearance as well as culture they formed what could best be classified as an ethnological incongruity. Of Polynesian stock somehow in the distant past they had made their way by sea far to the west of their natural habitat, winding up in what was generally considered to be strictly Melanesian territory. For what reason or when they had originally taken up residence in the Stewarts remained a mystery: doubtless their ancestors had been driven far from home waters by violent tropical gales and had no means of returning, so great was the damage done to their frail sailing craft. At any rate, probably due in large part of the hydrographic peculiarities of their tiny atoll, the comparative isolation of the Sikiana Islanders from the inroads of both white traders and their nearby Negroid contemporaries of the Solomons and the New Hebrides had rendered the descendents of the initial settlers rather unique as to time and place. Somewhat intrigued by the primitiveness of the colony's standard of living, Geiger took time off to have his picture taken with the chief, his family, and his dogs (with the unlit cigar as usual firmly clutched in his right hand) on the veranda of the lodge by Moss who had remembered to bring his camera along. The visiting Marines, however, did not extend their stay ashore beyond the customary bartering of American tobacco and candy bars in exchange for the few bits of native gear with which their owners were willing to part, and before dark the *Catalina* winged its way back to Guadalcanal.

But jaunts such as these to outlying islands did not last for more than a few days. On 3 November 1944, Geiger with his staff and Pierce aboard their twin-engine *Douglas* transport (*R4D-5,* No. 39072) flew off from Carney Field bound for the United States via Tarawa and Hawaii, arriving three days later at Anacostia's Naval Air Station. Following a week's stay at Washington, mostly devoted to conferences with the Commandant of the Marine Corps and its Director of Aviation, Major General Field Harris (who had relieved General Woods in July), Geiger was granted twenty days leave, and at once took off for Florida. Reunited with his wife at Pensacola, he also had a chance to renew old friendships in his home town, and in his spare time, considering that the wartime shortage of aged bourbon whisky had long since dried up all available local sources, he had ample opportunity (and good reason) to probe about the front lawn of his residence with a long metal rod, vainly searching for the long lost but not forgotten wooden keg, hidden somewhere under the sod six feet down, its contents now practically worth its weight in gold.

By the time the third anniversary of the Japanese raid on

Pearl Harbor had rolled around he was back on the West Coast, at San Diego, and on that date Geiger flew to Hawaii with his new pilot, Captain Edward Kicklighter, at the controls. At Admiral Nimitz's Headquarters he received preliminary briefings concerning two forthcoming amphibious landings of considerable magnitude: that of Lieutenant General Holland Smith's V MAC scheduled to seize Iwo Jima in the Volcano Islands in mid-February 1945, to be followed six weeks later by Lieutenant General Simon Bolivar Buckner's Tenth Army capture of Okinawa in the Ryukus. The latter operation, given the code name ICEBERG, was of paramount interest to Geiger, for the principal beach assault elements of the Tenth Army were to consist of Major General John Hodge's XXIV Corps and Geiger's III MAC, each of two divisions. Other major ground components slated to take part in the operation included the 2nd MarDiv (Major General Hunt),two Infantry Divisions, the Seventy-seventh (Major General Bruce) and the Twenty-seventh (Major General Griner), backed up by a third, the Eighty-first (Major General Mueller) in area reserve in New Caledonia, under Admiral Nimitz's control.

The basic concept of ICEBERG involving the capture not only of Okinawa but also of several of its small offshore islands had been arrived at only after considerable deliberation between Admiral Nimitz and General MacArthur. In substance, it was formulated on the premise that Okinawa rather than the larger island of Formosa could better serve as a base for long-range bombing against the Japanese homeland, being situated only 350 miles from Southern Kyushu. Furthermore, in American hands it was reasoned that Okinawa was well adapted for use as a fleet anchorage and repair base to support future naval operations against either the coasts of Japan or China: he who possessed Okinawa could dominate the East China Sea. The Joint Chiefs of Staff having reached this decision in mid-summer 1944, the responsibility for implementing it was given to Admiral Nimitz.

In October 1944, therefore, pursuant to his instructions CinCPOA had issued a joint staff study for operation ICEBERG, and at that time Admiral Nimitz had established a unified command headed by the Fifth Fleet's Vice Admiral Spruance, designating him as officer in command of the entire Ryukus campaign (TF-50), assigning Vice Admiral Turner as Commander, Joint Expeditionary Force (TF-51), and naming General Buckner as Commander, Expeditionary Troops ashore TF-56) in addition to his duties as Commander, Tenth Army.

At the moment of Geiger's arrival at Pearl Harbor, General Buckner and his capable team of assistants (among them, Marine Brigadier General Oliver Smith, serving as Buckner's Deputy Chief of Staff) were then engaged in drawing up a tentative Operation Plan (1-45) for ICEBERG, which was ultimately issued in January 1945. As a consequence, throughout Geiger's two-week stay in Hawaii (7—20 December 1944) in a temporary additonal duty status he was in a favorable position to get in on the ground floor, so to speak, of the detailed planning for the Okinawa campaign with specific reference to the employment of his III Corps. Moreover, he was, perforce, in almost daily personal contact with many of the senior commanders, Army as well as Navy and Marine Corps, who were to participate in the future operation. Whether or not Geiger was fully aware of its implications at that time (it remains a matter of opinion), the concurrent renewal of his long standing acquaintance with the Commanding General of the Tenth Army—particularly in the light of what subsequently transpired on the battlefield—was of utmost significance.

It will be recalled that Buckner and Geiger, when each held the rank of Major, together had attended the Army's Command and General Staff Course at Fort Leavenworth back in the mid-1920's, both being distinguished graduates. Throughout their respective careers in the Army and Marine Corps the two officers, an infantryman and an aviator, had kept in touch with one another, and had taken more than a casual interest in their opposite's activities inasmuch as each held the other in high professional esteem. Incidentally, the commander of the Tenth Army and the Commanding General of III Corps had much in common: both were large men who championed physical conditioning; were known to be fair-minded; and were equally positive in their attitudes, persistence and determination being the keynotes. In the same vein both general officers were prone to reach a decision only after carefully weighing all of the issues: once they passed judgement, there the matter rested, come what may. Perhaps the most pronounced difference was the manner of their approach. Whereas Buckner was severely formal when it came to planning, for he tended to follow staff manuals and rigidly prescribed procedure to the letter; Geiger, to the contrary, being less interested in detail and form and far more tolerant of discussion was generally more concerned with the spirit in his acceptance of completed staff work. Regardless of their attitude toward technical formalities, the former leader of the Aleutian campaign and the erstwhile ComAirCACTUS saw eye-to-eye in their confident approach toward solving a problem; hence, when purely by chance their paths were to cross some twenty years later in the Pacific, Buckner now the senior in rank was to prove conclusively his continued confidence in Geiger's demonstrated abilities by designating him his second in command.

The circumstances surrounding this decision were rather out of the ordinary. It is generally believed that Buckner had a premonition that he would not live to see the Okinawan campaign terminated, and that prior to undertaking it prudence dictated that he should nominate his successor. Granted that Geiger was the senior of his two Corps commanders, he was by virtue of date of rank junior to another Major General of the Army delegated to serve as the Island Commander, once Okinawa had been secured by the assault units of the Tenth Army. Although this Army officer was highly regarded by Buckner, the latter was of the opinion that Geiger had exhibited such splendid traits of leadership and sound judgement in four previous campaigns in the South and Central Pacific, he was better qualified for field command than the other individual.

Accordingly, General Buckner decided to send an official letter to Admiral Nimitz via the office of the Commanding General of the Army Forces in the Central Pacific (under CinCPOA) recommending Geiger as his successor. The intermediary, the senior Army officer present at Oahu (Hawaii), however, refused to forward the communication, and returned it to its originator with a penciled remark to the effect that the designation of a second-in-command of the Tenth Army was a matter which should be determined by the War Department in far distant Washington. Buckner, somewhat disturbed by the rebuff, nevertheless received the news more in the nature of a challenge. To find a way to circumvent the barrier interposed by his nominal, temporary senior in the chain of command posed no unsurmountable problem: once embarked for Okinawa he would no longer be subject to the jurisdiction of the Commanding General at Oahu, and he would be at perfect liberty to communicate directly with Admiral Nimitz. This Buckner did, whereupon, immediately following his death in combat on 18 June 1945, his Chief of Staff, General Post, without further delay notified General Geiger that as of that moment he was now in command of the Tenth Army, confirmed by Admiral Nimitz.

There were two other factors which might well have influenced General Buckner in the selection of his second-in-command. One was Geiger's well known reputation for cooperating unreservedly with his associates, Army as well as Navy. Personally, he got along very well with General Hodge, commanding the XXIV Corps, who had previously served as the Commanding General of the Americal Division when it relieved the 3rd MarDiv of Geiger's I MAC on Bougainville. By the same token Geiger had already served with General Bruce of the Seventy-seventh Infantry Division on Guam, and with General Mueller of the Eighty-first during the recently concluded Peleliu operation. Whenever Army and Marine Corps units had jointly taken part in prior campaigns of Geiger's III Corps, there had been a notable lack of friction between them, particularly at the higher echelons, for Geiger would under no circumstances condone any unnecessary inter-service rivalry nor did he play favorites, and his attitude in those respects was common knowledge. Similarly, his relations with Navy Task Force Commanders in amphibious operations could hardly have been improved upon: as far as Geiger was concerned it made no difference what kind of a uniform a man wore, his branch or arm of the service, or his outfit as long as the soldier or sailor, airman or Marine, got the job done properly. It is admitted that Geiger had a marked aversion towards a few individuals who appeared to relish staff billets in a combat command, but for the most part, his stony treatment if not thinly concealed scorn accorded them was reserved for persons of his own service. With this established reputation for promoting and maintaining harmonious relations between and among various elements of his often diverse command, this of itself was without doubt sufficient reason for Buckner to choose Geiger as his logical successor in the ensuing campaign.

The other element affecting Buckner's decision in all probability related to the prominent role assigned to the Tenth Army's Tactical Air Force (TAF) in operation ICEBERG. This sizable aviation component consisted in the main of the 2nd

Marine Air Wing (four MAG's and a fifth Air-warning Group) as well as several Army Air Corps squadrons, commanded by a Marine aviator holding the rank of Major General, and charged with the operations of all shore-based aircraft. With an Air Defense Command (ADC) and three Landing Force Air Support Control Units (LFASCU's) of which one each was provided for Tenth Army, XXIV Corps, and III Corps (all under command of Marine pilots), Marine fighter and torpedo-bomber squadrons aboard two fast carriers and two CVE's, and four "Grasshopper" observation squadrons, it was obvious that much of the defense against Japanese suicide pilots, the *kamikaze* ("divine wind"), not to mention close air support for the attacking riflemen on the ground was going to be largely an all-Marine Corps affair, once the two principal Japanese airfields inland from the landing beaches had been seized. Consequently, bearing in mind Geiger's appreciation of the vital part to be played by aviation in the pending operation and his knowledge of the proper manner of its employment, coupled with his proven ability as an infantry tactician, such were they that he of all officers assigned to the Tenth Army was undoubtedly best fitted to carry on with the mission in the unlikely event its commander were rendered *hors de combat.*

Following two weeks of intensive briefing on the background for the invasion of Okinawa (and with L-Day set for 1 April 1945), it was high time for Geiger to depart from Admiral Nimitz's Headquarters and to return to Guadalcanal to initiate Corps plans and to alert its Division commanders: on 20 December, Geiger, his Chief of Staff, Brigadier General Mervin Silverthorn (who had served in a similar capacity throughout the Guam and Peleliu campaigns), and several other members of his Corps staff who had been present at Pearl Harbor, took off from the Marine Corps air base at Ewa. Stopping en route at Tarawa the party landed two days later at Koli Point. Liaison with the 1st MarDiv (R), now under command of Major General del Valle, involved no strain as the Division and most of its supporting elements were centralized in the Solomons, either in the Guadalcanal-Tulagi area or at nearby Pavuvu in the Russells. Contacting the other main unit of III Corps which was simultaneously to storm the beaches at Okinawa, the 6th MarDiv (R) commanded by Major General Shepherd, required a flight to Guam, as it had not yet in its entirety been assembled for maneuvers and dress rehearsals at Guadalcanal. As for the remaining component, the 2nd MarDiv, although on a technicality it was not part of the III Corps for the actual landing, being rather a demonstration group ordered to make a feint off beaches in the far south of the Island of Okinawa (and thereafter revert to Tenth Army reserve on an on-call basis), Geiger notwithstanding wished to see how it was progressing, and stopped off at Saipan on his island-hopping tour of inspection of his scattered command.

On Christmas Eve 1944, he folded up the papers on his field desk, locked them in a safe, and ordered Lieutenant Moss to gas up the old *Catalina.* Joined by his aide and General Silverthorn, Geiger and his associates flew across Sealark Channel to Purvis Bay, Tulagi. The water landing at the fleet anchorage there was difficult: the harbor was positively crowded with scores of ships, and the pilot had to weave his way between the unlit moored vessels in semi-darkness. Taken by launch to the flagship of the Commander, Amphibious Group Three, U.S. Pacific Fleet, Vice Admiral Conolly greeted his old friends with open arms, put them up for the night, and treated them to a fine Christmas dinner the next day. It was an occasion Geiger was not going to forget. Among the high ranking officers present was a Major General Charles Mullen of the Army. Quite naturally, Conolly, Geiger, and Mullen sooner or later got around to discussing the coming Okinawa campaign and the eventual outcome of the war in the Pacific. The conversation at length centered on the duration of the conflict. One of the three officers wagered that regardless of the time schedule he would be the first to set foot in the City of Tokyo, whereupon the others immediately got hold of pencil and paper and drew up a written contract, stipulating: "— — each of the three undersigned proposes to reach Tokyo before anyone of the others. $100.00 will be paid into a purse for disbursement to the winner." Signed and duly witnessed on Christmas Day, each of the trio received his separate copy of the bet. Carefully tucking his into his wallet, Geiger then and there made up his mind that he would win the wager, and as will be subsequently related, in time he was able to collect the proceeds.

After months of strenuous schooling, including everything from street fighting to assaults on near duplicates of the type of Japanese defense installations to be expected on Okinawa, and weeks of ship-to-shore practice as well as detailed rehearsals, the

III Corps by early March 1945 was considered as combat ready as it were ever going to be for operation ICEBERG. Departing from Guadalcanal its two assault Divisions and their accompanying combat support units sailed for the staging rendezvous at Ulithi Atoll in the Western Carolines where they linked up with the XXIV Corps, recently arrived from Leyte in the Philippines. At Ulithi for the first time practically the entire Tenth Army including its Tactical Air Force was assembled, some 1,200 miles or 100 hours by sea from the target area. Against an estimated enemy strength of 80,000 on Okinawa (subsequently it was determined that the combination of the Japanese Thirty-second Army, the Island Garrison, and naval base personnel, commanded by Lieutenant General Ushijima, amounted to more than 100,000), General Buckner's impressive force numbered slightly in excess of 182,000 troops, of which at least 40% were Marines. Some idea of the scope of the Okinawa invasion could be gauged by the number of vessels gathered at Ulithi: an armada of approximately 1,400 ships of all types, a figure exceeding that employed at the first North African landings, and with more major combatant craft than had been present at Normandy. For this occasion, which up to that time had been regarded as the largest amphibious attack in history (and which, incidentally, turned out to be the most expensive single operation of the Second World War), Admiral Spruance was going to throw into the fray just about every fighting ship, landing craft, or piece of floating equipment of his mighty Fifth Fleet.

As for Geiger in his dual capacity as Commander, Northern Landing Force as well as III Corps, on 1 March he shifted his Headquarters afloat aboard the amphibious command vessel *AGC-13, USS Panamint,* flagship of Rear Admiral Lawrence Reifsnider commanding the Northern Attack Force. With some two weeks yet to go before *Panamint* weighed anchor and set a course northward for Ulithi Geiger decided that inasmuch as he was drawing flight pay, it behooved him to earn that extra stipend: on the 4th of the month he piloted a *Douglas* transport on a four-hour flight over and around Guadalcanal, thereby satisfying the minimum, monthly flight time requirement. At long last on the 16th the vessel steamed north toward the rendezvous area, and on the 25th in company with the landing ships and assault transports of Turner's Joint Expeditionary Force left the atoll destined for the western shores of Okinawa.

The Fifth Fleet, meanwhile, had not been idle. In mid-March Vice Admiral Mitscher's ubiquitous Task Force-58 had conducted air strikes against the *kamikaze* airfields in Kyushu, and commencing on the 23rd his heavy carriers turned their attentions to Okinawa and its vicinity. The following day, 8 of his fast battleships undertook their initial heavy bombardment of the beaches, and with the arrival of Rear Admiral Blandy's Amphibious Support Force (TF-52), the latter's 10 old dreadnoughts, 8 heavy and 3 light cruisers, and 24 destroyers joined forces to begin a week-long shelling of the landing sites. The combined preliminary air and naval gunfire bombardment, designed to pulverize the Japanese shore defenses, was of unprecedented dimensions: during the seven days preceding the L-Day landing on 1 April, Okinawa was on the receiving end of 13,000 tons of shells of varying caliber; additionally, more than 3,000 sorties were flown in the area by planes from fast and escort carriers, the attackers then blissfully unaware of the fact that their colossal aerial and surface barrage was for the most part a gigantic waste of ammunition and effort, Ushijima having elected not to contest the anticipated landings, at least as far as the beaches were concerned, but rather to withdraw inland to carefully prepared defense positions in depth in southern Okinawa.

While the Navy was busily engaged, certain selected elements of the Tenth Army following pre-arranged plans also got into the act as the main body of the Expeditionary Force slowly approached the Ryukus. On 26 March two regiments of the Army's Seventy-seventh Infantry Division, reinforced by a Fleet Marine Force, Pacific, reconnaissance battalion and naval support vessels of Rear Admiral Kiland's Western Attack Group, landed almost unopposed on the five main islands of Kerama Retto, about fifteen miles west of Okinawa proper. By the 30th General Bruce was able to declare them secure, and the next day an Army artillery group assaulted and captured Keise Shima, another cluster of coral islets some five miles east of Kerama. The successful seizure of these offshore bits of real estate was essential to the success of the major undertaking. The former was quickly converted into a logistical support, fueling, and repair base for seaplanes and naval auxiliary craft within close proximity to the principal objective. The latter could be effectively utilized as an emplacement site for Army heavy artillery within battery range (155-mm. Guns) of southern Okinawa, less than ten miles distant. An unexpected dividend realized by Kerama's capture was the discovery of nearly 400 small, Japanese suicide boats armed with depth charges, which the enemy had fully intended to let loose in night raids against crowded transport shipping of the American Expeditionary Force. Had the Japanese been able to unleash their "secret weapon" in conjunction with the disastrous effects of their daytime *Kamikaze* forays, the resultant damage which could have been inflicted on Admiral Turner's task force might well have proved incalculable; hence, the net gains achieved by the surprise preliminary landings on the small islands west of Okinawa were appreciable by any standards.

Thus, by the evening of 31 March—the air strength of the Okinawa garrison having been expended following three suicide attacks, and the offshore islands now being in American control—the stage was set for the all-out invasion of the Tenth Army over the Hagushi beaches on the western shore of Okinawa, for the ensuing day, Easter Sunday (which also happened to be April Fools' Day). So much has since been written about operation ICEBERG and so meticulously has it been examined and evaluated by official historians (which is not surprising considering that more than half a million persons of all services, including those of Britain's Royal Navy, participated in the campaign), primary emphasis in this account will be directed toward the operations of III Corps and the activities of its Commanding General.

At all events, while the 2nd MarDiv was conducting its demonstrations off the Minatoga beaches of the southeastern coast to confuse the enemy (an affair which resulted in heavy casualties to ships and embarked Marines from *kamikazes*), under cover of the most devastating prelanding bombardment of the Pacific war, the armored amphibians strung out in an almost continuous eight-mile line crunched over the reefs to discharge their human cargoes on the shores of Okinawa—genuine Japanese territory this time, not merely outlying terrain which had been previously overrun by the conquering sons of Nippon. Landing with four divisions in line abreast—from left to right (north to south) the 6th and 1st MarDiv's north of the village of Hagushi near the mouth of the Bishi Gawa (River), the Seventh and Ninety-sixth Infantry

Divisions to the south, each with two RLT's abreast and one in reserve—the III and XXIV Corps, respectively, of the Tenth Army made their way to shore relatively intact, on schedule, and unscathed. None of their amtracs were hit by hostile fire; the beaches were found to be practically deserted and elsewhere resistance was negligible; and the troops of the initial assault waves having walked in "standing up," casualties were incredibly inconsequential. Or, to state it alternately, what had heretofore been expected (based on past experience) to become a bitterly contested, yard-by-yard, and soaked-in-blood landing had degenerated into a giant-sized, routine ferrying operation, much to the amazement and evident relief of staff planners and combat riflemen, somewhat bewildered by this apparent stroke of good fortune.

Ushijima, of course, had planned it that way—it was all part of a trap. He had divined (particularly after what had transpired at Iwo Jima) that it would be senseless in the face of overwhelming superiority at sea held by the American Navy to defend Okinawa on the beaches, preferring rather to maintain the bulk of his forces in the interior beyond the effective range of carrier air and surface naval gunfire. Once having lured the invaders inland, his opponents would be forced to fight him on ground on his own choosing against strongly fortified bastions ingeniously contrived to make maximum use of critical terrain features, and incorporating an underground interlocking cave and blockhouse system more formidable than the casemates encountered on Saipan and Peleliu, across the narrows of southern Okinawa. While the Americans battered themselves to bits in futile frontal assaults against Japanese defense works which could not be outflanked (there being little room to maneuver), Ushijima planned to disrupt if not destroy the attackers' logistical and fire support means by suicide surface and aerial strikes employing the remaining major fleet units of the Japanese Navy, the one-man torpedo boats at Kerama Retto, and hundreds of *kamikazes* to be flown south from their airstrips in southern Kyushu. In substance, he reasoned that he could wage a costly war of attrition, which, admittedly a desperate gamble, could conceivably so deplete the strength of Admiral Nimitz's Pacific Fleet, Japan's chances for survival might be correspondingly improved.

In theory Ushijima's concept had merit; in practice it proved

293

unsound due to misunderstanding and miscalculation on the part of its proponent who had grossly underestimated the fortitude and the determination of his opponents. As related before, the suicide craft at Kerama Retto were easily removed from the play; Task Force–58 shortly was to send the last sortie of the Imperial Japanese Fleet from home ports to the bottom of the Pacific; the rapid seizure of Yontan and Kadena airfields in western Okinawa enabled the Tenth Army's Tactical Air Force to initiate land-based, close air support missions very early in the game; and the combination of naval aviators, ship and shore antiaircraft gunners, Navy, Marine, and Army, in time were to shoot the dreaded *kamikazes* out of the skies, albeit at frightful cost to the Fifth Fleet, expecially among the crews of those destroyers detailed to serve as radar-warning pickets. But above and beyond those considerations was the vital factor of morale: Ushijima for all his recognized talent had failed to take into consideration the resoluteness of the American commanders aboard ship and in the field. They had resolved to slug it out to the bitter end, confident that they would eventually win the campaign. On the other hand, Ushijima had underrated his adversaries' ability to absorb severe damage, meanwhile inflicting it in greater measure, and this oversight became the cause of his undoing. In the end, of course, he managed to absolve himself of any further responsibility: eighty-plus days after the Tenth Army landed, his positions now overrun and all of his combat troops either killed or captured, he succeeded in bowing out of the picture conveniently by committing ceremonial *hari-kari* in company with his chief of staff, the advancing American riflemen having worked their way forward to within proverbial stone's throwing distance from the entrance to his cave.

Regardless of what Ushijima might have waiting in store for them, on Easter Sunday, 1 April 1945, the assault echelons of Buckner's Tenth Army poured across Okinawa's silent landing beaches in a steady stream. By the evening of L-Day Tenth Army's two corps had established a beachhead some 7 miles in width with a depth of at least two miles; Yontan airfield had been secured by III Corps, and Kadena to the south in the zone of action of XXIV Corps; approximately 50,000 Marine riflemen and Army infantry with substantial increments of their divisional artillery had come ashore and dug themselves in; and even the Division and Corps

Command Posts had been set up on dry land. At a cost of only 100-odd casualties, and with the front lines at a point they had not been expected to reach until the third day (terrain having been found to be a greater obstacle to the movement inland than the few snipers encountered), the success of the landings had clearly exceeded the highest expectations of Admiral Turner and General Buckner.

Under such favorable circumstances execution of the planned scheme of maneuver was forthwith put into effect on L-Day plus 1: the central (inner) pair of the four divisions was ordered to advance as quickly as possible right across the island, dividing the Japanese forces more or less into two unequal portions, while the outer two divisions were to turn simultaneously north and south to engage the enemy wherever and whenever he might be located. In line with this directive the 1st Marine and Seventh Infantry Divisions continued their drive eastward toward Chimu and Nagagushu Bays; the 6th MarDiv, wheeling left, proceeded in a northeasterly direction destined for the Ishikawa Isthmus; while the Ninety-sixth Infantry Division, pivoting right, laid a course south toward Shuri Castle and Naha, Okinawa's principal municipality.

With III Corps assigned the general mission of sweeping clean any opposition on the northern end of the island, meanwhile XXIV Corps headed south toward what was believed to be the main enemy battle positions perpendicular to the American line of advance, it was evident that Geiger's command was expected to assume a subsidiary or supporting role. Initially, this was indeed the case; however, midway through the campaign III Corps, its mission in the north completed only after singularly hard fighting, was to be transferred south to assist XXIV Corps, and most assuredly thereafter was to contribute more than its fair share to the main effort long before the termination of hostilities on Okinawa.

For III Corps the first week ashore was more of a prolonged field exercise (with emphasis focused on the supply problem) than an active combat operation. Against unorganized and spotty opposition—there was no Japanese front lines—and but token resistance the advance was rapid, the retreating enemy refusing to make a determined stand. With the 6th MarDiv pushing steadily north up the west coast road net headed for Nago Bay and

Motobu Peninsula, and the 1st MarDiv now across to the eastern shore of Okinawa in its zone of action and occupying Katchin Peninsula, III Corps' progress was close to two weeks ahead of the proposed schedule. For General Shepherd's troops, however, the honeymoon could not last indefinitely: by 12 April it had been established that a force of some 2,000 Japanese under Colonel Udo had dug in on Yae Take, a critical hill mass dominating the Motobu Peninsula, and was displaying every indication of resisting any further American intrusion. To blast Udo's surrounded machine gunners and riflemen from their redoubt required almost a week of mountain warfare of the most rugged sort: flame throwers and demolition crews, supporting artillery fires, air bombardment, and even armored amtracs eventually turned the scale in the Marines' favor, the few Japanese who managed to survive the fire fight electing for the most part to blow themselves to bits in their caves with hand grenades rather than surrender.

Geiger, ever on the move and intent on seeing what was transpiring, followed day-to-day developments of the fighting on Motobu Peninsula with avid interest. Resolved to bring himself just as near as possible to the Japanese homeland, he frequently accompanied reconnaissance and combat patrols forward of the front lines, and in so doing managed to get a "too close for comfort" view of the effectiveness of Marine close air support: on at least one occasion the Corps Commander was forced to take cover in a ditch from low flying *Corsairs* whose pilots seemingly were inclined to engage anything on the ground that moved, be it friend or foe. Somewhat chagrined at the experience, Geiger nevertheless had only himself to blame for his predicament, and if nothing else, here was conclusive proof that given the opportunity Marine aviators could bring supporting fire to the battlefield whenever and wherever their services were required by the riflemen on the ground. For the moment, he was otherwise too occupied with his command duties to take time off to fly himself, but within a month's time he was able to "borrow" an artillery spotter (an *OY* "grasshopper" from VMO-3 based at Yontan airfield) for a bird's-eye of the campaign in southern Okinawa.

By 20 April, it was generally conceded that organized resistance on Motobu Peninsula as well as throughout the entire northern portion of Okinawa had been terminated. By that date the Seventy-seventh Infantry Division, following its capture and consolidation of Kerama Retto, had landed on Ie Shima (three miles off the tip of Motobu Peninsula), and had declared that islet secure by the 21st. The next day was marked by the flag-raising ceremony at 6th MarDiv's Headquarters at Nago, the Commandant of the Marine Corps, General Vandegrift, then on a tour of inspection being present along with Generals Geiger and Shepherd; nevertheless, although victory had been officially proclaimed as applied to two-third's of the Island of Okinawa, tracking down the survivors who had taken to the bush and had commenced a rigorous guerrilla campaign remained the continuing, mopping-up task of both the Marines and the Army for weeks to come.

Elsewhere on Okinawa throughout the month of April the picture was far less encouraging. Granted that thanks to Task Force–58 all hope of successful Japanese attack by sea on Tenth Army's shipping had vanished with the sinking of the monster battleship *Yamamoto* and her escorts on 7 April, a series of major, carefully planned *kamikaze* raids on Admiral Turner's vessels were inflicting extremely heavy damage; meanwhile General Hodge's XXIV Corps was experiencing very rough treatment as it worked its way south, battering with all its might against the main Japanese defense lines drawn across the island near its southern end.

To oppose the American advance the enemy had deliberately erected three successive defense rings each of which made maximum advantage of strategic high ground: a deep, mutually supporting system of broken ridges and sharp hill masses with steep cliffs thrown in for good measure, lying generally east and west at right angles to the invaders' direction of attack, honey-combed with caves and tunnels. For the Americans to overcome the automatic weapons sited in the Japanese emplacements invariably made it mandatory to register artillery pieces individually on each firing port, a time-consuming procedure which required enormous expenditure of ammunition (during the campaign field artillery fired over 1,700,000 rounds). To flush the enemy from his concealed positions, resort had to be made to what General Buckner referred to as the "blowtorch and corkscrew system"—a combination of napalm bomb strikes, flame throwers, and demolitions to be followed by vigorous bayonet assaults before final success could be achieved.

The first of these lines, the Machinato, was strung athwart

297

the island from north of Machinato to the eastern shore near the town of Tomai, following the trace of the Kakazu Ridge. The second and strongest line, in fact, Ushijima's principal battle position, two miles further south, was the Shuri defense complex, extending approximately from the Asa River Estuary (north of Naha) eastward across the island to Yonabaru. This line incorporated the key terrain features of Dakeshi and Wana Ridges (north of Shuri Castle) as well as three reciprocally supporting hills to the southwest designated as Sugar Loaf, Horseshoe, and Half Moon, with yet another, Conical Hill above Yonabaru airfield, serving as the eastern anchor. The third and final bulwark crossed the island two miles from its southern extremity, running eastward from the town of Itoman to Gushichan, otherwise known as the Kunishi Hill, Yuza-Dake, and Yaeyu-Dake line along the axial ridge in the center of the peninsula, where what was left of the Thirty-second Japanese Army was to make its last-ditch stand in its long and costly battle of attrition.

As if this were not enough, there existed an additional stronghold of Japanese resistance on the Oroku Peninsula, southwest of Naha, across the Kokuba Estuary, containing Naha airfield, the largest on Okinawa. In time the mission of seizing this was to be delegated to the Fourth Marines of the 6th MarDiv, it having been decided that rather than engaging the base of the peninsula which was held in force, the attacking Marines would launch an amphibious assault against its northern tip. The question of whether or not to conduct amphibious landings below the Shuri line as an alternative to continuing frontal attacks against the strong, inland Japanese defense works (which had slowed up the American advance almost to a dead stand) became a matter of no little debate as the campaign wore on. Although General Vandegrift and some of Buckner's field commanders, notably Geiger and Bruce of the Army's Seventy-seventh Division, urged that this be attempted, the Commanding General of the Tenth Army was contrary minded.

Actually, by the end of April he had the means at his disposal—both 1st and 6th MarDiv's of Geiger's III Corps as well as the much depleted Seventy-seventh—but certain of his staff officers were opposed to any new landings on the grounds that shipping shortages would create supply problems, aside from their views that once ashore the forces could not be adequately supported by artillery. Buckner was inclined to agree with his planners, with the result that other than the Oroku Peninsula affair for the remainder of the campaign the Marines were to fight side by side with Army counterparts following the precepts of conventional land warfare.

Be that as it may, III Corps had no cause to complain that then or later its services were not going to be fully utilized. Early in April, artillery being in short supply but in great demand, Buckner had given XXIV Corps not only Geiger's Corps artillery but also the heavy howitzers of the Eleventh Marines (normally in support of the 1st MarDiv). By the end of April he transferred 1st MarDiv lock-stock-and-barrel, to XXIV Corps thereby permitting withdrawal of the Twenty-seventh Infantry Division from the front lines, and sent the latter north to relieve the 6th MarDiv in northern Okinawa. Thus, by 1 May the 1st MarDiv had moved into the Machinato airfield area just north of the Asa River (the Machinato line having been pierced on 24 April), and a week afterwards, Geiger having been ordered to take over command of the 1st MarDiv zone as well as to bring down the 6th MarDiv on the extreme right (or seaward flank) of III Corps' new zone of action, his command was again reunited, ready for the contemplated all-out drive on the Shuri defenses. Commencing on 1 May and until the end of the Okinawa campaign, the American advance was thereafter to be undertaken by the two Corps (each of two Divisions) in line abreast: Geiger's III Corps on the right (west), Hodge's XXIV Corps on the left (east), meanwhile 2nd MarDiv (less one RLT) had been sent back to Saipan to gird its loins for the anticipated invasion of Japan (Operation OLYMPIC) scheduled for the fall of 1945.

On 11 May the long-awaited push on Ushijima's second ring got under way. Buckner's plan envisaged a simultaneous envelopment of both Japanese flanks (that on the west by the 6th MarDiv; that on the east by the Ninety-six Division) while a strong holding attack was to be made in the center conjointly by the 1st Marine and the Seventy-seventh Divisions. Having crossed the Asa River, 6th MarDiv first captured Sugar Loaf Hill followed by the seizure of Half Moon and Horseshoe, but only after a heavy loss of life incurred in ten days of constant fighting, While this was transpiring, Conical Hill (and subsequently Yonabaru and its airstrip) on the other end of the line was gained by the

Ninety-sixth Division (aided by the Seventh), and with the two extreme flanks of the three-mile-long battlefront across the island now in American control, forthwith it was up to the two central divisions either to envelope or to overrun by frontal assault the inner enemy bastion—ancient Shuri Castle. As for the 1st MarDiv's role, it required more than a week of exceedingly hard fought combat to force the Japanese defenders from Dakeshi and Wana Ridges, and it was not until 21 May that the ground fronting the outskirts of Shuri could be secured.

At this juncture the rains descended and the floods came: bogged-down in the mud the advance was brought to a standstill, it being well-nigh impossible for the attacking riflemen to overcome the enemy holed up in their caves and pillboxes without the assistance of tanks and vehicular mounted guns. To make matters worse, air support was consequently restricted, and the supply lines, dependent on trucks, almost ground to a halt. Despite the elements, on 23 May the 6th MarDiv conducted an eminently successful assault river crossing of the Asato, and was able to occupy the City of Naha, the westernmost anchor of the Shuri line. Inching its way forward from the west as well as south and in conjunction with elements of the 1st Marine and Seventy-seventh Divisions attacking from the north, the combined forces maintaining a steady pressure at last managed to eject the remaining Japanese from what was left of battered Shuri Castle, and by 31 May for Ushijima and the remnants of his retreating Thirty-second Army, the handwriting was on the wall.

Throughout the last week of May, Geiger, following true to form, had kept in close touch with the fighting at the front. At the conclusion of the 6th MarDiv's drive to seize Sugar Loaf Hill, he returned to Yontan airfield where he talked the Operations Officer of one of the Marine Observation Squadrons into loaning him a light reconnaissance aircraft. With Geiger at the controls and Captain Kicklighter along for company the pair made a flight of two hours' duration on 20 May over the area between Wana Ridge (where the 1st MarDiv was attempting to maintain a tenuous grip) and the northern face of Shuri Castle, scouting out routes of approach toward the next Division objective. Similarly, four days later, he performed a second aerial flight to obtain a closer view of the embattled 6th MarDiv, then fighting its way into Naha. Nor was he content to remain in the rear when the rains pinned the planes to the airstrips. On the ground as well as in the air the Corps Commander could always be depended upon to show up at the most unlikely spots at the most unexpected times. Or, as Buckner's Deputy Chief of Staff, Marine General Oliver Smith, was to relate many years after the campaign, invariably in selecting the site for his Corps' Command Post, Geiger chose a spot far from the "regulation distance" in rear of the front lines. With reference to the fighting before Naha, he could hardly have settled for a more exposed observation site. Here, he moved his CP to a point just north of the Naha Estuary when the area was still being swept by intense fire from its southern bank; in fact, his Command Post was in advance of those of his two Division commanders, quite in keeping with the temperament of the imperturbable man with the built-in cigar.

With two down and one to go, Tenth Army prepared itself for its ensuing onslaught against the third and final Japanese defense line across southern Okinawa, General Buckner sustaining relentless pressure all along his front line to keep the withdrawing enemy off balance. In addition, there remained the enemy stronghold on the Oroku Peninsula—principally Rear Admiral Ota's Base Force consisting of some 5,000 naval troops—which had to be eliminated as it constituted a threat to the right (western) flank of Buckner's advancing troops. Its capture was assigned to the 6th MarDiv. In spite of the weather and with but a minimum of time allotted for the planning, General Shepherd's command conducted what was later to be declared to be a model shore-to-shore amphibious landing on 4 June, and the assaulting regiments having once worked their way behind the Japanese lines, fought their way to Naha airfield, and overran it two days later. To encircle the enemy—by compressing the Japanese against the shores of the Kokubu Estuary near Tomigushi at the southeastern tip of the peninsula—required another week of steady fighting, and by 13 June General Shepherd could report his mission completed, there no longer being organized hostile resistance on the Oroku Peninsula. All that now remained for 6th MarDiv was to link up with 1st MarDiv, fighting hammer-and-tongs to wrest Kunishi Ridge from the Japanese as III Corps, side by side with its parent XXIV Corps, pushed on in the face of furious resistance toward Ara Sake (Cape), the extreme southern tip of Okinawa. One after another the enemy positions strung across the escarpment were outflanked and taken, the Eighth Regimental Landing Team of the 2nd MarDiv having been brought into action to assist the final drive to the sea.

Three days before the end of organized resistance on Okinawa was officially proclaimed, General Buckner's earlier premonition unfortunately proved to be correct. On 18 June, while visiting a Battalion Observation Post of the Eighth Marines, 300 yards from the front lines, in order to get a closer look at the fighting, a Japanese artillery shell exploded against a rock, and a fragment of the displaced coral struck and penetrated General Buckner's chest causing the death of the Commander, Tenth Army, within a matter of minutes. As a result of this tragic event, General Geiger was at once officially notified by the deceased's Chief of Staff that as of that moment he would assume command of the Tenth Army, thereby becoming not only the first Marine Officer ever to command a field army, but also the one and only American aviator ever to be so honored. The day afterward Geiger received a second accolade: promotion to three-star rank (as of 19 June with date of rank, 9 June 1945), the first Marine Aviator to advance to the grade of Lieutenant General, and now the senior pilot of the Marine Corps.

As for the fighting on Okinawa, it was all over but the shouting. While some Japanese committed suicide by jumping from steep cliffs, others brought an equally conclusive end to their travail by resorting to their customary procedure of self-disembowelment, only a very few deciding at the last moment to heed General Buckner's prior appeal to surrender as the more realistic solution to their dilemma. The withdrawal of the enemy having turned into a rout, his complete collapse was inevitable, and by 21 June General Geiger, the temporary commander of Tenth Army, formally announced the termination of organized hostile resistance in southern Okinawa, to be followed by the official flag-raising exercises at his Headquarters the next day, marking the capture of the Japanese stronghold in the Ryukus.

In retrospect, Ushijima's "last stand" had been a costly affair alike to defenders and invaders. Known enemy dead amounted to roughly 108,000 with an estimated 20,000 additional fatalities entombed in the wreckage of their underground caves; Japanese prisoners-of-war, some 7,400, accounting for the balance of the once proud Thirty-second Army. As for the American losses,

Tenth Army casualties totaled more than 38,000, including 7,000-odd killed in action, 2,500 Marines of III Corps (and attached Marine aviation) having lost their lives in operation ICEBERG, and 13,500 having been wounded. Ironically, the American Navy proportionately suffered even greater losses than its counterparts fighting ashore: with 38 ships sunk, 368 damaged (many severely), and 763 planes lost in combat, its dead numbered almost 5,000 with an equal number wounded. The Japanese, however, had been made to pay for it: nearly 4,200 of his aircraft, many of the *kamikaze* corps, were downed by American fighters of all three services and by antiaircraft gunners aboard ship as well as in the field. With regard to the Imperial Japanese Navy, what little remained was too inconsequential to be of any real fighting worth, once Task Force−58 had finished with it.

The nominal commander of the Tenth Army, meantime, was given scant opportunity to utilize his prerogatives. Twenty-four hours after the flag was raised, his relief in the form of General Joseph Stilwell, USA (of Burma fame and China lore), arrived by air, under orders from the War Department to carry on in Buckner's stead. Doubtless the various Corps and Division commanders of the Tenth Army would have been perfectly content to serve more or less indefinitely under their present, temporary over-all field commander−for Geiger, well known and well liked, was also uniformly respected as a combat leader−but the opinions of the higher echelons at Honolulu and Washington, far from the scene of the recently concluded campaign, prevailed to the extent it was deemed preferable for a field Army to be commanded by an Army officer rather than by a Marine. At any rate, they, too, played no favorites, and in the Army award of the Distinguished Service Medal, special mention was made of Geiger's exceptional performance in the Okinawan campaign, particularly his personal bravery and his inspiration of his command, which was "in large measure responsible for the success of the operation which secured a tremendously important base on the doorstep of the Japanese home islands."

During the final week of June while Tenth Army brought to an end its mop-up sweep of southern Okinawa, Geiger as Stilwell's deputy, for the first time in weeks found time hanging heavily on his hands. To acquaint himself with the general situation on the island−and perhaps just to demonstrate to his associates that here among them was a three-star General of Marines who could fly his own plane—Geiger flew for four hours in an *OY* (based at Naha airfield) on 27 June from one end of Okinawa to the other. But with the operation at an end and the pending invasion of Japan proper daily looming closer, it was high time for him to sit down once more with the planners at Guam and Pearl Harbor.

Therefore, on the very eve of the termination of MacArthur's campaign in the Philippines, and with every expectation of participating in the planned amphibious assault against the island of Kyushu, Geiger departed from Okinawa on 1 July, bound for Hawaii via Guam. The day after his arrival at Pearl Harbor, on 3 July 1945, he relieved Lieutenant General Holland M. Smith, as Commanding General, Fleet Marine Force, Pacific and from that moment until the end of the war in the Pacific, only six weeks away (but obviously then neither realized nor anticipated), he was to devote all of his efforts exclusively to preparing the Marine forces under his command for their contemplated role in operation OLYMPIC.

Chapter XIV

Collecting the Bet

As Commanding General, Fleet Marine Force, Pacific, the new incumbent found himself in charge of a sizable concern: very nearly the entire tactical field force (including attached aviation) of the Marine Corps west of San Diego. Excluding ships' detachments and Marine aviation squadrons aboard Navy aircraft carriers, Geiger was now responsible for the future operations of two Marine Amphibious Corps (V with Headquarters in Hawaii; III, in Guam) each of three Divisions (2nd, 3rd, and 5th; 1st, 4th, and 6th respectively), and three Marine Air Wings. In early August 1945 it had been anticipated that in the late autumn, about 1 November, General Walter Krueger's Sixth Army—XI and I Corps plus V MAC and 1st, 2nd, and 3rd MAW's—would undertake assault landings on southern Kyushu, Operation OLYMPIC. The second phase of the contemplated invasion of the Japanese homeland, Operation CORONET, the landing on eastern Honshu to be followed by a forty-mile advance across Kanto Plain to Tokyo, about 1 March 1946, envisaged the emplyment of III MAC along with the Eighth and Tenth Armies.

The very next day after Geiger assumed command at Pearl Harbor he took off for Maui to inspect one of the Divisions of V Corps in training there for its pending role in OLYMPIC. Neither of the two major invasions, of course, ever took place. On 6 August Hiroshima was subjected to atomic bomb drop; on 9 August Nagasaki received the second bomb; the following day the Japanese Government sued for peace; and on the 14th, President Truman received Japan's final acceptance of the proposed surrender terms, thereby terminating the War in the Pacific (less rounding up the die-hards).

With plans for the seizure of the principal ports and naval

facilities in the Tokyo Bay area receiving top priority, FMFPac was directed to provide an RLT for immediate occupation duty. Forthwith, on 12 August Geiger departed by plane for Admiral Nimitz's Headquarters at Guam. Ten days or more were spent there overseeing the mounting out of RLT-4 (from 6th MarDiv), assigned to a special Task Force (TF-31) of Admiral Halsey's Third Fleet, scheduled to land at Yokosuka on 30 August. Commanded by Brigadier General William Clement, USMC (ADC of 6th MarDiv), the three BLT's of the Fourth Marines successfully carried out their assigned mission on L-Day—at Yokosuka Navy Yard and airfield as well as across the harbor at Futtsu Cape—thereby becoming the first American troops to land on Japan's home soil. By mid-morning 30 August, the same flag that had first been raised on Guam and later on Okinawa was run up the staff of the Japanese naval headquarters building at Yokosuka, and the way was now clear to make final arrangements for the official surrender ceremonies slated for 2 September.

As for General Geiger, the senior Marine officer in the Pacific theater, to him was accorded the honor of representing the Marine Corps (along with General Clement) at the ceremony aboard USS *Missouri*. Boarding a seaplane at Saipan, Geiger accompanied Admiral Nimitz on the flight to Tokyo Bay, arriving there on the afternoon of L-Day. On 31 August, Geiger went ashore to observe developments at Yokosuka Navy Yard, and the following day, rather than join a group of officers who had decided to make a tour of Yokohama, he elected to continue northward another fifteen miles right into the heart of Tokyo.

This little private field excursion was not without the element of risk. Granted that the Japanese had offered not the slightest show of resistance to the initial landings at Tokyo Bay, by no means did this of itself guarantee the same spirit of cooperation among the residents of the Emperor's capital. To Geiger this was merely incidental: he had a $100.00 bet to collect, and he was bound and determined to cash in on it before either Admiral Conolly or General Mullen beat him to it. Proceeding past the startled Japanese sentries at the city limits, Geiger drove through the city to the Emperor's Palace. There, on the concourse, he had his picture taken—minus the cigar (for once) and exhibiting just the trace of a smile (equally rare)—proof positive that he had gotten closer into the enemy's camp than either of his two rivals.

Just to make it stick in case of argument, he proceeded to the grounds of the American Embassy, and called on the Swiss custodian, a Mr. Lingeller. The legal mind now went one step further: at Geiger's request he had Mr. Lingeller affirm in writing that on 1 September 1945 (the day before the surrender), at 1230, one Lieutenant General Roy S. Geiger of the United States Marine Corps had in fact arrived under his own steam at Tokyo, an act duly witnessed and attested by an accredited representative. Vastly relieved to hear that neither Conolly nor Mullen had won the race, Geiger in time forwarded the document to the other parties concerned, and three months later at Honolulu received General Mullen's check for the full amount, drawing to a successful conclusion Geiger's vow that he would not return to the United States before he he had made his way to Tokyo.

Having in turn duly witnessed the formal signing of the Japanese surrender terms aboard *Missouri* on the morning of 2 September, it was high time for Geiger to return posthaste to his Headquarters at Pearl Harbor where there were several matters requiring his undivided attention. Chief among these were the dispatch of Marine forces of occupation to both Japan and China, an intricate operation which had to be implemented without further delay despite the pressure to demobilize thousands of fundamentally "hostilities only" troops, technically eligible for discharge or rotation, further complicated by the stark reality that in the immediate period of postwar reduction, replacements were practically nonexistent. To comply with current JCS's directives, General Harry Schnidt's V Corps (less 3rd MarDiv) was at once sent to southern Japan. Corps Headquarters and 5th MarDiv established themselves at Sasebo, the locale of one of Japan's major navy yards, while 2nd MarDiv set up shop twenty-five miles to the south, amid what remained of bomb-gutted Nagasaki. Air support for the Corps was provided by elements of 2nd MAW: MAG-31 based at Yokosuka, and MAG-22 at Omura (north of Nagasaki), the primary mission of both groups being that of surveillance flights in support of occupation operations (i.e., demilitarization of the Japanese forces within assigned areas of responsibility). By December 1945, its mission accomplished, 5th MarDiv left for the United States for eventual disbandment; V Corps followed suit a month later; leaving 2nd MarDiv to carry on for another six months, at which time (July 1946) it too pulled stakes and sailed from Japan destined for Camp Lejeune.

Of equal importance and no less demanding was the task entrusted to General Keller Rockey's III Corps: that of accepting the surrender of Japanese forces remaining in North China, disarming them, and assisting in their repatriation back to Japan; keeping open, and maintaining rail communications for the Kailin coal mines which supplied vital stocks of fuel to much of China north of Shanghai; and, most difficult of all, exercising some degree of restraint (yet remaining nominally neutral) between three competing factions—Nationalist Chinese troops, Communist Eighth Route Army soldiers, and affiliated partisan bands—each struggling with might and main in an all-out civil war to gain their own ends in that strife-torn and exhausted land.

Arriving at Tientsin at the close of September, III Corps (less 4th MarDiv, left behind at Hawaii to disband) set up its Headquarters there along with those of the 1st MAW and the 1st MarDiv. One of the latter's reinforced regiments and two Marine Air Groups were sent to Peiping; a battalion was stationed at Chinwangtao; and other ground elements of the Division were spotted along the railway line leading north from Tangku to Chinwangtao. So much for the troop and aerial dispositions in Hopeh Province. To the south and east in Shantung, two weeks later 6th MarDiv (less RLT-4) backed up by two Marine Air Groups landed at Tsingtao, to discover that whereas the port was controlled by local followers of Chiang Kai-shek and a band of irregulars recognized by the Nationalists, the surrounding countryside to the contrary—in fact most of the Province—was held by the Communists; meanwhile, the Japanese were in command of the rail route leading into the interior.

In spite of the constant harrassing tactics of Communist guerrillas who repeatedly threatened Marines as well as Japanese, the surrender of the Imperial troops was accomplished within a relatively short period. In early October General Rockey acting for the Central Chinese Government accepted the surrender of some 50,000 Japanese in the Tientsin-Tangku-Chinwangtao area, and toward the end of that month, General Shepherd, CG of 6th MarDiv, along with Chiang Kai-Shek's personal, local representative similarly presided at the formal surrender of Japan's 5th Independent Mixed Brigade (about 10,000 soldiers) at Tsingtao. The duties of the Marine Forces of occupation in North

China, however, were far from terminated. Unlike their counterparts in Japan who had been able to complete their allotted task in a matter of weeks, it was to require many unenviable and dangerous months before they could be progressively withdrawn from the Orient, the last remaining units not taking their departure from Chinese soil until well into 1949.

Having made all possible arrangements to send V Corps to Japan and III to North China in accordance with JCS's directives, it was deemed expedient to bring Geiger back to Headquarters at Washington in order to acqaint him with developments relating to the postwar status of the Marine Corps. Flying eastward from Pearl Harbor on 18 September he arrived at Anacostia three days later. His stay at the nation's capital was of short duration, for the citizenry of Pensacola on hearing of his return to the United States let it be known far and wide that they were most anxious to extend an appropriate welcome to its most distinguished resident, a much decorated veteran and combat hero of five, major Pacific campaigns, not to mention being an erstwhile graduate of the Navy's flight school there back in the old "stick and string" era.

Ever loyal to the State of his birth and not a little intrigued with the prospect of what lay in store, Geiger accepted the invitation with pleasure and wasted no time winging his way on to the Gulf, more than content to get away from the confusion of a Washington trying to adjust itself to some semblance of a peacetime routine. The City Fathers of Pensacola, equally elated, proceeded to roll out the proverbial red carpet, and by municipal decree launched a parade and a pageant on a par with a Wall Street ticker-tape ovation. GEIGER DAY, 26 September 1945, was to be fondly remembered for months to come by everyone who participated. With the schools closed for the day so that the children might line the streets through which the motorcade passed, to the sound of cheers and blaring bands, the Lieutenant General triumphantly was driven to City Hall, there to receive the official greetings extended by the Mayor with the Keys to the City thrown in for good measure. Grinning from ear to ear, the recipient of these and other honors warmly thanked the donors for their kindness and their appreciation, and with holiday procedure proclaimed was whisked off to a day-long series of receptions, replete with congratulatory speeches and more fried chicken, cake, and ice cream than Geiger had ever dreamed of.

Before he had time to realize it, his thirty-day sojourn in the United States had passed, and by 20 October he was back at Pearl Harbor, then quite unaware that within a month's time he would again return to Washington, this time in a far more serious vein.

If the paradoxical issue of rapid demobilization concurrently with the requirement to supply troops for occupation duties defied an easy solution by Marine Corps planners in the autumn of 1945, of even greater concern affecting the future of the Marine Corps were outright threats to its continuation advocated by certain officials of the Army and the Air Force in the immediate postwar period. With the "merger bill" under lively discussion and with "unification now" a burning topic in the corridors and offices of the Pentagon, it was patently obvious that neither the Marine Corps nor Naval Aviation *per se* stood to profit by the proposed changes championed by the more outspoken members of the opposite camp. To add fuel to the fire, the recent introduction of atomic warfare had raised grave doubts as to the feasibility of future amphibious assault landings, the Marines' particular specialty, at least on the scale of those so lately undertaken in European as well as Pacific waters.

Understandably disturbed lest the Marine Corps be ultimately removed from the scene were pending legislation passed into law, its Commandant, General Vandegrift, had risen to its defense, and in testimony delivered before the Senate Military Affairs Committee, in October 1945, had spoken out forcefully and tellingly in behalf of his branch of the naval service. To assist him in presenting the Marine Corps' side of the picture, he called on the Commanding General, Fleet Marine Force, Pacific, to lend a helping hand, and it was primarily for this reason that under orders Geiger flew from Pearl Harbor to Washington in late November. Or, to state the case in Geiger's own words contained in the official transcript of his testimony delivered before the Senate Committee on Military Affairs, on 7 December 1945 (the fourth anniversary of the Pearl Harbor attack): "- - I have been called to Washington from my post in the Pacific to express my opinions concerning the proposed merger of the services, with particular reference to its effect on military operations. — — I have had the unique experience of being both an air and a ground commander in the Pacific War, and I believe my opinions represent an average of those who served with me in both the air and ground arms."

A carefully prepared statement, well substantiated by the written comments and recommendations of senior Army field commanders expressing their appreciation of and admiration for the feats of close air support provided by Marine Corps Aviation in Pacific campaigns, Geiger proceeded to delineate the flaws in arguments pressing for a separate Air Force as being "entirely inconsistent with any plan for unification." As for the future role of the highly vaunted Strategic Air Force, Geiger showed remarkable prescience in his comment: "– – I am inclined to agree with Air Chief Marshal Harris (of the RAF), who believes the long range strategic bomber may be the 'dodo' of the next war. I will go further by saying that atomic energy in conjunction with electronics will not only make piloted bombardment aircraft unnecessary but may result in such improved antiaircraft defenses as to render them virtually obsolete. As a result the strategic air force, the only possible pretext for a divorced air arm, would rapidly pass out of the picture."

Having gotten that off his chest, Geiger summarized his attitude regarding the War Department's plan of "depriving the President of these fundamental powers (i.e., the making of top strategic decisions in his capacity of Commander-in-Chief) and passing them into the hands of the so-called 'Chief of Staff of the Armed Forces' " by the following recommendations:

"First: Reject this retrospective unification blueprint outright, or at least insist that its proponents come forward with something up to date and constructive;

"Second: Let each department study the lessons of the war and place its own house in order in the light of the lessons learned;

"Third: Provide the President with the agencies necessary to assist him in the intelligent and expeditious discharge of his duties as Commander-in-Chief of the coordinate armed forces;

"Fourth: That Science, Labor, Industry, the Department of State, and all other factors in our national security be integrated into the structure as full-time partners.

"The program for National Security as proposed by the Navy Department fills these requirements. I commend it to you as the only true progressive proposal which has been set to writing, and one which deserves your careful consideration."

Evidently the views of CG, FMFPac, made quite an impression on the members present. Thanked by Senator Thomas (the Chairman, presiding), Senator Hill went one step further as evidenced by his comment: "Well, I will say this to you, General, that in my consideration of any consolidation, I do not contemplate and would not contemplate taking the air arm of the fleet from the Navy or the air arm of the Marine Corps from the Marines, and I do not see why they cannot go right ahead as autonomous units as they have in the past."

The legal mind tuned to the occasion, Geiger retorted: "You don't contemplate that but how many people do?"

To which Senator Hill, dialed in on the same frequency, replied: "Well, I think it possible to write the legislation so that it will not be done. I think it is possible to fix this thing so it will not be done, General. I think so. I think so."

Satisfied that for the time being he had done everything possible to assist in presenting the Marine Corps' side of the controversy, Geiger returned without further delay to Hawaii to resume his duties as commander of the Marine operational forces in the western Pacific. From 10 December 1945 until his relief eleven months later, he was an extremely busy individual, making frequent inspection tours to the forces in Japan and North China, attempting to solve the problem of finding trained replacements for time-expired Marine riflemen and aviators, and attending the atomic bomb tests at Bikini Atoll as the senior Marine Corps observer assigned to Operation CROSSROADS.

The winter of 1945-46 was largely devoted to hurried trips to Sasebo and Nagasaki—to witness the disbanding of 5th MarDiv followed by V Corps—and flights to Tientsin, Peiping, and Tsingtao—to observe the efforts of III Corps to maintain an uneasy peace in a region fast falling under the complete domination of the Communists. In December 1945, just to show the junior pilots that the "Old Man" knew what he was doing, he took over the controls of an *OY* borrowed from one of MAG-22's squadrons at Omura, and made three flights over the general Sasebo-Nagasaki area of western Kyushu. Again, the following spring, to demonstrate to some of the young "Spuds" that their Commanding General was not just another old "Fud," Geiger on 15 May 1946, then exactly 61 years, 3 months, and 20 days of age, took off in an *OY-3* from the airfield at Chinwangtao and flew back to Tientsin, electing to fly himself to III Corps Headquarters rather than repeat the 135-mile train ride made previously across bridges and through ravines constantly threatened by hit-and-run guerrillas whose specialty was blowing up rolling stock.

As for the demobilization issue, although the situation at times got out of control in some parts of Hawaii, dissatisfied Army and Air Force personnel being the principal instigators, the Marines for the most part behaved themselves. Geiger had let it be known that as far as he was concerned: "Marines do not meet and demonstrate," that any such show smacked of deliberate mutiny and was a clear cut display of lack of discipline. After all, what else could be expected of a leader whose sense of duty was so strong that at Guadalcanal as well as at Pelelieu he considered any man fit for duty who had strength enough to crawl, unassisted, to what passed as a sick bay for treatment of wounds or disease.

With this background it came as no surprise to those who had served under him in combat that when a small group of Marine noncommissioned officers approached him at Pearl Harbor with a petition pressing for early discharge and return to the United States, he took appropriate action. After reading the document he treated the party to his famous "twenty-foot stare" for several minutes in stony silence; told them just exactly what he thought of them; and having reduced each member to the rank of Private (not for their participation in the meetings, but for their demonstrated lack of leadership), had his Sergeant Major personally rip off their chevrons there and then before dismissing them. Just to show he meant business, Geiger promptly relieved the station commander who had heretofore had jurisdiction over the now demoted personnel. From that moment in January 1946, general demobilization of those entitled to it (and whose services could be spared) proceeded in an orderly, efficient, and thoroughly disciplined fashion, and there were no further incidents in his theater of command.

The summer months of 1946 were marked by his attendance at the atomic bomb tests in the Marshall Islands as the senior Marine Corps representative and observer. Flying from Honolulu to Kwajalein in late June, he boarded Vice Admiral William Blandy's flagship, *AGC-2, USS Blue Ridge,* and after steaming 250 miles to the northwest arrived at Bikini Atoll on the 29th. More than 200 ships, 150 aircraft, and 42,000 men were involved in one capacity or another in the two scheduled tests designed to provide data for study of atomic blast damage and radiation contamination. The first of these, Test ABLE, took place on 1 July. An air burst or bomb drop from "Dave's Dream" (a *B-29* bomber) into a group of some 75 vessels of varying types anchored within the target area, its spectacular results were recorded and summarized by an evaluation board set up by the Joint Chiefs of Staff. The second "experiment," Test BAKER, was conducted about three weeks later. This consisted of an underwater explosion (the bomb having been suspended below a landing craft) resulting in the sinking or disintegration of those vessels which had survived the original blast. It was claimed that the water of the lagoon had been rendered so lethal from radioactivity that four days after Test BAKER it was deemed unsafe for personnel to spend any "useful length of time" on the target vessels (or more properly, what remained of them). As a consequence, subsequent tests were run off at a new test site at Eniwetok Atoll, some 200 miles west of Bikini.

Having returned to Pearl Harbor to write his report, so impressed was Geiger with what he had observed first hand at Operation CROSSROADS, he recommended a complete reappraisal of the basic concept of amphibious operations, for it was his unreserved opinion that atomic weapons could raise havoc with expeditionary forces as then constituted. In due course his findings were forwarded to a special board convened at the Marine Corps Schools at Quantico endeavoring to develop the techniques of conducting future amphibious operations consistent with the limitations introduced by the atomic age. After three months of protracted study of the problem the board reached the conclusion that the answer lay in the development of assault helicopters (in lieu of surface landing craft), and without further fanfare the planners launched a Marine helicopter experimental squadron at Quantico, thereby initiating a vertical lift concept destined to prove its soundness at the outbreak of the subsequent Korean Emergency.

Geiger's remaining period as CG, FMFPac, was relatively uneventful. As before he continued to pilot his own plane, keeping up his flight time; otherwise, his attentions were for the most part devoted to administration and routine paper work. Perhaps it was just as well that the pace had slowed down, for his health was beginning to display signs that all was not going as smoothly as before. There seems to be little doubt that Geiger was aware that his health was failing, but he never discussed it, never complained, and carried on as usual with a few modifications. By mid-September it was apparent that he had given up smoking cigars. His explanation failed to convince those about him who had known him for years: he claimed that cigars were "too expensive," a rather naive excuse from a man who had practically "worn" a cigar as a person would wear a necktie all of his adult life. Always distrustful of doctors and by temperament inclined to ignore illness, he kept his own counsel, and did not seek medical advice. By late autumn, however, his appetite began to fall off, his color took on a different hue to the degree the change in his normal healthy appearance was most evident, and it was clear that whether he wished it or not, it was high time for a medical check-up.

Reluctantly turning over his duties to his assigned relief, General Turnage, on 15 November 1946, he departed by air the same day, and on the 17th joined Company A, Headquarters Battalion, at Marine Corps Headquarters, detailed to the Office of the Director of the Division of Aviation (General Harris). Following a visit to the Naval Medical Center at Bethesda where he was examined, he was advised to take leave to spend Christmas at his home at Pensacola, with the understanding that he would return to Bethesda thereafter for additional consultation.

Accordingly, on 14 December, accompanied by Captain Kicklighter, he flew to Pensacola for a month's leave. By this time there was no mistaking the fact that Geiger was seriously ill, and on 16 January 1947 it was necessary for him to return to Bethesda. Admitted to the Medical Center, he soon lapsed into semi-consciousness, and in the presence of his wife and family and one or more of his intimate friends passed away quietly on the 23rd of that month. As for the cause of his demise an autopsy performed at the hospital revealed cancer of the lung as the primary factor. Whether or not the condition could have been arrested or cured had it been detected at an earlier date falls within the realm of pure speculation, and in any event, even to conjecture would appear to be a matter best resolved by medical authorities rather than by the opinion of lay persons.

At the funeral cermonies at Arlington National Cemetery the six grey horses hitched to the caisson bearing the flag-draped casket, followed by the riderless horse with boots reversed in the stirrups and officer's sword slung backwards in the saddle frog, drew the remains of a four-star General of the Marine Corps. By Special Act of Congress under date 30 June 1947, Lieutenant General Roy S. Geiger had been posthumously elevated to the rank of full General, with date of rank effective 23 January, the only four-star General other than the Commandant of the Marine Corps to be so honored. And as a final token of respect to an officer who had served his Corps so devotedly for forty years on active duty, a Squadron of Marine *Corsairs* made three passes over his grave, the lead spot at the head of the flight being deliberately left unoccupied in General Geiger's honor. The State of Florida, similarly determined to pay homage to its deceased hero, rendered him singular honors: Jacksonville, Middleburg, and Pensacola at once passed resolutions and tributes to his memory.

Additional manifestations of respect and recognition were to follow in the months to come. Among these were the dedication of Geiger Hall, the splendid home of the Amphibious Warfare School at Quantico, and the troop transport, *USS Geiger,* commissioned in 1952. In September 1953, Camp Geiger at the Marine Corps Base at Camp Lejeune was named in his honor, his longtime friend and admirer, General Silverthorn, delivering the dedication address. In his speech extensive mention was made of many of Roy Geiger's outstanding qualities—his fearlessness, determination, and loyalty—his ability to inspire confidence, leadership in combat, and professional competence—General Silverthorn reiteratiing General Holland Smith's prior statement: "I imagine I am correct in asserting that no military aviator since the Wright Brothers has ever exercised quite interchangeably such air and ground commands, all in one war − − he has flown and commanded almost every kind of aircraft or aviation unit that ever existed."

In attempting any summary of Roy Geiger's many sided character two factors seem to stand out above all of his many desirable attributes: his utter resoluteness and his tremendous vitality. It has been said in many different ways, for many years, and in many tongues that the "unknown is the real destroyer of courage." To Roy the unknown did not seem to exist—he was convinced in his own mind that if he persevered long enough and hard enough, he could discover the proper solution to any baffling problem. In essence, he was a firm believer in the tenet that "fortune favors the brave"—to achieve results one must be willing to assume risks, and once having arrived at a selected course of action, it was only logical to pursue it relentlessly and to hope for the best. Undeterred by obstacles which might well have discouraged others of lesser determination (yet flexible enough to avoid them, provided the changes did not preclude gaining the desired ends), and disdainful of anxiety, Geiger was literally unaccustomed to fear. A man of direct action and of few words—he said what he meant, and he meant what he said—it was well-nigh impossible to dissuade him from an undertaking once he had made up his mind to see it through to its conclusion. As for his physical vigor and his stamina, if anyone could lay claim to a reputation for toughness, Geiger was eminently well qualified. It was not for nothing that he had earned the title "Rugged Roy," but it should not be overlooked that he did not expect others to attempt feats which he was not willing first to undertake himself.

But aside from his determination and his ruggedness were his extraordinary qualities as a leader. For him it was not enough to make others conform to his wishes or his commands. It was more important that his subordinates give their unqualified support to his decisions. By imparting some of his personality into everything a leader does or directs, a true commander by setting an exemplary personal example can usually approach if not achieve such an objective. Invariably Geiger was able to accomplish this aim, a field in which he excelled, for when it came to inspiring others to do their best by following the pattern he had demonstrated the "Old Man" was head and shoulders ahead of the pack.

Bibliography

BOOKS

Appleman, R.E. *The Last Battle*. Washington, 1948.

Blakeney, Jane. Heroes, *U.S. Marine Corps*, 1861-1955. Washington, 1957.

Condit, K.P. and E.T. Turnbladh. *Hold High the Torch*. Washington, 1960.

Davis, Burke. *Marine, The Life of Lieutenant General Lewis B. (Chesty) Puller, USMC (Ret.)* Boston, 1962.

DeChant, J.A., Captain *Devilbirds*. New York, 1947.

Griffith, S. B. II, Brigadier General, USMC (Ret.). *The Battle for Guadalcanal*. Philadelphia, 1963.

Halsey, W.F., Fleet Admiral, USN, and Lieutenant Commander J. Bryan, III, USN. *Admiral Halsey's Story*. New York, 1947.

Heinl, R.D., Jr., Colonel, USMC. *Soldiers of the Sea, The United States Marine Corps, 1775-1962*. Annapolis, 1962.

Hough, F.O., Lieutenant Colonel, USMC. *The Assault on Peleliu*. Washington. 1950.

———, Major V.E. Ludwig, USMC, and H.I. Shaw, Jr. *Pearl Harbor to Guadalcanal*. Washington, 1958.

Isely, J.A. and P.A. Crowl. *The U.S. Marines and Amphibious War*. Princeton, 1951.

Larkins, W. F. *U.S. Marine Corps Aircraft, 1914-1959*. Concord, California, 1960.

Lewis, C.L. *Famous American Marines*. Boston, 1950.

Lodge, O.R., Major, USMC. *The Recapture of Guam*. Washington, 1954.

McClellan, E.N., Major, USMC. *The U.S. Marine Corps in World War I.* Washington, 1920.

McCrocklin, J.H. (compiler). *Garde d'Haiti.* Annapolis, 1955.

Metcalf, C.H., Lieutenant Colonel, USMC. *A History of the United States Marine Corps.* New York, 1939.

———, (editor). *The Marine Corps Reader.* New York, 1944.

Miller, John, Jr. *Guadalcanal, the First Offensive,* Washington, 1949.

Millis, Walter. *Arms and Men.* New York 1956.

Montross, Lynn. *The United States Marines.* New York, 1956.

Morrison, S.E., Rear Admiral, USNR. *History of United States Naval Operations in World War II.* Volume V (Guadalcanal). Volume VI (Bougainville). Volume VIII (Guam). Volume XII (Palaus). Volume XIV (Okinawa). Boston, 1947-60.

Nichols, C.S., Major, USMC, and H.I. Shaw, Jr. *Okinawa, Victory in the Pacific.* Washington, 1955.

Pierce, P. N., Lieutenant Colonel, USMC, and Lieutenant Colonel F.O. Hough, USMC. *Compact History of the Marine Corps.* New York, 1960.

Potter, E.B. (editor). *The United States and World Sea Power.* Englewood Cliffs, N.J., 1955.

Pratt, Fletcher. *The Marines' War.* New York, 1948.

———. *Eleven Generals, Studies in American Command,* New York,1949.

Rentz, J.N., Major, USMCR. *Bougainville and the Northern Solomons.* Washington, 1948.

Shaw, H.I., Jr. and Major D.T. Kane, USMC. *Isolation of Rabaul.* Washington, 1963.

Sherrod, Robert. *History of Marine Corps Aviation.* Washington, 1952.

Smith, H.M., General, USMC. *Coral and Brass.* New York, 1949.

Thomas, Lowell. *Old Gimlet Eye.* New York, 1933.

Vandegrift, A.A. General, USMC (Ret.), and Captain R.B. Asprey, USMC (Ret.). *Once a Marine.* New York 1964.

W.H. Wise and Co., Inc., (publisher). *Battle Stations, Your Navy in Action.* New York, 1946.

Zimmerman, J.L., Lieutenant Colonel, USMCR. *The Guadalcanal Campaign.* Washington, 1949.

PERIODICALS:

Brainard, E.H., Major, USMC. "Marine Corps Aviation," *Marine Corps Gazette.* March, 1928.

Heinl, R.D., Jr., Lieutenant Colonel, USMC. "NGF Training in the Pacific," *Marine Corps Gazette,* June, 1948.

Henderson, F.P., Colonel, USMC. "NGF Support in the Solomons," *Marine Corps Gazette,* March–December, 1956.

Smith, H.M., General, USMC. "Development of Amphibious Tactics in the U.S. Navy," *Marine Corps Gazette,* June–October, 1948.

USMC HISTORICAL REFERENCE PAMPHLETS:

No. 20.–*Marine Corps Aircraft, 1913-1960.* Washington, 1961.

No. 21.–*The United States Marines in Nicaragua* (Revised). Washington, 1961.

Johnstone, J.H., Major, USMC. *A Brief History of the First Marines.* USMC Historical Reference Series No. 5., (Revised) Washington, 1960.

_____. *A Brief History of the Second Marines.* USMC Historical Reference Series No. 26., Washington, 1961.

Shaw, H.I., Jr. *The United States Marines in North China, 1945-49. USMC Historical Reference Series No. 23., Washington, 1960.*

_____. *The United States Marines in the Occupation of Japan.* USMC Historical Reference Series No. 24., Washington, 1961.

_____. *The United States Marines in the Guadalcanal Campaign.* USMC Historical Reference Series No. 29., Washington, 1961.

Wolf, G. S. *History of Marine Corps Aviation.* Service and Technical Branch, Division of Information, Headquarters United States Marine Corps, Washington, November, 1955.

U.S. GOVERNMENT DOCUMENTS:

Navy Department, Annual Reports and Appropriation Bills, including Annual Reports of the Commandant of the Marine Corps, 1912-1940.

Hearings before Subcommittee of House Committee of Appropriations concerning Navy Department Appropriation Bill for 1923, 20 March 1922.

United States Senate, Vol.24, Report of Proceedings, Hearing held before Committee on Military Affairs (S. 84, S. 1482, S. 1702 and H.R. 550), 7 December 1945, Washington, D.C.